DEDICATED

To my beloved wife, Doris
who died March 6, 1981.

Roy J. Campbell
109 Vale Street,
Battle Creek, Michigan, 49017

Hovey Bradford Campbell and his wife Alice Jane (Eddy)
His mother was Huldah Phinney.

Doris Olive (Coyle) Campbell
wife of the compiler. First wife.

The Compiler

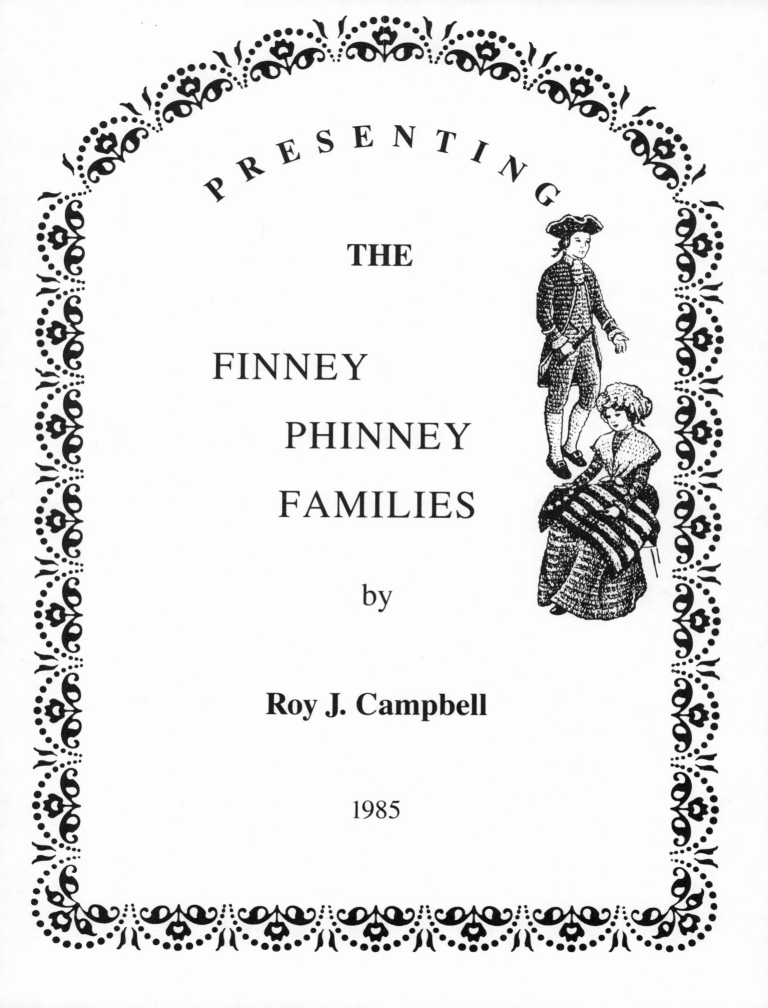

PRESENTING

THE

FINNEY

PHINNEY

FAMILIES

by

Roy J. Campbell

1985

The compiler of this book is Roy J. Campbell. Any material not in this book will be added to a second volume, should enough information of other Finney/Phinney Families to make another volume. Any information available will be kept on file for future volumes. Please send the material you have to Roy J. Campbell, 109 VAle Street, Battle Creek, Michigan 49017. Telephone number is (616) 968-8448.

1985.

Mayflower at Dock in Plymouth Harbor

Landing of the Pilgrims

Pilgrims' First Fort

Howland House   Built 1667

Replicas of Pilgrim Houses   Mayflower II in background

William Harlow House   Built 1677

EXPLANATION OF

Heraldry

The origin of coats of arms dates from the time of the Crusades in Medivial Europe. Heraldry is the last remnant of the ancient symbolism and a legitimate branch of Christian Art. Every genuine old coat of arms preaches a lesson of chivalric honour and Christian principle to those who inherit it. All the designs and colors on the shield have a symbolical meaning.

The Science of armory sprang into being during the Great Feudal Days. The Souvereign acquired the control of armorial bearings about 1300. In 1463 Richard II formed the office of arms into a corporation and founded and endowed the College of Arms to be the armorial headquarters for England.

The Term "COAT OF ARMS," is derived from the garment or "SURCOAT" which was worn over the armour, and which bore in embroidery a duplication of the design upon the shield. Without the shield there can be neither coat of arms nor achievement. It is the SHIELD which is of first and greatest importance, on which every thing else hangs and depends.

The Custom of using a coat of arms may be traced to very early times as to the Egyptians and the Roman Eagles. From these times grew the customs of clans and families distinguishing themselves from others by signs and emblems. After awhile it was considered a right of all noblemen to use a coat of arms. No two families allowed to use the same.

A Coat of Arms is composed of: a shield, crest, wreath, helmet, lambrequin, colors, motto, and some few show the supporters.

THE MEANING OF COLORS: (Or, gold, yellow, moon, fortitude, topaz, Sol.) (Ar., argent, silver, white, water, morning, infancey, hope, pearl, Luna.) (Gu., gules, red, fire, autumn, charity, jewels, ruby, Mars.) (Az., azure, blue, air, summer; childhood, justice, hopeful, sapphire, Jupiter.) (Vert, green, life, spring, youth, strength, dragon, emerald, Venus.) (Sa., sable, black, earth, winter, night, death prudence, discreit, diamond, Saturn.) (Pur., purple, purpure, thunder, evening, old-age, serious, temperance, amethyst, Royal, Mercury,) (Tawney, tenne', yellowish-brown, juncus,) (Murrey, sanguine, sardonix, vivacious, cruel, color of blood.) (Ppr., proper color or the color of nature. (Vair, composed of pieces of fur in shield-shape, denotes Royalty, color of bluish-grey.) (Ermine, the tails of the animal, black spots on a white field, denotes Royalty.)

The Crest is the ornament which surmounts the helmet. Only those families which were of tournament rank were entitled to crest.

The Wreath is a skein of silk with a gold or silver cord twisted round it. It is drawn as six alternate links of metal and color. It's origin was to hide the joining of the crest to the helmet.

The Helmet: everybody during the period of warfare wore a helmet, so every coat of arms has a right to a helmet.

The Mantling is a cloth suspended from a point on the top of the helmet. Its purpose in real war-fare was to save the armour from rust, to absorb the heat of the sun playing upon the metal armour, and entangle the sword of an adversary.

The Shield is the surface on which the armorial bearings are displayed. A shield behind which the knight defended himself. A broad piece of defensive armour commonly carried on the left arm. The escutcheon upon which emblems or charges of heraldry are depicted. It was often heart shape on the oldest monuments, coins and seals.

The Motto is a word, saying or sentence which gentlemen carry in a scroll under the arms and some times over the crest. It is usually a religious nature, sometimes used as a *slogan* or *battle-cry*. Many arms have neither motto nor crest.

The Supporters: these are marks of Royal favour dating from the 14th century. In those chivalrous past times no one took part in tournaments except of noble descent or war-like renown, who displayed their armorial shield attended by masquerade characters dressed in skins of animals, birds, etc., grotesque and fantastic costumes. These men supported the shield while the knight took part in the tournament.

Arms are the sign for technical rank of gentility. The possession and use of a coat of arms is a privilege. Who is entitled to a coat of arms? All persons who can prove descent from an ancestor whose armorial bearings have been acknowledged in any one of the Visitations are entitled to carry those arms by right of inheritance. The registry of its birth was at the time of the Holy Wars, and its cradle was rocked by the soldiers of the Cross.

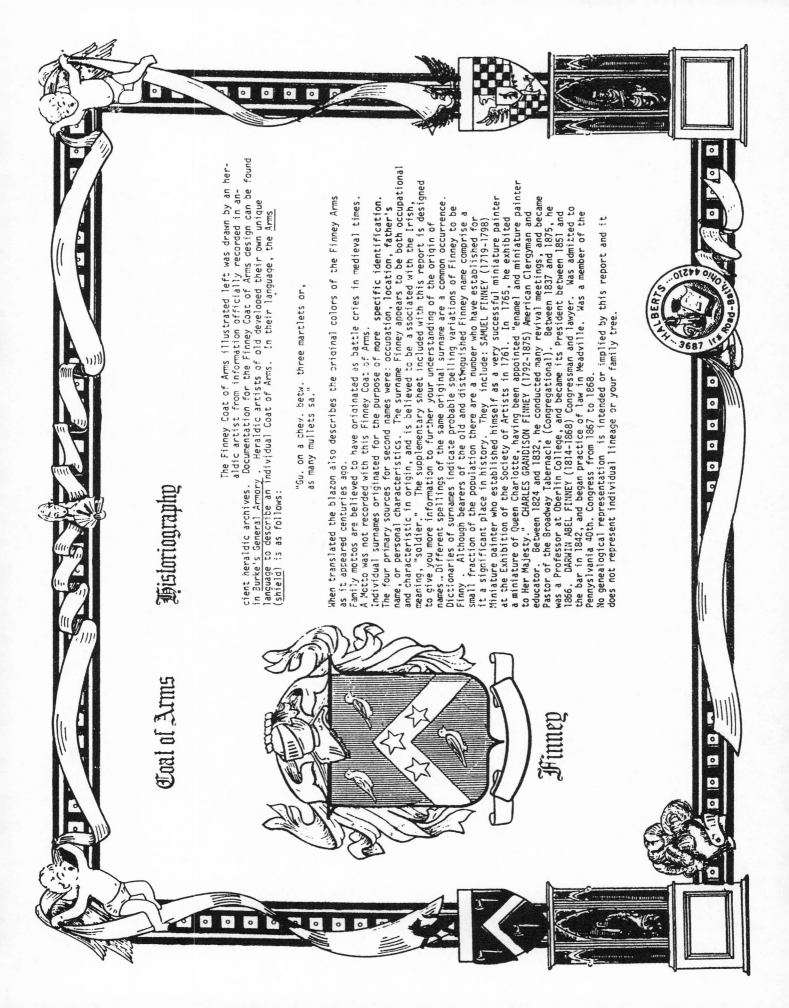

Coat of Arms

Historiography

The Finney Coat of Arms illustrated left was drawn by an heraldic artist from information officially recorded in an-
cient heraldic archives. Documentation for the Finney Coat of Arms design can be found
in Burke's General Armory. Heraldic artists of old developed their own unique
language to describe an individual Coat of Arms. In their language, the Arms
(shield) is as follows:

"Gu. on a chev. betw. three martlets or,
as many mullets sa."

When translated the blazon also describes the original colors of the Finney Arms
as it appeared centuries ago.
A Motto was not recorded with this Finney Coat of Arms.
Family mottos are believed to have originated as battle cries in medieval times.
Individual surnames originated for the purpose of more specific identification.
The four primary sources for second names were: occupation, location, father's
name, or personal characteristics. The surname Finney appears to be both occupational
and characteristic in origin, and is believed to be associated with the Irish,
meaning, "soldier." The supplementary sheet included with this report is designed
to give you more information to further your understanding of the origin of
names..Different spellings of the same original surname are a common occurrence.
Dictionaries of surnames indicate probable spelling variations of Finney to be
Finny. Although bearers of the old and distinguished Finney name comprise a
small fraction of the population there are a number who have established for
it a significant place in history. They include: SAMUEL FINNEY (1719-1798)
Miniature painter who established himself as a very successful miniature painter
at the Exhibition of the Society of Artists in 1761. In 1765, he exhibited
a miniature of Queen Charlotte, having been appointed "enamel and miniature painter
to Her Majesty." CHARLES GRANDISON FINNEY (1792-1875) American Clergyman and
educator. Between 1824 and 1832, he conducted many revival meetings, and became
Pastor of the Broadway Tabernacle (Congregational). Between 1837 and 1875, he
was a Professor at Oberlin College, and became its President between 1851 and
1866. DARWIN ABEL FINNEY (1814-1868) Congressman and lawyer. Was admitted to
the bar in 1842, and began practice of law in Meadville. Was a member of the
Pennsylvania 40th. Congress from 1867 to 1868.
No genealogical representation is intended or implied by this report and it
does not represent individual lineage or your family tree.

Finney

The material in this book was found in records from various sources. Much of the information was found over a period of ten years, and some was taken from the records in THE FINNEY FAMILY HISTORY 1732-1946, compiled by Minnehaha Finney, and some from other family records. Many of the entrees were found in the Mayflower Society Index and from SAR and DAR records.

This compiler wishes to thank and express his gratituded for the assistance with the many records furnished by Mr. Thomas R. Finney of Logansport, Indiana. His help in loaning me the material he had of the Finney Family were very helpful in the completion of these records. I also want to thank the other Finneys/Phinneys for their help also in records sent to me.

This book is written in alphabetical order as far as possible with the exception of the first part. In the index will be names of other related families and their offspring, that will be found no where else in this book. There are spaces left for notes and there are five blank pages in the back of the book for other information readers may use for any information they may have that is not in this book, or information about those that are but was not known at the time of this writing.

The Compiler.

HOW TO USED THIS BOOK

In locating people in this book, for example: JOHN FINNEY, look in FINNEY, find JOHN. A number back of his name means there is more about him at the place designated. Exampld: 54-532 means that by turning to page 54 you will find him at item 532.

In the index you will also find a number such as 49F which means that there is nothing more about him in this book, but he can be found at the page designated in THE FINNEY FAMILY HISTORY by Minnehaha Finney.

After the first section of the book the names will be listed in alphabetical order and will begin with FINNEY and then PHINNWY, than by the regular order. The Finney and Phinney names are listed Alphabetically, Sample: 1EF2 means that by turning to page 1EF you will find information at the 2nd entry. Example 1PH2 Means names is spelled with the PH and will be found at page 1PH at entry no. 2 The E before the F or PH means that his first name starts with E. Other names in this book will be found under their last names.

ABBREVIATIONS
****

b.	Born	F.	Finney
bpt	Baptized	Int.	Marriage Intent
c before dates. About		IN	Index
dau.	daughter	MF	Mayflower
desc.	descendant.	PH	Phinney.
DAR	Daughters American Revolution	SAR	Sons American Revolution.

sic - spelling is correct or was copied as found in records

Freeman, means that this person is now free from the person to whom he was an indentured servant, in order to get to America or because he was a non=desirable in England.

THE FINNEY/PHINNEY FAMILIES

Both the Bristol and Barnstable Lines
****
By

ROY J. CAMPBELL
A Descendant
****

      This family seems to have come from England before 1630 and consisted of a mother and three children; one daughter and two sons. "Mother" Finney d. in Plymouth, Mass. April 22, 1650"---aged upward of 80 years".

ISSUE:

!.   CATHERINE FINNEY b. c1586 d. June 7,1673. She m. GABRIEL FAL-LOWELL b. c1584 d. Dec. 18, 1667.

     ISSUE: *FALLOWELL.*

    1.   JOHN FALLOWELL d. before 1649.

    2.   ANN FALLOWELL m. THOMAS POPE of Plymouth who d. July 20, 1637

        Ann d. May 1, 1646.

2.   ROBERT FINNEY, b. c1608 d. 1687 m. Sept. 1,1641, PHEBE RIPLEY b. 1619 d. Oct. 9, 1710 in her 92nd year. Robert d. Jan. 7 or 9,1688. He had no children so left his property to his two nephews, children of his brother, John. There is a record stating he had a son "--of the first Robert" whose name was Josiah who had a large family. This could not be as Robert would not have left his estate to other than his own son. (See Special Section for this Josiah.)

*3,   JOHN FINNEY, the Pilgrim.

----

3. JOHN FINNEY, the Pilgrim b. 16__ d. c1703 son of "Mother" Finney.
    He m. (1) CHRISTIANA _____ who d. in Plymouth, Sept. 9,1649.
    He then m. (2) June 10, 1650 ABIGAIL COGGIN wife of Henry Cog-
    gin and dau of Thomas Bishop. She d. May 6, 1653 and he m. (3) June
    25,1654 ELIZABETH BAILEY, who was buried in BristolFeb. 9,1683/4.
    He received a land grant in Plymouth 1639/40. With his son, John, Jr.
    he was admitted a freeman of Barnstable, May 29, 1670 where John
    Jr. settled. For a time he was a resident of Scituate, Mass; but later
    joined the company which settled in Barnstable. In 1686 he sold his in-
    terest in the Mount Hope lands at Bristol to his son Jonathan. In 1702
    he moved to Swansea, Mass. where he died.
    ISSUE:

*4. JOHN FINNEY b. Dec. 24,1638. He m. Aug. 10, 1664 MARY ROGERS

 5, THOMAS FINNEY b. c1648 d. c1653.

By 3rd Wife all born in Barnstable

*6. JONATHAN FINNEY b. Aug. 14,1655.

 7. ROBERT FINNEY, b. Aug. 13,1656 d. 1690 moved to Plymouth.
     He afterwards joined the expedition to Canada under Phipps where
     he lost his life. His will is dated July 23,1690.

*8. HANNAH FINNEY 1657-____ m. (1) 1677 DEA. EPHRAIM MORTON
     son of Ephraim and Ann (Cooper) Morton. b. Jan 27,1648. She d.
     Feb. 18, 1732. Hannah m. (2) JOHN COOKE of Kingston, Mass. No
     issue by second husband.

 9. ELIZABETH FINNEY, b. March 15,1659 m. Dec. 19, 1773 HAILE
     BARTON b. c1753 son of Benjamin and Mary (Haile) Barton.

10. JOSIAH FINNEY b. Jan. 11, 1661; lived in Plymouth and had a
     large family. He m. Jan 19,1688 ELIZABETH WARREN, dau of
     Joseph Warren.

*11, JEREMIAH FINNEY b. Aug. 15,1662.

*12. JOSHUA FINNEY b. Dec. 1665.

---

4. JOHN FINNEY b. Dec. 24, 1638 son of JOHN and CHRISTIANA. He was the founder of the Barnstable line and changed the spelling of his name to P-H=I-N-N-E-Y. He m. MARY ROGERS the dau of Lt. John Rogers, son of Thomas Rogers of the *MAYFLOWER*. Mary Rogers was b. Sept. 22, 1644 and d. 1718. John d. 1718/19.

ISSUE:

*13. JOHN PHINNEY b. May 5, 1665.

14. MELETIAH PHINNEY b. Oct. 1666 d. 1667.

*15. JOSEPH PHINNEY b. Jan 28, 1668.

*16. THOMAS PHINNEY b. Jan 1672.

*17. EBENEZER PHINNEY b. Feb. 1674.

*18. SAMUEL PHINNEY b. Nov. 4, 1676.

*19. MARY PHINNEY b. Sept. 3, 1678 ; m. John Eastland.

*20. MERCY PHINNEY b. July 10, 1679.

*21. RELIANCE PHINNEY,

*22. BENJAMIN PHINNEY b. June 18, 1682.

*23. JONATHAN PHINEY, b. July 30, 1684.

24. HANNAH PHINNEY b. March 28, 1687 bpt. April 7, 1690 d. young.

25. ELIZABETH PHINNEY, b. March 28, 1687 bpt April 7, 1690. She d. young.

_____

6. JONATHAN FINNEY, b. Aug 14, 1655 d. May 1728 m. Int. Oct. 18, 1682 JOANNA KINNICUTT dau of JOHN and ELIZABETH KINNICUTT of Bristol. He was one of the first settlers in Bristol and made a freeman in 1680. He d. in Swansea, Mass. She d. Nov. 30, 1739. His descendants all spell their name with the "Ph" instead of the "F"

ISSUE:

26. JOANNA PHINNEY b. Nov. 30, 1683 m. a Mr. Clark.

27. JONATHAN PHINNEY, b. Nov. 3, 1686.

28. MEHETABEL PHINNEY bpt. Jan 19, 1688/9

29. ELIZABETH PHINNEY, bpt. 1695 d. June 30, 1730 She m. DAVID BRADFORD.

30. LYDIA PHINNEY, bpt 1695 m. HOPESTILL COTTON.

31. MARY PHINNEY, bpt. 1695.

32. EBENEZER PHINNEY bpt April 23, 1699.

33. HANNAH PHINNEY b. March 28, 1637 d. Feb. 10, 1689.

8. HANNAH FINNEY 1657-____ dau of John and his third wife ELIZABETH BAILEY. Hannah m. (1) DEA. EPHRAIM MORTON, son of Ephraim and Ann (Cooper)Morton. He was b. Jan. 27, 1648 d. Feb. 18,1732. She m. (2) JOHN COOKE of Kingston, Mass. There was no issue by the second husband. Hannah was born Sept. 2, 1657.

ISSUE: MORTON.

1. *HANNAH B. 1677 m. Benjamin Morton.*
2. *EPHRAIM. b. 1678.*
3. *JOHN, b. 1680 m. RELIANCE or REBECCA PHINNEY dau of his uncle John Phinney of Barnstable.*
4. *JOSEPH b. 1683.* *Were they twins?*
5. *EBENEZER b. 1683*

_____

11. JEREMIAH FINNEY, b. Aug. 15,1662 d. Feb. 18,1748 son of John and Elizabeth (Bailey) Finney. He m. Jan 7, 1684 ESTHER LEWIS dau of Thomas and Mary Lewis of Bristol, Mass. HE was a shipmaster. Esther was b. 1664 and d. April 11, 1748.

ISSUE:

34. JEREMIAH b. 1684 d. young.
35. MARY, b. March 26, 1686.
*36. HANNAH, b. Jan 14, 1687 d. Dec. 22, 1744 (?)
37. MEHETABLE b. May 8, 1687 d. Dec. 22, 1744 (?)
38. JOHN b. Aug. 3,1690 d young.
39. REBECCA b. Feb. 24,1691 m. March 11,1716 SAMUEL HARRIS of Swansee, Mass.
*40 ESTHER b. May 4, 1693 m. Int. Oct. 31, 1719 JOSEPH JOY.
41, DEBORAH bpt. Oct. 20, 1695.
*42. JOHN b. April 13,1696.
43. ABIGAIL b. April 17, 1697.
*44. JEREMIAH bpt. Sept 7, 1700.

_____

12.   JOSHUA FINNEY, b. Dec. 1665 d. Sept 7, 1714 son of JOHN and ELIZ-

ABETH (BAILEY) FINNEY. Marriage Intent May 31,1688 to MERCY WATTS of Bristol, Mass. She d. Feb. 12,1724. He moved to Bristol where his children were born. He moved to Swansea, Mass, where he died.

ISSUE:

*45.   JOSHUA FINNEY b. May 7, 1689.

46.   ELIZABETH FINNEY b. Sept. 25,1691/2 d. Sept. 19,1701.

47.   MARY FINNEY b. Sept. 25,1694.

*48.   JOHN FINNEY, b. Aug. 15,1696. He was known as "Doctor John"

*49,   SAMUEL FINNEY, b. May 29,1699.

*50.   JOSIAH FINNEY B. July 26, 1701.

51.   ELIZABETH FINNEY b. may 1,1707 m. Nov. 4,1753 NATHAN LUTHER of Swansea.

     A.   HULDAH LUTHER.

----

13.   JOHN PHINNEY b. May 5, 1665 d. 1746. He was the son of JOHN and MARY (ROGERS) FINNEY. He m. May 30, 1639 SARAH LUMBERT of Barnstable. She was the dau of Thomas and Elizabeth (Derby) Lumbert. Another account gives her birth as December 1666.

ISSUE:

*52.   ELIZABETH PHINNEY b. April 11, 1690.

53.   MARY PHINNEY b. Jan 20, 1692 d. Jan 1694.

*54,   JOHN PHINNEY b. April 8, 1696.

*55.   THOMAS PHINNEY b. May 25,1697 bpt. June 21,1697.

*56.   HANNAH PHINNEY b. April 8, 1700.

*57,   SARAH PHINNEY, b. Oct. 8, 1701 bpt. Nov. 9, 1702.

*58.   PATIENCE PHINNEY b. Sept. 12,1704.

*59.   MARTHA PHINNEY b. July 12,1706.

*60.   JABEZ PHINNEY, b. July 16,1708.

----

15.   JOSEPH PHINNEY B. Jan.28,1668 d. June 29, 1726 son of JOHN
and MARY (ROGERS) PHINNEY. He m. (1) MERCY BRYANT June
15,1693. She d. 1706. He m. (2) Sept. 19, 1706 ESTHER WEST Sept.
30.1680. Believe she died in Bridgewater 1778 age 96. She was
the dau of PETER and PATIENCE WEST. The will of Peter West
of Plympton, made July 25,1717 names daughter Esther. The will
of Joseph Phinney of Plympton made June 27,1726 names wife
Esther; sons, John, Joseph, and Peletiah, daughters Alice Hamblin,
Mary Hamblin, Mercy Phinney and Patience Phinney.
ISSUE:

   61.   ALICE PHINNEY b.April 1,1694. Marriage Int. Nov.21,1724
EBENEZER HAMBLIN JR. and m. Dec. 10,1724. The marriage record calls him "Eleazer" which was the name of
her sister's husband. Ebenezer was probably b. in Barnstable
March 18, 1698/9 to EBENEZER and SARAH (LEWIS) HAMBLIN.

 *62.   JOHN PHINNEY, b. Dec. 17,1696.

   63.   MARY PHINNEY b. May 5, 1700 m.Feb. 25, 1721 ELEAZER
HAMBLIN probably b.Aug. 22,1699 son of ISAAC and ELIZA=
BETH (HOWLAND) HAMBLIN. **Did she also m. Samuel Clark?**

   64.   MARCY (sic)Phinney b. Sept. 19,1707 living June 27,1726.

 *65.   JOSEPH PHINNEY b.April 10, 1709.

 *66.   PELATIAH PHINNEY, b. March 21,1710/1.

 *67.   PATIENCE PHINNEY b. Aug.19,1713; m. probably ROBERT
COOK in 1735 and had children.

   68.   EXPERIENCE PHINNEY b. April 8, 1716 d. Sept. 22,1724.

   69.   HANNAH PHINNEY b. April 8, 1720 d. Sept 5,1724.

----

16.   THOMAS PHINNEY, b.1671 d. 1755 son of JOHN and MARY (ROGERS)
PHINNEY. He m. Aug. 25,1698 the "the widow SARAH BEETLE" Sept.
1748 age 70. She was probably the dau of Richard Lockwood of Kit-
tary.Me. and the widow of Christopher Beetle whom she m. in 1686
Another record states he m. SARAH BUTLER b. 1678 d. Dec.1748.
ISSUE:

 *70.   GERSHOM PHINNEY b. March 21,1699/1700

 *71.   THOMAS PHINNEY, b. Feb.17, 1702/3.

   72.   ABIGAIL PHINNEY, b. June 8, 1704.

   73.   JAMES PHINNEY b. April 15,1706.

   74.   MERCY PHINNEY,b. Aug. 24,1708. She m. 1734 JOHN LINNELL
B. 1702 son of JOHN and RUTH (DAVIS)LINNELL

17.   EBENEZER PHINNEY, b. Feb. 18,1673 d. April 10, 1784, in Barnstable,
son of JOHN and MARY (ROGERS)PHINNEY. He m. Nov. 14, 1695
SUSANNA LINNELL dau of David and Hannah (Shelby)Linnell. Susanna
was b. 1673 and d. Nov. 23,1754.   David Linnell's will included wife
Hannah and daughter Susanna,dated 1688.   Ebenezer's will dated Nov.
26,1734 names grand-daughter, Lydia Phinney; sons,Samuel,Ebenezer
and David; daughters Mehitable, Mary and Rebecca.

ISSUE:

*75.   MEHITABLE PHINNEY b. Aug. 14,1696 m. SAMUEL HIGGINS.

*76.   MARY PHINNEY, b. March 23,1698.

77.   MARTHA PHINNEY b. April 22, 1700.

*78.   SAMUEL PHINNEY b. April 1, **1702**

*79.   REBECCA PHINNEY bpt June 11,1703.

80.   LYDIA PHINNEY (?) bpt July 7,1706.

*81.   EBENEZER PHINNEY, b. May 26,1708.

*82,   DAVID PHINNEY b. June 10,1710.

83.   SETH PHINNEY, (?) b. Sept 12,1714.

18.   SAMUEL PHINNEY, B. Nov.4,1676, son of JOHN and MARY (ROGERS)
PHINNEY. He m. April 30,1713. **BETHIA SMITH of Eastham. Believe**
she was the dau of John and Mary (Eldridge) Smith., b. Jan 16,1681/2.
ISSUE:

84.   BETHIA PHINNEY b. July 9,1726.

85.   THANKFUL PHINNEY, bpt July 29,1716.

86.   RHODA PHINNEY, b. Feb. 1, 1718/19

87.   MARY PHINNEY bpt June 16, 1723.

NOTES

19. MARY PHINNEY, b. Sept. 3. 1678 f/ before 1755 dau of JOHN and MARY (ROGERS)PHINNEY. She m. (1) Plymouth Oct. 29,1702 JOHN EASTLAND who d. 1726. He had previously m. (1) 1700 Elizabeth Janney. On Sept. 24,1726 an inventory of the estate of John Eastland was taken and in November £726 allowance was made for the widow, Mary. She m. (2) Int. Nov. 12,1726 JONATHAN BRYANT son of John and Abigail (Bryant)Bryant. He had previously been married to Margery_____ . Jonathan was b. March 23,1677 in Plymouth and d. before July 3, 1731. On July 3, 1731 claims against the estate were filed and on May 19, 1733 dower was set off to Mary Bryant, widow of Jonatehan of Plymouth, in holder deceased. Mary had died apparently before Jan. 24, 1756, when an accounting was rendered on the estate by an administrator *DE BON IS NON.*

ISSUE: *EASTLAND*

*88. ZERULAH b. Dec. 8, 1703.

*89. JOSEPH b. May 12, 1705.

*90. ELIZABETH b. Jan 31, 1708.

91. MAREY (sic) b. Nov. 1, 1710 d. Nov. 13, 17___ .

92. HANNAH b. Feb. 13, 1712-13 d. Dec. 2, 1717.

93. JEAN b. Sept. 15, 1715 d. Dec. 18, 1717.

94. JOSHUA b. April 13,1718 d. July 25, 1719.

95. MARY b. March 1, 1720.

---

20. MERCY PHINNEY, b. July 10, 1679 d. c1731. dau of JOHN and MARY (ROGERS)PHINNEY. She m. Jan 26,1715 ELEAZER CROCKER, b. July 21,1650, d. before Sept. 6, 1723 son of William and Alice Crocker. He had previously married in 1682 Ruth Chipman, a descendant of Pilgrim John Howland. On July 8, 1731 Isaac Hinkly of Barnstable was appointed guardian of Mercy Crocker, Minor, dau of Eleazer.

ISSUE: *CROCKER.*

1. *MERCY c1717.*

NOTES

8.

9.

21. RELIANCE PHINNEY, b. Aug. 27,1681 d. Dec. 4,1735 age 55, dau of
JOHN and MARY (ROGERS)PHINNEY.She ma. Dec. 27.1705 JOHN
MORTON b. July 20, 1680. age 59 son of Ephraim and Hannah (Finney)
Morton.

ISSUE: MORTON

1. JOHN b. Nov.15,1706 b. April 6,1765 (of Eel River.) No known marriage or children.
2. JONATHAN b.Feb.10, 1707/8 d. Dec. 29,1708.
3. JOSIAH b. Feb. 28,1708
4. JAMES b.May 13,1714.
5. DAVID b.March 19, 1716 m. May 8, 1739 REBECCA FINNEY.She was bpt. Sept. 27,
1727 dau of ROBERT and ANN (MORTON) FINNEY.

22. BENJAMIN PHINNEY,b. June 18,1682 d. before July·19,1758 son of
JOHN and MARY (ROGERS)PHINNEY. He m. (1)June 30,1709 in Barnstable MARTHA CROCKER, b. Feb. 22,1689/90. d. before Sept. 19,
1747. dau of Joseph and Temperance (Bursley) Crocker. Benjamin
and his wife, Martha were named in the will of Joseph Crocker. Benjamin m. (2) Nov 5,1747 ELIZABETH (YOUNG) AMES, dau of Henry
and Sarah (Snow) Young, of Eastham and probably the widow of Zephon
Ames.

ISSUE, by first wife.

*96. TEMPERANCE PHINNEY b. March 28, 1710.

*97. MELATIAH PHINNEY b. July 26,1712.

*98. BARNABAS PHINNEY b. March 28,1715.

99. SILAS PHINNEY, b. June 16. 1718 d. May 1720.

*100. ZACCHEUS PHINNEY b. Aug. 4, 1720.

*101. SETH PHINNEY b. June 27,1723.

102. LUSANNA PHINNEY, m_____DINMOCK before Nov. 21,1748.
when she witnessed her step-mother's deed.

NOTES

23.   JONATHAN PHINNEY b. July 30, 1684 d. between Sept 9, and Nov.
       6, 1738. He was the son of JOHN and MARY (ROGERS) FINNEY. He
       m. (1)c1717 ELIZABETH_____. He m. (2) Oct, 16,1735 DEBORAH
       WADE b. 1691 dau of Thomas and Elizabeth   (Curtis) .Wade.
       ISSUE:
       *103.   THANKFUL PHINNEY b. Barnstable Dec. 14, 1713.
       *104.   JOSEPH PHINNEY b. Barnstable Jan 24,1716.
        105.   JONATHAN PHINNEY b. Sept. 22, 1718 d. before Sept 21.1
                1739.
        106.   MEHITABLE PHINNEY bpt. Feb. 17, 1730.
        107.   TIMOTHY PHINNEY bpt. Feb. 17,1720.
       *108.   JOSHUA PHINNEY B. Jan 10, 1720
       *109.   ELIZABETH PHINNEY, b. 1718(?)m. JOHN MACOMBER.

                         _____

27.   JONATHAN PHINNEY b. Nov. 3, 1686 d. Nov; 26,1736 spm pf JONATHON
       and JOANNA (KINNICUTT) PHINNEY. He m. May 6, 1730 MERCY READ
       b. 1706 d. Nov 1767. He was a farmer and resided in Swansea. He was
       a mariner before he was a farmer. After his death his widow married (2)
       Benjamin Smith.
       ISSUE:
       *110.   HANNAH PHINNEY.
        111.   JONATHAN PHINNEY b. April 1733 d. May 1735.
        112.   JONATHAN PHINNEY b. Aug. 4, 1734 d. Sept 1739.
       *113.   ELISHA PHINNEY b. March 30, 1737 Posthumously.

                         _____

32.   EBENEZER PHINNEY bpt. April 23,1699&son of JONATHON and JOANNA
       (KINNICUTT) PHINNEY. He m. Int. May 28,1726 JANE FAUNCE dau.
       of Thomas and Jane (Nelson) Faunce. She was b. 1692 in Plymouth, Mass.
       It is possible he married his first wife in Norton, Mass. who was ABIGAIL
       CAMPBELL dau of Sylvanus Campbell.
       ISSUE:
        114.   NELSON PHINNEY b. July 8, 1728 d. Aug. 23,1730.

                         _____

36.   HANNAH FINNEY, b. Jan. 14, 1687 d. Dec. 22, 1744 dau of JEREMIAH
      ahd ESTHER (LEWIS)FINNEY. She m. Jan. 14,1706/7 THOMAS DIAMANT
      or DIMA son of Thomas and Hannah (James)Diamant. They moved from
      Long Island to Bristol in 1712. She d. in Bristol.
      ISSUE: *DIAMANT.*

      1.   *JAMES B. 1707 d. Oct 8, 1788. He was b. in Long Island.*
      2.   *JOHN b. c1709.*
      3.   *REBECCA b. in Long Island.*
      4.   *JEREMIAH b. 1710 in Long Island d. Nov. 10, 1798.*
      5.   *JONATHAN b. 1712 d. Feb. 25, 1797.*
      6.   *PHEBE b. 1717 d. Sept. 14,1790*
      7.   *LUCRETIA b. 1719 d. Jan 31, 1797.*
      8.   *DANIEL, b. Dec. 15, 1797 (?)*

                          _____

                          NOTES

40. ESTHER FINNEY, b. May 4, 1693 dau of Jeremiah Finney (11)
m. Int. Oct. 31,1719 JOSEPH JOY.
ISSUE: JOY
1. ESTHER b. 1770 d. Aug. 2, 1747.
2. JOSEPH b. June 25, 1773.
3. A CHILD b. 1726 d. July 1734.

---

42. JOHN FINNEY, b. April 13,1696 son of JEREMIAH and ESTHER (LEWIS)
FINNEY. He m. MARY CAMPBELL dau of Sylvanus and Mary Campbell.
of Norton, Mass. He purchased land in Norton in conjunction with his
cousin, Ebeanezer. He came to Norton in 1717 and moved to Easton in
c1766. There was only one child as far as is known by this compiler.
The child's name was ABIJAH FINNEY.

---

44. JEREMIAH FINNEY bpt. Sept. 7, 1700 son of JEREMIAH and ESTHER
(LEWIS) FINNEY. He m. Int. May 17,1727 ELIZABETH BRISTOW of Bristol, dau of Thomas and Elizabeth Bristow. She was b. Dec. 14,1706 d.
Nov. 8, 1730. He was a shipmaster living in Bristol.
ISSUE:
*115. JOSIAH FINNEY, b. July 1, 1728.
116. A CHILD b. Feb. 27, 1730
117. ELIZABETH FINNEY, b. 1731 d. May 14,1759.
*118. JEREMIAH FINNEY b. 1732 d. 1792.
£119. THOMAS FINNEY 1737-1792
*120. MARY FINNEY, b. 1742.
121. ESTHER FINNEY 1745-1746

NOTES.

46.   JOSHUA FINNEY b. May 7, 1689 d. _____ son of JOSHUA and MERCY
(WATTS)FINNEY. He m. MARTHA CARTER b. 1671 d. May 14, 1751.
They lived in Swansea, later moving to Lebanon, Conn. where they
purchased land in 1726 and moving there in 1750. Two of his brothers
John and Josiah moved to Litchfield county, Conn. He was a farmer.

ISSUE:

*122.   WILLIAM FINNEY.

123.   JOSIAH FINNEY, b. May 11, 1716 d. Nov. 29. 1746.

124.   MARY (MERCY) FINNEY. b. July 5, 1718 m. March 14,
1733/4 JOSEPH MANN d. before 1743.

125.   MARTHA FINNEY b. March 4, 1719/20

*126.   JOHN FINNEY

*127.   OLIVER FINNEY.

48.   JOHN FINNEY, b. Aug. 16, 1696 d. June 6, 1773 son of JOSHUA and
MERCY (WATTS)FINNEY. He m. Sept. 14, 1716 ANN TOOGOOD of
Swansea, Mass. who d. Aug. 11, 1778. He moved to Morton, Mass. then
purchased land in Lebanon, Conn. in 1738. He also owned land in
Kent, Conn. He seems to have been a physician although in deed he is
called a blacksmith. He was known as "Doctor John".
ISSUE:

128.   JOEL FINNEY b. Feb. 24, 1716/7

*129,   JOHN FINNEY b. Oct. 14, 1718.

*130.   NATHANIEL FINNEY.

131.   JOSHUA FINNEY, b. Feb. 24, 1723/4.

132.   ANN FINNEY b. April 30, 1727.

133.   MERCY FINNEY b. Jan. 1, 1729/30. m. Dec. 21, 1752 REUBIN
SACKET of East Greenwich, New Warren, Conn.

*134.   DAVID FINNEY.

135.   MARTHA FINNEY b. and d. June 12, 1738.

*136.   JABEZ FINNEY.

49. SAMUEL FINNEY, b. May 20, 1699 d. 1763 son of JOSHUA and MERCY
(WATTS)FINNEY. He m. March 12, 1726/7 ELIZABETH WOOD dau of
John and widow of Thomas **Tibbitts.** He was a blacksmith.

ISSUE:

137.   BENJAMIN FINNEY d. young.

138.   MERCY FINNEY b. March 25, 1732 m. Dec. 21, 1752 REUBIN
_____ of Warren, Conn. In 1765 she moved to Little Comp-
ton, R. I.

----

50. JOSIAH FINNEY b. July 26, 1701 d. 1774 son of JOSHUA and MERCY
(WATTS) FINNEY. He m. Jan. 1, 1723/4 ELIZABETH MANN. He was
one of the earliest settlers of Warren, Conn. Elizabeth d. 1775. Josiah's
will was proved Aug. 22, 1774.

ISSUE:

139.   ELIZABETH FINNEY b. Jan. 19, 1723/4

140.   JOSIAH FINNEY b. Jan 27, 1725/6 d. Sept 1726.

*141.   JOSIAH FINNEY, b. Feb. 24, 1727/8.

142.   KEZIAH FINNEY, b. March 5, 1730.

143.   LYDIA FINNEY b. March 6, 1732 d. c1770.

*144.   DAVID FINNEY.

*145.   JONATHAN FINNEY b. June 1, 1736.

----

52. ELIZABETH PHINNEY b. April 11, 1690 d. Dec. 30, 1786 age 96 dau
of JOHN and SARAH (LUMBERT)PHINNEY. She m. in Barnstable Nov.
25, 1714 NATHAN DAVIS b. Barnstable, March 2, 1690 son of Jabez and
Experience (Linnell)Davis. He d. in Harwinton, Conn. Sept 17, 1785. He
was 96 at his death.

ISSUE: D A V I S

1.   JABEZ b. 1715.

2.   SARAH b. and d. 1717.

3.   ELIZABETH. b. 1718.

4.   ISAAC b. 1720

5.   NATHAN.(?) b. 1735.

54. JOHN PHINNEY b. April 8, 1696 d. Dec.29, 1780 age 86 son of JOHN
     and SARAH (LUMBERT) PHINNEY.   He was b. in Barnstable and d. in
     Corban, Maine. He m. in Barnstable Sept 25,1718 MARTHA COLEMAN
     b. Barnstable March 4, 1698 d. Dec. 16, 1784 at age 47. She was the
     dau of James and Patience (Cobb) Coleman.
     ISSUE:

146.   ELIZABETH PHINNEY b. 1721.
147.   EDMUND PHINNEY b. 1723.
148.   STEPHEN PHINNEY, b. 1723.
149.   MARTHA PHINNEY b. 1727.
150.   PATIENCE PHINNEY, b. 1730.
151.   JOHN PHINNEY, b. 1732.
152.   SARAH PHINNEY b 1734.
153.   MARY PHINNEY b. 1736. Her middle name was GORHAM.
154.   COLEMAN PHINNEY b. 1732 (?)
155,   JAMES PHINNEY b. 1741.

55. THOMAS PHINNEY b. May 25,1697 bpt. June 21,1698 son of JOHN and
     SARAH (LUMBERT) PHINNEY. He m. March 31,1726 RELIANCE GOOD-
     SPEED b. Sept. 18, 1701 d. Jan 27,1784 dau of Ebenezer and Lydia (Cro-
     well) Goodspeed.
     ISSUE:

156.   ELI PHINNEY b. 1726/7.
157.   LYDY PHINNEY b. 1729 m. _____ HODGE.
158.   SARAH PHINNEY b. 1731/2 m. SYLVANUS HINKLEY.
*159.   ISAAC PHINNEY b.1734.
160.   PATIENCE PHINNEY, b. 1736 d. before 1754 m._____ BEARSE.
161.   ABIGAIL PHINNEY b. 1740.
162.   ELIZABETH PHINNEY b.1742.

56. HANNAH PHINNEY, b. April 8,1700 dau of JOHN and SARAH (LUMBERT) PHINNEY. She m. Oct. 6, 1720 at Barnstable ROGER GOODSPEED, b. Oct. 14,1698 d. before April 18, 1791. He was the son of Ebenezer and Lydia (Crowell) Goodspeed.

ISSUE: GOODSPEED.

1. THOMAS b. 1721   2. ISAAC b. 1723.   3. SARAH b. 1727

4. ELIZABETH b. 1731.   5. JOSEPH b. 1736.

---

57. SARAH PHINNEY b. Oct. 8, 1701 bpt. Nov. 9, 1702. She was the dau of JOHN and SARAH (LUMBERT) PHINNEY. She m. Int. Aug. 27,1724 THOMAS ADAMS b. Bristol, R.I. March 28,1698 son of Edward and Elizabeth (Walley) Adams.

ISSUE: ADAMS.

1. MARTHA b. 1725   2. THOMAS b. 1726   3. ELIZABETH b. 1728

4. WALLEY b. 1730   5. SARAH b. 1732   6. NATHANIEL b. 1734.

7. EDWARD b. 1736   8. HANNAH b. 1737/8   9. OBED (?)

---

58. PATIENCE PHINNEY b. Sept 12, 1704 dau of JOHN and SARAH (LUMBERT) PHINNEY. She m. in Barnstable March 12, 1727/8 JAMES COLEMAN b. April 11, 1704 d. Barnstable April 16, 1781 age 77 . He was the son of James and Patience (Cobb) Coleman. Her sister, Martha, also made her marriage intentions and married the same day. (See 59).

ISSUE: COLEMAN.

1. MARTHA b. 1728/9 died young 2. MARTHA b. 1732. 3. JAMES B. 1735

4. EBENEZER or JOHN b. 1737   5. MARY b. 1739   6. PATIENCEe.

NOTES

59. MARTHA PHINNEY b. July 12, 1706 dau of JOHN and SARAH (LUMBERT) PHINNEY. She m. in Barnstable March 12, 1727/8 JONATHAN LUMBERT b. April 16,1703 son of Joshua and Hopestill (Bullock)Lumbert. Martha and her sister Patience were married on the same day.

ISSUE: LUMBERT.

1. JONATHAN b. 1729.   2. MARTHAN b. 1731   3. MERCY b 1733/4   4. HOPESTILL b. 1737
5. SARAH b. 1739   6. SUSANNAH b. 1741.   7. SIMEON b. 1744.   8. JABEZ b.1748.

----

60. JABEZ PHINNEY b. July 16,1708 d. Dec. 1,1776 son of JOHN and SARAH (LUMBERT) PHINNEY. He m. Oct 5, 1732 JANE TAYLOR b. in Barnstable Oct. 15,1709 d. Barnstable July 10,1787 dau of Abraham and Mary (Butler) Taylor.

ISSUE:

163.   JOSEPH PHINNEY b. 1733 d. young

164.   MARY PHINNEY, b. 1735.

165.   ANNE PHINNEY b. 1738.

166.   HANNAH PHINNEY, b. 1741.

167.   JOSEPH PHINNEY, b. 1744.

168.   JOHN PHINNEY, b. 1745.

NOTES

17.

62. JOHN FINNEY, b. Dec. 17,1696 son of JOSEPH and MERCY (BRYANT) PHIN-
NEY. He m. (1)March 1, 1721 REBECCA BRYANT b. in Plymouth Dec. 8,1702
d. Kingston, Aug. 28,1741, dau of Jonathan and Margaret (West) Bryant. He m.
(2) April 5,1743 BETTY LOVELL of Abington. He m. (3) Dec. 25,1770 RUTH
SYLVESTER COOKE RING, b. June 26,1702 d. before Nov. 17,1779. She was the
dau of Israel and Ruth (Turner) Sylvester, a descendant of Pilgrim Stephen Hopkins.
ISSUE: By first wife:

169.   JONATHAN PHINNEY, b. Plymouth 1722/3 d. 1734/5
170.   JOHN PHINNEY, b. Plymouth 1724/5 d. 1750
171.   JONATEHAN PHINNEY, b. Kingston 1725/6 s. 1750.
172,   REBECCA PHINNEY b. Kingston 1730 d. 1747.
173.   JOHN PHINNEY b. Kingston, 1733 d. 1751,
174.   JOSEPH PHINNEYb. 1737 d. 1759.

---

65. JOSEPH PHINNEY b. April 10,1709 d. Dec. 21,1795 son of JOSEPH and ESTHER
(WEST) PHINNEY. He m. (1) Jan 9, 1734/5 MARY RICKARD d. Sept. 11, 1760
"Wife of Joseph" possibly Mary b. Oct. 29, 1711 in Plymouth to Joseph Rickard.
He m. (2) Jan. 14, 1762 ALICE HACKETT-RICHMOND CAMPBELL b. Jan. 18,
1714/5 d. after Nov. 27, 1763, dau of John and Elizabeth (Elliott) Hackett.
ISSUE: All by first wife.

175.   EXPERIENCE PHINNEY b. 1736.
176.   ACHSAH PHINNEY b. 1738.
177.   PELETIAH PHINNEY b. 1743.
178.   ALICE PHINNEY b. 1742/3 d. 1748/9
179.   AMY PHINNEY b. 1745.
180.   NOAH PHINNEY b. 1748,
181.   REBECCA PHINNEY b. 1750.

NOTES

66. PELETIAH PHINNEY b. March 21, 1710/11 son of JOSEPH and
     ESTHER (WEST) PHINNEY. He m. Dec. 28, 1738 MERCY WASHBURN
     b. May 29, 1718 dau of Josiah and Mercy (Tilson) Washburn.
     ISSUE:

     182. FREELOVE PHINNEY b. 1740
     183. LAURAINA PHINNEY b. 1741.
     184. ZERVIA PHINNEY b. 1742 d. young.
     185. ONESIPHORUS PHINNEY b. 1744.
     186. MARA PHINNEY, b. 1745.
     187. ZERVIA PHINNEY, b. 1748.
     188. ESTHER PHINNEY, b. 1751.
     189. KEZIA PHINNEY, b. 1753.
     190. BLISS PHINNEY, b. 1754.
     191. HANNAH PHINNEY b. 1758.
     192. JOHN PHINNEY, b. 1760

---

67. PATIENCE PHINNEY b. Aug. 19, 1713. dau of JOSEPH and ESTHER
     (WEST) PHINNEY. She probably m. ROBERT COOK in 1735.
     ISSUE: COOK.

     1. EBENEZER   2. SETH   3. SILAS. They all survivied infancy.

---

70. GERSHOM PHINNEY b. March 21, 1699/1700 d. 1762 son of THOMAS and
     SARAH (BEATLE) PHINNEY. He m. July 29, 1725 REBEKAH GRIFFITH
     b. June 18, 1703. and d. after Dec. 4, 1761. She was the dau of Stephen
     and Rebecca (Rider) Griffith.
     ISSUE:

     193. GERSHOM PHINNEY, bpt 1728.
     194. LAZARUS PHINNEY bpt. 1729
     195. SARAH PHINNEY, bpt 1730/1
     196. THANKFUL PHINNEY, m._____TAYLOR.
     *197. ISAAC PHINNEY 1733
     198. REBECCA PHINNEY bpt 1736 m._____BANGS
     199. TEMPERANCE PHINNEY, bpt 1736
     200. MEHITABLE PHINNEY, bpt 1741.
     201. JAMES PHINNEY bpt 1741.
     202. SETH PHINNEY, bpt 1745.
     203. RHODA PHINNEY bpt. 1748.

71,   THOMAS PHINNEY b. Feb. 17, 1702/3 d. 1778 son of THOMAS and
SARAH (BEATLE)PHINNEY. He m. (1) Nov. 1731 MARIAH LUMBERT on
LOMBARD, b. Oct. 1700 d. 1748.dau of Bernard Lumbert. He m. (2)(?)
Nov. 24,1748 ABIGAIL LUMBERT b. April 23, 1720 dau of Samuel and
Mary (Comer)Lumbert.

ISSUE:

204.   EDMUND PHINNEY.

205.   JAMES PHINNEY.

206.   SUSANNA PHINNEY.

207.   TEMPERANCE PHINNEY.

208.   FREELOVE PHINNEY.

---

75.   MEHITABLE PHINNEY b. Aug. 14,1696 d. May 28,1778 dau of EBENEZER
and SUSANNA (LINNELL) PHINNEY. She m. Oct 9,1718 SAMUEL HIG-
GINS. son of Jonathan and Lydia (Sparrow-Freeman)Higgins.

ISSUE: HIGGINS.

1, HANNAH b1719.		6. SAMUEL b. 1790	
2. EBENEZER b. 172£		7. SILVANUS b. 1736.	
3. MARTHA b. 1723		8. LYDIA b. 1737	
4. SYSABBA b 1725/ 6		9. ELIAKIM b. 1738/0	
	10. PRINCE b. 1740		

NOTES

76. MARY PHINNEY, b. March 23, 1698 d. c1796 age 98 dau of EBENEZER
and SUSANNAH (LINNELL) PHINNEY. She m. Dec. 22, 1724 at Barnstable JOB DAVIS son of Dolar and Hannah (Linnell) Davis. Job was b.
July 1700 and d. April 4, 1751 age 50.

ISSUE: DAVIS

1.	MARY b. 1725/6	5.	Mehitable b. 1733/4
2.	THOMAS b. 1726	6.	SETH b. 1736
3.	SHOBAL b. 1729	7.	HANNAH b. 1739
4.	MARY, b. 1731	8.	EBENEZER b. 1732.

---

78. SAMUEL PHINNEY b. April 1, 1702 son of EBENEZER and SUSANNAH
(KUINNELL) PHINNEY. He m. Int. Jan 23,1728 HANNAH RAY dau of
Peter and Tabitha (Newcomb) Ray. Hannah was b. in Edgartown, Oct.
16 1712. Dates of their deaths are unknown at this time.

ISSUE:

209. SUSANNAH PHINNEY b. 1730/1

210. NATHANIEL PHINNEY b. 1733.

211. PETER PHINNEY b. 1727.

212. WILLIAM PHINNEY, b. 1740.

213. HANNAH PHINNEY (?)

---

79. REBECCA PHINNEY bpt. June 11,1703 in Barnstable. She was the dau
of EBENEZER and SUSANNAH (LINNELL) PHINNEY. She m. STEPHEN
DAVIS b. Dec. 12, 1700 d. Barnstable June 4, 1782 age 81. He was the
son of Josiah and Ann (Taylor) Davis. Rebecca d. between NOv 1754 and
January 1777.

ISSUE: DAVIS

1.	PRINCE b. 1724	5.	SUSANNAH b. 1734.
2.	ANNA b. 1726	6.	SARAH b. 1737
3.	ISAACK b. 1729	7.	JONATHAN.
4.	REBECCA b. 1732	8.	STEPHEN
		9.	THANKFUL

---

81. EBENEZER PHINNEY b. May 26, 1708 d. after 1754, son of EBENEZER and SUSANNA (LINNELL) PHINNEY. He m. Sept. 23, 1730 REBECCA BARNES b. Plymouth, March 14, 1711 d after 1749. dau of Jonathan and Sarah (Bradford) Barnes., a descendant of Pilgrim William Bradford.
ISSUE:
214. SARAH PHINNEY b. 1732.
215. JONATHAN PHINNEY b. 1733.
216. MARTHA PHINNEY b. 1735
217. LEMUEL PHINNEY b. 1737.
218. SETH PHINNEY b. 1743/4 d. 1744/5
219. REBECCA PHINNEY b. 1747.

---

82. DAVID PHINNEY, b. June 10, 1710 d. Nov. 23, 1793 aged 84. He was the son of EBENEZER and SUSANNA (LINNELL) PHINNEY. He m. Sept. 27, 1733 MARY POPE b. Dec. 1713 d. Nov. 1, 1797 dau of John and Elizabeth (Bourne) Pope.
ISSUE:
220. DEBORAH PHINNEY b. 1735.
221. ELIJAH PHINNEY b. 1736 d. 1741.
222. ELIZABETH PHINNEY b. 1741 d. 1742.
223. MARY PHINNEY b. 1749.
224. SARAH PHINNEY bpt. 1754.

---

88. ZERULAH EASTLAND dau of MARY (PHINNEY) and JOHN EASTLAND b. Dec. 8, 1703. She m. Jan 12, 1723/4 BARNABAS SPOONER b. Feb. 5, 1699 d. c1734 son of John Spooner. Zerulah was also spelled as ZERVIAH.
ISSUE: SPOONER.
1. MOSES   2. JANE b. 1727/8   3. child(?)b.1735

NOTES

89. JOSEPH EASTLAND b. May 12, 1705 d. 1751 son of MARY(PHINNEY) EASTLAND . He m. March 6, 1728 FREELOVE SHEPHERD b. April 5 1697.She d. 1754 dau of Daniel and Mary (Brice)Shepherd.

ISSUE: EASTLAND.

!. VIRTUE b. 1729   2. JOHN b. 1732   3. MARY b. 1733/4 4. RELIANCE b. 1736.

90. ELIZABETH EASTLAND b. Jan 31, 1708 daughkter of MARY (PHINNEY) EASTLAND. She m. May 7,1730 AMOS TABER b. April 29, 1703 d. c1748. He was the son of Joseph and Elizabeth (Spooner) Tabor, and a descemdant of Pilgrim Francis Cooke He had been previously married to Elizabeth Lapham in 1724, by whom he had two children.

ISSUE: TABOR.

1. ANTIPAS b.c1731.   2. REBECCA b. c1733

96. TEMPERANCE PHINNEY, b. March 28, 1710 d. c1759 dau of **BENJAMIN** and MARTHA (CROCKER) PHINNEY. She m. Sept 22,1733 JAMES FULLER b. May 1, 1711. He was the son of Benjamin Fuller a descendant of Pilgrim Edward Fuller.

ISSUE: FULLER.

1. MARTHA b. 1734   5. JAMES b. 1743
2. JOHN b. 1735   6. JOSEPH b. 1743
3. SILAS bpt. 1739   7. BENJAMIN b. 1748
4. MARY b. 1741   8. BEERSHEBA bpt 1753.

NOTES

23.

97.   MELATIAH PHINNEY b. July 26, 1712 d. c1785 dau of BENJAMIN amd
MARTHA (CROCKER) PHINNEY. She m. May 15,1732 JOSIAH MOR-
TON b. Feb.28,1709/10   son of John and Reliance (Phinney)Morton.
ISSUE: MORTON

1. BENJAMIN b. 1733/4 d. 1735   6.   JOHN b. 1743 d. 1745.

2, SETH b, 1735   7.   MARY b. 1746.

3, BENJAMIN b. 1737 d. 1739   8.   JOHN b. 1748.

4. RELIANCE B. **1739** d. 1741   9.   JOSIAH b. 1750 d. 1751

5, NARTHA b. 1742   10.   JOSIAH b. 1752

11. SARAH b. 1755.

----

98.   BARNABAS PHINNEY, b. March 28,1715 d. 1747 son of BENJAMIN and
MARTHA (CROCKER). PHINNEY. He m. in Halifax Aug. 14,1745 MEHIT-
ABLE (CHURCHILL) NORTON, b. Nov 5, 1716 d. May 25,1797 dau of
James Norton. She m. (2) 1749 James Harlow and a descendant of
Pilgrim Richard Warren and William_Bonney.
ISSUE:

225.   ICABOD PHINNEY b. 1745.

----

100.   ZACCHUES PHINNEY b. Aug. 4, 1720 d/ 1751 son of BENJAMIN and
MARTHA (CROCKER) PHINNEY. He m. March 3, 1742/3 SUSAN DAVIS
She was b. in Falmouth Oct. 2,1725 dau pf Jabez and Anne (Dimrock)
Davis. She m. (2)1763 **THEODORE MORSE a descendant of Pilgrim Edward**
Doty. Zaccheus was from Barnstabie where he was born and died.
ISSUE:

226.   BENJAMIN PHINNEY b. 1744.

227.   TIMOTHY PHINNEY b. 1746.

228.   BARNABAS PHINNEY b. 1748.

229.   ZACCHEUS PHINNEY b. 1751.

101. SETH PHINNEY b. June 27,1723 d. after 1758 son of BENJAMIN and MARTHA (CROCKER)PHINNEY. He m. in Barnstable Oct. 26,1748 BETHIA BUMP or BUMPAS living in 1753. It is believed she was b. Aug. 23, 1729 dau of Samuel and Joanna (Warren) Bump and a descendant of Pilgrim Richard Warren.

ISSUE:

230. ZILPAH PHINNEY b. 1749.

231. SON b. and d. 1751

232. SON b and d. 1751 _____   Twins?

103. THANKFUL PHINNEY, b. Barnstable Dec. 24,1713. She was living in Conn. 1748 dau of JONATHAN and ELIZABETH PHINNEY. She m. (1) in Middleboro, Nov. 23, 1738 JOHN HAYFORD of Freetown b. Jan 7, 1712/3 d. Farmington,Oct. 16, 1742 son of John and Lydia (Pierce) Hayford. Thankful m. (2) to a man whose name was CARRINGTON.

ISSUE: HAYFORD

1. JOSEPH. B. 1739   2. JOHN d. 1742.   3. JOHN b.1743 "Son of John Deceased".

----

104. JOSEPH PHINNEY b, Barnstable Jan. 24,1716 d. Aug. 13,1793 son of JONATHAN and ELIZABETH PHINNEY. He m. Sept 18, 1746 PHEBE COLE of Berkley b. July 26, 1728 d. Middleboro June 10, 1796. She was the dau of John and Mary Cole.

ISSUE:

233. JONATHAN PHINNEY b. 1749.

234. PHEBE PHINNEY.

NOTES

108. JOSHUA PHINNEY b. Jan 10, 1720 d. Canterbury, Conn. Oct. 4,1787
      son of JONATHAN and ELIZABETH PHINNEY!. He m. in Canterbury,
      May 16, 1754 LUCY ENSWORTH bpt Sept. 17, 1732 d. Canterbury
      June 6, 1811, dau of Joseph and Mary (Cleveland) Ensworth.
      ISSUE:
      235. JOSHUA PHINNEY b. 1755.
      236. SAMUEL PHINNEY. b. 1758.

109. ELIZABETH PHINNEY b. c1718 d.cJan14,1775 dau of JONATHAN and
      ELIZABETH PHINNEY. She m. Jan 27,1746/7 JOHN MACOMBER born
      Taunton, Feb. 10, 1713 d. Middleboro June 14, 1775. He was the son
      of John and Elizabeth (Williams) Macomber.
      ISSUE: MACOMBER

      1.   ABIAH 2. ELIZABETH bc1760. 3. JOHN b. before 1761.
      4. SAMUEL b. before 1761 5. CYRUS b. before 1761
      6. ENOCH b. after 1763. 7. MARY b. after 1761.

      ----

110. HANNAH PHINNEY b. June 17,1731 dau of JONATHAN and MERCY.
      (READ) **PHINNEY** She m. 1747 RICHARD HAILE of Warren. He d.
      May 27,1797 son of Bernard Haile of Warren.
      ISSUE: HAILE.

      1.   HANNAH b. May 31, 1748.   5.   BERNARD b. April 11,1752.
      2,   ANNE b. Oct. 28,1751.   6.   JOHN b. April 11,1760.
      3.   JONATHAN b. March 22,1753.   7.   ELIZABETH b. Sept 25,1765.
      4.   BERNARD b. Aug. 4,1755.   8.   SAMUEL b. Sept 5,2770.

                              NOTES

113,   ELISHA PHINNEY b. March 30, 1737 posthumously. He was the son
of JONATHAN and MERCY (READ)PHINNEY. He was born after the
death of his father. His father d. in November 1736. Elisha m.(1) May
5,1763 JEMIMA TREADWELL b. Newport,R.I. Feb. 12,1761 dau of
John and Hannah (Claggett)Treadwell.   He m. (2) 1766 REBECCA PECK
of Rehobeth, Mass. dau of Henry and Rachel (Whittaker) Peck. She
was b. Feb. 11, 1748 and d. Oct. 28,1818. Elisha was a farmer.
ISSUE by first wife.

237. JONATHAN. PHINNEY b. Jan 30, 1764 d. Oct.11,1779.

ISSUE BY 2nd wife.

238. AARON PHINNEY b. April 24,1767 d. 1787 abroad.

*239. DANIEL PHINNEY b. Sept 14,1768.

*240. BENJAMIN PHINNEY, b. Oct. 8, 1771.

*241. JEMIMA PHINNEY, b. March 29, 1773.

242. ELISHA PECK PHINNEY, b.Oct. 31, 1774   m. Dec. 14,1806
      LYDIA BARTON dau of David and Rebecca (Brightman) Barton
      of Freetown, Mass. He d. April 16,1854   No Issue.

*243. REBECCA PHINNEY b. Sept. 22,1777

244. HANNAH PHINNEY, b.Oct. 11,1779; m. (1)_____ CORBAN.
      m.(2) DEA____BRUCE of New York.

245. NATHAN PHINNEY b. Oct. 5,1782 d. Jan. 3,1802 abroad.

NOTES

115. JOSIAH FINNEY, b. July 1, 1728 d. July 23, 1804 son of JEREMIAH and ELIZABETH (BRISTOW) FINNEY. He m. (1) May 19, 1751 MARY CAREY b. Dec. 3, 1732 d. Sept 18, 1760 dau of Allen and Hannah (Church) Carey of Bristol. He m. (2) Sept. 16, 1761 MARTHA GIBBS b. 1739 d. May 22, 1823. dau of James and Martha (Giddings) Gibbs. He was a farmer and a postmaster at one time, residing in Bristol.

ISSUE By first wife:

246. JEREMIAH FINNEY bpt Feb. 4, 1753 died at sea July 25, 1773.

247. ELIZABETH FINNEY bpt Dec. 8, 1754 d. Sept. 21, 1756.

248. ALLEN FINNEY, bpt. March 20, 1757 d. July 31, 1758.

249. MOLLEY FINNEY bpt. June 10, 1759.

BY 2nd wife:

*250. MARTHA FINNEY.

*251. CHARLOTTE FINNEY.

*252. SARAH FINNEY.

253. THOMAS GIBBS FINNEY b. 1768 died at sea Oct. 9, 1787.

254. GEORGE FINNEY b. 1770 died at sea May 9, 1792.

255. SUSANNA FINNEY, bpt July 1772 m. June 23, 1811 to CAPTAIN OLIVER FITCH. He was b. 1775 died Jan. 8, 1848.

256. ANN (NANCY) FINNEY b. Sept 19, 1773 d. Dec. 17, 1839. Umd.

257. ELIZABETH FINNEY bpt. June 18, 1780.

*258. RUTH THURSTON FINNEY, bpt. Oct. 9, 1781.

259. ABIGAIL FINNEY, (?) b. 1779 d. Oct. 16, 1796. She lived in Bristol.

NOTES

118. JEREMIAH FINNEY b. 1732/3 d. July 17,1807 son of JEREMIAH and ELIZABETH (BRISTOW) FINNEY. He m. (1) DEBORAH _____ b. 1740 s. Nov. 9,1791 m. (2)April 14,1792 MARY COY b. 1747 died Sept 20, 1821 dau of Samuel Coy. Jeremiah was a shipmastder. In the Revolutionary War he served as a private in 1778 in Col. Nathan Miller's **Regiment of R. I.**
ISSUE by first wife,
   260.   THOMAS FINNEY, b. 1758 d. March 8, 1760.
  *261.   LORING FINNEY, b. 1761.
   262.   ELIZABETH FINNEY, b. 1765 m. Feb. 26,1803 ISAAC LAFAY-
          ETTE NEWTON son of Richard and Lydia Newton of Wrent-
          ham, Mass.
   263.   DEBORAH FINNEY b. 1766 m. Dec. 22,1785 LUCIUS RHODES.
  *264.   REBECCA FINNEY b. 1769.
  *265.   MARY FINNEY b. 1770. m. PARKER CLARK.
  *266,   JOHN FINNEY bpt Sept 26,1773.
   267,   JEREMIAH FINNEY b. 1774 d. Jan 1, 1799.
  *268.   HANNAH FINNEY b. 1776 m. Nov. 5, 1795 ELISHA CARPENTER.

119. THOMAS FINNEY b. 1737 d. 1792 son of JEREMIAH and ELIZABETH (BRISTOW)FINNEY. He m. June 5, 1760 ELIZABETH CLARK of ply-mouth,Mass. b. 1742 d. March 3,1795.   Both are buried in Burial Hill.
ISSUE:
   269.   ELIZABETH CLARK FINNEY b. Aug. 22, d. Dec. 15,1761.
   270.   CLARK FINNEY b. Nov. 6,1762 d. Jan 17,1763.
   271.   MOLLY FINNEY b. Dec. 5,1763.
   272.   JOSIAH NORTON FINNEY, b. Nov. 10,1765.
   273.   RUTH FINNEY b. April 7,1768.
   274.   THOMAS FINNEY (?).

120.   MARY FINNEY b. 1742 dau of JEREMIAH and ELIZABETH (BRISTOW)
       FINNEY. She m. as his second wife, in1765 CORBAN BARNES b. 1732
       son of John and Dorcas (Corban)Barnes. of Plymouth, Mass.

       ISSUE: BARNES:

       1.   MARY b. 1765 m. Sept 16,1795 ELEAZER HOLMES
       2.   REBECCA b. 1768.
       3.   BETSEY b. 1777 m. (1) THOMAS DAVID m. (2) _____LEUCAS
              M. (3) _____MAYHEW.
       4.   CHARLOTTE,b. 1774 m. STEPHEN MARLOW.
       5.   CORBAN b. 1778.
       6.   PATTY b. 1781 m. ANSEL HOLMES.
       7.   DEBORAH b. 1785 m. ALDEN LEUCAS.
       8.   ABIGAIL b. 1789 m.(1)WILLIAM KEENE (2) ISSIAH CARVER.

       _____

122.   WILLIAM FINNEY, b. May 10, 1715 d. 1781 son of JOSHUA and MARTHA
       (CARTER)FINNEY. He was b. in Swansea, Mass and d. in Lebanon,
       Conn. He m. (1)Nov 8,1730 ELIZABETH CLARK of Swansea who died
       Oct. 1742. He m (2) Nov 2, 1747 Mrs. ABIGAIL BLACK. He purchased
       land in Lebanon, Conn where he died.

       issue;

       275.   WILLIAM FINNEY b. Dec.9, 1739.

       276.   ELIZABETH FINNEY b. May 25,1742.

       277.   IRENE FINNEY, b. March 27, 1749.

       278.   JOSEPH FINNEY, b. June 4, 1751.

                          _____

                          NOTES

126.   JOHN FINNEY, b. June 2,1721 d. 1788 son of JOSHUA and MARTHA
       (CARTER) FINNEY. He m. (1)Aug. 25,1743 RACHEL WOODWARD
       of Lebanon, Conn. who d. June 5, 1765. He m. (2) Oct. 17, 1765 SARAH
       THOMAS. He lived in Lebanon and Warren, Conn.
       ISSUE:
       *279.   JOEL FINNEY.
        280.   RACHEL FINNEY, b. 1745 m._____BARNUM.
        281,   LYDIA FINNEY b. Aug. 28,1746 m. AMAZIAH PHILLIPS of South-
               ington, Conn. He d. before 1788 .
        282.   ELEAZER FINNEY, b. 1754.
        283.   RUFUS FINNEY, b. May 18,1760 m. HANNAH FINNEY. (291)
        284.   JOHN FINNEY, b. Jan 12,1762,
        285.   DELADEMA FINNEY b. bpt July 1767.

                            _____

127.   OLIVER FINNEY b. Nov. 11,1728. Son of JOSHUA and MARTHA
       (CARTER)FINNEY. He m. Aug. 9,1749 ELIZABETH DUNHAM. He moved
       to Lebanon with his father later he lived in Warren. He bought land
       in Kent, Conn.
       ISSUE:
        286.   ELIZABETH FINNEY b. Sept 10, 1750.

                            _____

129.   JOHN FINNEY b. Oct. 14,1718 son of JOHN and ANN (TOOGOOD)FINNEY.
       He m. June 14,1744 HANNAH WASHBURN. He was b. in Swansea and
       moved with his father to Lebanonin 1728/9.
       ISSUE:
        287.   TIMOTHY FINNEY b. Aug. 28,1746.
        288.   MARTIN FINNEY, b.June 20,1751.
        289.   ELIEU FINNEY b. July 14,£755.
        290.   JOHN FINNEY b. July 19,1757.
        291.   HANNAH FINNEY b. March 10,1761 m. May 20,1770 her
               cousin RUFUS FINNEY son of John Finney. (283)

                            _____

                              NOTES

130.   NATHANIEL FINNEY b. Jan 3, 1720 son of JOHN and ANN (TOO-
        GOOD) FINNEY. He m. Sept 3, 1740 HANNAH WOOD of Swansea b.
        1718 d. Dec. 26, 1756 in Providence, R.I. In 1757 he moved from
        Swansea to Providence and then in 1760 he moved to NOVA SCOTIA
        settling in Sackville.

        ISSUE:

        292.   CALEB FINNEY.
                There were other children but not known at this time.

        _____

134.   DAVID FINNEY, b. Aug. 24, 1732 son of JOHN and ANN (TOOGOOD) FINNEY.
        He m. Feb. 26, 1759 ABIGAIL CLARK of Kent, Conn. He sold his property
        in Lebanon 1760 and moved to Duchess County N. Y.

        ISSUE:

        293.   ISAAC FINNEY b. Oct. 3, 1759.

        ----

136.   JABEZ FINNEY b. Nov. 21, 1757 son of JOHN and ANN (TOOGOOD)
        FINNEY. He m. Nov. 8, 1764 ELIZABETH _____ and lived in East
        Greenwich, R.I. where his father bought land in early 1717. He was
        a REVOLUTIONARY WAR soldier in 1778.

        ISSUE:

        *294.   GEORGE FINNEY.
         295.   HANNAH FINNEY m. Feb. 29, 1784 JOHN WEEDEN son of
                Caleb Weeden of East Greenwich.

                _____

                        NOTES

141. JOSIAH FINNEY b. Feb. 12, 1727/8 son of JOSIAH and ELIZABETH (MANN) FINNEY. He m. SARAH CARTER of Litchfield counry, Conn. She was b. Dec. 21,1732 and d. June 16,1777 dau of Thomas and Sarah (Gilbert) Carter. He was one of the earliest settlers of the county.

ISSUE:

296. JOSIAH FINNEY b. c1756.

297. LEVINA FINNEY, b. Oct. 28,1756.

298. SYLVESTER FINNEY b. March 15,1759.

299. SARAH FINNEY b. June 6, 1761 m. JUDAH ELDRED.

300. LUCINDA FINNEY, b. Jan 26,1763.

301. ZENAS FINNEY, b. Dec. 8, 1768.

302. CYRUS FINNEY, b. Oct. 6, 1771.

---

144. DAVID FINNEY, b. June 21,1734, son of JOSIAH and ELIZABETH (MANN) FINNEY. He m. (1) March 7,1754 JEMIMA WARNER who died Nov. 14, 1770. He m. (2) May 6, 1775 widow MARGARET FULLER. He moved to Conn. residing in Lebanon where he owned land at time of his second marriage.

ISSUE: All by first wife.

303. ELEAZER FINNEY b. Jan 20,1755.

304. ELIZABETH FINNEY, b. April 1, 1757.

305. URIAH FINNEY, March 17, 1761. He served in the Revolutionary War.

306. JEMIMA FINNEY, b. Aug. 15,1763.

307. BENJAMIN FINNEY, b. Aug. 9, 1771.

---

145. JONATHAN FINNEY, b. June 1, 1736 d. March 29,1773 son of JOSIAH and ELIZABETH (MANN) FINNEY. He m. Aug. 12,1757 PHEBE PHELPS and moved to Warren,Conn. where his father deeded him a farm of 112 acres on his marriage.

ISSUE:

308. JONATHAN FINNEY b. Nov. 8,1758.

309. BETHUEL FINNEY, b. June 11,1760. Lived in Lenox, Mass.

310. PHEBE FINNEY b. Feb. 22,1762.

311. RHODA FINNEY b. July 22 1763.

312. ZENA or ZERVIA FINNEY, b. Jan 14,1765.

312A ASENATH FINNEY.

312B. BERIAH FINNEY.

313. **LYDIA FINNEY** b. June 28, 1770 d. June 19,1771

*314. ABRAHAM FINNEY, b. April 20,1772.

159. ISAAC PHINNEY, b. Aug 26,1734 son of THOMAS and **RELIANCE** (GOOD-SPEED)PHINNEY. He m. ANNA THOMAS of Windham,Conn. March 12, 1763 as published in Barnstable . She was b. in Windham July 1,1744 dau of David and Mary (Johnson)Thomas. She was his 2nd wife.

ISSUE:

*315. LOT PHINNEY.

----

197. ISAAC PHINNEY b. May 10, 1733 d. 1790 son of GERSHOM and REBEKAH (GRIFFITH) PHINNEY. He m. in Chatham, Mass. Jan. 31, 1754 ELIZABETH KINEY or KENNEY. He was a R.W. soldier volunteering in 1777 from Williamsburg, Mass. during the Burgoyne Champaigne under Capt Samuel Fairfield. (History of Conn Valley Page 423)

ISSUE:

316. HEMAN (HIRAM) PHINNEY,b.Aug. 2, 1754.

317. DAVID PHINNEY b. March 28,1756 m. JUDITH NASH.

318. MERCY PHINNEY, b.Nov. 18, 1758 m. **NATHAN** ATWOOD.

319. SARAH PHINNEY, b. Aug. 8, 1760 m. ELISHA GRAVES(?)

320. TEMPERANCE PHINNEY, b. March 31 1752 m. ROSVILLE CLEVE-LAND.

*321. ISAAC PHINNEY, b. May 1,1764 m. HULDAH PRESTON.

322. NATHAN PHINNEY, b.Aug. 14,1766 m. SUSANNA ROGERS.

323. ZENAS PHINNEY, b. 1770 d. 1846 m. RHODA CLEVELAND, b. 1774 d. 1830.

NOTES

239.   DANIEL PHINNEY b. Sept. 14,1768 d. June 25,1857 son of ELISHA and his second wife REBECCA (PECK)PHINNEY.   He m. (1) June 14, 1798 ELIZABETH COOMER b. April 8, 1760 d. Nov 23,1823 dau of Thomas and Mary Coomer of Bristol.   He m. (2) ELIZABETH (ELIZA) CRANSTONK b. May 22, 1792 d. April 30, 1891 in Providence, dau of STEPHEN and SARAH CRANSTON, and widow of George Cole of Warren.   Daniel was a farmer, lived in Warren. There was no isse by first wife.

ISSUE:

*324.   EMMA PHINNEY b. April 13,1800 d. Nov. 25, 1860.

*325.   ELIZA KINNICUTT PHINNEY b. May 15,1802.

326.   THOMAS KINNICUTT COOMER PHINNEY b. March 21,1804.

327.   HANNAH PHINNEYb. June 20,1806 m. Feb. 24,1831 CAPT. AMBROSE BARNABY son of Daniel and Hope Barnaby b.1803 d. 1883.   He m. (2) HANNAH G. VINNECUM.

      1. AMBROSE BARNABY.

      2. MARGARET MASON BARNABY.

328.   REBECCA PHINNEY b. Dec. 3,1808 d Nov. 1,1851 m. Nov. 17, 1836 ROBERT MILLER son of Bernard and Lydia (Ingraham) Miller. b. June 3, 1803 d. March 3, 1852.

      1. GEORGE ROBERT MILLER.

329.   NATHAN PHINNEY b. April 17, 1812. d. Jan 27,1843 Unmd.

330.   ELISHA PECK PHINNEY, b. Sept 29,1814.

331.   NANCY PHINNEY b. Aug 29,1817 m. (1) March 29,1838 JOHN MASON BOSWORTH of Dartmouth, Mass. b. 1812. buroed Aug. 10, 1839 , (2) her first husbands brother ALVIN BOSWORTH. She d. May 19, 1857.

ISSUE: All by her first husband.

    1.   DANIEL VINNEY BOSWORTH.
    2.   JOHN BOSWORTH.
    3.   WILLIAM BOSWORTH.
    4.   JOSEPH BOSWORTH

NOTES

240. BENJAMIN PHINNEY, b. Oct. 8,1771 d. Dec. 21,1831 son of ELISHA and his second wife REBECCA (PECK) PHINNEY. He m. Aug. 31,1794, BETSEY VORCE b. Dec. 29,1776 d. Feb. 15,1857, dau of Mrs. Tabitha (Trafton)Vorce of Warren. He was a farmer residing in Swansea and afterwards in Warren. About 1796 he moved with his family to Montpelier, Vt. He served in the R. W. as Sergeant in the War of 1812 and was in Capt. Timothy Hubbard's Company. He d. in Montpelier.

ISSUE:

*332. LYDIA PECK PHINNEY b. April 8, 1795.

*333. HANNAH PHINNEY b. Oct. 8,1797.

 334. JOHN PHINNEY b. Aug 10,1799.

 335. ELISHA PHINNEY, b. Aug 1, 1801.

 336. ELIZA PHINNEY b. July 23,1803 d. June 28,1813.

 337. NATHAN PHINNEY, b. March 9, 1806.

 338. DEXTER PHINNEY b. Jan. 25,1808 drowned April 17,1811.

 339. TRUMAN PHINNEY b. March 26, 1810 d. Jan 15,1855 Unmd.

 340. CALISTA PHINNEY b. June 9,1812 m. May 25,1854 her husband's brother, NATHAN DODGE. She d. Oct. 20,1872.

       1. ELLA CALISTA DODGE.

 341. AMANDA PHINNEY, b. Aug. 11,1814 d. Aug. 25,1844 Unmd.

 342. WARREN PHINNEY, b. Sept. 6, 1816.

*343. CAROLINE PHINNEY b. April 17,1819.

 344. CHARLES HENRY PHINNEY, B. Jan. 12.1822 d. Jan 4, 1843. He d. at St Jago, Cape Verde Islands.

NOTES

241. JEMIMA PHINNEY, b. March 29,1773 dau of ELISHA and JEMIMA(TREAD-
WELL) PHINNEY. She m. HEZEKIAH KINGSLEY.

ISSUE: KINGSLEY.

1. NATHAN   2. ELISHA.   3. LUTHER   4. HENRY.

---

243. REBECCA PHINNEY, b. Sept 22, 1777 dau of ELISHA and JEMIMA
(TREADWELL)PHINNEY. She m. CAPT. WILLIAM CHAMPLIN b. May 5,
1776 son of Thomas and Phebe (Throop) Champlin of Bristol. He d. March
5, 1858.

ISSUE: CHAMPLIN

1. JOHN BOWMAN b. May 29,1798.
2. WILLIAM b. May 16,1800 m. ELIZA K. PHINNEY.
3. JULIA ANN b. April 21, 1802 d. Dec. 13,1891. She m.____HODGES.
4. CHARLOTTE b.Jan 11, 1805 d. April 4,1893. She m._____BARNEY.
5. MARY.
5. ELISHA (?)

---

250. MARTHA FINNEY, bpt Aug. 29, 1762 d. 1843 dau of JOSIAH and   hia
2nd wife MARTHA (GIBBS)FINNEY. She m. 1783 JOHN FALES son of
Nathaniel and Sarah (Little)Fales. John d. Oct. 4, 1813. Martha d. April
13,1843 in Providence.

ISSUE: FALES.

!. CHARLOTTE, b. Jan 5, 1784 d. Dec. 12,1848.
2. EEDELIA b. Jan 27,1783 d. July 14,1822.
3. TIMOTHY b.July 23,1788,
4. JAMES GIBBS b. Oct. 10, 1789 d. Oct. 21,1790.
5. BETSEY PAINE b. March 28, 1792.
6. ABBEY b.March 23, 1794.
7. MERCY CHURCH b. March 23,1796.
8. JOSEPH JACKSON B. April 10, 1798.
9. HENRY DeWOLF b. Feb. 8, 1800 d. Marach 30, 2801.
10. MARTHA GIBBS b. March 10,1802.

NOTES

251.   CHARLOTTE FINNEY, b. Feb. 10,1764 d. April 15,1829 dau of JOSIAH
        and his second wife MARTHA (GIBBS) FINNEY. She m. June 1,1784
        WILLIAM deWOLF of bristol b. Dec. 19,1762 d. April 19, 1829 son of
        Mark **Anthony**   and Abigail (Potter)deWolf.
        ISSUE: deWOLF.

        1, HENRY b. March 21 1785 d. Oct. 18, 1857.
        2. WILLIAM b. Dec. 8, 1788 d. Oct. 12,1830.
        3. CHARLOTTE b. June 17, 1793 d. April 22,1885 Unmd.
        4. MARIA b. Oct. 26, 1795 d. Dec. 16,1890.
        5. ABIGAIL b. April 18,1798 d. April 22,1817 m. _____DAVIS.

                        _____

252.   SARAH FINNEY b. 1767 d. 1820 dau of JOSIAH and his **second wife,**
        MARTHA (GIBBS)FINNEY. m. Nov. 15,1789 CAPT. HEZEKIAH USHER
        bpt May 12, 1763 d. at sea Sept 15,1795. Sarah d. at Bristol May 4,1820.
        ISSUE: USHER.

        1. ANN FRANCES bpt. May 24,1795.
        2. GEORGE FENNO bpt May 24,1795.
        3. HEZEKIAH bpt May 24,1795 d. Feb 5,1796.

                        _____

258,   RUTH THURSTON FINNEY, BPT Oct. 9,1781 dau of JOSIAH and his
        second wife MARTHA (GIBBS)FINNEY. She m. June 16,1811 ELKANAH
        FRENCH b. Feb. 4,1858 d. Sept 22,1856. She d. Feb. 4, 1858.
        ISSUE: FRENCH.

        1. **EMILY F.**   2.   ABBEY FINNEY m. her cousin GEORGE USHER.
        One child was born in November and died in December 1818.

                        _____

                        NOTES

261. LORING FINNEY, b. June 18, 1760 d. March 8, 1827 son of JEREMIAH and DEBORAH FINNEY. He m. Oct. 12,1785 EXPERIENCE PEARSE b. May 4, 1764 d. Dec. 11, 1835 in Bristol, dau of Samuel and Elizabeth Pearse. He was a shipmaster and served in the R.W. at the Battle of Rhode Island. He died in Bristol.

ISSUE:

345. THOMAS FINNEY b. March 23,1787 d. Sept. 12,1819 in North Carolina.

*346. MARY PEARSE FINNEY b. May 19, 1790.

347. LEVI LORING FINNEY b. Dec. 28,1791. Lost at sea June 26, 1812. Unmd.

348. ELIZABETH ATWOOD FINNEY, b. May 5, 1794 d. June 22, 1884. She m. (1) April 17,1836 SAMUEL LADIEU of Barrington, R.I. She m. (2) ISAIAH SYMMONS who d. June 19, 1877. No children.

----

264. REBECCA FINNEY, b. 1769 dau of JEREMIAH and DEBORAH FINNEY. She m. Nov. 10, 1785 CAPT. JESSE DAVIS, son of Icabod and Sylvia Davis of Freetown, Mass. who d.c 1842. Rebecca d. June 2, 1843.

ISSUE: *DAVIS*

1. *POLLY b. June 7, 1786.*

2, *LUCINDA b. March 25, 1790.*

3. *ANTHONY, b. Oct. 9, 1794.*

4. *DAVID b. July 9, 1798 d. Jan. 27, 1830.*

5, *AMANDA b. May 6, 1802.*

6. *JOHN JEREMIAH b. Dec. 4, 1808 d. Sept. 16, 1841.*

NOTES

265. MARY FINNEY b. 1770 dau of JEREMIAH and DEBORAH FINNEY. She m. April 24, 1788 CAPT PARKER CLARK son of Ezekiel and Hannah (Parker)Clark. of Rochester, Mass. Parker was b. April 26,1765 d. Feb. 26,1839 in Providence.

ISSUE: CLARK.

1. HENRY FINNEY CLARK b. Jan 1,1790 m. Sept 20,1815 ALICE TAYLOR dau of Edward and Alice (Dexter)Taylor.She d. June 20,1820 in Indiana.

2. GEORGE GIBBS CLARK b. Oct. 1792 m. (1) March 30, 1818 ANNE ELIZ WESTCOTT (2) Nov. 4,1833 MARY DRING BOLLES d. Oct. 31,1869.

3. MARY CLARK b. Feb. d. July 25,1794.

266, JOHN FINNEY bpt Sept 1773 son of JEREMIAH and DEBORAH FINNEY. He m. July 8, 1798 AVIS BOWEN of warren, Rhode Island, dau of James and Ruth (Arnold)Bowen. Avis was b. Feb.24,1780.

ISSUE:

349. AVIS FINNEY.

NOTES

268. HANNAH FINNEY, b. 1776 d. June 30, 1805 dau of JEREMIAH and
DEBORAH FINNEY. She m. NOv. 5, 1795 ELISHA CARPENTER, son
of Peter and Abigail (Briggs)Carpenter of Norton, Mass. He was b.
April 26,1766 d. Nov. 21,1822.

ISSUE: *CARPENTER.*

1.   *MARY b. March 24, 1798 m. a Mr. WHITE*
2.   *LOUISA b. Nov. 28, 1799 m a Mr. HOWARD*

---

279. JOEL FINNEY b. Sept. 1,1744 d. 1798 son of JOHN and RACHEL (WOOD-
WARD) FINNEY. He m. 1768 ANN SACKETT.

ISSUE:

350. ANN FINNEY b. Jan 25,1769.

351. HEMAN FINNEY, b. Dec. 17, 1770.

352. JOEL FINNEY b. July 26, 1772.

353. RACHEL FINNEY, b. April 28, 1774.

354. ELIJAH FINNEY b. April 28, 1776.

355. LIDES FINNEY, b. 1780.

355A BELINDA FINNEY b. May 4, 1782.

355B JONATHAN SACKETT FINNEY, b. 1786.

355C ANSON FINNEY b. 1786.

355D MIRANDA FINNEY, b. 1788.

---

294. GEORGE FINNEY b. 1773 son of JABEZ and ELIZABETH FINNEY. He
m. May 4, 1792 HENRIETTA MATHEWS b. June 1, 1772 dau of Caleb
and Susanna (Pierce) Mathews. of East Greenwich, R.I. He resided for
a time in East Greenwich.

ISSUE:

356. BETSEY ANN FINNEY b. April 19, 1793.

357. GEORGE FINNEY, b. April 11, 1795.

314. ABRAHAM FINNEY b. April 20, 1772 son of JONATHAN and PHEBE
(PHELPS) FINNEY m. HULDAH GIFFORD. He moved to Lee, Mass.

ISSUE:

358. EZRA FINNEY m. JULIA MASON.

A. EZRA FINNEY.

B. SETH m. SALLY CHURCHILL 1798

C. ELKANAH C. k

D. HANNAH m. EPHRAIM HOWARD.

E. MARY OTIS m. AUGUSTUS BURGESS

*See SPECIAL SECTION
for information on
B, C, D, and E.*

41.

315. LOT PHINNEY, b. April 6, 1766 d. April 20, 1851 son of ISAAC
and ANNA (THOMAS) PHINNEY. He m. (1)1786 ELIZABETH DUR-
LAND b. in New York and d. before 1805 probably in Granville.
They were probably in Wilmot. Nova Scotia.
ISSUE:

*359.   LEVI PHINNEY M. ELIZABETH FALES GATES.

———————

321. ISAAC PHINNEY b. May 1, 1764 d. Aug. 5, 1868 son of ISAAC and
ELIZABETH (KENNEY) PHINNEY. He m./HULDAH PRESTON   dau
of Ephraim and Lydia (Peck) Preston. Isaac and Huldah are both
buried in a private cemetery at Peck Hill, N.Y. Huldah was born
1774 and d. Cazenovia, N.Y. July 10, 1853.
ISSUE:

360.   CLARASA PHINNEY b. Aug. 22,1785 Williamsburg., Mass.

361.   SARAH (SALLY) PHINNEY b. Aug. 10,1788, Williamsburg.

*362.   SETH PHINNEY b. May 27, 1791 Williamsburg.

363.   SUBMIT PHINNEY b. Aug. 17,1793 m. RICHARD CULVER.

364.   MERCH PHINNEY, b. July 20,1796 Williamsburg

365.   NATHAN PHINNEY d. Aug. 18, 1884 m. CATHERINE _____

366.   SALMON (SOLOMON) PHINNEY m. BETSEY _____
        d. 1891.

———————

324. EMMA PHINNEY b. April 13,1800 d. Nov. 25,1860 dau of DANIEL
and ELIZABETH (CRANSTON) PHINNEY. She m. Aug. 23,1818
THOMAS EASTERBROOKS b. Dec. 17, 1797 d. July 31, 1858, son
of Icabod and Rhoby (Cole) Easterbrooks of Warren.
ISSUE: *EASTERBROOKS.*

1.   *SALLY*   2. *BENJAMIN*   3. *BETSEY.*

4.   *ADELINE*   5. *NATHAN*   6. *BURRILL BOSWORTH.*

NOTES

325. ELIZA KINNICUTT PHINNEY, b. May 15,1802 dau of DANIEL and RE-
BECCA (PECK) PHINNEY. She m. Sept. 15,1823 her cousin, CAPT.
WILLIAM CHAMPLIN son of Capt. William and Rebecca (Phinney)Cham-
blin of Warren. He d. 1831.
ISSUE: CHAMPLIN.

1. WILLIAM.   2. JOHN BOWMAN   3. ALEXANDER.

---

332. LYDIA PECK PHINNEY, b. April 8, 1725 dau of BENJAMIN and BETSEY
(VORCE) PHINNEY. She m. Jan 12,1823 JOSIAH PARKER of Oxford,
Mass. son of Thomas and Abigail Parker.
ISSUE: PARKER.

1. LEANDER.   2. MANVILLE JOSIAH.   3. SABRINA   4. LEROY.

---

333. HANNAH PHINNEY, b. Oct. 8, 1797 d. Aug. 23,1831 in March 2, 1818
NATHAN DODGE b. March 6, 1798 d. Aug. 30, 1878 son of Solomon and
Nancy (Taggert) Dodge of Montpelier, Vt. He m. her sister CALISTA
PHINNEY after his first wife died.
ISSUE: DODGE.

1. POLLY.   2. LUTHER   3. COLLAMORE   4. HENRY   5. LEE
6. JONATHAN   7. OMARI ALONZO   8. NATHAN PRINTICE. 9.CAIRA CAROLINE

343. CAROLINE PHINNEY b. April 17,1819 dau of BENJAMIN and BETSEY
(VORCE) PHINNEY. She m. Jan. 25, 1844 THOMAS CRANE BARROWS
b. Feb. 5, 1819 d. Feb. 3, 1895. He was the son of Silas and Betsey
(Greenbough) Barrows of Montpelier, Vt.
ISSUE: BARROWS.

1. LAURA ISABELLA.   2. ABBIE LIZZIE   3. ELLEN CAROLINE
4. NELLIE   5. EMILY.

NOTES.

346.   MARY PEARCE FINNEY, b. May 19, 1790 d. March 13,1866 dau of
LORING and EXPERIENCE (PEARSE) FINNEY. She m. Dec. 31,1813
CAPTAIN JOSIAH COGGESHALL son of Capt. William and Molley
(Finney) Coggeshall.
ISSUE: COGGESHALL
1.   MARY, 2, LORING FINNEY. 3. MARTHA 4. WILLIAM
5. GEORGE.

359.   LEVI PHINNEY, son of LOT and ELIZABETH (DURLAND) PHINNEY.
He was b. 1796 and d. Oct. 1875.. He m. RUTH GATES dau of John;
and Elizabeth (Fales)Gates. Ruth was b. 1802 d. Jan 7, 1867.
ISSUE:
367.   INGLIS PHINNEY, b. 1824 d. 1909. He was b. in Victoria Vale
Nova Scotia and d. Middleton. He m. c1846 MATILDA CRAIG Who
was b. in Armagh, Ireland April 11,1829 d. Middleton May 27 1921 dau
of William and Charlotte (Brown) Craig. He was educated in Acadia
University and was a school teacher.   There were no children known
at this time.

362.   SETH PHINNEY, b. May 27, 1791 d. 1872 son of ISAAC and HULDAH
(PRESTON) PHINNEY. He m. LYDIA JANE_____. b. 1792 died
1859 in Clinton Coiunty, Michigan. .Seth was b in Williamsburg, Mass
He d. in Bingham Township, Clinton County, Michigan.
ISSUE:
*368.   HULDAH PHINNEY b. May 3, 1814.
*369.   GEORGE PHINNEY b. 1816.
*370.   LOVINA PHINNEY b. 1818.
*371.   EMILY PHINNEY b. April 8, 1821
*372.   ALMINA PHINNEY.
*373.   HARRIET MARIA PHINNEY.

NOTES

368.   HULDAH PHINNEY, b. May 3, 1814   d. 1894   dau of SETH and LYDIA
        JANE PHINNEY.   She was b. in Cazenovia, N.Y. and died in Delta,
        Michigan. Dec. 19, 1894.   She m. ELSON MONROE CAMPBELL 1831.
        He was b. 1810 and d. Delta, Michigan Aug. 3, 1895.   They were
        probably m in Cazenovia, N.Y. as they came to Michigan from Cazeno-
        via with two little girls and settled in or near Wacousta, Michigan.
        A son, HOVEY BRADFORD CAMPBELL wrote an obituary about his mother.
        ISSUE: CAMPBELL.

        1,   LYDIA b. 1853 d. before 1894 m. March 17,1850 SAMUEL HART DeWitt, Michigan.

        2.   SARAH E. b. 1835 d. Feb. 1,1913 m. June 6,1852 JAMES MERRITT AVERY. He was
              b. Feb. 8, 1831 in Canada. They are buried in Nirvana, Michigan.
                   A.   Nettie Avery m. a Mr. Tripp in Texas
                   B.   Adolphus.
                   C.   AMY AVERY M. A Mr. Johnson.
                   D.   JOHN E. b. 1873 d. 1938 m. MABEL G._____ They had:
                        1.   JOHN MERRITT AVERY.
                        2.   RUBY AVERY.
                        3.   GLENN.
                        4.   DOROTHY.
                        5.   MINNIE Avery m. HAROLD STRAYER and they had
                                  Herold Strayer Jr.
                        6.   ORA AVERY.

        3. SETH b, 1842 d. 1919 buried Grand Ledge, Mich cemetery. He m. SARAH A._____.

        4. HOVEY BRADFORD b. Jan 8, 1844 at Eagle, Michigan d. April 15, 1922 buried at
             North Engle Cemetery.
        5. CLARK CAMPBELL.
             (See ENCYCLOPEDIA of the CAMPBELL FAMILIES written by Compiler Roy J. Campbell)

                              _____

369.   GEORGE PHINNEY, b. 1816 d. 1893 son of SETH and LYDIA JANE
        PHINNEY, he m. CAROLINE BROWN b. 1841 d. March 17, 1873.
        They are buried in North Eagle, Michigan cemetery.
        ISSUE:

        *374.   JAMES M. PHINNEY .

        *375.   NELLIE PHINNEY.

         376.   RENA PHINNEY m. GEORGE WILLIS buried in Tenn.

         377.   HENRY PHINNEY, m. ADA_____ They had GEORGIA
                PHINNEY.

         378.   LYDIA PHINNEY m. _____POOL

        *379.   FRANK PHINNEY m. IDA FERRIS.

        *380.   ORA PHINNEY.   m. WESLEY SIGNS.

                              _____

370. LOVINA PHINNEY b. Oct. 8, 1818 d. Dec. 27, 1885 dau of SETH and LYDIA JANE PHINNEY. She m. DAVID McCAUSEY b. May 27, 1815 in Washington County, N.Y. Lovina was born in Madison County, N.Y. and died in Portland, Michigan.

ISSUE: *McCausey.*

1. *HENRY b. 1843 d. 1922.*

    A. *NOAH McCausey m. a Mr. Sprague.*

371. EMILY PHINNEY, b. April 8, 1821 d. Aug. 8, 1902 dau of SETH and LYDIA JANE PHINNEY. She was born in New Hampshire and d. in Geneva, Kansas. She m. Sept. 3, 1839 JONATHAN HOVEY SPICER. He was b. April 12, 1816 in Plymouth, N.H. He was a grandson of Jabez Spicer descendant of William Brewster, of the *Mayflower.* They were in Clinton Co, Michigan and moved to Geneva, Kansas in 1852.

ISSUE: *SPICER*

1. *DUANE DELOYAL SPICER.*

372. ALMINA PHINNEY b. 1828 d. Feb. 18, 1882 dau of SETH and LYDIA JANE PHINNEY. She m. HIRAM TRIM as her second husband. She m. (1) JOHN THORNBER.

ISSUE: *THORNBER.*

1. *JENNIE m. JAMES WADDELL.*

2. *NINA m. ALBERT BARNES HUMISTON.*

3. *HATTIE m. (1) Mr. Smith (2) AARON LOWDON.*

4. *WESLEY.*

373. HARRIET MARIA PHINNEY b. 1831 d. Sept. 20, 1873 dau of SETH and LYDIA JANE PHINNEY. She m. Jan 1, 1850 WARREN BLAN= CHARD b. Sept. 3, 1820 in N.Y. d. not known. She m. (2) WILLIAM DENSMORE Oct. 29, 1867 (*Mich. V.R.*)

ISSUE: *BLANCHARD.*

1. *ELMER b. April 22, 1852 m. HELEN A. HALLADAY.*

    A. *GLENN*   B. *GUY.*

2. *CHAUNCEY LOUIS b. March 18, 1862 d. Dec. 30, 1938 m. CORA CHENY.*

3. *MERRITT JOHN DENSMORE b/April 4, 1869 m. Rhoda Goodwin.*

374. JAMES M. PHINNEY b. 1860 d. 1926 son of **GEORGE** and CAROLINE (BROWN) PHINNEY. He m. MARY C. _____ and both are buried in S. Bingham Cemetery, Clinton County. Michigan.

ISSUE:

*381.   ALBERT PHINNEY 1890.

———————

375. NELLIE PHINNEY, birth and death unknown. She was the daughter of GEORGE and CAROLINE (BROWN) PHINNEY. m. (1) JAKE SIGNS whom she divorced then m. (2) GEORGE ASH. She is buried in De-Witt, Michigan.

ISSUE: SIGNS/ ASH.

1. CLYDE SIGNS   2. MYRTLE ASH 3.ROBERT ASH 4. MARVEL ASH
  Marvel ash m. HERMAN THIBERT OF WAUCOUSTA, MICHIGAN.

———————

379. FRANK PHINNEY b. 1871 d. 1949 son of GEORGE and CAROLINE (BROWN) PHINNEY. He m. IDA FERRIS b. 1872 d. 1953. Both are buried in North Eagle Cemetery, Eagle, Michigan.

ISSUE:

382.   OTIS PHINNEY.

383.   GERTRUDE PHINNEY.

384.   FLOSSIE PHINNEY m LEWIS WILSON.

   1. ELIZABETH WILSON.
   2. GEORGE WILSON
   3. LEO WILSON.

385.   ANDREW PHINNEY.

386   MELVIN PHINNEY.

387.   IRWIN PHINNEY.

388.   HAROLD PHINNEY.

389.   ETHEL PHINNEY of Houston, Texas

———————

380. ORA PHINNEY dau of **GEORGE** and **CAROLINE (BROWN) PHINNEY.**

She married WESLEY SIGNS.

ISSUE: *SIGNS.*

1. *BERTHA m. ORIN STEVENS.*
2. *NETTIE m. WILLIAM KENNY.*
3. *LAURA b. 1890 m. 1907 RAY SEARLES.*

    A. *GLEN SEARLES.*

    B. *DONALD SEARLES.*

    C. *GLERALD SEARLES.*

    D. *DELMAR SEARLESS*

    E. *LAWRENCE SEARLES.*

    F. *JENNIE SEARLES m. a Mr. VEZAR.*

    G. *CHARLENE SEARLES m a Mr. HILL*

    H. *ANNA BELLE SEARLES.*

---

381. ALBERT PHINNEY **b.** 1890 son of JAMES M. and MARY C. PHINNEY.

It is not known at this time whom Albert married. His children are:

listed however:

ISSUE:

390.   LORETTA PHINNEY.

391.   EDNA PHINNEY m a Mr. price.

392.   CASSIE PHINNEY m. DANIEL SHAFER.

393.   CLARENCE PHINNEY.

NOTES

FINNEY FAMILIES

These families are related to the families in the front of this book. It is obvious that these families go back to the Bristol and Barmstable lines. It is hoped by this compiler that if your family is not shown in this book that you will send him the information you have about your family and if there is enough names, and there must be, a new, continued volume will be written. The compiler's name and address will be in the front of the book.

Due to the numbering systerm used this section will begin with five hundred.

****

500. ROBERT FINNEY b. in Scotland or England   c1630 son of _____
m. ISABELL_____ c1655.
ISSUE:
501. HENRY FINNEY b. Nov. 30, 1657.
502 JAMES FINNEY B. July 4, 1659.
503. WILLIAM FINNEY, b. May 4, 1664.
504. MARYE (sic) FINNEY b. Aug. 29, 1666.
*505. ROBERT FINNEY, b. 1668.

——————

505. ROBERT FINNEY, b. Londonderry, Ireland 1668 son of ROBERT and ISABELL FINNEY. He m. DOROTHEA_____ dau of _____ b. 1690. He d. March 1753 and was buried at Thunder Hill, Pa. They came to America in 1720 settling in New London Township, Chester, Pa. The **THUNDER HILL ESTATE** was a 900 acre estate bought from Michael Harlan and was property next to the 15,000 acres owned by Letitia Penn dau of William Penn.
ISSUE:
*506. JOHN FINNEY m. twice.
*507. ROBERT FINNEY.
*508. LAZARUS FINNEY.
*509 LETITIA FINNEY m. WILLIAM McKEAN.
*510. WILLIAM FINNEY m. JEAN STEPHENSON.
*511. THOMAS FINNEY m. MARY CHESTER.
*512. ANNA FINNEY m. JOHN McCLANAHAN.

——————

506. JOHN FINNEY, known as Doctor John, b. in Ireland d. March 1774 in Newcastle, Delaware. He m. (1) ELIZABETH FRENCH dau of Robert and Mary (Sandeland)French. Elizabeth's mother was the widow of Maurice Trent. John m. (2) SARAH RICHARDSON dau of John Richardson.

ISSUE:

*513. ANN DOROTHEA FINNEY b. 1735 d. 1817 m. JOHN FINNEY.

*514. DAVID FINNEY d. May 1806 m. ANN THOMPSON.

515. ROBERT FINNEY d. 1771 Unmd.

516. ELIZABETH FINNEY d. May 30, 1788.

517. JOHN FINNEY, Jr. b. Nov. 1749 d. Jan 19, 1753. He was Sarah's son.

518. INFANT died.

519. INFANT died.

---

507. ROBERT FINNEY b. Ireland d. 1782 son of ROBERT and DOROTHEA FINNEY. He was a doctor and never married. He inherited the Thunder Hill Estates.

---

508. LAZARUS FINNEY, b. Northern Ireland d. 1740 Chester Co, Pa. He was the son of ROBERT and DOROTHEA FINNEY. He m. CATHERINE SYMONTON. She m. (2) Col. John Frew of E. Nottingham and New London, Pa. Lazarus was the first tavern keeper in New London, Pa., beginning in 1729 and was still standing in 1949 and was used as a tavern. Catherine was granted letters of administration in the estate and it was settled in 1746.

ISSUE:

*520. ROBERT FINNEY b. 1727 d. Oct. 29, 1822.

*521. JOHN FINNEY b. 1730 d. July 5, 1782 Newcastle.

522. DOROTHEA FINNEY, m. JOHN OCHILTREE.

*523 CATHERINE FINNEY.

NOTES

509. LETITIA FINNEY d. 1742 Chester Co, Pa.,dau. of ROBERT and DORO-
THEA FINNEY. She m. WILLIAM McKEAN b. 1707.

ISSUE: McKEAN.

1. THOMAS b. 1734 d. 1817 was one of the signers of the DECLARATION
OF INDEPENDENCE, and later was Governor of Pennsylvania. He m.
1763 MARY BORDEN who d. 1773. She was the dau of JOSEPH of Bor-
dentown, N.J. Thomas m. (2) SARAH ARMITAGE b. Newcastle, Delaware
They had 12 children.

_____

510. WILLIAM FINNEY b. 1700/10 in Northern Ireland. He d. 1748 Chester
Co., Pa. His will dated Jan 12, 1749 and he was buried in Thunder-
hill cemetery. He m. JANE STEPHENSON *dau of _____
He was the son of ROBERT and DOROTHEA FINNEY.

ISSUE:

*524. JAMES FINNEY b. 1726 m. 1747 MARTHA MAYES.

525. ELIZABETH FINNEY, b. 1728 d. 1816 m. ANDREW HENDERSON.

526. ARCHIBALD FINNEY, b. 1730 m. _____LAUGHEAD dau of
Robert Laughead.

527. THOMAS FINNEY b. 1732 d.1770/1 m. 1757 SUSAN STEWART.

528. WILLIAM FINNEY b. 1734 d. young.

529. LAZARUS FINNEY b. 1737/8 died young.

*530. MARTHA FINNEY, b. 1740 m a Mr. JOSEPH LAUGHRON.

*531. ROBERT FINNEY, b. 1742 d. APRIL 17.1827.

*532. JOHN FINNEY, b. 1745 m. ANN DOROTHEA dau of Dr. John.

*533. WALTER FINNEY b. 1747 d. 1820.

534. JEAN FINNEY,b. 1759/60 m. DAVID HUNTER and lived in
Pittsburgh, Pa.

_____

511. THOMAS FINNEY b. in Ireland d. 1767 Chester Co.,Pa. He was the
son of ROBERT and DOROTHEA FINNEY, He m. Oct. 27,1736 in Christ
Church, Philadelphia, Pa. MARY CHESTER.

ISSUE:

535. ROBERT FINNEY.

536. DOROTHEA FINNEY,

537. ERIN(ANN) FINNEY.

_____

_____

*Jane is also referred to as Jean Stephenson. (Stevenson)

512. ANNA FINNEY, b. Ireland d. after 1778 Chester Co., Pa. She m. JOHN McCLANAHAN.

ISSUE: McCLANHAN.

1, ELIJAH.   2. JOHN.

---

513. ANN DOROTHEA FINNEY, b. 1735 d. 1817 dau of JOHN and ELIZA= BETH (FRENCH) FINNEY. She m. her cousin JOHN FINNEY son of William and Jean (Stephenson) Finney. (See 532 for her children)

---

514. DAVID FINNEY, d. May 1806 son of JOHN and ELIZABETH (FRENCH) FINNEY. He m. ANN THOMPSON who came from County Antrim, Ireland. David was at one time Justice of the Supreme Court of Delaware.

ISSUE:

538. JOHN FRENCH FINNEY d. 1794.

539. ELIZABETH FINNEY, m. JAMES MILLER.

540. ANN DOROTHEA FINNEY d. May 1792 m WILLIAM MILLER. He was a brother to her sister's husband.

*541. DAVID THOMPSON FINNEY b. Jan. 20,1773 d. May 22,1863. He m. MARY JAMES.

542. WASHINGTON FINNEY, David's twin, m. CHRISTINE BECKMAN.

543. SARAH FINNEY m. FRENCH McMULLEN.

---

520. ROBERT FINNEY b. 1727 d. Oct. 29, 1822 son of LAZARUS and CATH- ERINE (SYMONTON) FINNEY, m. Sept. 1746 in Union,Co, Pa. DIANA SPENCER.

ISSUE:

544. LAZARUS FINNEY b. Sept 9,1751 d. Oct. 3,1883. He was a Revolutionary War Veteran. He m. (1)ELIZABETH FULTON and (2) ELIZABETH OCHELTREE.

---

521.   JOHN FINNEY, b. 1730 d. July 5, 1782 son of LAZARUS and CATHERINE

(SYMONTON) FINNEY. He m. RUTH LLOYD dau of Joseph Lloyd. They
were married in Old Swedes Holy Trinity Church, Wilmington, Delaware,
built in 1698 and they are buried in the same church yard.
ISSUE:

*545.   JOSEPH FINNEY, b. April 2,1765 d. March 22,1837.

546.   JAMES FINNEY, b. 1768. He settled after 1800 in Gibson Co.
Indiana . He m. (1) MARY COGHORN.. He m. (2) Dec. 21,1837
JEAN SARAH MAKENSON.

*547.   ROBERT FINNEY, b. 1783 in Va. d. July 10,1866.

548.   JOHN FINNEY, lived in Grayson Co Va in 1825.

549.   WILLIAM FINNEY, m. MARGARET JEFFERSON. Their childrwn
lived in Murfreesboro, Tenn soon after 1800.

---

523.   CATHERINE FINNEY, dau of LAZARUS and CATHERINE (SYMONTON)
FINNEY, m. July 25,1758 JAMES LOUGHEAD and went to Phildelphia
where he was a merchant . On Aug. 11. 1772 he submitted a petition
to be appointed vendue Master for Philadelphia. No children are mentioned.

---

524.   JAMES FINNEY b. in Pennsylvania 1726 the first child of WILLIAM and
JEAN (STEPHENSON) FINNEY. He m. MARTHA MAYES. He d. 1802.
ISSUE:

550.   THOMAS FINNEY b. 1747/8 m. June 12, 1770 MARGARET
SWAN.

*551.   JAMES FINNEY, 2nd b. 1750.

552.   JEAN FINNEY, B. 1752 m. ROBERT SMITH.

553.   WILLIAM FINNEY, b. 1758 m. ANNE MORTON b. Nov. 2,1781
d. 1816.

554.   MARGARET FINNEY, b. 1758 m. JAMES McCUTCHEON.

555.   JOHN FINNEY, b. 1760 m. MARY TAYLOR.

556,   MARY FINNEY, b. 1762 m. a Mr. PEDEN.

557.   ANDREW PINNEY, b. 1764 m. JANE HOWE.

558.   ROBERT FINNEY, b. 1765 m. MARY (POLLY) PEDEN d. July
16, 1850. Their family see P2RF-1.

---

530. MARTHA FINNEY b. 1740 dau of WILLIAM and JEAN (STEPHENSON) FINNEY. She m. JOSEPH LAUGHRON. She evidently died young and so did her husband as she left her children to be raised by her brother. William Finney. The children were not named.

---

531. ROBERT FINNEY, b. 1742 in Chester Co.,Pa. He d. April 17, 1827. He was the son of WILLIAM and JEAN (STEPHENSON) FINNEY, and a private in the Rev. War on Capt. Thomas Strawbridges Co of Militia commanded by Lt. Col. Even Evans. He was on Co Muster Roll Dec. 5, to 25, 1776 inclusive., 4th Battalion, Chester Co Militia. He m. (1) a Miss. Laughead and (2) JANE _____ (Military Service Records, Wash. DC)

ISSUE:

559.   JENNETT FINNEY b. 1765-75. She m. DAVID MEAD founder of Meadville, Pa. He was known as General David Mead, 1796

*560.   JAMES FINNEY b. 1787.

---

532. JOHN FINNEY b. 1745 son of WILLIAM and JEAN (STEPHENSON) FINNEY. He m. his cousin ANN DOROTHEA FINNEY dau of Dr. John Finney. He was the ruler elder in the New London Presbyterian Church, and lived many years in Londonderry, Township, Chester Co. He engaged in agriculture persuits. He was Justice of the Peace, commissioned Feb. 1. 1806 and sworn in May 20, 1806.

ISSUE:

561.   JOHN FINNEY JR. He was commissioned Justice of the Peace May 24, 1816 and sworn in July 8, 1816.

NOTES

533. WALTER FINNEY b. 1747 d. 1828 son of WILLIAM and JEAN
(STEPHENSON) FINNEY. He m. MARY O'HARA. He was a Major
in the American Revolution and attained notice in the Revolution
and Indian Wars. Fort Finney, Ohio and Fort Finney, Indiana are named
after him. No children are shown.

---

541. DAVID THOMPSON FINNEY, b. Jan 20,1773 d. May 22,1863. He was
the son of DAVID and ANN(THOMPSON) FINNEY. He m. March 9,
1797 MARY JAMES dau of Major John and Elizabeth James. She was
b. Sept. 10, 1775 and d. July 13,1859 in Holmes Co.,Ohio.
ISSUKE:

*562. JOHN FRENCH FINNEY, b. Feb. 9, 1798.

*563. DAVID THOMPSON FINNEY, Jr. b. Nov. 27,1799.

564, ELIZABETH FINNEY, B. Aug. 16,1801.

*565. WASHINGTON FINNEY, b. May 4,1803.

566. MARY JANE FINNEY. b. July 4, 1806.

567. ANN EVANS FINNEY b. Dec. 19,1808.

*568. WILLIAM JAMES FINNEY b. Dec. 6, 1811.

*569. RACHEL JAMES FINNEY, b. Dec. 1, 1813 m DAVID MARCHAND.

570. THOMAS McKEAN FINNEY b. Nov. 12,1817.

NOTES

545.   JOSEPH FINNEY, b. April 2, 1765 d. March 22, 1837. He was the son
       of JOHN and RUTH (LLOYD) FINNEY. He m. (1) Dec. 13,1783;
       RACHEL BARKLEY (2) by 1807 ANN KESSTER b. Jan 9, 1774 in North
       Carolina. She d. March 15, 1853 in Indiana. She was the dau. of
       John and Sarah Kesster. Joseph dealt in realestate and was also a
       school teacher in 1826.
       ISSUE:
       *571.   JOSEPH FINNEY b. Sept. 18,1784 d. March 8, 1867.
       *572.   JOSHUA FINNEY b. 1790.
       *573   RICHARD KING FINNEY, b. March 8, 1808.
        574   MARGARET (PEGGY) RECTOR FINNEY b. June 27,1812, Grayson
               Co.,Va. She d. after 1880 in Indiana. She is buried in Rush
               Creek cemetery, north of Sylvania, Ind. She never married. In
               1880 she lived with her nephew Wesley and his wife Mary and
               their children.

               _____

547.   ROBERT FINNEY b. 1783 in Virginia, son of JOHN and RUTH (LLOYD)
       FINNEY. He d. July 10,1866 West Milton, Miami Co.,Ohio. He m.
       HANNAH HICKMAN b. 1783 in Pa. He was a soldier in the War of 1812.
       in Ky. militia on the Wabash River Frontier.
       ISSUE:
       575.   JOSEPH FINNEY b. 1815. He was a school teacher in Ohio.
       576.   RUTH FINNEY b. 1818.

               _____

               NOTES

551. JAMES FINNEY b. 1750 son of JAMES and MARTHA (MAYES) FINNEY. He was called "James, the second" He m. (1) MARTHA CRUNKLETON b. April 20,1774. He m. (2) ELIZABETH BRADEN. He m. (3) REBECCA RHEAH.

ISSUE:

577. MARAGARET FINNEY b. 1774/5 m ROBERT BRADEN. No children.

*578. ROBERT FINNEY, b. 1777/8 m. MARGARET GOTHRIE.

579. MARTHA FINNEY b. 1780 m. WALTER FRANCIS c1806

580. ELIZABETH FINNEY b. 1782 m. a Mr. McMILLEN c1806.

581. JOHN FINNEY b. 1784 m. ELIZABETH (BETSEY) CANNON, Dec. 10, 1816.

Wife No. 2 children:

582. WALTER B. FINNEY b. 1786/7.

Wife No 3. children.

583. JAMES FINNEY, b. 1806/7

584. THOMAS FINNEY b. c1808/9 in Ohio.

---

560. JAMES FINNEY b. 1787 son of ROBERT and JANE FINNEY. He m. twice. His second wife was SARAH_____. They had 14 children.

ISSUE:

585. JANE FINNEY.

586. ROBERT FINNEY.

587. JOSEPH FINNEY.

588. WILSON FINNEY.

589. SARAH FINNEY.

590. DAVID MEAD FINNEY.

591. CATHERINE FINNEY b. 1833 in Pennsylvania.

592. DANIEL FINNEY, b. 1834.

593, ALEXANDER FINNEY. b. 1837 in Pennsylvania.

594. GEORGE FINNEY b. 1839 in Pa m. MARGARET_____.

595. JAMES FINNEY.

596. SARAH FINNEY.

597. LUISA SUE ANN FINNEY. b. 1853.

598. HIRAM FINNEY b. 1845.

---

562. JOHN FRENCH FINNEY, b. Feb. 9, 1798 son of DAVID and MARY (JAMES)FINNEY. He m. REBECCA BUTLER b. 1809. He was a farmer and the census of 1850 states he was worth $5,000 in real-estate.

ISSUE:

*599. DAVID FINNEY, b. 1827. He m. RACHEL D._____ ،

600. JONATHAN FINNEY b. 1830 in Ohio.

601. JOHN FINNEY b. 1835 in Ohio m. REBECCA_____.

602. MARY FINNEY b. 1833 in Ohio.

*603. THOMAS FINNEY, b. Oct. 21,1841 m. EMMA G. WHITMAN.

604. REBECCA FINNEY b. 1843 in Ohio.

605. GEORGE FINNEY b. 1843 in Ohio.

---

563. DAVID THOMPSON FINNEY, Jr. b. Nov. 27,1799 son of DAVID and MARY (JAMES) FINNEY. He m. HANNAH BUTLER who was born 1804.

ISSUE:

606. SARAH FINNEY b. 1839.

607. JAMES FINNEY b. 1835 m. MARY E. _____.

608. ANN FINNEY b. 1840.

809. JANE FINNEY b. 1847 in Ohio

610. LUCRETIA FINNEY b. 1847 in Ohio.

611. JONATHAN FINNEY b. 1849.

NOTES

565. WASHINGTON FINNEY, b. May 4, 1805 son of DAVID THOMPSON and
MARY(JAMES) FINNEY. He was b in Pennsylvania and m. MARTHA
_____ b. 1811 in Pa.

ISSUE:

612. DAVID FINNEY b. 1832.

613. SAMUEL FINNEY, b. 1835.

614. JOHNSTON FINNEY b. 1837.

615. MARGARET FINNEY, b. 1837.

616. RACHEL FINNEY b. 1841.

617. MARY R. FINNEY b. 1843.

618. CLARISSA D. FINNEY b. 1845.

619. CLEMENDA L. FINNEY, b. 1847.

568. WILLIAM JAMES FINNEY b. Dec. 6, 1811 son of DAVID THOMPSON
and MARY (JAMES) FINNEY. He m. LOUISA_____ b. 18__

ISSUE:

620. THOMAS FINNEY b. 1850 Holmes Co. Ohio m. LOIS _____
b. 1828 in Pennsylvania.

621. ANN FINNEY b. 1854.

622. WILLIAM FINNEY, b. 1856.

623. ARTHUR FINNEY, b. 1861.

569. RACHEL FINNEY b. Dec. 4, 1813 dau of DAVID THOMPSON and MARY
(JAMES) FINNEY. She m. DAVID MARCHAND b. 1811, and they went
to live in Holmes Co, Ohio. in 1850.
ISSUE: *MARCHAND.*

1. *MARY E. b. 1846 in Holmes Co., Ohio*

2. *JOANNA FINNEY b. 1848.*

NOTES

571. JOSEPH FINNEY b. Sept 18,1784 d. March 8, 1867 son of JOSEPH and
RACHEL BARKLEY FINNEY. He m. Sept 10, 1805 in Greene Co.
Tenn. MARY POLLY LONG b. April 2,1786 in Va d. Sept .27,1872.
Both are buried Linebarger Cemetery near West Union ,Indiana. Between
1795 and 1809 they lived most of the time in Greene Co, Tenn. part
of the time in Surry Co, North Carolina. He served in the War of 1812
2nd Surry Reg. N.C. Militia. He enlisted on Feb. 1,1814.and was discharged Sept. 4, 1814. He was granted land later and there was a widow's
pension on the war service. In 1826 they settled in Anapolis one mile
west of the town where they spent the rest of their lives. He was a
farmer, a Mason, and an United Brethern.

ISSUE:

*624. ROBERT FINNEY b. Aug. 23,1808.

625. JOSEPH FINNEY, b. Dec. 19,1808 Greene Co, Tenn. d. May 5,
1854 in Clinton Co Indiana. He m.LORENA MORGAN dau of
KENSHEN and SARAH MORGAN.

626. JOHN LONG FINNEY b. Dec. 16,1810 N.C. He d. before 1903
in Kansas . He m.(1) ELIZABETH CAMPBELL (2) Feb. 2,1840
m. PARKE DELANEY HUNT.

627. NANCY FINNEY b. Oct. 16,1812 Surry Co.,N.C. She m. THOMAS
B. WADE.

*628. HAWKINS COOK FINNEY, b. Aug. 28, 1815 d. Jan. 1,1889. He
m. (1) Nov. 16,1837 MARTHA COUNTE. He m. (2) Mrs. SARAH
S. WALTERS. Her maiden name was WILEY. He m. (3) MARY
E. COSSETT.

*629. POLLY FINNEY b. Jan. 21,1818 d. June 21, 1898 in Indiana.

*630. ELIZABETH FINNEY, b. March 9,1820 d. Aug. 27, 1900.

631. RACHEL FINNEY b. March 27, 1821 d. April 21,1860 in Ill.
She m. Nov. 4, 1838 NACY HARRISON JONES.

*632. WESLEY FINNEY b. May 10, 1823.

*633. FANNEY FINNEY b. Feb.16, 1825 d. Dec. 18,1891.

634. CATHERINE FINNEY, b. Jan 1 ,1828 d. after 1881. She m.
DAVID BRADFORD.

*635. MARY ANN FINNEY m. JOHN HAMILTON WEAVER.

572. JOSHUA FINNEY, b. 1790 son of JOSEPH and RACHEL (BARKLEY) FINNEY. He m. JURIAH COLLINS b. 1796 in N.C. after 1850. She d. He served in the War of 1812 in Green Co , Tenn. He was a farmer and a school teacher. His old home is on Boone Trail ten miles southwest of Yadkinville, N.C. No children were listed.

----

573. RICHARD KING FINNEY b. March 8, 1808 in Va. He was the son of JOSEPH and RUTH (LLOYD) FINNEY. He d. Feb. 22, 1875 and is buried in Rush Creek Cemetery, Indiana. He was a farmer and purchased land in Penn Twp on Jan. 13,1836. He later bought land and lived on Rush Creek where he died. He m. April 25, 1847 REBECCA DAVIES. b. Sept 11 1809 Berks Co, Pa. She d. Sept 29,1891. She was the dau of Joseph and Lydia (Kennedy)Davies. Joseph and Lydia both died enroute to Indiana and their five children continued the journey alone, reaching Parke County in 1827. They were Quakers.

ISSUE:

*636. JOSEPH DAVIES FINNEY b. April 12,1848 d. March 15.1928 at Kingman,Ind.

637. LYDIA ANN FINNEY b. Nov 7, 1849 d. Jan 2,1930. She m. WILLIAM R. PATTON. b. 1850 d. April 15,1929 at Kingman,Ind. There were no children.

NOTES

578,   ROBERT FINNEY b. 1777/8 son of JAMES and MARTHA (CRUNKLETON) FINNEY. He m. MARGARET GUTHRIE c1806.

ISSUE:

638.   JOSEPH FINNEY, b. c1807.

639.   MARIA FINNEY.

640.   ROBERT P. FINNEY, m. (1)MARY HITCHCOCK Dec. 11,1844. He m. (2) LYDIA ANN JENKINS. Nov. 8,1846. There is no other record.

641.   JANE FINNEY, m. SAMUEL CARNAHAN Jan. 27,1847.

642.   DAVID FINNEY.

*643.   THOMAS G. FINNEY, b. June 12,1826.

644.   SARAH FIN.NEY.

645.   WILLIAM G. FINNEY moved to Washington D.C. and was in Ford's theater when President Lincoln was shot.

———————

599.   DAVID FINNEY, b. 1827 son of JOHN FRENCH and REBECCA BUTLER FINNEY. He m. RACHEL D._____.

ISSUE:

646.   THOMAS FINNEY b. 1853.

647.   ALBERT E. FINNEY. b. 1855.

648.   JEMIMA FINNEY b. 1859.

649.   CLARIE FINNEY b. 1863.

———————

603.   THOMAS FINNEY b. Oct. 21,1841 son of JOHN FRENCH and REBECCA (BUTLER) FINNEY. He m. April 11,1864 EMMA G. WHITMAN. They moved to Paxton, Kansas.

ISSUE:

650.   MARY FINNEY b. Paxico, Kansas.

651.   CHRISTIANA FINNEY.

652.   HALLIE FINNEY.

*653.   JOHN EDGAR FINNEY.

———————

624.   ROBERT FINNEY, b. Aug. 23,1808 son of JOSEPH and MARY POLLY (LONG) FINNEY. He m. MATILDA HUNT who was b. Sept. 20,1815. She d. Oct. 16,1896 in Tuscola, Ill. She was the dau of Zimri and Mary (Dix)Hunt.

ISSUE:

654.   ELIJAH COOK FINNEY, b. April 14,1836 d. Jan.24,1917 in Ill.

655.   DANIEL WILLIAM FINNEY b. Oct. 8, 1837 d. June 17, 1905. He m. GILLA HUFFMAN dau of Lawson Huffman.

*656.   DAVID WESLEY FINNEY, b. Aug. 22, 1839 d. Nov. 1,1916. in Kansas He m. HELEN McCONNELL.

657.   PAMELA ANN FINNEY, b. Jan 1,1841 d. March 3,1843.

658.   ZIMRI DIX FINNEY, b. March 18,1842 d. Jan 14,1876 in Kansas. He m. RACHEL STEWART dau of Abraham and Mary Stewart. He was in service during the Civil War.

*659.   ROBERT JOHNSON FINNEY, b. Dec. 10,1844 d. Dec. 11,1912.

660.   MARY ELIZABETH FINNEY, b. June 10,1847 d. 1929 .

*661.   JOSEPH HARRISON FINNEY,b. Jan 10,1849 d. Sept 9,1897.

662.   MALINDA CATHERINE FINNEY, b. Feb. 4, 1855. In 1940 she was living in Tuscola, Ill. She m. WILLIAM DAVID GOLDMAN son of George and Elizabeth (Tucker)Goldman.

NOTES

628. HAWKINS COOK FINNEY, b. Aug 28, 1813 d. Jan. 1, 1889. He was the son of JOSEPH and MARY POLLY(LONG) FINNEY. He m. (1) Nov. 16, 1837 MARTHA COUNTE or KONUTZ. He m. (2) MRS. SARAH S. WALTERS. He m. (3) MARY E. COSSETT. Sarah's maiden name was "WILEY"

ISSUE:

  *663. JOHN V. FINNEY, b. 1837 m. MARY RANSOPHER Nov. 1864.

  664. DAVID FINNEY b. 1861.

  665. FRANCES FINNEY, b. 1844 m. JOSEPH KINDER.

  666. LEVONIA FINNEY b. 1847.

  667. AMANDA FINNEY, b. 1849

  668. JOSEPH FINNEY, b. 1851.

  669. WESLEY FINNEY, b. 1851 m. CATHIE KNAPP.

  670. LUCRETIA FINNEY, b. 1854.

  671. ABIGAIL FINNEY b. 1856.

  672. EMILY FINNEY b. 1858 m. SAMUEL E. GRIFFIN.

Taken from the 1860 census report showing Martha as Hawkin's wife. Records of Thomas Finney of Logansport, Indiana.

---

629. POLLY FINNEY, b. Jan 21, 1818 d. June 21, 1898 in Indiana. She was the dau. of JOSEPH and MARY POLLY (LONG) FINNEY. She m. July 10, 1839 ALEXANDER EPHLIN b. 1821 North Carolina. son of David and Catherine Ephlin.

ISSUE: EPHLIN.

1,   JOSIAH b. 1836 in Indiana m.HANNAH J. _____ b. 1838.

    A. ADDA b. 1868.

    B. WILLIAM b. 1869.

    C. THEODOSIA b. 1872 in Indiana.

NOTES

630. ELIZABETH FINNEY, b. March 9, 1820 dau of JOSEPH and MARY POLLY (LONG) FINNEY. She d Aug. 27, 1900. She m. DANIEL MATER a minister b. May 1, 1810 Butler Co, Ohio. He was the son of George and Susannah (Pierce) Mater. Daniel and his brother John were co-founders of Offerbein United Brethren Church, Bellmore, Indiana.

ISSUE: *MATER.*

1. GEORGE WESLEY SCOTT b. 1850 d. 1854.
2. JOHN WINFIELD RUSSELL b. July 28, 1852 d. May 9, 1927.
He m. SARAH ANN DARR and was a builder and contractor/ Their child was GRACE DELLA MATER b. Oct 9, 1879 in Danville, Ill. and she ma: JOSEPH DANIEL BOLTON.

3 DANIEL HARRISON RILEY b. 1854 d. Feb. 18, 1904 in Ill. He m. MARY E. BELL.
4. MARY JANE b. Jan. 3, 1857 d. Aug. 9, 1938 in Terre Haute, Indiana. She m. C. LEE PHILLIPS
5. HIRAM REASANT MOORE b. Feb. 4, 1959 s. 1921. He m. MARY EVA WATSON.

---

632. WESLEY FINNEY b. May 10, 1823 in Indiana son of JOSEPH and MARY POLLY (LONG) FINNEY. He d. Oct. 3, 1904 in Kansas. He m. MARY MATILDA HINSHAW b. Oct. 20 1829 d. Feb. 1900. She was the dau of Jesse and Hannah (Moon) Hinshaw of Indiana. He moved to Indiana with his stock and household furnishings in a freight train.

ISSUE:

*673. SAMANTHA JANE FINNEY, b. Aug. 7, 1851 d. April 1937 in Kansas

674. JAMES ANDERSON FINNEY, b. 1854 d. 1848(?) Should those dates be reversed, or perhaps to 1884?

*675. MARY C. FINNEY, b. May 8, 1857 d. Aug. 22, 1926.

*676. ANNA E. FINNEY b. May 24, 1859 d. March 1928.

677. POLLY HANNAH FINNEY, b. March 23, 1864 d. Dec. 12, 1886. She m. Dec. 25, 1885 at her father's home JAMES CUMMINGS. b. 1858.

*678. JOHN WESLEY FINNEY,

*679. LOUISA MAY FINNEY b. Jan 8, 1867.

*680. DANIEL WEBSTER FINNEY, b. Nov. 7, 1868 d. Dec. 10, 1927.

*681. CLARA ELLEN FINNEY, b. May 27, 1872 d. Dec. 12, 1945.

---

633.   FANNEY FINNEY, b. Feb.16, 1825 d. Dec. 18,1891 dau of JOSEPH and
MARY POLLY (LONG) FINNEY, She 'm. JABEZ RAYL.

ISSUE: RAYL

1.   ASHBURY b. 1854.

2.   HIRAM b. 1856.
3.   ELWOOD b. 1861
4.   AMANDA b. 1863.
5.   WILLIAM b. 1865.

635.   MARY ANN FINNEY, b. Jan 22, 1832 d. Aug. 2, 1908 dau of JOSEPH and
MARY POLLY (LONG) FINNEY, She m. JOHN HAMILTON WEAVER.

ISSUE: WEAVER.

1.	JANE ANN b. 1861.	5.	WILLIAM H. b. 1869.
2.	JOSEPH A. b. 1863.	6.	GEORGE b. 1872.
3.	ANDREW b. 1865.	7.	PEARLEY b. 1874.
4.	MARY E. b. 1867	8.	BARTNAPH b. 1876,

636.   JOSEPH DAVIES FINNEY, b. April 12,1848 d. March 15,1828 son of
RICHARD KING FINNEY. He m. (1) Aporil 16,1868 AMANDA E. MILLI-
KAN b. Sept. 13,1847 dau of Jonathan and Elizabeth (Brown) Millikan. He
married (2) June 5,1886 MRS. SARAH M. FISHER. who died May 15,1920.

ISSUE:

*682.   WILLIAM ARVEL FINNEY, b. Sept. 27, 1869.

683.   ASA ALBERT FINNEY, b. Nov. 24,1872 d. June 11,1909. He m.
ANNA WILLIAMSON. There were no children.

684.   CHARLES L. FINNEY, b. May 3, 1875. d. May 4, 1875.

*685.   RICHARD HARRISON FINNEY, b. May 11, 1877 .

NOTES

643. THOMAS G. FINNEY, b. June 12,1826 d. April 2, 1906 son of ROBERT
and MARGARET (GUTHRIE)FINNEY. He m. (1) SUSANNA COCHEREL
May 2,1844 (2) MARGARET J. NASH May 1848.
ISSUE:

    686.   ZEB FINNEY, b. 1849.

    687.   SAMUEL FINNEY, b.1850

*688.   WILLIAM FINNEY, b. June 3, 1855 d. Feb. 7, 1941.

    689.   THOMAS FINNEY,

    690.   JOHN FINNEY.

    691.   MARY FINNEY m. _____HOGG.

    692.   DAUGHTER. Name unknown.

---

653. JOHN EDGAR FINNEY, son of THOMAS and EMMA G. (WHITMAN) FIN-
NEY. His marriage was not shown but his children were listed.
ISSUE:

    693.   WHITMAN D. FINNEY b. in Kansas.

    694.   WILLIAM F. FINNEY, b. in Kansas.

---

656. DAVID WESLEY FINNEY, b. Aug 22,1839 d. Nov. 1, 1916 in Kansas. He
was the son of ROBERT and MATILDA (HUNT) FINNEY. He m. HELEN
McCONNELL. He served many terms in the political offices of Kansas,
sometimes as a legislature, and he served two terms as Lt. Governor of
the state. During the period 1881 to 1886 Finney County, Kansas was
named for him by an act of Legislature. He also served in the Civil War
He was a merchant, mill owner and farmer. No children were listed in the
records examined.

From Kansas records and Historical Society archives..

NOTES

659.　ROBERT JOHNSON FINNEY B. Dec. 10, 1844 d. Dec. 12,1912. He was the son of ROBERT and MATILDA (HUNT) FINNEY. He m. July 8,1867 MALISSA DICKENSON THOMPSON b. Feb. 9, 1845. He m. (2) Dec. 1, 1910 Rockville, Ind. GERTRUDE MAY ATKINSON b. April 27, 1883 dau of Simon and Mary Atkinson. He was a railroad mail clerk as well as a merchant. He was also sheriff of Parke County, Indiana.

ISSUE:

*695.　CHARLES EDWARD FINNEY, b. April 29, 1869.

696.　ROBERT JOHNSON FINNEY b. Sept. 28, 1911. He m. DORIS_____ They lived in Chesterton, Ind. No children listed.

661.　JOSEPH HARRISON FINNEY, b. Jan. 10,1849 d. Sept 9,1897. He was the son of ROBERT and MATILDA (HUNT) FINNEY. He m. twice (1) CATHERINE ALICE PORTER. and (2) SARAH AGNES VALODIN. No children are shown.

663.　JOHN V. FINNEY b. 1837 son of HAWKINS and MARTHA (COUNTE) FINNEY. He m. June 1865 MARY RANSOPHER dau of _____ He m. (2) PRISCILLA LOWRY, dau of William and Emeline Lowry, on April 11, 1877. (See family group 663 in Appendix)

673.　SAMANTHA JANE FINNEY, b. Aug. 7,1851 d. April 1937 dau of WESLEY and MARY MATILDA (HINSHAW) FINNEY. She m. Feb.27, 1868 ABNER COPELAND b. 1838 in N.C. d. 1909 Wayside, Kansas. Both are buried in Harrisonville Cemetery near Wayside.

ISSUE: *COPELAND.*

1.　AUSTIN b. 1874 in Indiana

2.　CLARISSA b. Oct. 5,1879 d. Sept. 5, 1970 Unwd.

3.　EZRA b. Oct. 19, 1886 d. Nov. 6, 1966.

4.　ELBERT b. 1877 called "EPPS"

5.　EMERY b. Nov. 19,1889 d. Jan. 5, 1964.
　　A. GEORGE COPELAND

6.　SAMUEL lived in Washington State or in Canada

7.　CHARLES O. b. March 6, 1892 d. Aug. 31,1969. He m. Nov. 30, 1920 Marie Hudson b. Dec. 13,1897 d. Dec. 25, 19__. They had Ralph and Henry Copeland.

+++++++++

675. MARY C. FINNEY, b. May 8, 1857 dau of WESLEY and MARY MATILDA (HINSHAW) FINNEY. She d. Aug. 22, 1926. She m. Sept. 5, 1880 WIL= LIAM H. ALLEN.

ISSUE: *ALLEN.*

1. *CLARA m. NICHOLSON.*
2. *MYRTLE m. (1) GEORGE M. HENNICKS.* Devorced.
3. *LILLIAN.*
4. *LAGA.*
5. *HERMAN.*

---

676. ANNA E. FINNEY b. May 24, 1859 d. March 1928 dau of WESLEY and MARY MATILDA (HINSHAW) FINNEY. She m. March 14, 1878 TILGHMAN WOOD b. 1851 d. 1927.

ISSUE: *WOOD.*

1. *PERRY b. 1886 d. 1962.*
2. *NELLIE b. 1883 d. 1929.*

---

678. JOHN WESLEY FINNEY b. Feb. 14, 1862 in Indiana son of WESLEY and MARY MATILDA (HINSHAW) FINNEY. He m. Oct. 6, 1886 NANCY BROOKS. He d. Oct. 6, 1945.

ISSUE:

697. EVA (EVIE) FINNEY.

698. STELLA FINNEY m a Mr. HILBERT. They live in Yates Center, Kansas.

---

679. LOUISA MAY FINNEY b. Jan 8, 1867 dau of WESLEY and MARY MAT- ILDA (HINSHAW) FINNEY. She m. Sept 20, 1889 ANSON MADISON and lived in Gage, Oklahoma.

ISSUE: *MADISON.*

1. *DEWEY* 2. *CALVIN* 3. *WILLIAM* 4. *ETHEL*
There were eight other children .none listd by name.

NOTES

680.   DANIEL WEBSTER FINNEY b. Nov. 7, 1868 in Indiana. He was the son of WESLEY and MARY MATILDA (HInshaw) Finney. He d. Dec. 10,1927. He m. Dec. 13,1896 MARY ANN FARLOW, dau of Nathan and Martha (Cloud) Farlow. She was b. March 12,1873 and d. Jan 2,1952 in Indeperdence, Kansas. They are both buried in Mt Hope Cemetery, Independence, Kansas.

   ISSUE:

   699.   MABEL ESTELLA FINNEY b. July 9,1899 d. Feb. 13,1903.

   *700.   CARL CHESTER FINNEY, b. May 13,1905.

---

681.   CLARA ELLEN FINNEY, b. May 27, 1872 dau of WESLEY and MARY MATILDA (HINSHAW) FINNEY. She m. ELMER FARLOW Feb. 23,1895. He was b. Nov. 12,1869 d. Sept 18,1981.

   ISSUE: FARLOW

   1.   MERLE b. June 28,1899 d. June 17, 1967. He m. ELIZABETH COSTELLO b. Oct. 28,1900. Living in 1979. She was the dau of ELISHA j. and Sarah H. Costello. They had MARY BELLE FARLOW who m. WILLIAM W. BUTTS.

   2.   ORVILLE m. IRMA _____ and lived in Tulsa,Oklahoma.

---

682.   WILLIAM ARVEL FINNEY, b. Sept 17,1865 son of JOSEPH and AMANDA (MILLIKAN) FINNEY. He m. Nov. 22,1889 CLAUDIA BAILEY in Colorado.

   ISSUE:

   701.   EDNA MAY FINNEY, b. Nov. 22, 1899. She m. (1)WALTER ROBINSON and (2)SYDNEY TYSON.

NOTES

685.   RICHARD HARRISON FINNEY, b. May 11, 1877 son of JOSEPH
     DAVIES and AMANDA E. (MILLIKAN)FINNEY. He m. June 30,1926
     ETTA LUCILLE NEWMAN b. Dec. 7,1898 dau of Embert and Nancy
     Effie (Atkinson)Newman.
     ISSUE:

     702.   CHARLES LEE FINNEY b. Oct. 21,1929, Kingman, Indiana

     703.   MARCIA HELEN FINNEY, b.Feb. 20, 1932,Kingman, Indiana.

---

688.   WILLIAM G. FINNEY, b. June 3, 1855 d. Feb. 7, 1941 son of THOMAS
     C. and MARGARET (NASH) FINNEY. He m. (1) MARY ISABEL LESTER
     She had a child but both mother and child died at the child's birth.
     (2) m. SUSAN ROSINE LESTER and (3) m. LAURA A. BOWMAN.
     ISSUE: One child was born and died at birth including the mother
              as mentioned above.

  *704.   JOSEPH FIELDING FINNEY, b. Alba, Mo. Nov. 25,1876 .

   705.   FRANK LESLIE FINNEY b.Aug. 15,1879 . He m. ALICE SEA.
         1904 d. Dec. 13,1961 in Los Angeles, California. Family 1FF9

---

695   CHARLES EDWARD FINNEY, b. April 19, 1869 son of ROBERT JOHNSON
     and MELISSA DICKENSON (THOMPSON)FINNEY. He m. June 20,1895 in
     Indianapolis, Ind. JESSIE GROSE, dau of Madison and Mary (Rader)Grose.
     Jessie was b. Nov. 30,1871 in Newcastle, Ind.
     ISSUE:

   706.   DOROTHY MILDRED FINNEY, b.and d. June 11,1898.

   707.   CHARLES WESLEY FINNEY b.Nov. 30. 1899. He lived in 1940
         at 2344 W. Park Avenue, Oklahoma City, Okla. He m. (1)March
         10, 1921 in Tucson, Arizona GLADYS CLINE b. April 1898 in
         Goshen,Indiana. He m. (2) in Fullerton, California June 30. 1928
         BEULAH BLANCHE BERDEN b. April 23,1905 Hydro, Okla.
         Charles attended the University of Arizona and was a 32nd degree
         Mason, Scottish rites; Methodist, a newspaper man, City Editor
         Arizona Republic, Pheonix, Arizona., news editor Pasedena, Cal.
         Star News . He was acting and assistant Managing Editor, New
         Bedford, Mass. Standard Times.

   708.   MARION FINNEY, b. Feb. 25,1905 d. same day.

---

700.   CARL CHESTER FINNEY, b. May 13, 1905 son of DANIEL WEBSTER and MARY ANN (FARLOW) FINNEY. He m. VIVIA JAY McCLURE.

ISSUE:

*709.   TOMMIE MILTON FINNEY, b. Oct. 30, 1927.

*710.   MARY JAY FINNEY, b. March 3, 1930.

 711.   VIRGINIA LEE FINNEY, b. Nov. 23, 1938.

 712.   DAVIEL ROBERT FINNEY b. Nov. 13, 1935 d. same day.

*713.   JAMES EDWARD FINNEY, b. June 22, 1937.

*714.   DAVID WESLEY FINNEY, b. July 22, 1949.

---

704.   JOSEPH FIELDING FINNEY, b. Nov. 25, 1876, Alva, Mo. He was the son of WILLIAM G. and SUSAN (LESTER) FINNEY. He m. STELLA SCOTT ENGLER July 11, 1908 in Logansport, Indiana. She d. July 27, 1949 in Fayetteville, Arkansas.

ISSUE:

*715.   OWEN ENGLER FINNEY, b. July 9, 1909, Muncie, Indiana

*716.   FORREST FIELDING FINNEY, b. Nov. 25, 1910.

*717.   THOMAS RYAN FINNEY, b. Nov. 30, 1914.

---

709.   TOMMIE MILTON FINNEY, b. Oct. 30, 1927. He was the son of CARL CHESTER FINNEY. He m. LORIS GRISWOLD and (2) ROSE MARY (HIGH) AMERINE.

ISSUE:

718.   TOMMIE MILTON FINNEY JR. b. July 5, 1947.

719.   CHRISTOPHER WALKER AMERINE FINNEY (Adopted)

720.   REBECCA LEE AMERINE FINNEY, (Adopted)

721.   KAREN DEANNE FINNEY b. Nov. 16, 1954.

NOTES

710.   MARY JAY FINNEY b. March 3,£930 dau of CARL CHESTER and VIVIA JAY (McCLURE) Finney. She m. CHARLES LEROY PLUM.

ISSUE: *PLUM.*

1.   *ROBERT MICHAEL b. May 5, 1952 m. Patricia Montgomery. They had one child.*

2.   *JUDITH ANN b. May 22, 1954 m. STEVE PIERCE.*

3.   *DOROTHY JEAN b. Sept. 27, 1955 m. THEODORE ADAMS.*

4.   *SUSAN LYNN b. Dec. 10, 1960.*

---

713.   JAMES EDWARD FINNEY b. June 22,1937 son of CARL CHESTER and VIVIA JAY (MCCLURE) FINNEY. He m CAROL SHELLEY.

ISSUE:

722.   SHELLEY DIANE FINNEY b. Dec. 5, 1963.

723.   DANIEL EDWARD FINNEY b. July 12, 1967.

---

714.   DAVID WESLEY FINNEY, b. July 22,1949 son of CARL CHESTER and VIVIA JAY (McCLURE) FINNEY. He m. (1) BECKY BURCH and (2) RONDA RAY LEE BOWEN.

ISSUE:

724.   JEREMY SCOTT FINNEY b. Nov. 4, 1973.

725.   STACY MICHELLE BOWEN Step-daughter b. Dec. 4, 1969

726.   BRETT MATTHEW BOWEN, Step=son b. Oct. 10, 1971.

727.   JONATHAN DAVID FINNEY b.March 11, 1977

728.   AARON JAMES FINNEY, b. Oct. 14, 1978.

---

715.   OWEN ENGLER FINNEY, b. July 9, 1909 son of JOSEPH and STELLA SCOTT (ENGLER) FINNEY. He m. MARILYN BRANT.

ISSUE:

729.   BARBARA ANN FINNEY b. Aug 6, 1964

NOTES

716. FORREST FIELDING FINNEY, b. Nov.25,1910 son of JOSEPH FIELDING
and STELLA SCOTT (ENGLER)FINNEY. He m. EDNA RUTH HART.
ISSUE:
*730. SHIRLEY ANN FINNEY. b. March 19, 1933.
*731. DAVID OWEN FINNEY, b. Oct. 4, 1934.
*732 WALLACE RAY FINNEY b. Feb. 6, 1941.

----

717. THOMAS RYAN FINNEY, b. Nov. 30,1914 son of JOSEPH FIELDING
and STELLA SCOTT (ENGLER) FINNEY. He married FLORA MAY
ROBERTS.
ISSUE:
*733. THOMAS RYAN FINNEY, Jr. b. Feb. 6,1941.
*734. JOSEPH MICHAEL FINNEY, b. March 4, 1943.
*735. FRANK LEWIS FINNEY, b. Nov. 29,1945.
 736. BRENDA ALICE FINNEY, b. July 13,1953 m. DAVID EUGENE LOOKER.

730. SHIRLEY ANN FINNEY,b. March 19,1933 dau of FORREST FIELDING
and EDNA RUTH (HART)FINNEY. She m. LARRY LEE LIBY. They
had two children names unknown at this time.

731. DAVID OWEN FINNEY, b. Oct. 4, 1934 son of FORREST FIELDING
and EDNA RUTH (HART)FINNEY. He m. MARY LaRUE WHALEY. They
had five children names unknown at this time.

732. WALLACE RAY FINNEY b. Feb. 6,1941 son of FORREST FIELDING and
STELLA SCOTT (ENGLER)FINNEY. He married LOIS MARIE GRAVEDONI
and they had two children names unknown at this time.

733. THOMAS RYAN FINNEY, Jr. b. Feb. 6, 1941 son of THOMAS RYAN
and FLORA MAY(ROBERTS) FINNEY, He m. PAULA LEE FOUST. He
was the third child in the family and not the first as listed.,althouigh
the dates of his birth and those of his brothers and sisters would seem to
make him the first child. Thomas and Flora had three children names
unknown at this time.

734. JOSEPH MICHAEL FINNEY b. March 4, 1943 son of THOMAS RYAN and FLORA MAY (ROBERTS) FINNEY. He m. KAREN SUE SHERMAN. She d. May 30, 1974 They had three children names unknown at this time.

735, FRANK LEWIS FINNEY b. Nov. 29, 1943 son of Thomas Ryan and FLORA MAY(ROBERTS) FINNEY. He m. BARBARA JEAN GEIER. They had four children names unknown at this time.

Most of these records came from the files and records of Thomas Finney of Logansport, Indiana who was kind enough to loan me the compiled records of *THE FINNEY FAMILY HISTORY 1732-1946* By Minnehaha Finney. His assistance was gratefully accepted and appreciated.

The Compiler.

FAMILY GROUPS

FAMILY GROUP NO. 1   Husband's Full Name JOHN FINNEY

Husband's Data	Day Month Year	City, Town or Place	County or Province, etc.	State or Country	Add. Info. on Husband
Birth	22 Aug 1823	Bowling Green		Kentucky	
Chr'nd					
Mar.	23 Oct. 1845	Berger	Franklin	Mo	
Death	19 April 1909				
Burial		Finney Family Cemetery, Robertsville, Mo			

Places of Residence

Occupation
Other wives, if any No (1) (2) etc.
Make separate sheet for each mar.   Church Affiliation   Military Rec.

Dau of John Heart of Mill Creek

His Father John Finney   Mother's Maiden Name Elizabeth Heart/\

Wife's Full Maiden Name **Louisey Elizabeth Roark**

Wife's Data	Day Month Year	City, Town or Place	County or Province, etc.	State or Country	Add. Info. on Wife
Birth	12 Feb 1824	Berger	Franklin	Mo	
Chr'nd					
Death	7 Jan 1900				
Burial		Finney Family Cem, Robertsville Mo.			

Places of Residence

Occupation if other than housewife
Other husbands, if any No (1) (2) etc.
Make separate sheet for each mar.   Church Affiliation

Her Father William Roark   Mother's Maiden Name Nancy Breeding

Sex	Children's Name in Full (Arrange in order of birth)	Children's Data	Day Month Year	City, Town or Place	County or Province, etc.	State or Country	Add. Info. on Children
F	1 Nancy J. Finney	Birth	12 Nov 1847	Robertsville Mo			
	Full Name of Spouse*	Mar.	Single				
		Death	10 Apr 1920				
		Burial					
M	2 William R Finney	Birth	27 June 1849	Robertsville Mo			
	Full Name of Spouse*	Mar.					
		Death	1 Feb 1890	"	"		
		Burial					
M	3 John M. Finney	Birth	23 Dec. 1853	"	"		
	Full Name of Spouse*	Mar.	Single				
		Death	~27 Apr 1894				
		Burial					
M	4 JAMES FINNEY	Birth	11 Sept 1855	"	"		
	Full Name of Spouse*	Mar.	Single				
		Death	6 Sept 1953	"	"		
M		Burial					
m.	5 Elige T Finney	Birth	12 Oct 1861	"	"		
	Full Name of Spouse*	Mar.	Single				
		Death	26 Dec. 1909	"	"		
		Burial					
M	6 ZIMRI C. FINNEY	Birth	5 May 1863	"	"		
	Full Name of Spouse*	Mar.	Single				
		Death	19 July 1931	" "	"		
		Burial					
M	7 Benjamin F. Finney	Birth	18 Jan 1866	"	"		
	Full Name of Spouse*	Mar.					
		Death	12 Dec 1866	"	"		
		Burial					
M	8 TIMOTHY Finney	Birth					
	Full Name of Spouse*	Mar.					
		Death					
		Burial					
F	9 MARY FINNEY	Birth	8 Feb 1878	"	"		
	Full Name of Spouse*	Mar.					
		Death	8 Feb 1878	"	"		
		Burial					
	10	Birth					
	Full Name of Spouse*	Mar.					
		Death					
		Burial					

*If married more than once No each mar (1) (2) etc and list in "Add info. on children" column Use reverse side for additional children, other notes, references or information.

Family Record

Father — FINNEY, JOHN

Event	Day	Month	Year	Town	County	State	Notes	Source No.
Birth			16					
Death			c1703					
Buried								
Married	10 June		1650					

Occupation Farmer Military Church

Places Lived

Other Wives (2) Abigail Coggin widow of Henry dau of Thomas Bishop
(3) Elizabeth Bailey

His Father's Name _____
His Mother's Maiden Name _____ "MOTHER"

Mother — CHRISTIANA

Event	Day	Month	Year	Town	County	State	Notes	Source No.
Birth								
Death	9 Sept.		1649					
Buried								

Occupation Military Church

Places Lived

Other Husbands

Her Father's Name _____
Her Mother's Maiden Name _____

Children

Sex	Full Given Name	Event	Day	Month	Year	Town	County	State	Source No.
M	1. JOHN FINNEY	Birth	24.	Dec.	1638				
	Spouse - Mary Rogers	Death			1718/9				
		Married							
M	2. THOMAS FINNEY	Birth			c1648				
	Spouse -	Death			c1655				
		Married							
M	3. JONATHAN FINNEY	Birth	14	Aug.	1665				
	Spouse - Joanna KINNICUTT	Death		May	1728				
		Married	Int.18 Oct.		1682				
M	4. ROBERT FINNEY	Birth	13	Aug.	1656				
	Spouse -	Death		July	1690				
		Married							
F	5. HANNAH FINNEY	Birth			1657				
	Spouse - Deacon EPHRAIM MORTON	Death	18	Feb.	1732				
		Married			1677				
F	6. ELIZABETH FINNEY	Birth	15	March	1653				
	Spouse - HAILE BARTON	Death							
		Married	19	Dec.	1773				
M	7. JOSIAH FINNEY	Birth							
	Spouse - ELIZABETH WARREN	Death	!!	Jan	1661				
		Married	15	Jan.	1688				
M	8. JEREMIAH FINNEY	Birth	15	Aug.	1662				
	Spouse - ESTHER LEWIS	Death	18	Feb.	1746				
		Married	7	Jan	1684				
M	9. JOSHUA FINNEY	Birth		Dec.	1665				
	Spouse - MERCY WATTS	Death	7	Sept	1714				
		Married	Int 31	May	1688				
	10.	Birth							
	Spouse -	Death							
		Married							

In the circles, identify by number your sources of information — then list each on the reverse side.

☐ Additional children listed on the reverse side.

Family Record

Father — FINNEY, JOHN

FINNEY/PHINNEY
Surname

Event	Day	Month	Year	Town	County	State	Notes	Source No.
Birth	24 Dec		1638	PLYMOUTH		MASS		
Death			1718/19	Barnstable,		MASS		
Buried								
Married								
Occupation				Military			Church	
Places Lived								
Other Wives								

His Father's Name ___ JOHN FINNEY
His Mother's Maiden Name ___ CHRISTIANA

Mother — ROGERS, Mary

Event	Day	Month	Year	Town	County	State	Notes	Source No.
Birth	22	Sept,	1644	Eastham		MASS		
Death			1718					
Buried								
Occupation				Military			Church	
Places Lived								
Other Husbands								

Her Father's Name ___ Lt. JOHN ROGERS (Mayflower)
Her Mother's Maiden Name ___ HANNAH

Children

Sex	Full Given Name	Event	Day	Month	Year	Town	County	State	Source No.
M	1. JOHN PHINNEY — Spouse - SARAH LUMBERT	Birth / Death / Married	5	May	1665				
F	2. MELETIAH PHINNEY — Spouse -	Birth / Death / Married		OCT	1666				
M	3. JOSEPH PHINNEY — Spouse - MERCY BRYANT	Birth / Death / Married	28	Jan	1668				
M	4. THOMAS PHINNEY — Spouse - SARAH BEETLE	Birth / Death / Married		JAN.	1672				
M	5. EBENEZER PHINNEY — Spouse - SUSAN LINNELL	Birth / Death / Married			1674				
M	6. SAMUEL PHINNEY — Spouse - BETHIA SMITH K	Birth / Death / Married	4	NOV	1676				
F	7. MARY PHINNEY — Spouse - JOHN EASTLAND	Birth / Death / Married	3 / / 24	SEPT / / Oct	1678 / / 1702				
F	8. MERCY PHINNEY — Spouse - ELEAZER CROCKER	Birth / Death / Married	10 / / 26	July / / Jan	1679 / / 1715				
F	9. RELIANCE PHINNEY — Spouse - JOHN MORTON	Birth / Death / Married	27 / 4 / 27	AUG / DEc / DEc	1681 / 1735 / 1705				
M	10. BENJAMIN PHINNEY — Spouse - 1. Martha CROCKER 2. ELIZABETH AMES	Birth / Death / Married	18 / Before 19 / 30	June / July / June	1692 / 1758 / 1709	2n wife Elizabeth (Young) Ames			

Additional children listed on the reverse side.

In the circles, identify by number your sources of information — then list each on the reverse side.

Family Record

Finney/ Phinney

Surname

Father — FINNEY. JONATHAN

Event	Day	Month	Year	Town	County	State	Notes	Source No.
Birth	14	Aug.	1665					
Death		May	1728					
Buried								
Married	Int.18 Oct. 1682							

Occupation Farmer   Military   Church

Places Lived Bristol and Swansea, Mass.

Other Wives

His Father's Name John Finney

His Mother's Maiden Name Elizabeth Bailey

Mother — KINNICUTT, ELIZABETH

Event	Day	Month	Year	Town	County	State	Notes	Source No.
Birth								
Death	30	Nov.	1739					
Buried								

Occupation   Military   Church

Places Lived

Other Husbands

Her Father's Name

Her Mother's Maiden Name

Children

Sex	Full Given Name	Event	Day	Month	Year	Town	County	State	Source No.
F	1. JOANNA PHINNEY Spouse - CLARK	Birth	30	Nov.	1683				
		Death							
		Married							
M	2. JONATHAN PHINNEY Spouse - MERCY READ	Birth	3	Nov.	1686				
		Death	26	Nov.	1736				
		Married	6	May	1730				
F	3. MEHITABLE PHINNEY Spouse -	Birth	bpt. 19 Jan 1688						
		Death							
		Married							
F	4. ELIZABETH PHINNEY Spouse - BRADFORAD	Birth	Bpt.		1695				
		Death	30	June	1730				
		Married							
F	5. LYDIA PHINNEY Spouse - HOPESTILL COTTON	Birth	Bpt		1695				
		Death							
		Married							
F	6. MARY PHINNEY Spouse -	Birth	Bpt		1695				
		Death							
		Married							
M	7. EBENEZER PHINNEY Spouse -	Birth	Bpt. 23 Apr.1699						
		Death							
		Married							
F	8. HANNAH PHINNEY Spouse -	Birth	28	March	1687				
		Death	10	Feb.	1689				
		Married							
	9. Spouse -	Birth							
		Death							
		Married							
	10. Spouse -	Birth							
		Death							
		Married							

In the circles, identify by number your source of information — then list each on the reverse side.

☐ Additional children listed on the reverse side.

Finney
Surname

Father — FINNEY, Jeremiah

Event	Day	Month	Year	Town	County	State	Notes	Source No.
Birth	15	Aug	1662					
Death	18	Feb.	1748					
Buried								
Married	7	Jan	1684					

Occupation Shipmaster   Military   Church

Places Lived

Other Wives

His Father's Name John Finney

His Mother's Maiden Name Elizabeth Bailey

Mother — LEWIS ESTHER

Event	Day	Month	Year	Town	County	State	Notes	Source No.
Birth			1664 K					
Death	11	April	1748					
Buried								

Occupation   Military   Church

Places Lived Bristol, Mass.

Other Husbands

Her Father's Name Thomas Lewis

Her Mother's Maiden Name Mary (   ) Lewis

Children

Sex	Full Given Name	Event	Day	Month	Year	Town	County	State	Source No.
M	1. Jeremiah Finney Spouse –	Birth Death Married		Young	1684				
F	2. Mary Finney Spouse –	Birth Death Married	26	March	1686				
E	3. Hannah Finney Thomas Diamant	Birth Death Married	14 22 14	Jan Dec Jan	1687 1748 1706	Date must be in error Probably Long Island			
F	4. Mehetable Finney Spouse –	Birth Death Married	8 22	May Dec	1687 1744(?)	Or this date is in error			
M	5. JOHN Finney Spouse –	Birth Death Married	3	Aug Young	1690;				
F	6. Rebecca Finney Spouse – Samuel Harris	Birth Death Married	24 11	Feb March	1691/2 1716				
F	7. Esther Finney Spouse – Joseph Joy	Birth Death Married	4 INT 31	May Oct	1693 1719				
F	8. Deborah Finney Spouse –	Birth Death Married	20	Oct	1695				
M	9. John Finney Spouse – Mary Campbell	Birth Death Married	13	Sptil	1696	Dau of Sylvanus and Mary Campbell			
F	10. Abigail Finney Spouse –	Birth Death Married	17	April	1697				

In the circles, identify by number your sources of information — then list same on the reverse side.

[X] Additional children listed on the reverse side.

Family Record

	Family No.
FINNEY	
	Surname

Father — FINNEY, Joshua

Event	Day	Month	Year	Town	County	State	Notes	Source No.
Birth		Dec	1665					
Death	7 SEPT		1714					
Buried								
Married	INT 31 MAY		1688					

Occupation Farmer   Military   Church

Places Lived Bristol and Swansea, Mass.

Other Wives

His Father's Name JOHN FINNEY

His Mother's Maiden Name ELIZABETH BAILEY

Mother — WATTS, MERCY

Event	Day	Month	Year	Town	County	State	Notes	Source No.
Birth								
Death	12 FEB.		1724					
Buried								

Occupation   Military   Church

Places Lived BRISTOL, SWANSEA, MASS.

Other Husbands

Her Father's Name

Her Mother's Maiden Name

Children

Sex		Full Given Name	Event	Day	Month Year	Town	County	State	Source No.
	1.	JOSHUA FINNEY	Birth	7 MAY 1689					
			Death						
		Spouse – ELIZABETH BRISTOW	Married	INT 17 MAY 1727		Dau of Thomas & Elizabeth Bristow			
F	2.	ELIZABETH FINNEY	Birth	25 Sept 1691/2					
			Death	19 Sept 1701					
		Spouse –	Married						
F	3.	MARY FINNEY	Birth	25 Sept 1694					
			Death						
		Spouse –	Married						
M	4.	JOHN FINNEY	Birth	15 AUG 1696					
			Death						
		Spouse –	Married						
M	5.	SAMUEL FINNEY	Birth	20 MAY 1699					
			Death	1763					
		Spouse – ELIZABETH WOOD	Married	12 March 1726/7		Dau of John Wood widow of	Thomas Tibbiits		
M	6.	JOSIAH FIN:NEY	Birth	26 July 1701					
			Death	Aug 1774					
		Spouse – ELIZABETH MANN	Married	1 Jan 1723/4					
F	7.	ELIZABETH FINNEY	Birth	1 MAY 1737					
			Death		WARREN, CONN.				
		Spouse –	Married						
	8.		Birth						
			Death						
		Spouse –	Married						
	9.		Birth						
			Death						
		Spouse –	Married						
	10.		Birth						
			Death						
		Spouse –	Married						

In the circles, identify by number your sources of information — then list each on the reverse side.

☐ Additional children listed on the reverse side.

Family No.

Father — PHINNEY, JOHN   PHINNEY

Surname

Event	Day	Month	Year	Town	County	State	Notes	Source No.
Birth	5 May		1665					
Death			1746					
Buried								
Married	30 May		1689					
Occupation								
Places Lived		Military				Church		
Other Wives								

His Father's Name   JOHN PHINNEY

His Mother's Maiden Name   MARY ROGERS (Mayflower)

Mother — LUMBERT, SARAH

Event	Day	Month	Year	Town	County	State	Notes	Source No.
Birth			1666					
Death								
Buried								
Occupation								
Places Lived		Military				Church		
Other Husbands								

Her Father's Name   THOMAS LUMBERT

Her Mother's Maiden Name   ELIZABETH Derby

Children

Sex	Full Given Name	Event	Day	Month	Year	Town	County	State	Source No.
F	1. ELIZABETH PHINNEY	Birth	11	April	1690				
	Spouse — NATHAN DAVIS b. 2 March 1620 d. 17 Sept. 1785	Death	30	Dec	1786				
		Married	25	Nov	1714	Barnstable			
F	2. MARY PHINNEY	Birth	20	Jan	1692				
	Spouse —	Death							
		Married							
M	3. JOHN PHINNEY	Birth	8	April	1696				
	Spouse — MARTHA COLEMAN	Death	29	Dec	1780				
		Married	25	SEpt	1718	Barnstable			
M	4. THOMAS PHINNEY	Birth	25	MAY	1697				
	Spouse — RELIANCE GOODSPEED	Death							
		Married	31	March	1726	dau Ebenezer & LYDIA (Crowell)			
F	5. HANNAH PHINNEY	Birth	9	April	1700				
	Spouse — ROGER GOOSAPWWS	Death							
		Married	6	Oct.	1720	Barnstable			
F	6. SARAH PHINNEY	Birth	8	Oct.	1701				
	Spouse — THOMAS ADAMS	Death							
		Married	INT 27	Aug	1724				
F	7. PATIENCE PHINNEY	Birth	12	Sept	1704				
	Spouse — JAMES COLEMAN	Death							
		Married	12	March	1737/8				
F	8. MARTHA PHINNEY	Birth	12	July	1706				
	Spouse — JONATHAN LUMBERT	Death							
		Married	12	March	1727/8				
M	9. JABEZ PHINNEY	Birth	16	JULY	1708				
	Spouse — JANE TAYLOR	Death	1	DEC	1776				
		Married							
	10.	Birth							
	Spouse —	Death							
		Married							

In the circles, identify by number your sources of information — then list each on the reverse side.

☐ Additional children listed on the reverse side.

Family Record

Father — PHINNEY, Joseph

Event	Day	Month	Year	Town	County	State	Notes	Source No.
Birth	28 Jan.		1668					
Death	29 June		1726					
Buried								
Married	15 June 1693							
Occupation	Farmer			Military		Church		
Places Lived								
Other Wives	2nd wife ESTHER WEST.							

His Father's Name   John Finney/Phinney

His Mother's Maiden Name   Mary Rogers

Mother — BRYANT, Mercy   1st wife.

Event	Day	Month	Year	Town	County	State	Notes	Source No.
Birth								
Death			1706					
Buried								
Occupation				Military		Church		
Places Lived								
Other Husbands								

Her Father's Name

Her Mother's Maiden Name

Children

Sex	Full Given Name		Event	Day	Month	Year	Town	County	State	Source No.
F	1. ALICE PHINNEY		Birth	1 April		1694				
			Death							
	Spouse - EBENEZER HAMBLIN, Jr		Married	10 Dec. 1724						
M	2. JOHN PHINNEY		Birth	17 Dec.		1696				
			Death							
	Spouse - (1)REBECCA BRYANT		Married	1 March 1721						
FF	3. MARY PHINNEY		Birth	5 May		1700				
			Death							
	Spouse - ELEAZER HAMBLIN		Married	25 FEB 1721						
F	4. MARCY (SUC)PHINNEY		Birth	19	Sept.	1707				
			Death							
	Spouse -		Married							
M	5. JOSEPH PHINNEY		Birth	10 APRIL		1709				
			Death							
	Spouse -		Married							
M	6. PELATIAH PHINNEY		Birth	21 March 1710						
			Death							
	Spouse -		Married							
F	7. PATIENCE PHINNEY		Birth	19 Aug		1713				
			Death							
	Spouse - ROBERT COOK		Married			1735				
F	8. EXPERIENCE PHINNEY		Birth	8 April		1716				
			Death							
	Spouse -		Married							
F	9. HANNAH PHINNEY		Birth	8 April 1720						
			Death	5 Sept		1724				
	Spouse -		Married							
	10.		Birth							
			Death							
	Spouse -		Married							

Information — then list same on the reverse side.

☐ Additional children listed on the reverse side.

Family Record

Father — PHINNEY, THOMAS

Event	Day	Month	Year	Town	County	State	Notes	Source No.
Birth			1671					
Death			1755					
Buried								
Married	25 Aug.		1698					

Occupation Farmer   Military   Church

Places Lived

Other Wives SARAH BUTLER b. 1678 d. 1748 possibly the same person as Sarah Beetle. See dates of deaths.

His Father's Name _____

His Mother's Maiden Name _____

Mother — SARAH BEETLE WIDOW OF Christopher Beetle.

Event	Day	Month	Year	Town	County	State	Notes	Source No.
Birth								
Death			1748					
Buried								

Occupation

Places Lived   Military   Church

Other Husbands

Her Father's Name Richard Lockwood

Her Mother's Maiden Name _____

Children

Sex	Full Given Name	Event	Day	Month	Year	Town	County	State	Source No
M	1. GERSHOM PHINNEY	Birth	21	March	1699				
	Spouse –	Death							
		Married							
M	2. THOMAS PHINNEY	Birth	17	Feb.	1702				
	Spouse –	Death			1778				
	(1) MARIAH LUMBERT	Married	Nov.		1731				
F	3. ABIGAIL PHINNEY	Birth	8	June	1704				
	Spouse –	Death							
		Married							
M	4. JAMES PHINNEY	Birth	15	April	1706				
	Spouse –	Death							
		Married							
F	5. MERCY PHINNEY	Birth	24	Aug.	1708				
	Spouse –	Death							
	JOHN LINNELL b. 1702	Married			1734	Son of John and Ruth (Davis)			
	6.	Birth							
	Spouse –	Death							
		Married							
	7.	Birth							
	Spouse –	Death							
		Married							
	8.	Birth							
	Spouse –	Death							
		Married							
	9.	Birth							
	Spouse –	Death							
		Married							
	10.	Birth							
	Spouse –	Death							
		Married							

In the circles, identify by number your sources of information — then list each on the reverse side.

☐ Additional children listed on the reverse side.

Family Record

Father — PHINNEY EBENEZER

Event	Day	Month	Year	Town	County	State	Notes	Source No.
Birth	18	Feb.	1673					
Death	10	Apro;	1784					
Buried								
Married	14	Nov.	1625					

Occupation FARMER Military Church

Places Lived

Other Wives

His Father's Name JOHN FINNEY

His Mother's Maiden Name MARY ROGERS

Mother — LINNELL, SUSANNA

Event	Day	Month	Year	Town	County	State	Notes	Source No.
Birth			1673					
Death	23	Nov	1754					
Buried								

Occupation WIFE Military Church

Places Lived

Other Husbands

Her Father's Name DAVOD :OMME::

Her Mother's Maiden Name HANNAH SHELBY

Children

In the circles, identify by number your sources of information — then list each on the reverse side.

Sex	Full Given Name	Event	Day	Month	Year	Town	County	State	Source No.
F	1. MEHITABLE PHINNEY	Birth	14,	Aug	1696				
	Spouse -	Death	9	Oct	1718				
	SAMUEL HIGGINS	Married							
f	2. MARY PHINNEY	Birth	23	March	1698				
	Spouse JOB DAVIS	Death	22	Dec.	1720				
		Married							
F	3. MARTHA PHINNEY	Birth	22	April	1700				
	Spouse -	Death							
		Married							
M	4. SAMUEL PHINNEY	Birth	1	Sptil	1702				
	Spouse HANNAH RAY	Death							
	b, 16Oct. 1712	Married	Int 23	Jan	1728				
F F	5. LYDIA PHINNEY	Birth	Bpt. 7	July	1706				
	Spouse -	Death							
		Married							
M	6. EBENEZER PHINNEY	Birth	26	May	1708				
	Spouse -	Death			1753				
	REBECCA BARNES	Married	23	Sept	1730				
M	7. DAVID PHINNEY	Birth	10	June	1710				
	Spouse - B. Dec. 1713	Death	23	Nov.	1793				
	MARY POPE	Married	27	Sept	1733				
M	8. SETH PHINNEY	Birth	12	Sept	1714				
	Spouse -	Death							
		Married							
	9.	Birth							
	Spouse -	Death							
		Married							
	10.	Birth							
	Spouse -	Death							
		Married							

Additional children listed on the reverse side.

PHINNEY
Sur

Father — PHINNEY, SAMUEL

Event	Day Month Year	Town	County	State	Notes	To
Birth	4 Nov 1676					
Death						
Buried						
Married	4 April 1713					
Occupation						
Places Lived		Military		Church		
Other Wives						

His Father's Name   JOHN PHINNEY
His Mother's Maiden Name   MARY ROGERS

Mother — SMITH, BETHIA

Event	Day Month Year	Town	County	State	Notes	B
Birth	16 Jan 1631					
Death						
Buried						
Occupation						
Places Lived		Military		Church		
Other Husbands						

Her Father's Name   JOHN, SMITH
Her Mother's Maiden Name   MARY ELDRIDGE

Children

Sex	Full Given Name	Event	Day Month Year	Town	County	State
F	1. THANKFUL PHINNEY	Birth	BPT 29 July 1716			
	Spouse -	Death				
		Married				
F	2. RHODA PHINNEY	Birth	1 Feb. 1718/9			
	Spouse -	Death				
		Married				
F	3. MARY PHINNEY	Birth	Bpt.16 June 1723			
	Spouse -	Death				
		Married				
F	4. BETHIA PHINNEY	Birth	9 July 1726			
	Spouse -	Death				
	5.	Married				
		Birth				
	Spouse -	Death				
	6.	Married				
		Birth				
	Spouse -	Death				
	7.	Married				
		Birth				
	Spouse -	Death				
	8.	Married				
		Birth				
	Spouse -	Death				
	9.	Married				
		Birth				
	Spouse -	Death				
	10.	Married				
		Birth				
	Spouse -	Death				
		Married				

In the circles, identify by number your source of information — then list on the reverse side.

[ ] Additional children listed on the reverse side.

Family Record

Father — EASTLAND, JOHN

Event	Day	Month	Year	Town	County	State	Notes	Source No.
Birth								
Death			1726					
Buried								
Married	29 Oct. 1702							
Occupation				Military		Church		
Places Lived								
Other Wives	(1) 1700 ELIZABETH JONES.							

His Father's Name _____

His Mother's Maiden Name _____

Mother — PHINNEY, Mary

Event	Day	Month	Year	Town	County	State	Notes	Source No.
Birth	3 Sept	1678						
Death			1754					
Buried								
Occupation	Wife			Military		Church		
Places Lived								
Other Husbands	(1) Jonathon Bryant b. March 23, 1677 d. 1731							

Her Father's Name   John Phinney

Her Mother's Maiden Name   MARY ROGERS

Children

Sex	Full Given Name	Event	Day	Month	Year	Town	County	State	Source No.
M	1. Zerulah Eastland	Birth	8 Dec	1703					
		Death							
	Spouse – BARNABAS SPOONER	Married	12 Jan	1723/4					
M	2. JOSEPH EASTLAND	Birth	12 May	1705					
		Death		1751					
	Spouse – Freelove Shepherd	Married	6 March	1728					
F	3. ELIZABETH EASTLAND	Birth	31 Jan	1708					
		Death							
	Spouse – AMOS TABER	Married	7 May	1730					
F	4. MAREY (sic) EASTLAND	Birth	1 Nov.	1710					
		Death	13 Nov	17__					
	Spouse –	Married							
F	5. HANNAH EASTLAND	Birth	13 Feb.	1712/3					
		Death	2 Dec.	1717					
	Spouse –	Married							
F	6. JEAN EASTMAN	Birth	15 Sept	1715					
		Death	18 Dec.	1717					
	Spouse –	Married							
M	7. JOSHUA EASTLAND	Birth	13 April	1718					
		Death	25. July	1719					
	Spouse –	Married							
F	8. MARY EASTLAND	Birth	1 March	1720					
		Death							
	Spouse –	Married							
	9.	Birth							
		Death							
	Spouse –	Married							
	10.	Birth							
		Death							
	Spouse –	Married							

In the circles, identify by number your sources of information — then list each on the reverse side.

☐ Additional children listed on the reverse side.

Family Record

PHINNEY
Surname

Father — PHINNEY, BENJAMIN

Event	Day Month Year	Town	County	State	Notes	Source No.
Birth	18 June 1682					
Death	before 19 July 1758					
Buried						
Married	(1)30 June 1709					
Occupation	Farmer		Military		Church	
Places Lived						
Other Wives	ELIZABETH (YOUNG) AMES dau of Henry and Sarah (Snow) young widow of Zephon Ames.					

His Father's Name JOHN FINNEY

His Mother's Maiden Name MARY ROGERS (Mayflower)

Mother — CROCKER MARTHA

Event	Day Month Year	Town	County	State	Notes	Source No.
Birth	22 Feb. 1689					
Death	Before 19 Sept. 1747					
Buried						
Occupation			Military		Church	
Places Lived						
Other Husbands						

Her Father's Name JOSEPH CROCKER

Her Mother's Maiden Name Temperance BURSLEY

Children

b

Sex	Full Given Name	Event	Day Month Year	Town County State	Source No.
F	1. TEMPERANCE PHINNEY	Birth	28 March 1710		
		Death	1759		
	Spouse JAMES FULLER B. 1 May 1711	Married	22 Sept 1733		
F	2. MELATIAH PHINNEY	Birth	26 July 1712		
		Death	1785		
	Spouse – JOSIAH MORTON b. 28 Feb. 1709	Married	15 May 1732		
M	3. BARNABAS PHINNEY	Birth	28 March 1715		
		Death			
	Spouse – MEHITABLE (Cgrchill)Norton	Married	14 Aug 1745	She was b. 5 Nov. 1716 d. 1797	
M	4. SILAS PHINNEY	Birth	16 June 1718		
		Death			
	Spouse –	Married			
M	5. ZACCJEIS •PHINNEY	Birth	4 Aug 1720		
		Death			
	Susan Davis b. 2 Oct 1725	Married	3 March 1742/3	b/ Falmouth dau of JabezDavis	
M	6. SETH PHINNEY	Birth	27 June 1723		
		Death			
	Spouse – Bethia Bump b. c23 Aug 1729	Married	26 Oct. 1748		
F	7. LUSANNA PHINNY	Birth			
		Death			
	Spouse – DIMMOCK	Married			
	8.	Birth			
		Death			
	Spouse –	Married			
	9.	Birth			
		Death			
	Spouse –	Married			
	10.	Birth			
		Death			
	Spouse –	Married			

☐ Additional children listed on the reverse side.

Family Record

Father —FINNEY, Joshua

Event	Day	Month	Year	Town	County	State	Notes	Source No.
Birth	7 May 1689							
Death								
Buried								
Married								
Occupation	FARMER			Military		Church		
Places Lived								
Other Wives								

His Father's Name Joshua Finney
His Mother's Maiden Name Mercy Watts.

Mother — CARTER, MARTHA

Event	Day	Month	Year	Town	County	State	Notes	Source No.
Birth			1671					
Death	14 Aug. 1751							
Buried								
Occupation				Military		Church		
Places Lived								
Other Husbands								

Her Father's Name
Her Mother's Maiden Name

Children

Sex	Full Given Name	Event	Day Month Year	Town	County	State	Source No.
M	1. WILLIAM FINNEY Spouse 1. Elizabeth Clark (2)Abigail Black	Birth Death Married	10 May 1715 1781 8 Nov. 1780	1st wife.			
M	2. Josiah FINNEY Spouse -	Birth Death Married	!! May 1716 29 Feb. 1746				
F	3. MARY (CERCY) FINNEY Spouse - Joseph Mann	Birth Death Married	5 July 1718 before 1743 14 March 1733/4				
F M	4. MARTHA FINNEY Spouse -	Birth Death Married	4 March 1718/9 1788				
	5. JOHN FINNEY Spouse - 1,Rachel Woodward 2. Sarah Thomas	Birth Death Married	2 June 1721 25 Aug. 1743	1st wife			
M	6. OLIVER FINNEY Spouse - ELIZABETH DUNHAM	Birth Death Married	11 Nov. 1728 August 1749				
	7. Spouse -	Birth Death Married					
	8. Spouse -	Birth Death Married					
	9. Spouse -	Birth Death Married					
	10. Spouse -	Birth Death Married					

In the circles, identify by number your sources of information — then list each on the reverse side.

☐ Additional children listed on the reverse side.

Family Record

FINNEY
Surname

Father — FINNEY, JOHN (Doctor John)

Event	Day	Month	Year	Town	County	State	Notes	Source No.
Birth	16	AUG	1696					
Death	6	JUNE	1773					
Buried								
Married	14	SEPT	1716					

Occupation Listed as Blacksmith but is also reported as a doctor Church

Places Lived

Other Wives

His Father's Name   JOSHUA FINNEY

His Mother's Maiden Name   Merry Watts

Mother — TOOGOOD, ANN

Event	Day	Month	Year	Town	County	State	Notes	Source No.
Birth								
Death	11	Aug.	1778					
Buried								

Occupation Wife   Military   Church

Places Lived

Other Husbands

Her Father's Name

Her Mother's Maiden Name

Children

Sex	Full Given Name	Event	Day	Month	Year	Town	County	State	Source No.
M	1. JOEL FINNEY	Birth	24	FEB.	1716/7				
	Spouse –	Death							
		Married							
M	2. JOHN FINNEY	Birth	14	Oct	1718				
	Spouse –	Death							
	HANNAH WASHBURN	Married	3	Sept.	1740				
M	3. NATHANIEL FINNEY	Birth	3	JAN	1720				
	Spouse –	Death							
	HANNAH WOOD	Married	3	Sept.	1740				
M	4. JOSHUA FINNEY	Birth	24	Feb	1723/4				
	Spouse –	Death							
		Married							
F	5. ANN FINNEY	Birth	30	APRIL	1727				
	Spouse –	Death							
		Married							
F	6. MERCY FINNEY	Birth	1	Jan	1729/30				
	Spouse –	Death							
	REUBIN SACKET	Married	21	Dec	1752	E. Greenwich'.	New Warrem.	Conn.	
M	7. DAVID FINNEY	Birth	24	AUG.	1732				
	Spouse –	Death							
	ABIGAIL CLARK	Married	26	FEB.	1759	Kent		Conn.	
F	8. MARTHA FINNEY	Birth	12	June	1738				
	Spouse –	Death							
		Married							
M	9. JABEZ FINNEY	Birth	21	Nov	1737				
	Spouse –	Death							
	ELIZABETH	Married	8	Nov.	1764				
	10.	Birth							
	Spouse –	Death							
		Married							

In the circles, identify by number your sources of information — then list each on the reverse side.

☐ Additional children listed on the reverse side.

Family Record

Father — FINNEY, JOSIAH

Event	Day	Month	Year	Town	County	State	Notes	Source No.
Birth	26 July		1701					
Death			1774					
Buried	1 Jan		1723/4					
Married								
Occupation			Military			Church		
Places Lived	WARREB, CONN.							
Other Wives								

His Father's Name JOSHUA FINNEY
His Mother's Maiden Name MERCY WATTS

Mother — MANN, ELIZABETH

Event	Day	Month	Year	Town	County	State	Notes	Source No.
Birth								
Death			1775					
Buried								
Occupation			Military			Church		
Places Lived								
Other Husbands								

Her Father's Name
Her Mother's Maiden Name

Children

Sex	Full Given Name	Event	Day	Month	Year	Town	County	State	Source No.
F	1. ELIZABETH FINNEY	Birth	19 JAN		1723/4				
		Death							
	Spouse -	Married							
M	2. JOSIAH FINNEY	Birth	27 Jan		1725/6				
		Death		SEPT	1726				
	Spouse -	Married							
F	3. KIZIAH FINNEY	Birth	5	MARCH	1730				
		Death							
	Spouse -	Married							
F	4. LYDIA FINNEY	Birth	6	March	1732				
		Death			c1770				
	Spouse -	Married							
M	5. DAVID FINNEY	Birth	21	June	1734				
		Death							
	Spouse (1) MARGARET FULLER (2) JEMIMA WARNER	Married	7	MARCH	1754				
M	6. JONATHAN FINNEY	Birth	1	June	1736				
		Death							
	Spouse - PHEBE PHELPS	Married	12	Aug.	1757				
	7.	Birth							
		Death							
	Spouse -	Married							
	8.	Birth							
		Death							
	Spouse -	Married							
	9.	Birth							
		Death							
	Spouse -	Married							
	10.	Birth							
		Death							
	Spouse -	Married							

In the circles, identify by number your sources of information — then list each on the reverse side.

☐ Additional children listed on the reverse side.

Family Record

Family No.

FHINNEY

Surname

Father — PHINNEY, THOMAS

Event	Day	Month	Year	Town	County	State	Notes	Source No.
Birth	25	May	1699					
Death								
Buried								
Married	31	MARCH	1726					
Occupation		Military				Church		
Places Lived								
Other Wives								

His Father's Name _____ JOHN PHINNEY

His Mother's Maiden Name _____ SARAH LUMBERT

Mother — GOODSPEED, RELIANCE

Event	Day	Month	Year	Town	County	State	Notes	Source No.
Birth	18	Sept	1701					
Death	27	JAN	1784					
Buried								
Occupation		Military				Church		
Places Lived								
Other Husbands								

Her Father's Name _____ EBENEZER GOODSPED

Her Mother's Maiden Name _____ LYDIA CROWELL

Children

Sex	Full Given Name	Event	Day	Month Year	Town	County	State	Source No.
M	1. ELI PHINNEY	Birth		1726/7				
	Spouse –	Death						
		Married						
F	2. LYDY PHINNEY	Birth		1729				
	Spouse –	Death						
		Married						
F	3. SARAH PHINNEY	Birth		1731/2				
	Spouse – SYLVANUS Hinkley	Death						
		Married						
M	4. ISAAC PHINNEY	Birth		1734				
	Spouse –	Death						
	DANNA THOMAS	Married	12	March 1763	Windham		Conn.	
F	5. PATIENCE PHINNEY	Birth		1736				
	Spouse – BEARSE	Death	Before	1754				
		Married						
F	6. ABIGAIL PHINNEY	Birth		1740				
	Spouse –	Death						
		Married						
F	7. ELIZABETH PHINNEY	Birth		1742				
	Spouse –	Death						
		Married						
	8.	Birth						
	Spouse –	Death						
		Married						
	9.	Birth						
	Spouse –	Death						
		Married						
	10.	Birth						
	Spouse –	Death						
		Married						

In the circles, identify by number your sources of information — then list each on the reverse side.

☐ Additional children listed on the reverse side.

Family Record

CAMPBELL

Family No.

Surname

Father — CAMPBELL, elson monroe

Event	Day	Month	Year	Town	County	State	Notes	Source No.
Birth			1810					
Death	3 Aug. 1895			Delta,		Michigan		
Buried								
Married			1831					

Occupation _____ Military _____ Church _____

Places Lived Cazenovia, N.Y.   WACOUSTA, Michigan

Other Wives _____

His Father's Name _____

His Mother's Maiden Name _____

Mother — PHINNEY HULDAH

Event	Day	Month	Year	Town	County	State	Notes	Source No.
Birth								
Death								
Buried								

Occupation _____ Military _____ Church _____

Places Lived _____

Other Husbands _____

Her Father's Name Seth Phinney

Her Mother's Maiden Name Lydia Jane

Children

Sex	Full Given Name	Event	Day	Month	Year	Town	County	State	Source No.
F	1. Lydia Campbell	Birth			1851				
		Death			1898				
	Spouse - Samuel Hart	Married	17 March 1850			DeWitt, Michigan			
F	2. SARAH E. CAMPBELL	Birth			1835				
		Death	1 Feb. 1913						
	Spouse - James Merritt Avery	Married							
	3. SETH CAMPBELL	Birth			1842				
		Death			1919				
	Spouse - Sarah A.	Married				Grand Ledge, Michigan			
M	4. HOVEY BRADFORA CAMPBELL	Birth	* Jan. 1844			Eagle, Michigan			
		Death	15 April 1922						
	Spouse - ALICE JANE EDDY	Married				N. Eagle Cemetery, Eagle, Mich			
M	5. CLARK CAMPBELL	Birth							
		Death							
	Spouse -	Married							
	6.	Birth							
		Death							
	Spouse -	Married							
	7.	Birth							
		Death							
	Spouse -	Married							
	8.	Birth							
		Death							
	Spouse -	Married							
	9.	Birth							
		Death							
	Spouse -	Married							
	10.	Birth							
		Death							
	Spouse -	Married							

In the circles, identify by number your sources of information — then list each on the reverse side.

Additional children listed on the reverse side.

FAMILY Finney – Mayes   Family Group No 524

Husband's Name __James Finney 1st – Rev. War Pvt. – 4th Great Grand-Parents__   GENERATION

Address __(Youghiogheny Valley), Allegheny Co., PA.__   Wife's Maiden Name __Martha Mayes__

Date of Birth __1726__ Where __Chester Co., PA.__   Address _____ Same _____

Date of Marriage __1747__ Where __Chester Co., PA.__   Date of Birth _____ Where _____

Other Wives _____   Date of Death __July 8th 1804__ Where __Allegheny Co., PA.__

Date of Death __Aug. 3rd 1802__ Where __Allegheny Co., PA.__   Cemetery _____

Cemetery _____   Other Marriages _____

Father's Name __William Finney__   Father's Name __Thomas Mayes__

Mother's Maiden Name _____   Mother's Maiden Name __Margaret (   )__

M or F	CHILDREN Arrange in order of birth	When Born			Where	Married To	When Married			Where	When Died			Where	Chart
		Mo.	Day	Year			Mo.	Day	Year		Mo.	Day	Year		
M	Thomas			1747	Lancaster Co. PA.	Margaret Swan	6		1770	Co., PA. Cumberland					
M	James 2nd Pvt. Rev. War			1750	"	#1-Martha M. Crunkleton	4	20	1774				1829	Harrison Co., PA.	
						#2-Elizabeth Braden									
						#3-Rebecca Rheah									
F	Jean			1752	" "	Robert Smith									
M	William – Pvt. Rev. War			1754	" "	Anne Morton	11	2	1781	Westmoreland, PA.	9	18	1816	Allegheny Co., PA.	
F	Margaret			1758	" "	James McCutcheon									
M	John – Rev. War Pvt.	12	18	1760	" "	Mary Taylor	10	23	1808	Jefferson Co., OH.	1	30	1839	Harrison Co., OH.	
F	Mary			1762	" "	( ) Peden									
M	Andrew			1764	" "	Jane Howe ****									
M	Robert			1765	" "	Mary (Polly) Peden					7	16	1850	Blythedale Allegheny Co., PA.	

**** Andrew & Jane (Howe) Finney, parents of Easter or (Hester Finney) Large, w/o Jonathon Large.(See inside Paper)

From Ella Wood Finney– D.A.R. Membership Application #35198‑Feb. 8th 1945.– 2nd great grand-daughter of James Finney 1st.
From Bible records, Rond Hill Tombstones Records & Family Records in Possession of Miss Ella Wood Finney.
James 2nd, 3rd great grand-father of Thomas R. Finney.
Robert, b/o James 2nd, 3rd great grand-father of Herb Nolan, husband of Mary Nolan.
John, b/o James 2nd, Rev. War Vet. ** Ohio Rev. War Soldiers by D.A.R. * Page 401 & 139 same Finney, John was living with
James 2nd in Harrison Co., OH. *** And died there.
William, b/o James 2nd Pvt. in Capt. Morton's Co. 2nd Westmoreland Battallion.

FAMILY Finney - Crunkleton - B   GENERATION ____ # 5

Husband's Name James Finney - 3rd Great Grandfather Family Group No 551 Wife's Maiden Name #1 - Martha Crunkleton

Address LancasterCo., PA. WestmorelandCo.,PA. & Harrison Co.,Ohio   Address _____

Date of Birth ___ 1750 ___ Where Lancaster.Co., PA.   Date of Birth _____ Where _____
Date of Marriage #1- 4-20-1774 Where Lancaster Co., PA.   Date of Death _____ Where _____
Other Wives #2-Elizabeth Braden. #3 Rebecca Rhean   Cemetery _____
Date of Death Sept. 1st 1829 Where Harrison Co., Ohio   Other Marriages _____

Cemetery _____

Father's Name James Finney s/o William & Jean Stephanson   Father's Name Robert Crunkleton
Mother's Maiden Name Martha Mayes d/o Thomas & Margaret Mayes   Mother's Maiden Name Margaret (   )
                                                                 From Franklin Co., PA.

M or F	CHILDREN Arrange in order of birth	When Born Mo.	Day	Year	Where	Married To	When Married Mo.	Day	Year	Where	When Died Mo.	Day	Year	Where	Chart
						Co.,PA.									
F	Margret			1774/75	Westmoreland	Robert Braden	About		1794						
M	Robert	Abt.	"	1777/'78	"	Margret Guthrie	"		1806	(See Finney-Crunkleton-Guthrie-Caldwell-D)			Died Young		
F	Martha	"		1780	"	Walter Francis	"		1806	(See Guthrie-Caldwell-Finney- C)					
F	Elizabeth	"		1782	"	Joseph McMillen	"		1808						
M	John	"		1784	"	Betsey Cannon	12	10	1816						
	By Elizabeth Braden														
M	Walter B.	"		1786/7	Fayette Co.,PA.										
	By Rebecca Rheah				"										
M	James	"		1804/5	Harrison Co., Ohio										
M	Thomas	"		1808/10	"										

James Finney, came from Fayette Co.,PA. in 1800/06 with son in law Robert Braden to 600 NW C. Short Crk.Harrison Co., O
 " married Rebecca Rheah - Ohio Valley Genealogies. & Harrison Co., Census 1820 - Page 50.
 " Family History - 1732-1946 Mrs. Lynn Yocum 1303 Milam Way - Carrollton, TX. 15006.

FAMILY Finney-Crunklton-Guthrie-Caldwell - D   Family Group No 578

GENERATION

Husband's Name __Robert Finney__ ------ 2nd Great Grand-Parents -------   Wife's Maiden Name __Margaret Guthrie__

Address _____

Date of Birth __1777/78__ _____ Where _____
Date of Marriage __Abt. 1806__ _____ Where _____ __PA.__
Other Wives __None__ _____
Date of Death _____ Where _____
Cemetery _____
Father's Name __James Finney__
Mother's Maiden Name __Martha Crunkleton__

Address _____
Date of Birth __Dec. 11th 1784__ Where _____
Date of Death __Jan. 23rd 1865__ Where __Harrison Co.,OH.__
Cemetery _____
Other Marriages __None - d. at 81 y. 12 d.__
Father's Name __Robert Guthrie__
Mother's Maiden Name __Elizabeth Jane Caldwell__

M or F	CHILDREN Arrange in order of birth	When Born			Where	Married To		When Married			Where	When Died			Where	Chart
		Mo.	Day	Year				Mo.	Day	Year		Mo.	Day	Year		
M	Joseph															
F	Maria															
M	Robert P.					Lydia Ann Jenkins	#2	11	8	1840	Harrison Co., OH.					
						Mary Hitchcock	#1	12	11	1844	Harrison Co., OH.					
F	Jane					Samuel Carnahan		1	27	1847	Harrison Co., OH.					
M	David															
M	Thomas G.(Guthrie)	6	12	1820	Co., OH. Harrison	Margaret J. Nash	#2	5	4	1843	Harrison Co., OH.	d. 2-12-1919				
						Susanna Cocherel	#1	5	2	1844	Harrison Co., OH.	d. 4-2-1906				
F	Sarah															
M	William G. (Guthrie)				Moved to Washington, D.C. 1861 * Was in Ford Theater when President Lincoln was shot.											

Robert Finney- Martha or Margaret(Guthrie) Finney -*- William G. Finney at Ford Theater. from
History of Upper Ohio Valley - Harrison Co., & Belmont Co., Ohio.

FAMILY __Finney - Stephenson__ GENERATION __#3__

Husband's Name __William Finney - 5th Great Grand Parents__ Family Group No 510

Wife's Maiden Name __Jean Stephenson__

Address __Chester Co., Penn.__

Date of Birth __1700-1710__ Where __Northern Ireland__

Date of Marriage _____ Where _____

Other Wives _____

Date of Death __1751__ Where __Chester Co., Penn.__

Cemetery __Thunder Hill, Chester Co., PA.__

Father's Name __Robert Finney__

Mother's Maiden Name __Dorothea (   )__

Address _____

Date of Birth _____ Where _____

Date of Death _____ Where _____

Cemetery __Thunder Hill, Chester Co., PA.__

Other Marriages _____

Father's Name _____

Mother's Maiden Name _____

M or F	CHILDREN Arrange in order of birth	When Born Mo. Day Year	Where	Married To	When Married Mo. Day Year	Where	When Died Mo. Day Year	Where	Chart
M	James Col. War Rev. War	1726	Penn. Chester Co.,	Martha Mayes	1747		1802		
F	Elizabeth	1728	"	Andrew Henderson			1816	Penn. Chester Co.	
M	Archibald	1730	"	( ) Loughead d/o Robt. Loughead					
M	Thomas Col. War	1732	"	Susanna Stewart	2 15 1757		1770-71	Penn. Dauphin Co.,	
M	William	1734	"	Patented land Westmreland Co., Penn. died young.			died young.		
M	Lazarus	1737-8	"	died young.			died young.		
F	Martha	1740	"	( ) Laughron Left her children in care of William Finney. m. ( ) Laughron.					
M	Robert Pvt. Rev. War	1742	"	#2 Jane ( ) #1-( ) Lagghead (Cousin)			4 17 1827 Meadville,	Crawford Co.,Penn.	
M	John	1745	"	Ann Dorthea Finney Died 10	2 1820 @ Thunder Hill		1814 Chester Co.,	Penn.	
M	Walter Maj.Rev. War	1747	? Penn. Chester Co.	Maj. Robert Finney (Frontiersmen) By Allan W.	Mary O'Hara		Eckert		
F	Jean or Jane	1749/50		David Hunter					

Martha (Finney) Laughron s/o William Finney above - Left her children in Delaware 1764 inthe care of William. William
died young.

Remarks on Thomas Finney above from the Minnehaha Clive Finney Family History, Page # 86.
(FREE), Thomas, James, James Jun, & Thomas Jun. - "   "   "   # 91.
Thomas & James Finney, sons of James & Martha Mayes "   "   "   # 104

FAMILY Finney Family group No. 628

GENERATION

Husband's Name Hawkins Cook Finney
Address Forest Township Cinton Co., IN.
Date of Birth Aug. 28th 1815 Where E. Tenn. Hawkins Co.
Date of Marriage Nov. 16 1837 Where E. Tenn.
Other Wives Hawkins Cook Finney m. Sarah B. Carter
Date of Death Jan 1 1889 Where Forest Township Clinton Co., IN.
Cemetery
Father's Name Joseph Finney
Mother's Maiden Name Mary Polly Long

Wife's Maiden Name Martha Konutz (Counte)
Address Same
Date of Birth - - 1817 Where Alabama
Date of Death Where
Cemetery
Other Marriages
Father's Name
Mother's Maiden Name

M or F	CHILDREN Arrange in order of birth	When Born Mo.	Day	Year	Where	Married To	When Married Mo.	Day	Year	Where	When Died Mo.	Day	Year	Where	Char
M	John V.	10	18	1837	Coles Co., Ill.	#2-Priscilla Lowry Mary Ransopher	4 11	21	1877 1861	Clinton Co., IN. Forest Co...					
M	David			1839	Indiana										
F	Frances E.			1843	"	Joseph Kinder									
F	Levonia			1846	"										
F	Amanda A.			1848	"	Samuel Walters									
M	Joseph L.			1850	"										
M	Wesley T.			1850	"	Cathie Knapp									
F	Lucretia A.			1854	"										
F	Abigail			1856	"										
F	Emily F.			1858	"	Samuel E. Griffin									

FAMILY Finney & Nash - Great Grand Parents   Family Group No 643   GENERATION __Margret J. Nash__   7th

Husband's Name __Thomas G. Finney__

Address _____   Harrison Co. Marriages

Date of Birth __June 3rd 1826__ Where _____   Page 595.

Date of Marriage __May 4th 1848__ Where __Harrison Co., Ohio.__

Other Wives _____

Date of Death __Feb. 12th 1919__ Where __Petersburg,In.__

Cemetery __Birdseye, In.__

Father's Name __Robert Finney__

Mother's Maiden Name __Margret Guthrie__

Wife's Maiden Name __Margret J. Nash__

Address _____

Date of Birth __April 28th 1829__ Where _____

Date of Death __April 2nd 1906__ Where __Birdseye, In.__

Cemetery _____

Other Marriages _____

Father's Name _____

Mother's Maiden Name _____

M or F	CHILDREN Arrange in order of birth	When Born			Where	Married To	When Married		Where	When Died			Where	Chart
		Mo.	Day	Year			Mo.	Day	Year		Mo.	Day	Year		
M	Zeb														
M	Samuel														
M	William G. Finney	6	3	1855		#1- Isabell Lester	7	11	1874	Alba, Mo.					
						#2- Susan Rosine Lester	8	23	1875		2	7	1941	Petersburg, In.	
M	Thomas					#3- Laura A. Bowman	3	29	1882	Pike Co., In.					
M	John														
F	Mary					Hogg									
F															

1860 - 1870 Census for Dubois, Crawford & Pike Counties of Indiana

Family Group No 663

FAMILY Finney - Ransopher - Lowry

GENERATION

Husband's Name John V. Finney

Address Forest Twp. Clinton Co., IN.

Date of Birth Oct. 18th 1837 Where Coles Co., IL.

Date of Marriage June 1865 Where Clinton Co., IN.

Other Wives #2- Priscilla Lowry, d/o William &Emeline Lowry 4-11-1877

Date of Death Where

Cemetery

Father's Name Hawkins Cook Finney

Mother's Maiden Name Martha Konutz (Countee)

Wife's Maiden Name Mary Ransopher

Address Clinton Co., IN.

Date of Birth Where

Date of Death Dec. 1875 Where Clinton Co.

Cemetery

Other Marriages None

Father's Name

Mother's Maiden Name

M or F	CHILDREN Arrange in order of birth	When Born			Where	Married To	When Married		Where	When Died			Where	Char
		Mo.	Day	Year			Mo.	Day Year		Mo.	Day	Year		
F.	Savannah													
M	James H.													
M	Stephan													
F	Samantha													
	Dillie													
F.	Mattie													
F.	Priscilla													
M	John													
	By Priscilla Lowry													
M	Clinton													
M	Omir A.													

FAMILY ___Finney___

Family Group No. 688

Husband's Name ___William G. Finney___

Married to
#1- 7-11-1875
#2- 9-23-1875
#3- 3-29-1882

Address _____

Date of Birth __12-7-1855__ Where __Dubois Co.,IN.__
Date of Marriage __7-11-1874__ Where __Alba, MO.__
Other Wives #2- Susan Rosine Lester * #3 Laura A. Bowman
Date of Death __2-7-1941__ Where __Petersburg, IN.__
Cemetery __Walnut Hill, Petersburg, IN.__
Father's Name __Thomas G. Finney__
Mother's Maiden Name __Margret J. Nash__

GENERATION ___8th___

Wife's Maiden Name #1-Mary Isabel Lester

Address _____
Date of Birth __9-21-1854__ Where __Washington Co., IN.__
Date of Death __1875__ Where __Alba, MO.__
Cemetery __Cedar Bluff, North of Alba, MO.__
Other Marriages ___None___

Father's Name ___Joseph Lester___
Mother's Maiden Name ___Mary Blocksom___

#2- Wife Susan Rosine
buried at Purcell, MO.
with her 2nd husband
William N. Parsons.
#3- Wife Laura A. buried
Walnut Hill, Petersburg,.

M or F	CHILDREN Arrange in order of birth	When Born			Where	Married To	When Married			Where	When Died			Where	Chart
		Mo.	Day	Year			Mo.	Day	Year		Mo.	Day	Year		
F	Un-named - Mary Isabel & child died at birth					***	*	*	*	**			1875	Alba, MO.	
	By 2nd Wife Susan Rosine Lester														
M	Joseph Fielding	11	25	1876	Alba,MO.	Stella S. Engler	7-11-1908			Logansport, IN.	7		1949	Fayetteville, Ark.	
M	Frank Leslie	8	15	1879	" "	Alice Sea	4-22-1904				12	13	1961	Los Angeles, Cal.	
	By 3rd Wife Laura A. Bowman														

FAMILY Finney - Engler   Family Group 704

Husband's Name Joseph Fielding Finney— Spanish American & W.W. 1
Address Walton, IN.
Date of Birth 11-25-1876 Where Alba, MO.
Date of Marriage 7-11-1908 Where Logansport, IN.
Other Wives None ?
Date of Death 7-27-1949 73 Where Fayetteville, AR.
Cemetery Walton, IN. I.O.O.F.
Father's Name William G. Finney 86
Mother's Maiden Name Susan Rosine Lester 75

GENERATION

Wife's Maiden Name Stella Scott Engler
Address Same
Date of Birth 10-21-1882 Where Walton, IN.
Date of Death 4-10-1959 76 Where Walton, IN.
Cemetery Walton, IN. I.O.O.F.
Other Marriages None

Father's Name Owen Engler 81
Mother's Maiden Name Sarah Emma Scott 91

M or F	CHILDREN Arrange in order of birth	When Born			Where	Married To	When Married			Where	When Died			Where	Chart
		Mo.	Day	Year			Mo.	Day	Year		Mo.	Day	Year		
M	Owen Engler	7	9	1909	Muncie, IN.	Marilyn Brant	6	11	196	Logansport, IN.	11	20	1975	Walton, IN.	66
M	Forrest Fielding	11	25	1910	Logansport, IN	Edna Ruth Hart	6	4	1932	Yorktown, IN.	7	25	1984	Muncie, IN.	73
M	Thomas Ryan	11	30	1914	Muncie, IN.	Flora May Roberts	5	18	1942	Lake Charles,					

Family Group No 715

FAMILY Finney – Brant

Husband's Name __Owen Engler Finney__

Address __Walton, IN.__

Date of Birth __7-9-1909__ Where __Muncie, IN.__

Date of Marriage __6-11-1964__ Where __Logansport, IN.__

Other Wives __None__

Date of Death __11-20-1975__ Where __Walton, IN.__

Cemetery __Walton, IN. I.O.O.F.__

Father's Name __Joseph Fielding Finney__

Mother's Maiden Name __Stella Scott Engler__

GENERATION

Wife's Maiden Name __Marilyn Brant__

Address __Same__

Date of Birth __7-25-1935__ Where _____

Date of Death _____ Where _____

Cemetery _____

Other Marriages __Billy Winters #2__

Father's Name __Oral John Brant__

Mother's Maiden Name __Agnes Pauline Harmon__

M or F	CHILDREN Arrange in order of birth	When Born			Where	Married To	When Married		Where	When Died			Where	Chart
		Mo.	Day	Year			Mo.	Day Year		Mo.	Day Year			
F	Barbara Ann	8	6	1964	Logansport, IN.									

FAMILY   Finney – Hart   Family Group No 716

Husband's Name   Forrest Fielding Finney
Address   2304 North Hollywood – Muncie, IN. 47304
Date of Birth   11-25-1910   Where   Logansport, IN.
Date of Marriage   6-4-1932   Where   Yorktown, IN.
Other Wives   None
Date of Death   July 25th 1984 Where   Muncie, IN.
Cemetery   Elm Ridge Mausoleum in Muncie,IN.
Father's Name   Joseph Fielding Finney
Mother's Maiden Name   Stella Scott Engler

GENERATION   Edna Ruth Hart
Wife's Maiden Name   Same
Address
Date of Birth   8-14-1914   Where   Elkins, WV.
Date of Death   Where
Cemetery
Other Marriages

Father's Name   Humbolt Theodis Hart
Mother's Maiden Name   Stella Maude Eisner

M or F	CHILDREN Arrange in order of birth	When Born			Where	Married To	When Married			Where	When Died			Where	Chart
		Mo.	Day	Year			Mo.	Day	Year		Mo.	Day	Year		
F	Shirley Ann	3	19	1933	Muncie,IN.	Larry Lee Liby	6	15	1952	Muncie, IN.					
M	David Owen	10	4	1934	"	Mary LaRue Whaley Gravedoni	2	12	1955	Junction City, KS.					
M	Wallace Ray	2	6	1941	"	Lois Marie	8	18	1962	Negaunee, MI.					

Forrest F. Finney

MUNCIE — Forrest F. Finney, 73, 2304 Hollywood, died at 7 a.m. Wednesday at his residence.

He was born Nov. 25, 1910, in Logansport to Joseph F. and Stella S. Engler Finney. He was married on June 4, 1932, to Ruth Hart, who survives. He was a printer for the Muncie Star.

Also surviving are one daughter, Shirley A. Liby, Muncie; two sons, David O., Los Angeles, Calif., and Wallace R., Key West, Fla.; one brother, Thomas R. Finney, Logansport; and nine grand-children.

He was preceded in death by a brother, Owen E. Finney, Walton.

Services will be 10 a.m. Friday in Meeks Mortuary, with the Rev. Elden Petry officiating. Entombment will be in Elm Ridge Mausoleum in Muncie. Friends may call from 2 to 4 p.m. and 7 to 9

10th from Robert Finney
13th from Francis Cooke
13th Generation Americans

FAMILY Finney – Roberts   Family group No 717

GENERATION _____

Husband's Name ___ Thomas Ryan Finney – World War 2 ___

Address ___ Rt. #7 Box 31 Logansport, IN. ___

Date of Birth __ 11-30-1914 __ Where __ Muncie, IN. __

Date of Marriage __ 5-18-1942 __ Where __ Lake Charles, LA. __

Other Wives ___ None ___

Date of Death _____ Where _____

Cemetery _____

Father's Name ___ Joseph Fielding Finney ___

Mother's Maiden Name ___ Stella Scott Engler ___

Wife's Maiden Name ___ Flora May Roberts ___

Address ___ Same ___

Date of Birth __ 5-11-1919 __ Where __ Lake Charles, LA. __

Date of Death _____ Where _____

Cemetery _____

Other Marriages _____

Father's Name ___ William George Roberts ___

Mother's Maiden Name ___ Alice Louisa Bidwell ___

M or F	CHILDREN Arrange in order of birth	When Born Mo.	Day	Year	Where	Married To	When Married Mo.	Day	Year	Where	When Died Mo.	Day	Year	Where	Chart
M	Joseph Michael	3	4	1943	Victoria, TX.	Karen Sue Sherman	8	30	1969	Logansport, IN.					
M	Frank Lewis	11	29	1945	Lake Charles, LA.	Barbara Jean Geier	6	3	1973	Metea, IN.					
M	Thomas Ryan Jr.	2	25	1949	"	Paula Lee Foust	4	12	1969	Logansport, IN.					
F	Brenda Alice	7	13	1953	"	David Eugene Looker	12	11	1971	"	5	30	1974	Logansport, IN.	

Rotation for S.A.R.

#1– Finney, Joseph F. b. 11-25-1876 – Alba, MO.
#2–   "   , William G. b. 12-7-1855 – Dubois Co., IN.
#3–   "   , Thomas G. b. 6-3-1826 – Harrison Co., OH.
#4–   "   , Robert 3rd b. 1777/8 – Westmoreland Co., PA.
#5–   "   , James Jr. b. 1750 – Lancaster Co., PA.
#6–   "   , James Sr. b. 1726 – New London Twp. Chester Co.,PA.
#7–   2   , William b. Abt. 1700 New London, Ireland.
#8–   "   , Robert Jr. b. 1668 –   "   "   "
#9–   "   , Robert Sr. b. Abt. 1630 Either Scotland or England.
                                        ******

10th Generation – Finney, Thomas Ryan b. 11-30-1914 Muncie, IN.

NAMES ALPHABETICALLY ARRANGED

Containing information not previously recorded in this book. The arrangement begins with the name FINNEY followed by PHINNEY, then continues through the alphabet. The letter F preceded by a number means that the information recorded was talem from *THE FINNEY FAMILY HISTORY 1747 – 1946* compiled by Miss. Minnehaha Finney, a descendant.

FINNEY:

1. AARON JAMES, b. Oct. 14,1978 son of David Wesley Finney (P73-728)

2. ABIGAIL b. April 17,1697 dau of Jeremiah and Esther (Lewis) Finney. (P4-43)There is very little about her and only appears when she has signed legal papers with her husband. (P4-43)

3. ABIGAIL (BLACK) wife of William Finney. Her children by Mr. Finney were IRENE and JOSEPH.(P30-122)

4. ABIGAIL b. 1770 d. Oct. 16,1796 dau of Josiah and Martha (Gibbs)Finney. (P28-259)

5. ABIGAIL (Coggin)dau of Thomas Bishop widow of'Henry Coggin wife of John Finney. (P2-3)

6. ABIGAIL, b. 1856 dau of Hawkins Finney (P64-671)

7. ABIJAH b. June 17,1729 son of John and Mary (Campbell)Finney. (He was not originally listed with the family. (P12-42)

8. ABRAHAM,b. April 20,1772 son of Jonathan and Phebe (Phelps) Finney. (P33-314)

9. ADELINA M. b. May 28,1915 dau of ELIJAH and his second wife, MARIE (DOUGAL-MARSHALL) FINNEY.

    Taken from the "FINNEY FAMILY HISTORY 1742-1942" compiled by Minnehaha Finney. These records will be numbered with the number of the page in the records followed by the letter "F" (78af) 1EF-8

10. (ADELBERT) HOWARD FINNEY, son of Ezra Thompson Finney Jr. and Mary(Flower) dau pf Benjamin Franklin and Clarissa (Wilder)Flower. Mary Flower was born in North Bloomfield, Trumbull County, Ohio. Adelbert, was born in Bristolville, Trombull Co, Ohio. July 8,1876. He d. at his home, Montclair, N.J. June 22, 1952. He was an attorney. He m. Sept 25,1901 a daughter of Amos Steckel and Ellen White.

    ISSUE:

    1. Howard Jr. b. Oct. 6, 1903.

!. AGNES, dau of Thomas and Susan (Stewart) Finney. She was the sixth child in the family and was bpt. July 29, 1784. She m. JAMES PATTERSON. Her name is found mostly in deeds or legal papers she signed with her husband. She d. c1817 when the estate was settled. They had twelve children.

ISSUE: *PATTERSON:*

1. *JOHN died before his father leaving his wife and four children.*
2. *SUSANNA B. 1777 d. 1849 m. her cousin WILLIAM PATTERSON.*
3. *THOMAS b. 1781 d. 1860 (Xorrection made by Helen Patterson) He died April 7,1848. He m. SARAH CRAIG.*
4. *WILLIAM, b. 1782 d. 1860 m. SARAH STEWART.*
5. *JAMES, b. 1784 d. 1855 m.(1)MARY WATT. (2) MARY SWANGIE.*
6. *MARGARET b. 1787 d. 1856 Unmarried.*
7. *ELIJAH b. 1788 d. 1875 Unmarried.*
8. *JOSEPH b. 1792 d. 1855 Unmarried.*
9. *SAMUEL, b. c1794. There is no proof he existed except he had three daughters.*
10. *FINNEY HENRY b. 1796 drowned in the Youghiogheny river.*
11. *ROBERT, b.c1798 d. 1845 m. REBECCA WILSON.*
12. *NANCY, b. 1802 d. 1855 Unmarried.*

2. ALBERT E. son of David b. 1855 (P62-647)

3. ALEXANDER b. 1837 son of James (P57-593)

4. ALICE, b. Dec. 23,1881 dau of William and Lizzie (Reynolds) Finney. (P5WF2-3)

5. ALICE, (SEA) wife of Frank (P71-705)

6. ALLEN bpt. March 20, 1757 son of Josiah and Martha (Gibbs) (P28-248)

7. ALMA (LANGE) b. April 9, 1903 m. James David Finney.

A. NEIL FINNEY. (1JF-12)

8. ALPHRETTA b. Dec. 30, 1848 at Mansfield. Ohio, dau of William and Jane Patterson Finney. She m. JOHN CROUCH. She d. Sept 24,1928 IN 169

ISSUE: *CROUCH*

!. *WILLIAM WILLIS b. May 13,1877 m. GERTRUDE MAXWELL.*
2. *JAMES BOYD b. Feb. 15,1887 m. MARY ESTELLA STANTZ.*

9. AMANDA b. 1849 dau of Hawkins Cook Finney (P64-667)

1. ANABELLE b. Oct. 14,1906 dau of William Herbert and Susanna (Bell) Finney.   She m. Alva Clement Jacobson ——— 2WF 4-3

    ISSUE: JACOBSON

    1. ROBERT WESLEY.   2. CLARK HERBERT   3. Helen Louise d. Jan. 4, 1947.

    ————————

2. ANDREW b. 1764 son of James m. Jane Howe ——————————— 53-557
3. ANN, b. April 30,1727 dau of John and Ann (Toogood)Finney.————— 13-132
4. ANN, b. 1840 dau of David Thompson and Hannah (Butler)————— 58-608
5. ANN DOROTHEA d. May 1792 dau of David and Ann (Thompson)   52-540
6. ANN DOROTHEA dau of Dr. John wife of John ————————— 51-532
7. ANN DOROTHEA, dau of David wife of William Miller——————— 52-540
8. ANN EVANS b. 1808 dau of David Thompson and Mary (James)——— 53-567
9. ANN (MORTON) wife of Robert and mother of Rebecca who m. David Newton (See Reliance Finney.———————————————— 9-21-5
10. ANN (NANCY)b. Sept 19,1773 d. Dec. 17,1839 dau of Josiah and Martha(Gibbs).————————————————————— 28-256
11. ANN (THOMPSON) wife of David .————————————————— 52-514
12. ANN (TOOGOOD) d. Aug. 17, 1778awife of John ——————————— 13-48
13. ANN b. 1854 dau of William James and Louisa.——————————— 59-621
14. ANN b. 1769 dau of Joel and Ann Sacket ——————————————— 41-350
15. ANN (KESSTER) wife of Joseph———————————————————— 56-545
16. ANNA b in Ireland and d. after 1778 dau of Robert and Dorothea, wife of John McClanahan ——————————————————————— 49-512
17. ANNA (WILLIAMS) wife of Asa Finney who was the son of Joseph Davies. ————————————————————————————— 66-683
18. ANNA E. b. May 29,1859 d. March 1928; dau of Wesley and Mary Matilda (Hinshaw) ————————————————————————— 69-676
19. ANNE MARGARET b. Feb. 7, 1920 dau of Frank Wylie and Susie (Littlejohn). She m. Aug. 1940 ROBERT EARL WHITE b. Oct. 16, 1919 at Glassport, Pa. She is a trained   nurse ————————— 141F

    ISSUE: WHITE

    1, SUZANNE PEARL b. March 29, 1942 at Glassport, Pa.

    ————————

FINNEY:

1. ANSON, son of Joel and Ann (Sackett)Finney. He was b. 1786(P41-355C)

2. APRIL ANN dau of Charles Lawrence Finney..She is living with her parents in Germany (See Charles Lawrence)   1CF-11±2

3. ARCHIBALD b. 1730 son of William and *Jean (Stevenson)Finney. (51-526)

4. ARTHUR b. 1861 son of William and Louisa Finney. (P39-623)

5. ASA b. 1872 son of Joseph and Amanda (Milliken)Finney.(P66-683)

6. ASENATH, son of Jonathan and Phebe (Phelps)Finney (P33-312A)

7. AVIS, child of John and Avis (Bowen)Finney. (P40-349)

NOTES

---

*Jean Stevenson is sometimes changed to Jane Stevenson Stephenson is spelled for Stevenson in places.

1. BARBARA ANN b. Aug. 6,1964 dau of Owen Engler _____ 73-729
2. BECKY (BURCH) wife of David Wesley _____ 73-714
3. BELINDA b. May 4, 1782 dau of Joel and Ann (Sacket) _____ 41-355A
4. BENJAMIN son of Samuel and Elizabeth (Wood) _____ 14-137
5. BENJAMIN, b. Aug. 9, 1771 son of David and Jemima (Warner) _____ 33-307
6. BENJAMIN, F. b. 1866 son of John and Louisey. Finney. He was b. in Robertsville, Mo. His mother was the dau of William and Nancy (Breeding) Roark. Benjamin d. Dec. 12,1866. (See John Finney) 5JF4-7
7. BERIAH b. Nov. 14,1768 son of Jonathan; and Phebe (Phelps) _____ 33-312B
8. BETHUEL b. June 11, 1760 son of Jonathan and Phebe (Phelps) _____ 33-309
9. BETSEY ANN b. April 19,1793 dau of George and Henrietta (Mathews) _____ 41-356
10. BEULAH, (BIRDEN) wife of Charles Wesley _____ 71-707
11. BELLE, dau of Robert and Margaret (Patterson). She m.Melvin Reynolds _____ 1SF-8-1

ISSUE: *REYNOLDS*

1. *PAUL McCLURE REYNOLDS,Lived with his grandmother,Sarah Jane McClure in the latter years of her life.*

---

12. BRENDA ALICE b. July 13, 1953 m. David Eugene Looker. She was the dau of Thomas Ryan _____ 74-736

FINNEY:

1. CALEB, son of Nathanial and Hannah (Wood)_____ 32-292

2. CARL CHESTER b. May 13, 1905 son of Daniel Webster_____ 72-700

3. CATHERINE b. c1586 dau of "Mother"_____ 1-1

4. CATHERINE, dau of Lazarus and Catherine (Symonton)_____ 50-523

5. CATHERINE b. 1828 d. after 1881 dau of Joseph_____ 60-634

6. CATHERINE, dau of James_____ 57-591

7. CATHERINE (Symonton) wife of Lazarus_____ 50-508

8. CHARLES EDWARD b. April 29, 1869 son of Robert_____ 68-695

9. CHARLES KEY b. 1823 in Westmorland Co. Va. He d. Feb. 26, 1905. He m.(1) FRANCES COOKE b. Jan 29, 1848 in Metagorda, Tex. and d. Sept. 20, 1933 in New Orleans, La. She was the dau of Hamilton Leon and Temperance (Haley) Cooke. It is possible he m. twice (2) ELIXA U. FINNEY b. Oct. 8, 1839. It is possible the first wife listed should be the second wife according to the dates involved.

   ISSUE:

   1. JOHN L. FINNEY b. Jan 2, 1858 d. April 9, 1878.

   2. ROBERT B. FINNEY b. Jan 12, 1858 d. April 20, 1878.

   *3. DAVID PURCELL FINNEY, b. Oct. 21, 1876 in New Orleans 2DF7

   *4. FRANCES KEY FINNEY b. Nov. 27, 1909_____ 1FF5
   Frances Finney's records)

   _____

10. CHARLES L. b. 1875 son of Joseph and Amanda (Millikan___ 66-684

11. CHARLES LAWRENCE b. May 10, 1933 in Hillsdale, Ind. He was the son of Rufus and Mildred Catherine (Millikan) Finney. He m. Feb. 22, 1961 in Warsaw, Ind. LaVONNE LOWMAN b. Dec. 10, 1939 dau of Kivan and Yvonne Lowman. He was a career soldier with 27 years service with two tours of service in Germany, two in Viet Nam and one in Korea. While in Germany he ranked commanding Sergeant-Major of which there are only 160 in the entire army_____ 4RF5-3

    ISSUE:

    1. KATHY CHAPMAN, Step-daughter.

    2. APRIL ANN FINNEY b. July 18, 1962._____ 4AF-2

FINNEY:

1. CHARLES LEE b. Oct. 21,1929 Kingman, Ind. son of Richard and Lucile (Newman) _____ 71-702

2. CHARLES WESLEY, b. Nov. 30, 1899 son of Charles Edward and JEssie (Grosse) _____ 71-707

3. CHARLOTTE b. Feb. 10, 1764 d. April 15,1829 dau of Josiah and Martha (Gibbs) _____ 38-251

4. CHARKOTTE (Gates) wife of Dwight MacDill _____ 4DF2

5. CHLORENE (Anderson)wife of Francis Wylie _____ 1FF6

6. CHRISTIANA dau of Thomas and Emma G. (Whitman) _____ 62-651

7. CHRISTOPHER WALKER AMERINE _____ 72-219

8. CLAIRE, dau of William Herbert _____ 2WF4-4

9. CLARA ELLEN dau of Wesley and Mary (Hinshaw) _____ 70-681

10. CLARIE, dau of David and Rachel D. _____ 62-649

11. CLARISSA, dau of Washington and Martha _____ 59=618

12. CLARE, son of Thomas _____ 29-270

13. CLAUDIA (BAILEY) WIFE OF William Arvel _____ 70-682

14. CLEMENDA L. dau of Washington and Martha _____ 59-619

15. CLYDE , son of William and Lizzie (Reynolds). He was born Sept. 22, 1877 and m. Feb. 8, 1898 SYLVIA RHODES b. July 4, 1880. _____ IN-590

ISSUE:

1. HAROLD RHODES FINNEY b. March 8, 1900 _____ 1HF-9

2. MANNA MAGETTA FINNEY b. Sept. 27, 1904. _____ 131F

3. MARY ELIZABETH FINNEY, b. Jan 9, 1907. _____ 131F

4 VIOLA MYRTLE FINNEY b. Aug 21, 1911 _____ 131F

5. REYNOLDS MONROE FINNEY b. July 24,1916 _____ 132F

6. VAUGH LA RENE FINNEY B. Sept 29, 1919 _____ 132F

NOTES

FINNEY:

1.   DANIEL b. 1834 son of James and Sarah _____ 57-592

2.   DANIEL EDWARD b. July 12,1967 son of James Edward _____ 73-723

3.   DANIEL WEBSTER, b. Nov. 7,1868 d. Dec. 10,1927 son of

      Wesley and Mary Matilda (Hinshaw)_____ 65-680

4.   DANIEL WILLIAM b. Oct. 8,1837 son of Robert _____ 63-655

5.   DARBY ANN Step-dau of Donald Allen_____ 3DF4-1

6.   DAVID son of John and Elizabeth (French) _____ 50-514

7.   DAVID son of Robert and Margaret (Patterson). He was b.

      May 4, 1855 and d. May 31,1936. He m. Oct. 19,1881

      SARAH PATTERSON who was b. Nov. 1872 d. Nov. 24,1889.

      He m. (2) Dec. 15,1892 HARRIET WAY b. Nov. 28,1872_____IN 724

      ISSUE: By first wife:

        1.   HOWARD PATTERSON FINNEY b. May 31,1882 m. Feb.

           16,1922 NANCY GAMBLE_____1HF 19

        2.   SAMUEL GUY FINNEY d. young; studied for the ministry.

      *3.   FRANK WYLIE FINNEY b. April 14,1884 m. March 11,

           1913 SUSIE LITTLEJOHN _____1FF-7

        4.   ROBERT COLEMORE b. Sept.22,1888 m. MARY FERGUS.

           Children by 2nd wife._____ 3RF-1

        5.   ZELAH b. Aug. 21,1893 _____1ZF-4

        6.   ANNA MARGARET b. Dec. 24,1894_____131F

      *7.   PORTER MILROY b. March 30,1896 m. Dec. 18,1922

           EDNA HOUSEHOLDER _____ 1PF-10

        8.   HAROLD CHARLES b. 1898

      *9.   IVA ELBERTA b Feb. 13,1901_____1-1F-3

     *10.   OLIVER ERBARDT b. Aug. 6, 1904_____1-OF-1

     *11.   REBECCA RUTH b. Sept. 15,1908 _____ 1RF-1

                        _____

8.   DAVID b. 1832 son of Washington and Martha _____ 59-612

9.   DAVID son of Robert and Margaret (Guthrie _____ 62-642

10.   DAVID b. 1827 son of John French and Rebecca Butler _____ 58-599

11.   DAVID b. Aug. 21,1732 son of John and Ann (Toogood) _____ 13-134

12.   DAVID b. 1864 son of Hawkins Cook _____ 64-668

FINNEY:

1.   DAVID, son of Josiah and Elizabeth (Mann)_____ 33-144

2.   DAVID, son of David Thompson _____ 55-563

3.   DAVID, b. March 2?,1893 son of William and Lizzie (Reynolds 5WF2-4

4.   DAVID GARY, b. Sept 16,1937 in Hillsdale, Ind. He was the
son of Rufus E and Mildred Catherine (Millikan)Finney.   He
m. Oct. 11, 1969 in Bulawayo, Rhodesia. Africa JUDITH LEE
LANDRY b. March 4, 1940 in Wateska, Ill. She was a graduate of Lincoln Christian College and has a degree in Christian
education. They both served in Rhodesia as missionaries for
nine years . They reside in Rockville,Ind. **No children are**
known at this time. _____ 4RF-5:4

5.   DAVID MEAD,.   son of James and Sarah_____ 57-590

6.   DAVID OWEN, b. Oct. 4,1934 son of Forest Fielding_____ 74-731

7.   DAVID PURCELL b. Oct. 21,1876 son of Charles Key and
Frances (Cooke)Finney. He was b. in New Orleans, La and m.
EMMA LOUISE SCHROEDER. *(Records of Frances Finney
Mills.)* _____ 1CF-9

8.   DAVID THOMPSON, b. Jan 20,1773 son of David   _____ 58-563

9.   DAVID WESLEY, son of Robert and Matilda Hunt_____ 67-656

10.   DAVID WESLEY, son of Carl Chester _____ 72-714

11.   DEBORAH bpt Oct. 20, 1695 dau of Jeremiah and Esther _____ 4-41

12.   DEBORAH   dau of Jeremiah a;nd Deborah_____ 29-263

13.   DEBORAH ANN, dau of Richard Otis and Helen Maxine
(Sharer) Finney. She was b. Nov.26,1956. She m. RICKY STARK
whom she divorced and who was the father of MICHAEL AN-
THONY b. April 19,1976. She m. BRYAN SHANNON b. Dec
1956. The date of her last marriage is unknown at this time.
She m. BRYAN SHANNON b. Dec. 1956._____ IN-647
ISSUE by last husband:

     1.   *CHRISTOPHER WAYNE SHANNON. b. Dec. 6,1977.*

     2.   *MISTY DAWN b. March 17, 1980.*

FINNEY:

1. DELADEMA, bpt. July 1767 dau of John and Rachel (Woodward) Finney. (P31-285)

2. DELILA ROSINE b. June 8,1911 dau of Frank Leslie Finney and Alice (Sea) Finney. (P71-705- P1FF-9=2)

3. DIANA (SPENCER) wife of Robert Finney. (P52-520)

4. DONALD ALLAN, son of Richard Otis and Helen Maxine(Sharer) Finney. He was b. July 15,1952; m. Nov. 6,1976 DANA LOIS COOK b. April 5,1953, dau of Morris and Caroline Cook of Effington, Ill. **They were married in Rockville Christian Church by Rev. David Finney. Dana had prviously been married.** (P1RF-18)
   ISSUE:
   1. DARBY ANN, b. Dec. 17,1974. Step-daughter.
   2. TAMMY DAWN, b. Nov. 18,1978.
   3. KENNETH ALLAN, b. July 14,1979.

5. DONALD ELSWORTH, son of Rufus E. and Mildred Catherine (Millikan) Finney. He was b. Nov. 9, 1927 d. Jan 23,1976. He never married. He attended Hillsdale High School and became a Staff Sergeant in the U.S. Airforce during World War II. He was a Lieutenant in the Indiana State Police in charge of stolen car detail and served 27 years with the State Police from 1948 to 1976. He attended numerous training schools and was a 32nd degree mason; a member of the Methodist Church and is buried in Holt's Prairie Cemetery. (4RF-5)

6. DOROTHEA wife of Robert. She was probably b in Ireland.(P49-505)

7. DOROTHEA, dau of Lazarus and Catheri;ne (Symonton)Finney. She m. JOHN OCHILTREE. No children are shown. (P50-522)

8. DOROTHEA,dau of Thomas and Mary (Chester)Finney (P51-536)

9. DOROTHY MILDRED b. and d. June 11,1898 (P71-706)

10. DWAINE LEE b. May 15,1919 son of_____ d. one day old (22F)

FINNEY:

1. DWIGHT MacDILL, b. May 27, 1876 son of James and Elizabeth (Short) Finney. He m. June 4, 1902 WAVE W. WOOSTER dau of Charles Coffman and Nannie (Cullum) Wooster. Charles was a soldier in the Civil War and descended from General David Wooster of the Revolutionary War. (P1JF13-5)

ISSUE:

     1.   JAMES DAVID FINNEY b. April 24, 1903.   1JF 12

     2.   NANNIE ELIZABETH FINNEY, b. Dec. 17, 1905.   1NF 10

     3.   JULIA PEARL FINNEY, b. June 11, 1908.   8JF1

     4.   WAVE WOOSTER FINNEY, b. Jan 16, 1911.   1WF5

     5.   DWIGHT MacDILL JR. b. Oct. 6, 1916.   4DF½2

  *6.   JOHN CHARLES FINNEY, b. Nov. 7, 1920.   1N-569

----

2. DWIGHT MacDILL Jr. (3DF-1-5) b. Oct. 6, 1916 He m. May 27, 1938 CHARLOTTE MAE GATES b. Oct. 28, 1921 in Kansas.

ISSUE:

     1.   CONENE MAE FINNEY, b. Feb. 16, 1940.

     2.   GARRON DWIGHT FINNEY, b. Nov. 27, 1941.

     3.   JANET LOU FINNEY, b. Mar. 22, 1944.

     4.   PATRICIA ANN FINNEY, b. July 25, 1945.

NOTES

1. **EDNA MAY,** b. Nov. 22,1899 dau of William Arvel and Claudia (Bailey)Finney. She m. (1) WALTER Robinson,and (2) SYDNEY TYSON. No children are shown. (P70-701)

2. **EDNA ROTH (HART)** wife of FORREST FIELDING FINNEY. Her children are listed under FORREST FIELDING (P74- 716)

3. **EDNA (HOUSEHOLDER)** wife of PORTER MILROY FINNEY. Her children: (See Porter Milroy (P1PF-10)

4. **ELEAZER,** b. 1754 son of John and Rachel (Woodward)Finney. (P31-282)

5. **ELEAZER** b. Jan 20,1755 son of David and Jemima (Warner)Finney. (P33-303)

6. **ELIGE** b. Oct. 12,1861 d. Dec. 26,1909. Never married. He was the son of John and Louisey Elizabeth (Roark) Finney. (See John Finney P5JF 4-5)

7. **ELIEU** b. July 14,1755 son of John and Hannah (Washburn)Finney. (P31-289)

8. **ELIJAH,** b. May 26,1799 d. Oct. 29,1870 son of William and Margaret (Stewart)Finney. He m. 1827 ELIZABETH CULBERTSON b. 1800 d. Oct. 2,1839. He m. (2) MRS MARIA DOUGAL MARSHALL who had a daughter. Maria was b. Feb. 24,1807 d. May 29, 1892. Elijah's first wife died when the last child was born and the child died with her.

ISSUE: By first wife.

1. WILLIAM PATTERSON b. 1829 d. 1916.
2. JOSEPH d. in infancy
3. ABIGAIL ANN b. 1833 d. 1907 m. _____ Garrett.
4. JAMES JOHNSON, b. 1837 d. 1899.
5. ELIJAH JR. b. 1839 d. 1865. m. ELIZABETH CULBERTSON.
    By 2nd wife:
6. THOMAS ALEXANDER b. 1842 d. 1862.
7. MARGARET. b. 1845 d. May 21, 1935 .
8. JOHN CRAIG b. 1846 d. 1929
9. ADALINA M. b. 1846 d. May 28,1935.

2EF

FINNEY:

1.	ELIJAH JR. son of Elijah and Elizabeth (Culbertson)	1EF8-5
2.	ELIJAH COOK son of Robert and Matilda (Hunt)	63-654
3.	ELIJAH, son of Joel and Ann Sacket	41-354
4.	ELINOR BELL dau of Robert Colemore and Mary (Fergus)	3RF1-1
5.	ELIZABETH, dau of John and Christiana Finney. She was b. March 15,1659 m. Dec. 19,1773 HAILE BARTON b. c1753. son of Benjamin and Mary (Haile)Barton	2-9
6.	ELIZABETH, dau of Joshua and Mercy (Watts)	5-46
7.	ELIZABETH, sister to No.6. wife of Nathan Luther	5-51
8.	ELIZABETH, dau of Jeremiah and Elizabeth (Bristow)	12-117
9.	ELIZABETH, dau of Josiah and Elizabeth (Mann)	14-139
10.	ELIZABETH, (Bristow) wife of Jeremiah	28-115
11.	ELIZABETH, dau of Josiah and Mary (Carey)	28-247
12.	ELIZABETH, dau of josiah and 2nd wife Martha (Gibbs)	28-257
13.	ELIZABETH, dau of Jeremiah and Deborah	29-262
14.	ELIZABETH, dau of William and Elizabeth (Clark)	30-276
15.	ELIZABETH, dau of Oliver and Elizabeth (Dunham)	31-286
16.	ELIZABETH, dau of David and Jemima (Warner)	33-304
17.	ELIZABETH, dau of John and Elizabeth (French)	50-516
18.	ELIZABETH, dau of Josephj and Mary Polly (Long)	60-630
19.	ELIZABETH, dau of William and Jean (Stephenson)	51-525
20.	ELIZABETH, dau of David and Ann Thompson)	52-539
21.	ELIZABETH, dau of David Thompson and Mary (James)	55-564
22.	ELIZABETH, dau of James	57-580

NOTES

1. ELIZABETH ATWOOD dau of Loring and Experience (Pearse)   39-261
2. ELIZABETH (BRADEN) wife of James _____ 57-551
3. ELIZABETH (CAMPBELL) wife of John Long _____ 60-626
4. ELIZABETH (FRENCH) wife of John _____ 50-506
5. ELIZABETH (FULTON) 1st wife of Lazarus _____ 52-544
6. ELIZABETH (HEART) dau of John Heart, wife of Joh Family   5JF4
7. ELIZABETH (SHORT) wife of James Patterson. Her children   1JF13
8. ELLEN (SIMPSON) dau of Frank Wylie and Suksie (Littlejohn)
   Finney. She m. BLAINE EDWARD CHEASLEY _____ 1FF7-1
   ISSUE: *CHEASKEY*
   1. *MARY ELLEN B. May 30, 1937*
   2. *JAMES ALLISON b. May 8, 1939*
   3. *LINDA ANN b. NOV. 7, 1944.*

9. EMILY, dau of Hawkins Cook _____ 64-672
10. EMMA G. (WHITMAN) wife of Thomas _____ 62-603
11. ERIN (ANN) dau of Thomas and Mary (Chester) _____ 51-537
12. ESTHER, dau of Jeremiah and Mary (Lewis) Her children ___ 12-40
13. ESTHER, b. Sept 11,1912 dau of William Herbert and Susanna
    (Bell) Finney. She m. May 3,1934 WOODROW M. KETHCART
    b. March 23,1913. _____ IN 339
    ISSUE: *KETHCART*
    1. *BARBARA ANN*

NOTES

FINNEY:

1. ETTA LUCILE (NEWMAN)wife of Richard Harrison Finney.
   (P71-685)

2. EVA. (EVIE)dau of John Wesley and Nancy (Brooks)Finney.
   (P69-697)

3. EVELYN (EISELE) wife of William Herbert Finney,Jr. (21F)Her
   name is spelled E I S L E (29F). _____2WF-5

4. ELIXA W. or U b. Oct. 8, 1839 wife of Charles Key Finney
   (P1CF-9)

5. EZRA son of Abraham and Huldah (Gifford)Finney. He m. JULIA
   MASON (P41-358)

6. EZRA son of Ezra and Julia (Mason)Finney. (P41-358A)

7. EXPERIENCE (PEARSE)wife of LORING FINNEY. (P39-261)

NOTES

1. FANNEY, b. Feb. 16,1825 d. Dec. 18,1891 dau of Joseph and Mary Polly (Long) Finney. She m. JABEZ RAYL. (P66-633)
2. FLORA MAY (ROBERTS) wife of Thomas Ryan Finney (P74-717)
3. FORREST FIELDING, son of Joseph and Stella Scott (Engler) Finney. (P74-716)
4. FRANCES SUSAN b. Jan 9,1946 adopted child of Francis Wylie and Chloriene (Anderson)Finney. (147F)   1FF-6
5. FRANCES KEY, b. 1909 dau of Charles Key and Frances (Cooke) Finney. She m. WILLIAM WARD MILLS.   1CF9-4
ISSUE:

   1. WILLIAM WARD MILLS,Jr. b. June 17,1935, Hattiesburg, Miss.
   Records of Frances Finney Mills, Baton Rouge, La.

6. FRANCIS WYLIE b. April 30,1918 son of Frank Wylie and Susie (Littlejohn)Finney. He m. Oct. 20,1939 CHLORIENE ANDERSON, b. June 9, 1910. They adopted FRANCIS SUSAN FINNEY. (P1FF-4)
7. FRANK WYLIE, b. April 14,1884, son of David and Sarah (Patterson) Finney. He m. Marach 11,1913 SUSIE LITTLEJOHN (P 1DF 7-3)
ISSUE:

   1. ELLEN SIMPSON FINNEY, b. Jan 1914.
   2. WILLIAM DAVID FINNEY, b. Jan 23,1916,
   3. FRANK WYLIE JR b. April 30, 1920 .
   4. ANNA MARGARET, b. Feb. 7, 1920.

8. FRANK LEWIS, b. Nov. 29,1945 son of Thomas Ryan and Flora May (Roberts)Finney. He m. BARBARA JEAN GEIER. (P.75-735)
9. FRANK LESLIE b. Aug. 15,1879 son of William G. and Susan Rosine (Lester)Finney. (P71-705)
ISSUE:

   1. RUBY JEWEL FINNEY b. April 12,1905 m. _____TERRY.
      A. FRANK PATRICK TERRY.
   2. DELILA ROSINE FINNEY b. June 8,1911 m. MARION LEE THOMAS They had two children names unknown at this time.

FINNEY:

1. GARRON DWIGHT, b. Nov. 27, 1941 son of Dwight and Charlotte (Gates) Finney. (P4DF2-2)

2. GEORGE b. 1773 son of Jabez and Elizabeth Finney (P41-294)

3. GEORGE b. April 11, 1795 son of George and Henrietta (Mathews) Finney. She was the dau of Caleb and Susanna (Pierce)Mathews. (P41-357)

4. GEORGE, b. 1839 son of James and Sarah Finney (P57-594)

5. GEORGE QUENTIN, son of Rufus E and Mildred Catherine (Millikan) Finney. (4RF5-4)

6. GEORGE, b. 1843 son of John French and Rebecca (Butler) Finney. (P58-605)

7. GEORGE, b. 1770 d. at sea May 9, 1787 son of Josiah and his second wife, Martha (Gibbs)Finney. (P28-254)

8. GERTRUDE MAY (ATKINSON) 2nd wife of Robert Johnson Finney. (P68-659)

9. GILLA (HOFFMAN) wife of Daniel William Finney (P63-655)

10. GLADYS (CLINE) b. April 1898 wife of Charles Wesley Finney. (P71-707)

NOTES

FINNEY:

1.   HALLIE, dau of Thomas and Emma G. (Whitman)Finney. (P62-652)

2.   HANNAH, b. 1657 dau of John and Elizabeth (Bailey) Finney. (P4-8)

3.   HANNAH, b. Jan. 14,1687 dau of Jeremiah and Esther (Lewis)Finney. (P11-36)Her children.

4.   HANNAH, b. March 10,1761 dau of John and Hannah (Washburn) (P31-291)

5.   HANNAH, dau of Jabez and Elizabeth Finney (P32-295)

6.   HANNAH, b. 1776 dau of Jeremiah and Deborah Finney. (P41-268)

7.   HANNAH (HICKMAN) b.1783 wife of Robert Finney. (P56-547)

8.   HAROLD CHARLES, b. 1898 son of David and his second wife, Harriet (Way)Finney. (P1DF7-8)

9.   HAROLD RHODES, b. March 8, 1900 son of Clyde and Sylvia (Rhodes) Finney. (P2CF1 5-1)

10.   HARRIET JANE, dau of Porter Milroy and Edna Householder)Finney. (133F)   1PF10-1

11.   HARRIET(WAY) wife of Harold Charles Finney. (P1HF-8) Her children (P1DF-7)

12.   HAWKINS COOK, b. Aug. 28,1815 son of Joseph and Mary Polly (Long)Finney. (P60-628)

13.   HELEN (McCONNELL)wife of David Wesley Finney. (P67-656)

14.   HELEN SUSANNA, b. Nov. 9, 1904 dau of William Herbert and Susanna (Bell) Finney. (20F)   2WF4-2

15.   HELEN VIRGINIA, dau of Porter Milroy and Edna Householder. (P1PF10)

16.   HENRY, son of Robert and Isabell Finney (P49-501)

17.   HEMAN, son of Joel and Ann (Sackett) Finney (P41-351)

18.   HIRAM, son of James and Sarah Finney b. 1845. (P57-598)

19.   HOWARD PATTERSON, son of David and Sarah (Patterson)Finney. He was b. May 31,1882.   (1DF7-1)

20,   HULDAH (GIFFORD) wife of Abraham Finney. (P.41-314)

FINNEY FAMILIES

FINNEY:

1. IRENE, b. March 27, 1749 dau of William and Abigail (Black) Finney; (P30-277)

2. ISAAC, b. Oct. 5, 1759 son of David and Abigail (Clark) Finney. (P32-293)

3. IVA ELBERTA, b. Feb. 13,1901 dau of David and his second wife,Harriet Way Finney. Iva m. June 9, 1925 Colin L. For-sythe. _____ 1DF7-9

ISSUE: FORSYTHE

1. DAVID WILLIAM b. July 25, 1926.

2. ELBERTA BELL b. March 11,1928.

FINNEY"

1.   JABEZ, son of John and Ann (Toogood) _____ 32-136
2.   JAMES, son of Robert and Isabell _____ 49-502
3.   JAMES, son of William and Jean (Stephenson) _____ 53-524
4.   JAMES, son of John and Ruth (Lloyd) _____ 53-546
5.   JAMES, the Second, son of James and Martha (Mayes) _____ 57-551
6.   JAMES, son of Robert and Jane _____ 57-560
7.   JAMES, son of James and his second wife, Sarah _____ **57-595**
8.   JAMES, SON OF DAvid Thompson and Hannah (Butler), _____ 58-607
9   JAMES ANDERSON son of Wesley and Mary (Hinshaw) _____ 65-674
10. JAMES EDWARD, son of Carl Chester and Vivia(McClure)____ 73-713
11. JAMES BOYD b. Sept 4, 1914 son of William Herbert and
     Susanna (Bell) Finney. He m. June 20, 1943 **NEVA GATEWOOD**
     b. Sept 3,1917. _____ 2NF. 4-7
     ISSUE:

     1.   JAMES LEE FINNEY b. July 24,1944.
     2.   ROGER BOYD FINNEY b. May 5, 1947.
     _____

12. JAMES DAVID, b. April 24,1903 son of Dwghjt and Wave W.
     (Wooster) Finney. He m. April 24,1924 ALMA LANGE. She
     was b. April 9. 1903. _____ 4DF1-1
     ISSUE:

     1.   NEIL, b. Nov. 13,1927.
     _____

13. JAMES PATTERSON, son of William and his first wife, Jane
     (Patterson) Finney. James was b. 1837 d. 1918 he m. ELIZA-
     BETH (SHORT) March 22, 1865, _____ IN 623.
     ISSUE:

     1.   MINNEHAHA FINNEY b. Jan 24, 1867 _____ 5MF-r
     2.   WILLIAM HERBERT FINNEY b. March 21,1869 _____ 2WF-4
     3.   ROSCCAE RAITT FINNEY, Aug. 13, 1871 _____ 4RF2
     4.   SARAH JANE PEARL FINNEY b. July 15,1873 _____ 2S F 6
     5.   **DWIGHT** MacDILL FINNEY b. May 27,1876 _____ 4DF1
     _____

14. JAMES, son of James and Rebecca (Rheah) _____ 57-583

FINNEY:

1. JAMES, b. 1805 son of William and Margaret (Stewart)Finney. He never married. (77F) 6WF1-5

2. JAMES PATTERSON, b. 1862 son of Samuel and Mary (Lowry) Finney. (78aF) (1SF-6-6

3. JAMES CULBERTSON, b. 1833 d. 1908. son of Thomas and Nancy (Culbertson)Finney. (P1TF-4

4. JAMES LEE, b. July 24,1944 son of James Boyd and Neva (Gatewood) Finney. (P.1JF11-1)

5. JAMES, son of Robert and Polly Peden (2RF1-1)

6. JAMES, b. 1726 son of William and Jean (Stevenson) Finney. P51-524)

7. JAMES MADISON, b. Feb. 17, 1859 d. Aug. 23,1936. He m. Margaret Davis b. 1864 d. 1938. They were m. Feb. 20,1886 in Clark Co, Ill.
    ISSUE:

    1. NELLIE FINNEY, m._____HILLARD. She was b. Dec. 10, 1886 d. Dec. 10,1961.

    2. MYRTLE FINNEY, b. Nov. 24,1887 m._____LARRISON.

    3. LULA FINNEY, B. Feb. 28,1889 d. Feb. 20,1923. She m. a Mr. Cox.

    4. LENNA FINNEY b. Nov 6, 1890 d. May 31,1968: She m. a Mr. Huddlestun.

    5. JAMES OVAL, b. Nov. 11, 1897 m. HELEN ALEXANDER. (P2JF-8)

    6. ARTHUR OMER b. Feb. 10,1900 d. April 13,1970.

    7. OWEN LEE FINNEY b. Oct. 21,1901 d. Jan 25,1979.

    _____

8. JAMES OVAL, b. Nov. 11, 1897 son of James Madison and Margaret (Davis)Finney. He m. HELEN ALEXANDER June 12,1904.
    ISSUE:

    1. MARION FRANCES b. June 29,1927. She m. LOWELL LIVINGSTON. in 1949.

        A. JAMES LIVINGSTON m. DONNA HOWARD.

        B. JOAN LIVINGSTON m. a Mr. JENNINGS

            1. JODY JENNINGS.

            2. STACEY JENNINGS.

Records of Marion (Finney) Livingston.

_____

FINNEY:

1. JANE, dau of Robert and Polly (Peden)Finney. She m. ROBERT McCONNELL. (134F) (2RF1-6

2. JANE, dau of James and Sarah Finney (P57-585)

3. JANE (HOWE) wife of Andrew Finney (P53-557)

4. JANE, b. 1847 dau of David Thompson and Hannah(Butler)Finney. (P 58-609)

5. JANE, dau of Robert and Margaret (Guthrie)Finney. (P62-641)

6. JANE(STEPHENSON) WIFE OF William Finney (86F) In one place she is called JEAN and in another she is called JANE. (P.53-524)

7. JANE (PATTERSON) b. April 4,1816 wife of William Stewart Finney, She died in child-birth leaving nine children, Her children (5WF-1)

8. JANET LOU, b. March 22,1944 dau of Dwight MacDill and Charlotte (Gates)Finney. (4DF2-3)

9. JEAN b. 1752 dau of James and Martha (Mayes)Finney. (P53-552)

10. JEAN, b. 1759 dau of William and Jane (Stevenson) Finney.(P.51-534)

11. JEAN FLORENCE (MURDOCH)b. Nov. 1, 1920 wife of William David Finney. (P4M8) Her family (P2WF- 3)

12. JEAN SARAH (Makenson) wife of James Finney. (P53-546)

13. JEAN (STEVENSON) wife of William (P.51-510) Jean's maiden name is spelled two ways STEPHENSON.

14. JEMIMA b. Aug.15,1763 dau of David and Jemima (Warner)Finney. (P33-306)

15. JEMIMA (WARNER) wife of David Finney (P33-306 Her children (P33-144)

16. JEMIMA b. 1859 dau of David and Rachel Finney (P62-648)

17. JEMIMA dau of David and Jemima (Warner) _____ 33-306

18. JENNET dau of Robert. She m. DAVID MEAD_____ 54-559

19 JEREMIAH, son of John, the Pilgrim. _____ 2-11

20. JEREMIAH son of Jeremiah anmd Esther (Lewis)_____ 4-44

21. JERIMIAH, son of Josiah and Martha (Gibbs) _____ 28-246

22. JEREMIAH, kson of Jeremiah and Deborah _____ 29-267

FINNEY:

1. JEREMY SCOTT, b. Nov. 4, 1973 son of David Wesley and his first wife Becky (Burch)Finney. (P73-724)

2. JESSIE (GROSE) b. Nov. 30,1871 wife of Charles Edward Finney. (P71-695)

3. JOEL b. Feb. 24,1716/7 son of John and Ann (Toogood)Finney. (P. 13-128)

4. JOEL b. Sept. 1,1744 d. 1798 son of John and Rachel (Woodward) Finney (P.41-279)

5. JOEL, son of Joel and Ann (Sackett)Finney (P41-352)

6. JOHN, bpt.Sept 26,1773 son of Jeremiah and Deborah Finney. (P40-266)

7. JOHN b. Jan 12, 1762 son of John and Rachel (Woodward)Finney. (P.31-284)

8. JOHN, b. July 19,1757 son of John and Hannah (Washbuurn) Fommeu. (P31-290)

9. JOHN, son of Robert and Dorothea Finney. (P50-506)

10. JOHN, b. Nov. 1749 son of John and Sarah (Richardson) Finney. (P.50-517)

11. JOHN, b. 1730 d. July 5, 1782 son of Lazarus and Catherine (Symonton) Finney. (P53-521)

12. JOHN b. 1745 son of William and Jane (Stevenson)Finney, (P54-532)

13. JOHN, FRENCH, d. 1794 son of David and Ann (Thompson) Finney (P.52-538)

14. JOHN, son of John and Ruth (Lloyd) Finney (P53-548)

15. JOHN, b. 1760 son of James and Martha (Mayes)Finneyi. (P53-.

16. JOHN, son of John and Ann Dorothea (Finney) Finney. (P54-532)

17. JOHN FRENCH, b. Feb.9,1798 son of David Thompson and Mary (James)Finney. (P58-562)

18. JOHN, b. 1784 son of James and Martha (Crunkleton)Finney. (P57-581)

19. JOHN, b. 1835 son of John French and Rebecca (Butler)Finney. 58-

20. JOHN LONG b. Dec. 16,1810 son of Joseph and Mary Polly (Long) Finney. (P60-626)

21. JOHN EDGAR, son of Thomas and Emma G. (Whitman)Finney.(P67-653.

FINNEY:

1. JOHN son of Thomas G and Margaret G. (Nash)Finney. (P67-690)

2. JOHN WESLEY, b. Feb. 14,1862 in Indiana son of Wesley and
   Mary Matilda (Hinshaw)Finney. 69-678

3. JOHN V. son of Hawkins and Martha (Counte)Finney. (P68-663)

4. JOHN, m. ELIZABETH HEART, dau of John Heart of Mill Creek,
   Mo. John was b. Aug. 22,1823 d. April 19.1909. He m. Elizabeth
   Oct. 23,1845. at Berger, Mo. It is unknown who John's parents were
   at this time.

   ISSUE:

   1. NANCY J. FINNEY, b. Nov. 12,1847, Robertsville, Mo.
   2. WILLIAM R. FINNEY b. June 27,1849.
   3. JOHN M. FINNEY, b. Dec. 23,1853 d. April 27,1894.
   4. JAMES FINNEY b. Sept. 11,1855 d. Sept 6,1953.
   5. ELIGE T. FINNEY, b. Oct. 12,1861 d. Dec. 26,1909
   6. ZIMRI G. FINNEY, b. May 6,1863 d. July19,1931.
   7. BENJAMIN F. Finney, b. Jan 18,1866 d. Dec. 12,1866
   8. TIMOTHY FINNEY.
   9. MARY FINNEY, b. Feb. 8,1878 and died the same day.
   All of these children were born and died in Robertsville, Mo.

   ---

5. JOHN, son of Robert and Nancy (Neven) Finney.   2RF2-1

6. JOHN CHARLES, b. Nov. 7, 1920 son of Dwight and Wave (Wooster)
   Finney (26F)He m. JANE ANN POOLER, b. Aug. 26,1925 dau of

7. Arthur Charles and Olive Virginia Pooler. John had a very good Army
   recordhaving been a soldier in the 2nd World War. He served in the
   Asiatic Pacific Theater and had won the World War II Victory Metal,
   Good Conduct Metal; the American Campaign Metal ; The Bronze
   Arrowhead and the Phillippine Liberation Ribbon with two bronze
   stars. He was engaged in campaigns in the Philippines and in Oki-
   nowa and was never wounded. **His family**   IN-569

   ---

8. JOHN CRAIG, b. 1846 d. 1929 son of Elijah and his second wife
   Maria (Dougal-Marshall) Finney. (76F)   1EF8-8

FINNEY:

1. JOHN, **the pilgrim** d. 1703 son of "Mother" Finney _____ 1&2-3
2. JOHN, b. Dec. 24, 1638 son of John and Christiana _____ 3-4
3. JOHN, son of Jeremiah and Esther (Lewis) _____ 4-38
4. JOHN, son of Jeremiah and Esther (Lewis) _____ 12-42
5. JOHN, son of Joshua and Mercy (Watts) _____ 13-48
6. JOHN, son of Joshua and Martha (Carter) _____ 31-126
7. JOHN, son of John and Ann (Toogood) _____ 31-129
8. JOHN JR son of John and Ann Dorothea _____ 54-561
9. JOHNSTON, son of Washington and Martha _____ 59-614
10. JONATHAN, son of Josiah and Elizabeth (Mann) _____ 33-145
11. JONATHAN, son of Jonathan and Phebe (Phelps) _____ 33-308
12. JONATHAN, son of John French and Rebecca (Butler) _____ 58-600
13. JONATHAN, son of David Thompson and Hannah (Butler) ____ 58-611
14. JONATHAN DAVID, son of David Wesley and Becky (Burch) 73-727
15. JONATHAN SACKETT, son of Joel and Ann (Sacket(t) _____ 41-355B
16. JOSEPH, son of William and Abiogail (Clark) _____ 30-278
17. JOSEPH, son of John and Ruth (Lloyd) _____ 53-545
18. JOSEPH, son of Joseph and Rachel (Barkley) _____ 60=571
19. JOSEPH, son of Robert and Hannah (HIckman) _____ 56-575
20. JOSEPH, son of James and Sarah _____ 57-587
21. JOSEPH son of Joseph and Mary Polly (Long) _____ 60,625
22. JOSEPH DAVIES, son of Richard King and Rebecca (Davies) 66-636
23. JOSEPH, son of Robert and Margaret (Guthrie) _____ 62-638
24. JOSEPH HARRISON, son of Robert and Malinda (Hunt) _____ 68-661
25. JOSEPH FIELDING, son of William G. and Susan Rosine

    (Lester) _____ 72-704
26. JOSEPH MICHAEL, son of Thomas Ryan and Flora May

    (Roberts) _____ 75-734
27. JOSEPH b. 1851 son of Hawkins Cook _____ 64-668

_____

FINNEY:

1. JOSIAH, son of Joshua and Mercy (Watts) _____ 14-50
2. JOSIAH son of Jeremiah and Elizabeth (Bristow) _____ 28-115
3. JOSIAH, son of Joshua and Martha (Carter) _____ 13-123
4. JOSIAH, son of Josiah and Elizabeth (Mann) _____ 33-141
5. JOSIAH NORTON, son of Thomas and Elizabeth (Clark) _____ 29-272
6. JOSIAH, son of Josiah and Sarah (Carter) _____ 33-296
7. JOSIAH, son of John and Elizabeth (Bailey) _____ 2-10
8. JOSHUA, son of John and Elizabeth (Bailey) _____ 5-12
9. JOSHUA, son of John and Mercy (Watts) _____ 13-46
10. JOSHUA son of John and Ann (Toogood) _____ 13-131
11. JOSHUA, son of Joseph and Rachel (Barkley) _____ 61-572

NOTES

FINNEY:

1. JULIA PEARL b. June 11, 1908 dau of Dwight M. and Wave
   Washington (Wooster) Finney. She m. March 28, 1929 CARL
   HERSCHEL BROADBENT. b. Sept. 4, 1906 _____ 4DF1-3
   ISSIE: *BROADBENT*
   1.   CARLDON   2. NEIDA VONNE   3.. BEVERLY JO.

2. JURIAH (COLLINS) wife of Joshua Finney _____ 61-572

3. JUSTINE LILLIA b. June 19,1926 dau of William Herbert and
   Susanna (Bell) Finney. She m. Sept 9, 1945 HAROLD OLSON
   b. Oct. 6, 1921 in Lindsborg, Kansas. He was a pilot in the
   United States Air Force. in World War II and made fifty--
   four missions over Germanyj and was given the air metal
   with six Oak Leaf Clusters;   the distinguished Flying Cross
   and Eight Battle Stars. _____ 2WF4-10

NOTES

1. KAREN DEANNE b. Nov. 16,1954 dau of Tommie Milton and his second wife,Rose Mary (High-Amerine)Finney. (P72-721)

2. KENNETH ALLAN, b. July 14,1979 son of Donald Allan and Dana Lois (Cook)Finney (P3DF-4-3)

3. KEZIAH b. March 5, 1730 dau of Josiah and Elizabeth (Mann)Finney. (P14-142)

NOTES

FINNEY:

1.   LAURA A. (BOWMAN) 3rd wife of William C. _____ 31-688

2.   LAZARUS, son of Robert and Dorothea _____ 50-508

3.   LAZARUS, son of William and Jane (Stephenson) _____ 51-529

4.   LAZARUS, son of Robert and Diana (Spencer). He was b. Sept. 9,1751 d. Oct. 3,1883. It is believed by this compiler that the dates are in error as it would make him living 132 years. However, these were the dates in the records examined. _____ 52-544

5.   LETITIA, dau of Robert and Dorothea _____ 51-509

6.   LEVI LORING, b. Dec 28,1791 son of Loring and Experience (Pearse). _____ 39-347

7.   LEVINIA, dau of Josia and Sarah (Carter) _____ 33-297

8.   LIDES, dau of Joel and Ann (Sacket) _____ 41-355

9.   LILLIE, b. Aug. 1879 dau of William and Lizzie (Reynolds) Finney. She m. April 25, 1900 JOHN SHALER b. June 12,1872
   ISSUE: *SHALER.*
   1. *MAE b. Feb. 12, 1901 m. July 16,1922 IRA WILLIAMS b. March 17,1903. They had one child HAROLD WILLIAMS.*

10.   LIZZIE (Reynolds) wife of William. Their children _____ 5WF-2

11.   LIZZIE (SHORT) wife of James Patterson Finney. Her children __ 1JF 13

12.   LORENA (MORGAN) wife of Joseph, dau of Kenshen and Sarah Morgan. _____ 60-625

13.   LORING, son of Jeremiah and Deborah _____ 29-261

14.   LOUISA MAY, dau of Wesley and Matilda (Hinshaw) _____ 65-679

15.   LOUISEY ELIZABETH (ROARK) wife of John. For children _____ 5JF5

16.   LUCINDA (NICHOLS) wife of William _____ 2RF1-5

17.   LUCINDA, dau of Josiah and Sarah (Carter) _____ 33-300

18.   LUCRETIA dau of David Thompson and Hannah (Butler) _____ 58-610

19.   LUCRETIA, dau of Hawkins Cook _____ 64-670

20.   LOUISE SUE ANN, dau of James and Sarah _____ 57-597

21.   LULA, dau of James Madison and Margaret (Davis) _____ 2JF7-3

FINNEY:

1.   LAVONIA,   dau of Hawkins Cook _____ 64-666

2.   LYDIA, dau of **Donathan**, and Phebe (Phelps) Died young ____ 33-313

3.   LYDIA ANN dau of Richard King and Rebecca (Davis)._____61-637

4.   LYDIA,   dau of Josiah and Elizabeth (Mann)._____ 14-143

5.   LYDIA (JENKIN:S) wife of Robert P. _____ 62-640

6.   LYDIA, dau of John and Rachel (Woodward)_____ 31-281

FINNEY:

1. MABEL ESTELLA, dau of Daniel and Mary Ann (Farlow)Finney. (P70-699)

2. MABEL (WARREL)b. Oct. 5,1896 wife of David Finney., who was the son of William and Lizzie (Renolds) Finney. (132F)   5WF-2

3. MAGGIE, wife of Hiram Ayers. (Margaret)(56 &60 F)She was b. Dec. 18,1840. Hiram was b. Aug. 31,1833. Margaret d.Feb. 10,1833. Hiram d. Aug. 3, 1917.

   ISSUE: A Y E R S.

   1. IDA DORA b. Oct.17,1866 d. April 28,1867.

   2. EUNICE CLYDE b. Feb. 25,1868 m. WILLIAM HENRY CRUMBLING..

   3. JAMES CRAIG b. June 17, 1871 never married.

   4. WILLIAM HOMER b. Jan 8, 1874 m. Nov. 26, 1902 GRACE ANNA GAMBILL.

   5. RALPH ERSKINE b. Feb. 11,1880 m. VIOLET MAY SCOTT. and (2)April 12,1916 MARY ELIZABETH LAWRENCE.

   _____

4. MALINDA CATHERINE b. 1855 dau of Robert and Matilda (Hunt) Finney. (P63-662)

5. MALINDA (HUNT), b. Sept 20,1815 wife of Robert Finney. (P63-624)

6. MARCIA HELEN b. Feb. 20,1932 dau of Richard Harrison and Amanda E. (Milliken)Finney. (P71-703)

7. MARGARET (BADDERS) wife of Oliver Erbardt Finney. They were married May 31,1928. (134F)   They had a son. RICHARD DAVID b. Dec. 18,1931 at Glassport, Pa.   IN-23

8. MARGARET, b. 1774/5 dau of James and Martha (Crunkleton) Finney. (P57-577)

9. MARGARET, b. 1758 dau of James and Martha (Mayes)Finney. (P53-554)

10. MARGARET b. 1839 dau of Washington and Martha Finney. (P59-615)

11. MARGARET, b. 1826 d. 1895 dau of Thomas and Nancy (Culbertson) Finney. She never married. (78aF)

12. MARGARET, b. 1845 d. May 21,1935 dau of Elijah and his 2nd wife Maria (Dougal-Marshall) Finney. (P1EF-8)

13. MARGARET b. 1840 d. 1883 dau of William Stewart and his 1st wife Jane (Patterson) Finney. She m. HIRAM AYERS.

   ISSUE: AYERS.   See No 3 above for children.

FINNEY:

1. MARGARET LORRAINE,b. Aug 7,1916 dau of William Herbert and
    Susanna (Bell)Finney. She m. May 1,1936 CLARENCE ANDREW WALKER.
    He was b. Nov. 24,1914.   **2WF4-8**
    ISSUE: W A L K E R

    1. VIRGINIA CLAIRE b. Sept. 13,1944.

    ---

2. MARGARET (Guthrie) b. c1806 wife of Robert b. 1777 (P62-578)
3. MARGARET (PEGGY)RECTOR, b. 1812 dau of Joseph and Ann
    (Kesster) Finney. (P56-574)
4. MARGARET (NASH) b. May 1848 wife of Thomas G. Finney.
    (P67-643)
5. MARGARET (JEFFERSON0 wife of William who was the son of
    John and Ruth (Lloyd) Finney. (P53-549) They had children but
    none were listed by name.
6. MARGARET (SWAN) wife of Thomas (P53-550)
7. MARIA, dau of Robert and Margaret (Guthrie)Finney (P62-639)
8. MARIA (DOUGAL-MARSHALL)wife of Elijah Finney. She was his
    second wife. (P1EF-8)
9. MARILYN (BRANT) wife of Owen Engler Finney (P73=715)
10. MARION, b. Feb. 25,1905 dau of Charles Edward and Jessie
    Grose)Finney. (P71-708) She d. one day old.
11. MARTHA, b, March 4m1719/20dau of Joseph and Martha (Carter)
    Finney. (P13-125)
12. MARTHA, b and d. June 12,1738 dau of John and Ann (Toogood)
    Finney. (P13-135)
13. MARTHA, dau of Josiah and Martha (Gibbs) Finney (P37=250)
14. MARTHA b. 1740 dau of William and Jean (Stephenson)
    (P54-530)
15. MARTHA, b. 1780 dau of James (P57-579)
16. MARTHA, b. 1811 wife of Washin;gton Finney. (P59-565)
17. MARTHA (MAYES) WIFE OF James Finney. (P53-524)
18. MARTHA (COUNTE) wife of Hawkins Finney. (P64-628)
19. MARTHA (CRUNKLETON)wife of James Finney (P57-551)

3MF
FINNEY:

1.   MARTIN, b. June 20,1751 son of John and Hannah (Washburn)
      Finney (P31-288)

2,   MARY, b. March 26,1686 dau of Jeremiah and Esther (Lewis)
      Finney (P4-35)

3.   MARY, b. Sept. 25,1694 dau of Joshua and Mercy (Watts)Finney.
      (P5-47)

4.   MARY, b. 1742 dau of Jeremiah and Elizabeth (Bristow) Finney.
      (P30-120)

5.   MARY (MERCY), b. July 5,1718 dau. of Joshua and Martha (Car-
      penter)Finney. (P13-124)

6.   MARY b. 1770 dau of Jeremiah and Deborah Finney. (P40-265)

7.   MARY, dau of John French and Rebecca (Butler) Finney (P58-602)

8.   MARY, dau of Thomas G. and Margaret (Nash) Finneyi. (P67-691)

9.   MARY, b. 1762 dau of James and Martha (Mayes)Finney (P53-556)

10.   MARY ANN, dau of Joseph and Mary Polly (Long) Finney (P66-635)

11.   MARY ANN (Farlow) wife of Daniel Webster (P70-680)

12.   MARY C. b. May 8,1857 dau of Wesley and Mary Matilda
      (Hinshaw) Finney. (P69-675)

13.   MARY (CAMPBELL)wife of John Finney. (P12-42)

14.   MARY(CHESTER) wife of Thomas Finney. (P51-511)

15.   MARY (COGHORN) wife of James b. 1768 son of John and
      Ruth(Lloyd) Finney. (P53-546)

16.   MARY (CAREY)wife of Josiah and his first wife. (P28-115).

17.   MARY (COY) wife of Jeremiah Finney (P29-118)

18.   MARY E. wife of James Finney (P58-607)

19.   MARYE (sic)b. Aug. 29,1666 dau of Robert and Isabel Finney.
      (P49-504)

20.   MARY (FERGUS) b. Oct. 23,1891 wife of Robert Colemore Finney.
      (133F)   3RF-1

21.   MARY PEARCE m. Captain Josiah Coggeshall . (P44-346)

22.   MARY E. (COSSETT) 3rd wife of Hawkins Cook Finney (p64-628)

23.   MARY, dau of thomas and Emma (Whitman)_____ 62-650

FINNEY:

1. MARY ELIZABETH, b. June 10,1847,dau of Robert and Malinda (Hunt)Finney (P63-660)

2. MARY JANE b. May 10,1843 dau of William Stewart and Jane (Patterson)Finney.   5WF1-4

3. MARY JANE, b. July 4,1806 dau of David Thompson and Mary(James) Finney. (P55-566)

4. MARY (JAMES) wife of David Thompson Finney (P55-541)

5. MARY MATILDA (HINSHAW) wife of Wesley Finney (P65-632)

6. MARY JAY, dau of Carl Chester and Vivia Jay (McClure) Finney. (P73-710)

7. MARY ISABEL (LESTER) 1st wife of William G. Finney. (P71-688)

8. MARY (HITCHCOCK) wife of Robert P. Finney (P62-640)

9. MARY (LOWRY)wife of Samuel Finney. (P2JF-2)

10. MARY (O'HARA) wife of Walter Finney. (P55-533)

11. MARY (POLLY) dau of William and Margaret (Stewart)Finney.
    She was b. 1796 d. Dec. 31,1867 Unmarried (76F)   6WF1-2

12. MARY POLLY (LONG)b.April 2,1786 wife of Joseph Finney. (P60-571)

13. MARY POLLY (PEDEN) d. July 16,1850. wife of Robert Finney. (P53-558)

14. MARY R. b. 1843 dau of Washington and Martha Finney.(P59-617)

15. MARY (ROGERS)dau of Lt. John Rogers of the MAYFLOWER. (P3-4)

16. MARY (TAYLOR)wife of John Finney (P53-555)

17. MEHITABLE bpt Jan 19,1688 dau of Jonathan and Joanna Finney. (P3-28)

18. MEHITABLE, b. May 8,1687 dau of Jeremiah and Esther (Lewis) Finney. (P4-37)

19. MERCY, dau of John and Ann (Toogood)Finney. (P13-133)

20. MERCY, b. March 25,1732 dau of Samuel and Elizabeth (Wood)Finney. (P14-138)

21. MICHAEL CHARLES, son of John Charles and Jane Ann (Pooler) Finney. (30aF) He was b. April 4, 1947/ IN 569-1

22. MINETTE ELIZABETH b. July 29,1903 dau of William Herbert and Susanna (Bell) Finney . Wife of Ray Edward Harruff Her children. (IN 295)

FINNEY:

1. MINNEHAHA OLIVE, b. Thursday Jan 24,1867 at Pittsburg, Ind. dau of James P. and Elizabeth (Short) Finney. _____ (1JF13-1)

2. MIRANDA, b. 1788 dau of Joel and Ann (Sackett) Finney. (P41-355D)

3. MOLLY, b. Dec. 5, 1763, dau of Thomas and Elizabeth (Clark) Finney. _____ (P29-271)

4. MOLLEY (sic)dau of Josiah and Mary (Carey) his first wife. (P28-249)

5. "MOTHER" first of the Finney family to come to American Colonies. _____ (P-1)

NOTES

FINNEY:

1. NANA MAGETTA dau of Clyde and Sylvia (Rhodes) _____ 2CF2

2. NANCY, dau of Robert and Margaret (Patterspm)_____ 2RF2-5

3. NANCY, dau of Joseph and Mary Polly (Long) _____ 60-627

4. NANCY (CULBERTSON) wife of Thomas_____ 1TF-4

5. NANCY (GAMBLE) wife of Howard Patterson Finney. He was ___ 1DF7-1
   b. May 31,1882 and m. Nancy Feb. 16,1922. In 1930 they
   lived in McKeespor. He was the son of David and Sarah (Patterson)Finney _____ 1HF-19

6. NANCY J. b. Nov. 12, 1847 s. April 10,1840 dau of John and
   Louisey Elizabeth (Roark)Finney. *(Records of Frances Mills)* ___ 5JF5-1

7. NANCY JEAN dau of William David and Jean Florence (Murdock). Their family _____ 2WF3-4

8. NANCY (NEVEN) wife of Robert Finney. She was his first
   wife. Their family_____ 2RF4

9. NANCY B. wife of John McKee; dau of William and Margaret
   (Stewart) Finney. She d. 1861 and John m. (2) Caroline Cobean
   (McConnell)who had a daughter.
   ISSUE: *McKEE*
   1. *JOSEPH m. SUSAN McCONNELL, his father's step-daughter.*
   2. *WILLIAM*
   3. *JOHN d. in 1864 age 13 years.*

10. NANNIE ELIZABETH b. Dec. 17,1905 dau of Dwight and Wave
    (Wooster)Finney. She m. April 28, 1926 WILLIAM ROSS YOKUM.
    He was b. July 10, 1903 _____ IN7732.
    ISSUE: *YOKUM*
    1. *OWEN OLIVER b. May 3, 1933*
    2. *LYNN DAVID b. Jan 2, 1943.*

11. NATHANIEL, son of John and Ann (Toogood) _____ 13-130

12. NELLIE, dau of James Madison; m. a Mr. Hillard _____ 23F7-1

FINNEY:

1. OLIVER ERBARDT, b. Aug. 6, 1904 son of David and Sarah (Patterson) Finney. He m. May 31, 1928 MARGARET BADDERS. (1DF7-10.
   ISSUE:
   1. RICHARD DAVID b. Dec. 18, 1931.

   ———————

2. OLIVER, b. Nov. 11, 1728, son of Joshua and Martha (Carter) Finney.   (P31-127)

3. OWEN ENGLER b. July 9, 1909 Muncie, Indiana, son of Joseph Fielding and Stella Scott (Engler)Finney. ———————————— (P73-715.

   ———————

NOTES

FINNEY:

1.   PAMILA ANN, b. January 1, 1841 d. March 3, 1843 dau of Robert and Matilda (Hunt) Finney. (P63-657)

2.   PARKE DELANEY (HUNT) wife of John Long Finney. (P60-626)

3.   PATRICIA ANN b. July 25, 1945 dau of Dwight MacDill and Charlotte (Gates) Finney. (30F)   4DF2-4

4.   PEARL, b. July 15, 1873 wife of Andrew Milton Stevenson. They were m. Dec. 21, 1898.

     ISSUE: STEVENSON

     1.   ELIZABETH ISABEL b., Aug. 7, 1900 d. May 26, 1909 of Scarlet Fever.

     2.   DAVIDA FINNEY b. June 8, 1902 d. Sept 4, 1931 of Peritonitis.

     3.   JAMES PAUL b. Dec. 31, 1903 m. Sept. 4, 1937 JOSEPHINE READ b. Jan. 23, 1909 He is an attorney.

     4.   RUTH MINNEHAHA b. Aug. 26, 1906 m. Sept. 12, 1933 CARL DONALD SHULTZ b. June 10, 1906 . They have two children (See Schultz for children). IN 624

5.   PHEBE b. Feb. 22, 1762 dau of Jonathan and Phebe (Phelps) Finney. (P33-310)

6.   PHEBE, (PHELPS) WIFE OF Jonathan Finney. (P33-145)

7.   POLLY (PEDEN) wife of Robert Finney. It is evident that Mary Polly and Polly Peden is one and the same person. (P53-558)

8.   POLLY b. Jan 21, 1818 dau of Joseph and Mary Polly (Long) Finney. (P64-628)

9.   POLLY HANNAH dau of Wesley and Mary Matilda (Hinshaw) Finney. (P65-677)

10. PORTER MILROY, b. March 30, 1896 son of David and his 2nd wife HARRIET (WAY) FINNEY. He m. Dec. 18, 1922 EDNA HOUSEHOLDER (133F) 1DF7-7

     ISSUE:

     1.   HARRIET JANE FINNEY b. June 23, 1925.

     2.   ROBERT DAVID FINNEY b. Nov. 19, 1926.

     3.   HELEN VIRGINIA FINNEY,

NOTES

FINNEY:

_____   _____

1. ROBERT, Sr. m. POLLY PEDEN' as a first wife . They had seven childrden. He m. (2) DORIS_____. _____ IN 5€1

   ISSUE:

   1. JAMES.
   2. THOMAS
   3. JOHN.
   4. ROBERT JR.
   5. WILLIAM m. LUCINDA NICHOLS.
   6. JANE m. ROBERT McCONNELL
   7. SARAH m. JOSEPH WADDELL.

   _____

2. ROBERT JR. son of Robert and Polly (Peden)Finney m. (1) NANCY NEVIN (2) MARGARET PATTERSON. She was b. Aug. 15 1818. Robert was b. c1816 He had four children by Nancy.

   1. JOHN A. FINNEY.
   2. ROBERT FINNEY.
   3. JOSEPH FINNEY.
   4. MARY FINNEY m. JOHN MUSGRAVE WATT.

   Children by Margaret:

   5. NANCY (131F)
   6. SARA JANE m. ALEXANDSER McCLURE. ____ 1SF-8
   7. WILLIAM b. Nov. 1851 m. LIZZIE REYNOLDS. _____ 5WF-2
   8. DAVID m. SARAH PATTERSON and (2) HARRIET WAY. (1DF=7)

   _____

3. ROBERT JOHN b. Dec. 31, 1942 son of William and Jean Florence (Murdoch) Finney. (147F) _____ 2WF-3÷3

4. ROBERT, son of Robert and Nancy (Neven) Finney. (2RF2-2)

   _____

   NOTES

FINNEY:

1,   ROBERT COLEMORE b. Sept '22,1888 son of David and Sarah (Patterson) Finney. He m. Aug. 24,1915 MARY FERGUS. She was b. Oct. 23,1891. 1DF7-4

ISSUE:

1.   ELEANOR BELL (P2EF4)
2.   LOIS MARIE
3.   RUTH NORMA.

---

2.   ROBERT DAVID, b. Nov. 19, 1926 son of Porter Milroy and Edna(Householder) Finney. (133F) (1PF-10-2)

3.   ROBERT, b. c1630 m. ISABELL (P49-500)

4.   ROBERT, b. in Ireland 1668 son of Robert and Isabell (P49-505)

5.   ROBERT, son of Robert and Dorothea Finney (P49-507)

6.   ROBERT, d. 1771 son of John and Elizabeth (French)Finney. (P50-515)

7.   ROBERT, b. 1727 son of Lazarus and Catherin;e (Symonton) Finney (P50-520)

8.   ROBERT, b. 1742 son of William and *Jean (Stevenson)Finney.(P54-531)

9.   ROBERT, son of Thomas and Mary (Chester) Finney. (P51-535)

10.   ROBERT, b. 1783 son of John; and Ruth (Lloyd) Finney (P.53-547)

11.   ROBERT, B. 1765 son of James and Martha (Mayes) Finney. (53-558)

12.   ROBERT, b. 1777/8 son of James and Martha (Crunkleton)Finney. (P62-578)

13.   ROBERT, b. Aug. 23,1808 son of Joseph and Mary Polly (Long) Finney. (P60-625)

14.   ROBERT P. son of Robert and Margaret (Guthrie) Finney. (P62-640)

15.   ROBERT, m. MARGARET GUTHRIE (P62-578)

16.   ROBERT b. c1608 son of "Mother" Finney (P1-2)

17.   ROBERT, b. Aug. 13,1656 son of John, the Pilgrim (P2-7)

18.   ROBERT, son of James and Sarah Finney. (P57-586)

---

* Also spelled Stephenson.

1. ROGER BOYD, son of James Boyd and Neva (Gatewood) Finney. He was b. May 5, 1947. (1JF-11-2)

2. ROSCOE RAITT, b. Aug. 13,1871 son of James P. and Elizabeth (Short) Finney. He d. Feb. 4, 1885 (P.1JF-13-3)

3. RUBY JEWEL, b. April 12,1905 dau of Frank Leslie and Alice (Sea) Finney. She m. a Mr. TERRY. (P.1 FF 9-1)
    ISSUE: TERRY.

    1. FRANK PATRICK.

    _____

4. RUFUS, b. May 18,1760 son of John and Rachel (Woodward) Finney. He m. HANNAH FINNEY, dau of John and Hannah (Washburn) Finney. (P.31-283&291)

5. RUFUS, b. Aug. 13,1908. son of George and Mattie L. Finney. He m. MILDRED CATHERINE MILLIKEN b. Nov. 28, 1907 d. Jan. 27, 1980. She was the dau of Otis and Mary Ellen (Rheah) (Leavett) Milliken.
    ISSUE:

    1. DONALD ELSWORTH FINNEY (3DF-5)
    2. RICHARD OTIS FINNEY. (RF 16
    3. CHARLES LAWRENCE FINNEY (1CF-11)
    4. DAVID GARY FINNEY, (2DF-2)
    4. GEORGE QUENTIN FINNEY, (1GF-5)

    _____

6. RUTH b. April 7,1768 dau of Thomas and Elizabeth (Clark) Finney. (P.29-273)

7. RUTH b. 1818 dau of Robert and Hannah (Hickman)Finney.(P56-576)

8. RUTH THURSTON bpt Oct. 9,1781 dau of Josiah and Martha (Gibbs) Finney. (P.38-258)

9. RUTH (LLOYD) wife of John Finney (P53-521)

10. RUTH NORMA dau of Robert Colemore and Mary (Fergus)Finney. (3RF1-3)

FINNEY:

1. SAMATHA JANE b. Aug 7,1851 d. April 1937 dau of Wesley and Mary Matilda **(Hinshaw)** Finney. Her children (P68-673)

2. SAMUEL b. May 20,1699 son of Joshua and Mercy (Watts)Finney. (P14-49)

3. SAMUEL, b. 1835 son of Washington and Martha Finney. (P59-613)

4. SAMUEL, b. 1850 son of Thomas G. and Susanna (Cocherel)Finney. (P67-687)

5. SAMUEL, GUY, son of David and Sarah (Patterson) Finney.(P.1DF7-2)

6. SAMUEL b. 1813 son of William and Margaret (Stewart) Finney. He m. Oct. 14,1849 MARY LOWRY b. June 15,1821. Samuel died Aug. 29,1876 and Mary d. May 10,1892._____ 6WF1-7

   ISSUE:

   1. WILLIAM LOWRY FINNEY b. 1850 d. 1916.
   2. THOMAS JOHNSON b. 1852 d. 1915.
   3. MARGARET JANE b. 1854 d. 1938. She m. a Mr. MARTIN.
   4. SARA AGNES b. 1856 d. 1881m a Mr. WILSON.
   5. SAMUEL STEWART b. 1858 d. 1933
   6. JAMES PATTERSON, b. 1862 d. 1892.

   _____

7. SAMUEL PHILANDER b. Jan 17,1853 d. May 11,1853.son of William Stewart and Jane (Patterson) Finney. (78F) _____ 5WF7

8. SARA JANE; b. Sept 5,1848 dau of Robert and Margaret (Patterson) Finney. She m. ALEXANDER McCLURE. (P.2RF2-6)

   ISSUE: McCLURE.

   1. BELLE m. MELVIN REYNOLDS (P1BF-11))
   2. MARTHA CURRY m. ED HARPER
   3. ROBERT m. SUE SHARP.

   _____

9. SARAH, dau of Robert and Margaret (Patterson)Finney. She m. JOSEPH B. WADDELL (P2RF1-7)

10. SARAH,1767-1820 dau of Josiah and his second wife,Martha (Gibbs) Finney. Her children (P38-252)

11. SARAH b. June 6, 1761 dau of Josiah and Sarah(Carter) Finney. (P33-299)

12. SARAH, dau of David and Ann(Thompson) Finney. (P52=543)

FINNEY:

1. SARAH, dau of James and Sarah Finney. (P57-589)

2. SARAH, b. 1839 dau of David Thompson and Hannah (Butler) Finney. (P58-606)

3. SARAH, dau of Robert and Margaret (Guthrie) Finney.(P62-644)

4. SARAH AGNES,b. Jan. 16,1845 dau of William Stewart and Jane (Patterson) Finney. (78aF) _____ 5WF1-6

5. SARAH AGNES (VALODIN) wife of Joseph Harrison Finney. (P68-661)

6. SARAH JANE PEARL, b. July 15,1873 dau of James P. and Elizabeth (Short) Finney. (P.1JF 13-4)

7. SARAH M. (FISHER) 2nd wife of Joseph Davies Finney. (P66-636)

8. SARAH (PATTERSON) wife of David Finney (P.1DF7)

9. SARAH (RICHARDSON) wife of John Finney dau of John Richardson. (P50-506)

10. SARAH (THOMPSON) 2nd wife of William Finney. (P.5WF1) Children. See P.5WF-1)

11. SARAH (THOMAS) wife of John Finney (P31-126)

12. SARAH (WALTERS) second wife of Hawkins Cook Finney. (P64-628)

13. SHELLEY DIANE b. Dec. 5, 1963 dau of James Edward and Carol (Shelley)Finney. (P73-722)

14. SHIRLEY ANN, b. March 19,1933 dau of Forrest Fielding and Edna Ruth (Hart)Finney. (P74-730)

15. STEPHEN DAVID, b. July 24,2940 son of William : David and Jean Florence (Murdoch)Finney. (2WF-1 -1

16. STELLA, dau of John Wesley and Nancy (Brooks) Finney. (P69-698)

17. STELLA SCOTT (ENGLER) wife of Joseph Fielding Finney.(P72-704)

18. SUSAN ROSINE (LESTER) second wife of William G Finney. (P71-688)

19. SUSIE LITTLEJOHN) wife of Frank Wylie Finney(P1FF-7)

20. SUSANNA (BELL) wife of William Herbert Finney (P2WF.4

21. SUSANNA, bpt July 1772 dau of Josiah and his second wife, Martha (Gibbs) Finney. (P28-255)

22. SUSANNA, b. Dec. 22,1846 dau of William Stewart amd Jane (Patterson)Finney (P5WF- 1-5

FINNEY:

1. SUSANNA (SUSIE) b. 1801 d. May 25,1868 dau of William and Margaret (Stewart) Finney.   (6WF-4-4

2. SYLVESTER b. March 15,1759 son of Josiah and Sarah **(Carter)** Finney; (P33-298)

3. SYLVIA (RHODES) wife of Clyde Finney (P2CF-15)

NOTES

FINNEY:

1. THOMAS GIBBS b. 1768 d. at sea, son of Josiah and Martha
   (Gibbs) _____ 28-253

2. THOMAS RYAN SON OF Joseph and Stella Scott (Engler) 74-717

3. THOMAS son of Thomas Ryan _____ 74-733

4. THOMAS b. July 9, 1795 in Pennsylvania; m. Jan 4, 1827
   Nancy (Culbertson) b. Jan 29, 1806 in Guernsey Co, Ohio.
   In the early eighteen=thirties they lived on a farm near
   Mansfield, Ohio! Thomas d. May 26,1856; and Namcy d.
   Feb. 11, 1877. They had seven children.

5. TOMMIE LEE , son of William Herbert and Rбrзum (Eisele) 2WF5-1

6. TOMMIE MILTON son of Carl Chester   Family _____ 72-709

7. TOMMIE MILTON, son of Tommie Milton _____ 72-718

NOTES

FINNEY:

    1.   URIAH b. March 17,1761 son of David and Jemima (Warner)Finney.
        He served in the Revolutionary War from 1778 to 1780 (P33-305)

NOTES

FINNEY:

---

    1.   VAUGH LA RENE b. Sept 29,1919 child of Clyde and Sylvia
        (Rhodes)Finney(P2CF.15-6)

    2.   VIOLA MYRTLE b. Aug 21, 1911 dau of Clyde and Sylvia (Rhodes)
        Finney (P2CF15-4)

    3.   VIRGINIA LEE b. Nov. 23,1938 dau of Carl Chester and Vivia
        Jay' (McClure) Finney. (P72-711)

NOTES

FINNEY:

1. WALLACE RAY. son of Forrest Fielding and Stella Scott (Engler) _____ 74-732

2. wALTER, son of William and Jane (*Stevenson) _____ 55-533

3. WALTER B. son of James and 2nd wife Elizabeth (Braden) _____ 57-582

4. WASHINGTON twin to David Thompson, son of David _____ 52-542

5. WAVE WOOSTER dai pf Dwight and Wave Washington (Wooster) She m. Aug. 8, 1931 JAMES LOWELL CREIGHTON b. July 25,1909. Wave was b. Jan. 16,1911. _____ 4DF1-4

   ISSUE: *CREIGHTON.*

   1. Dorothy Jean

6. WESLEY, son of Joseph and Mary Polly (Long) _____ 65-632

7. WESLEY. spm pf Hawkins C. _____ 64-669

8. WHITMAN, son of John Edgar and (Wife unknown) _____ 67-693

9. WILLIAM, son of Joshua and Martha **(Carter)** _____ 30-122

10. WILLIAM, son of William and Elizabeth (Clark) _____ 30-275

11. WILLIAM, son of Robert and Isabell _____ 49-503

12. WILLIAM, son of Robert and Dorothea. He m. Jane Stephenson 51-510

13. WILLIAM, son of William and Jane Stephenson_____ 51-528

14. WILLIAM son of John and Ruth (Lloyd) He m. MARGARET JEFFERSON_____ 53-549

15. WILLIAM, son of William James and Mary (James)_____ 59-622

16. WILLIAM ARVEL, son of Joseph Davies and Amanda (Milliken) 70-682

17. WILLIAM, G. son of Robert and Margaret (Guthrie) ._____ 62-645

18. WILLIAM , son of Thomas G. and his first wife Margaret (Nash) 67-689

NOTES

*Jane Stevenson, is also known at JEAN STEPHENSON¬

FINNEY":

1. WILLIAM, F. son of John Edgar and wife unknown (P67-694)

2. WILLIAM JAMES, b. Dec. 6, 1811 son of David Thompson and Mary (James) Finney. (P59-568)

3. WILLIAM DAVID, b. Jan 23,1916 son of Frank Wylie and Susan (Littlejohn)Finney. (P1FF7- 2)He m. Sept 16,1939 JEAN FLORENCE MURDOCH b. Nov. 1,1920.

    ISSUE:

    1. STEPHEN DAVID. b. July 24, 1940
    2. WILLIAM THOMAS b. Aug. 27, 1941.
    3. ROBERT JOHN b. Dec. 31, 1942.
    4. NANCY JEAN b. Feb. 20,1944.

    ----

4. WILLIAM HERBERT b. March 21,1869 son of James P. and Elizabeth (Short) Finney. He m. SUSANNA BELL dau of William Coleman and Elizabeth (Smith) Bell. (See also 3WF-1)

    ISSUE:

    1. MINETTE ELIZABETH b. July 29,1903 (20F)   IN?295
    2. HELEN SUSANNA b. Nov.9,1904.
    3. ANABELLE b. Oct. 14,1906.
    4. CLAIRE b. March 8, 1908. m. GEORGE CRUMBAKER   IN 173
    *5. WILLIAM HERBERT JR.
    6. ESTHER b. Sept 11,1912 Her family 3EF-13
    7. JAMES BOYD b. Sept. 4,1914. m. NEVA GATEWOOD   !JF-11
    8. MARGARET LORRAINE b. Aug 7, 1916   2MF-1
    9, DWAINE LEE, b. May 15,1919 (22F)   3DF-10
    10. JUSTINE LILLIE b. June 9,1925   8JF-3

    ----

5. WILLIAM HERBERT son of William Herbert and Susanna (Bell) Finney. He m. EVELYN EISELE June 9, 1937. William was electrocuted while repairing a "High line" at Fort Collins, Colo., June 15,1943.

    ISSUE:

    1. TOMMIE LEE FINNEY b. Feb. 2, 1938.
    2. WILLIAM HERBERT b. April 6,1943.

FINNEY,

1. WILLIAM HERBERT (See also 2WF4.

Records of **THE FINNEY FAMILY HISTORY 1732 – 1946**

BY

MINNEHAHA FINNEY

* * * * * * * *

William Herbert, son of Rev. James Patterson and Elizabeth (Short) Finney, was born March 21, 1869 at Manhattan, Kansas. He died of diabetes mellitus, May 2,1931, at 3 a. m. at his home in Turkey Creek township, his age at the time of his death being 62 years, 1 month and 11 days.

When a youth, while at home, and not otherwise engaged, he helped with the farm work in which he felt a special interest. He took a great interest in the homestead which his parents took in Mitchell county in 1879, he being 10 years old at the time. He attended school at district 74 and later Beloit High School; in 1889 he went to Tarkio, Mo, and at once entered on his college studies in the institution located there. He was a diligent student and pleasant with his associates. After a course of study requiring six years, he graduated at Tarkio college, June 13,1895. For a year after his graduation he engaged in business of different kinds, as opportunity afforded. In the fall of 1896, he entered the Theological Seminary at Xenia, Ohio, graduating in 1898. He was an earnest, devoted Christian, very active in Christian effort in his younger years.

He came back to Mitchell county in 1899 to begin farming. He was married on October 22,1902 to Susannah Bell , who preceded him in death October 17,1926. They began housekeeping on the farm in the Pleasant View neighborhood where they had lived ever since. To that union ten children were born, one, of whom died in infancy. Two boys and seven girls survive and are as follows; Minette, Helen, Anabell, Claire,William, Esther,Boyd, Maragaret and Justine. Aside from his family of children, Mr. Finney is survived by his sisters, Miss. Minnehaha Finney in Egypt, and Mrs. Pearl Stevenson, Sterling, Kansas and his brother, Dwight M. Finney, Beloit, Kansas.

Robert Finney was a staunch member of the Pleasant View M.E. Church. He was always a sympathetic companion to his children in their Christian life. His worth as a community leader cannot be estimated. His efforts for Turkey Creek township were upon his mind to the very last for the township for which he had been trustee for the last twelve years..

FINNEY:

WILLIAM HERBERT (Cont.)

He always advocated that good roads came before education could come for the youth. His children shall always remember him as "Dad" which to them meant love, sympathy and interest in them. On receiving the cablegram,notifying his sister, Minnehaha, In Egypt, as a missionary, of her brother's death she answered with the scripture reference,first Thessalonians 4;13 **"But I would not have you to be ignorant, brethern, concerning them which are asleep, that ye sorrow not, even as others which have no hope!"**

The services were held Sunday at 3 PM at the Beloit M.E. Church with the Rev. L.R. Hendrick in charge. Internment was made in Elmwood cemetery.

NOTES

FINNEY:

1. WILLIAM STEWART, b. Dec. 18,1807 son of William and Margaret (Stewart) Finney. He m. May 5,1936 '(1) JANE PATTERSON b. April 4,1816. She d. Jan 26,1853 in childbirth. He m. (2) Mrs. SARA (THOMPSON) STEWART Nov. 7, 1853. She had a son, Newton Stewart, by her first husband. He grew up with his step-brothers and sisters.

   ISSUE, by first wife.

   1. JAMES PATTERSON FINNEY b. 1837 d. 1918 (P1JF13)
   2. WILLIAM FINNEY, b. 1839 d. 1853.
   3. MARGARET FINNEY b. 1840 d.1883 m. HIRAM AYERS (P1MF3)
   4. MARY JANE FINNEY b. 1843 d. 1923 n, DENNY BURNS SIMP-SON. (56F)
   5. SUSANNA FINNEY b. 1845 d. 1851.
   6. SARAH AGNES FINNEY, b. 1846 d. 1850
   7. ALPHRETTA FINNEY b. 1848 d.1926 m. JOHN CROUCH(2AF8)
   8. MARTHA EUNICE FINNEY, b. 1851 d. 1863.
   9. SAMUEL PHILANDER FINNEY b. 1853 d. same year.

   ———————

2. WILLIAM b. Nov. 1851 son of Robert and Margaret (Patterson)Finney. He m. Dec. 27,1876 LIZZIE REYNOLDS b. Jan 1,1856 d. 1908.
   ISSUE:

   1. CLYDE FINNEY, b Sept 22,1877 m. Feb. 8, 1898 SYLVIA RHODES. (P2CF14) for children.
   2. LILLIE FINNEY, b. Aug. 1879 (1LF9)
   3. ALICE FINNEY died young. (2AF4)
   4. DAVID FINNEY b. March 22, 1893 (P2DF3)

   ———————

3. WILLIAM, son of Robert and Polly (Peden) Finney. He married Lucinda Nichols (P2RF1-5

4. WILLIAM b. 1754 son of James and Martha (Mayes) Finney. He m. ANNE MORTON Nov. 2, 1781 and died. 1816.(P 53-553)

5. WILLIAM LOWRY b. 1850 son of Samuel and Mary (Lowry) Finney. 1SF6-1

6. WILLIAM SHANNON b. 1843 son of Thomas and Nancy (Culbertson) Finney. He d.1884. (78aF) **Parents** _____ 1TF4

7. WILLIAM R. b. June 27,1849 d. Feb. 1, 1890 son of John and Louisey Elizabeth (Roark) Finney. (p 5JF4-2)

FINNEY:

1. WILLIAM, son of Thomas and Susanna (Stewart). He was b. 1762 and d. May 11, 1821. He m. MARGARET STEWART b. Aug. 17, 1774 died Dec. 17, 1858.

   ISSUE:

1.	THOMAS b. July 9, 1795	1TF4
2.	MARY (Polly) b. 1796.	4MF11
3.	ELIJAH b. May 26,1799	1EF8
4.	SUSANNA (SUSIE) b. 1801	3SF1
5.	JAMES b. January 1805	2JF1
6.	WILLIAM STEWART b. Dec. 18, 1807	5WF1
7.	SAMUEL b. 1813	1SF6
8.	NANCY b. 1821	1NF-9

2. WILLIAM b. 1856 son of William James and Louisa _____ 59-622
3. WILSON, son of James and Sarah _____ 57-588

NOTES

FINNEY

1. ZEB, b. 1849 son of Thomas G. _____ 67-686

2. ZENA or ZERTIA b. Jan 14,1765. Child of Jonathan _____ 33-312

3. ZENAS b. 1764 child of Josiah and Sarah (Carter) _____ 33-301

4. ZELAH, dau of David and Sarah (Patterson)wife of ALBERT
   ROTH. Their children _____ IN 596

5. ZIMRI G. b. May 6,1863 d. July 19, 1911 son of John and
   Louisey Elizabeth (Roark)Finney _____ 5JF4-6

6. ZIMRI DIX b. March 18, 1842 d. Jan 14,1876. He m. RACHEL
   STEWART. He was the son of Robert and Matilda (Hunt) _____ 63-658

—————

NOTES

These families spell their name differently but are still part of the original family spelling their name F-I-N-N-E-Y, due to John Finney b. 1638. (Number 4) who married Mary Rogers, dau of Lt. John Rogers, son of Thomas Rogers who came to America on the *Mayflower*. Thomas and his son, John came together and the rest of the family came later. It is not known why John Finney spelled his name differently, but it is at this point that one family is known as the Bristol branch and the other as the Barnstable branch.

_____

PHINNEY:

1.	AARON, son of Elisha and hkis first wife Jemima (Treadwell)	27-238
2.	ABIGAIL, dau of Thomas and Sarah	6-72
3.	ABIGAIL, dau of Thomas and Reliance (Goodspeed)	15-161
4.	ABIGAIL (CAMPBELL) dau of Sylvanus, 1st wife of Ebenezer	10-32
5.	ABIGAIL (LUMBERT) wife of Thomas	20-71
6.	ACHSAH, child of Joseph and Mary (RIckard)	18-176
7.	ALBERT son of **James** and Mary C. Their children.	48-381
8.	ALICE, dau of Joseph and Mercy (Bryant) wife of EBENEZER HAMBLIN, JR.	6-61
9.	ALMINA dau of Seth and LYdia Jane	46-372
10.	AMANDA, dau of Benjamin and Betsey (Vorce)	36-341.
11.	AMY, dau of Joseph and Mary (Rickard)	18-179
12.	ANDREW, son of Frank and Ida (Ferris)	47-385
13.	ANNA (THOMAS) wife of Isaac	34-159
14.	ANNE dau of Jabez and Jane (Taylor)	17-165

_____

NOTES

162.

PHINNEY:

1.	BARNABAS, son of Benjamin and Martha (Crocker)	24-98
2.	BARNABAS, son of Zaccheus and Susan (Davis)	24-228
3.	BENJAMIN, son of John and Mary (Rogers). He was not listed in the oriaginal entry.	10-23
4.	BENJAMIN, son of Elisha and Jemima (Treadwell)	16-240
5.	BENJAMIN son of Zachues and Susan (Davis)	24-226
6.	BETHIAH, dau of Samuel and Bethya (Smith)	7-84
7.	BETHIAH (BUMP) wife of Seth	25-101
8.	BETHYA (SMITH) wife of Samuel	7-84
9.	BLISS, child of Peletiah and Mercy (Washburn)	19-190

———————

NOTES

1. CALISTA b. June 9, 1812 dau of Benjamin and Betsey (Vorce) Phinney. (P36-340)

2. CAROLINE b. April 7, 1819 dau of Benjamin and Betsey (Vorce) Phinney. (P43-343)

3. CAROLINE (BROWN) wife of George Phinney. (P45-369)

4. CASSIE, dau of Albert :wife of DANIEL SHAFER. (P48-381)

5. CHARLES HENRY, son of Benjamin and Betsey (Vorce) Phinney. (P36-344)

6. CLARASA b. Aug. 22, 1785 dau of Isaac and Huldah (Preston) Phinney. (P42-360)

7. CLARENCE, son of Albert (P48-393)

8. CLARISSA A. dau of James and Lois (Cody) Phinney. She m. G. V. NASH and had one child CLARENCE NASH. (From the Mason records)

9. COLEMAN, b. 1732 (?)son of John and Martha (Coleman)Phinney. (15-154)

10. CLEMENT, d. 1841 His father is unknown and he married RUTH _____. He d. Dec. 5, 1841. His children;

    ISSUE:
    1. JACOB M. PHINNEY b. Dec. 20, 1837 d. Aug. 22, 1838.
    2. JACOB M. PHINNEY, b. May 13, 1840.
    3. AUGUSTUS PHINNEY b. Dec. 22, 1841.

    ----

11. CLEMENT b. _____ d. ____ father is unknown. He m. SARAH_____
    ISSUE:
    1. RUTH MARIE PHINNEY.

NOTES

PHINNEY:

1. DANIEL, b. Sept 14,1768 son óf Elisha and Jemima (¨Treadwell)
    Phinney. (P35-239)

2. DAVID b. June 10,1710 son of Ebenezer and Susanna (Linnell)
    Phinney. (P22-82)

3. DAVID, b. March 28, 1756 son of Isaac and Elizabeth Kenney (P34-317)

4. DEBORAH, b. 1735 dau of David and Mary (Pope)Phinney. (P22-220)

5. DEBORAH, (WADE)b. 1651 d. 1738 wife of Jonathan Phinney.(P10-23)

6. DEXTER,b. Jan 25,1808 son of Benjamin and Betsey (Vorce)Phinney.
    (P36-338)

NOTES

PHINNEY:

1. EBENEZER, son of John and Mary (Rogers) _____ 7-17
2. EBENEZER, son of Jonathan and JOanna (Kinnicutt)._____ 10-32
3. EBENEZER, son of Ebenezer and Susanna (LInnell)_____ 22-81
4. EDMUND son of John and Martha (Coleman) _____ 15=147
5. EDMUND, son of Thomas and Mariah (Lumbert)_____ 20-204
6. EDNA, dau of Albert, wife of a Mr. PRICE _____ 48-391
7. ELI, son of Thomas and Reliance (Goodspeed) _____ 15-156
8. ELISHA, son of Jonathan and Mercy (Read) _____ 27-113
9. ELISHA, son of Benjamin and Betsey (Vorce) _____ 36-335
10. ELISHA PECK, son of Elisha and his second wife Rebecca **(Peck)** 27-242
11. ELISHA PECK, son of Daniel and his 2nd wife Elizabeth (Cran-
    ston) _____ 35.330
12. ELIZA, dau of Benjamin and Betsey (Vorce)_____ 36-336
13. ELIZA KINNICUTT dau of Daniel and Elizabeth (Cranston)_____ 43=325
14. ELIZABETH, dau of Thomas and Reliance (Goodspeed)_____ 15-162
15. ELIZABETH, dau of John and Sarah (Lumbert) _____ 14-52
16. ELIZABETH dau of Jonathan and Joanna (Kinnicutt_____ 3-29
17. ELIZABETH, dau of Johnand Martha (Coleman) _____ 15-146
18. ELIZABETH, dau of Jonathan an, wife of JOHN MACOMBER ____ 26-109
19. ELIZABETH, twin of Hannah, dau of John and Mary (Rogers) ____ 3-25
20. ELIZABETH (DURLAND) wife of Lot _____ 42-315
21. ELIZABETH (COOMER) wife of Daniel_____ 35-239
22. ELIZABETH, (ELIZA) (Cranston) 2nd wife of Daniel_____ 35-239
23. EMILY, dau of Seth and Lyidia Jane _____ 44-371
24. EMMA, dau of Daniel and wife of THOMAS EASTERBROOKS. ___ 42-324.
    Her children _____ 42-324
25. ESTHER, dau of Peletiah and Mercy (Washburn)_____ 19-188
26. ESTHER(WEST) wife of Joseph _____ 19-66
27. ETHEL dau of Frank and Ida (Ferris) _____ 47-389
28. EXPERIENCE dau of Joseph and his 2nd wife Esther (West) ____ 6-68
29. EXPERIENCE, dau of Joseph and Mary (Rickerd) _____ 18-175

1FPH

PHINNEY:

1. FLOSSIE, dau of Frank and Ida (Ferris) Wife of LEWIS WILSON   47-384
2. FRANK, son of George and Caroline (Brown)_____   47-379
3. FREELOVE, dau of Thomas and Abigail (Lumbert)_____ 20-208
4. FREELOVE, dau of Peletiah and Mercy (Washburn) _____ 19-182

———————

1GPH

1GPH

PHINNEY

1. GEORGE, son of Seth and Lydia Jane _____ 45-369
2. GERSHOM, son of Thomas and Sarah; (Beetle)_____ 19-70
3. GERSHOM, son of Gershom and Rebecca (Griffith)_____ 19-193
4. GERTRUDE, dau of Frank and Ida (Ferris) _____ 47-383
5. GEORGIA, dau of Henry_____ 45-377

———————

NOTES

PHINNEY:

1. HANNAH, dau of John and Mary Rogers _____ 3-24

2. HANNAH, dau of Jonathan and Joanna (Kinnicutt)_____ 3-33

3. HANNAH, dau of John and Sarah (Lumbert)_____ 16-56

4. HANNAH, dau of Joseph and his 2nd wife, Esther (West)_____ 6-69

5. HANNAH, dau of Jonathan and Mercy (Read) wife of RICHARD'

   HAILE. Their children_____ 26-110

6. HANNAH, dau of Jabez and Jane (Taylor) _____ 17-166

7. HANNAH, dau of Peletiah and Mercy (Washburn) _____ 19-191

8. HANNAH, dau of Samuel and Hannah (Ray),_____ 21-213

9. HANNAH, dau of Elisha and his 2nd wife, Rebecca (Peck) _____ 27-244

10. HANNAH, dau of Daniel and his 2nd wife, Elizabeth (Cranston)

    wife of Capt. AMBROSE BARNABY. Her children _____ 35-327

11. HANNAH, dau of Benjamin, wife of NATHAN DODGE. Her children 43-333

12. HAROLD, son of Frank and Ida (Ferris)_____ 47-388

13. HARRIET MARIA dau of Seth and Lydia Jane. Her children_____ 46-373

14. HELEN LOIS dau of James and Helen Linklane (Rich) Phinney.

    She was b. November 19, 1848 in Dartford, Wisconsin. She m.

    Henry Clay Sloan. (Sloane) *Mason Family records. See Appendix.*

15. HEMAN (Hiram) son of Isaac and Elizabeth (Kiney) _____ 34-316

16. HENRY, son of George and Caroline (Brown)_____ 45-377

17. HULDAH, dau of Seth and Lydia Jane. Their children _____ 45-368

18. HULDAH (PRESTON) wife of Isaac _____ 42-321

NOTES

PHINNEY:

1. ICABOD son of Barnabas and Mehitable (Churchill)(Norton)Phinney. (P24-225)

2. INGLIS, son of Levi and Ruth (Gates) Phinney. (P44-367)

3. IRWIN, son of Frank and Ida (Ferris) Phinney (P47-387)

4. ISAAC son of Thomas and Reliance (Goodspeed) Phinney.(P34-159)

5. ISAAC, son of Gershom and Rebekah (Griffith) Phinney (P34-197).

6. ISAAC, son of Isaac and Elizabeth (Kiney or Kenney) Phinney (P42-321).

NOTES

PHINNEY:

1.   JABEZ, son of John and Sarah (Lumbert)_____ 17-60
2.   JAMES, son of Thomas and Sarah _____ 6-73
3.   JAMES, son of John and Martha (Coleman)_____ 15-155
4.   JAMES, son of Gershom and Rebekah (Griffith) _____ 19-201
5.   JAMES, son of Thomas and Mariah (Lumbert)_____ 20-205
6.   JAMES, son of George and Caroline (Brown) _____ 47-374
7.   JAMES MILTON, son of James and Lois (Cody) He was b in
     Vernon Center, Oneida county, N.Y. July 4, 1821. He moved
     to Wisconsin with his wife , Helen L. *(From Mason Records)*
     See Appemdix
8.   JAMES MILTON, m. in Penfield, Monroe Co. N.Y. Nov. 24,
     1847 (*See Appendix. From the Mason records.*
9.   JANET(TAYLOR) pr JANE wife of Jabez _____ 17-60
10. JEMIMA (TREADWELL) wife of Elisha _____ 27-113
11. **JEMIMA**, dau of Elisha, wife of Hezikiah Kingsley _____ 37-241
12. JOANNA, dau of Jonathan and Joanna (Kinnicutt)_____ 3-26
13. JOHN, son of John and Christiana,husband of MARY ROGERS___ 3-4
14. JOHN son of John and Sarah (Lumbert) _____ 15-54
15. JOHN, son of John and Rebecca (Bryant) _____ 18-170
16. JOHN, son of John and Rebecca (Bryant)_____ 18-173
17. JOHN, son of Joseph and his first wife Mercy (Bryant) _____ 18-62
18. JOHN, son of John and Martha (Coleman)_____ 15-151
19. JOHN, son of Jabez and Jane (Taylor) _____ 17-168
20. JOHN, son of Peletiah and Mercy (Washburn)_____ 19=192
21. JOHN, son of Benjamin and Betsey (Vorce)_____ 36-334
22. JOHN, son of John and Mary (Rogers)_____ 5-13
23. JONATHAN, son of John and Christiana _____ 3-6
24. JONATHAN, son of John and Mary (Rogers)_____ 10-23
25. JONATHAN, son of Jonathan and Joanna (Kinnicutt)_____ 10-27
26. JONATHAN, son of Jonathan and Elizabeth _____ 10-105
27. JONATHAN, son of Jonathan and Mercy (Read)_____ 10-111-112
28. JONATHAN, son of John and his first wife, Rebecca (Bryant) _____18-169

PHINNEY:

1.	JONATHAN, son of John and his first wife Rebecca (Bryant)	18=171
2.	JONATHAN, son of Ebenezer and Rebecca (Barnes)	22-215
3.	JONATHAN, son of Joseph and Phebe (Cole)	25=233
4.	JOSEPH, son of John and Mary (Rogers)	3-15
5.	JOSEPH, son of Joseph and Mercy (Bryant)	18-65
6.	JOSEPH, son of Jabez snf Jand (Taylor)	**17-163-167**
7.	JOSEPH, son of John and Rebecca (Bryant)	18-174
8.	JOSHUA, son of Jonathan and Elizabeth	26-108
9.	JOSHUA, son of Joshua and Lucy (Ensworth)	26-235
10.	JUDITH, (NASH) wife of David	34-317

NOTES

PHINNEY:

    1,   KEZIA, dau of Peletiah and Mercy (Washburn)_____ 19-189

1LPH

PHINNEY:

1.	LAURAINA, dau of Peltaiah and Mercy (Washburn)	19-183
2.	LAZARUS, son of Gershon and Rebekah (Griffith)	19-194
3.	LEMUEL, son; of Ebenezer and Rebecca (Barnes)	22-217
4.	LEVI, son of Lot and Elizabeth (Durland)	44-359
5.	LORETTA, dau of Albert	48-390
6.	LOVINA, dau of Seth and Lydia Jane	46-370
7.	LOT, son of Isaac and Anna (Thomas).	34-315
8.	LUSANNA, dau of Benjamin and Martha (Crocker)	9-102
9.	LYDIA, dau of Jonathan and Joanna (Kinnicutt) wife of Hopestill Cotton	3-30
10.	LYDIA, dau of Ebenezer and Susanna (Linnell)	7-80
11.	LYDIA JANE wife of Seth	44-362
12.	LYDIA, wife of a Mr. Pool	45-378
13.	LYDIA, (PECK) dau of Benjamin and Betsey (Vorce).	43-332
14.	LYDY, dau of Thomas and Reliance (Goodspeed).	15-157

NOTES

PHINNEY:

1. MARA, b. 1745 dau of Peletiah and Mercy Washburn Phinney. 19-186

2. MARCY (sic) dau of Joseph and Esther (West) Phinney. _____ 6-54

3. MARIA, b. Oct. 11, 1804 d. Dec. 8, 1862; m. CAPT JONATHON
PARKER. He was a ship captain and master mariner.

   ISSUE: PARKER

   1. JANE WILLIAMS PARKER b. Aug. 3, 1826 m. Jan 27,1848
   Joseph Parker. Hodges. They had two children.

   2. MARIE LOUISE b Nov. 20,1829 d. Oct. 21, 1855.

   3. SARAH J. b. Oct. 31,1833 m. Jan 1, 1848 JOSEPH ALLEY.

   4. CAPT. WILLIAM B. b. Oct. 29. 1836 d. Barnstable Aug. 17,
   1903. He m. (1) JUNE 14,1850 SOPHIA B. CROCKER d. Feb. 14,
   1872. He m. (2) JENNIE BEARSE d. 1919. He had one chhild by
   his first wife and two by the second.

   5. HARRIET S. b. April 17, 1842 d. Single.

   6. FRIDERICK ELTON b. June 19,1844 d. 1922. He m. ANNA LOUISE
   CROCKER and theyi had one daughter.

   7. EMILY H. b. April 30,1847 d. Aug. 24, 1849.

   _____

4. MARTHA, dau. of John and Sarah (Lumbert) _____ 17-59

5. MARTHA, dau of Ebenezer and Susanna (Linnell) _____ 7-77

6 MARTHA, dau of John and Martha (Coleman) _____ 15-149

7. MARTHA, dau of Ebenezer and Rebecca (Barnes) _____ 22-216

8. MARY, b. Norton, Mass, Nov. 12,1727 d. possibly in Easton, Mass
1819, aged 90 years. She was the dau of John, and Mary (Campbel)
(sic) Phinney. She m. EBENEZER JONES b. Raynham, Mass.
Oct. 1, 1726 son of Joseph Jones. He was a sergeant in the local
militia in 1754.

   ISSUE: JONES (Recorded in Easton)

   1. ISAAC JONES b. Raynham, March 6, 1750

   2. EBENEZER JONES b. in Easton, March 22, 1752

   3. JOSEPH JONES b. Feb. 21,1757.

   4. MARY JONES b. Easton Nov. 14,1758.

   _____

NOTES

PHINNEY:

1. MARY, dau of Joseph and Mercy (Bryant) wife of ELEAZER
   HAMBLIN _____ 6-63
2. MARY, dau of Jonathan and Joanna (Kinnicutt) _____ 3-31
3. MARY, dau of John and Sarah (Lumbert) _____ 5-53
4. MARY, dau of Ebenezer and Susanna (Linnell) wife of JOB DAVIS 21-76
5. MARY, dau of Samuel and Bethya (Smith) _____ 7-87
6. MARY. dau of John and Martha (Coleman) _____ 15-153
7. MARY, dau of Jabez and Jane (Taylor) _____ 17-164
8. MARY, dau of David and Mary (Pope) _____ 22-223
9. MARY ANN dau of Rev. Samuel C. and Lorine (Mason records) 1SPH-1
10. MEHETABEL dau of Jonathan and Joanna (Kinnicutt) _____ 3-28
11. MEHETABLE, dau of EBenezer, wife of SAMUEL HIGGINS _____ 20-75
12. MEHITABLE, dau of Jonathan _____ 10-106
13. MEHETABLE, dau of Gershom and Rebekah (Griffith) _____ 19-200
14. MELETIAH, child of John and Mary (Rogers) _____ 3-14
15. MELATIAH, dau of Benjamin and Martha (Crocker) wife of
    JOSIAH MORTON. Their children _____ 24-97
16. MELVIN, son of Frank and Ida (Ferris) _____ 47-386
17. MERCY, dau of Thomas and Sarah _____ 6-74
18. MERCY, dau of John and Mary (Rogers) _____ 8-20
19. MERCY dau of Isaac and Elizabeth (Kiney) wife of NATHAN
    ATWOOD. _____ 34-318
20. MERCY, (Washburn) wife of Peletiah _____ 19-66
21. MERCH, child of Isaac and Huldah (Preston) _____ 42-364

NOTES

PHINNEY:

1. NANCY, dau of Daniel and Elizabeth (Coomer)_____ 35-331
2. NATHAN, son of Elisha and Rebecca (Peck) _____ ___ 27-245
3. NATHA:N, son of Isaac and Elizabeth (Kiney)   m. SUSANNA
    ROGERS _____ 34-322
4. NATHAN, son of Daniel and Elizabeth (Cranston)_____ 35-329
5. NATHAN, son of Benjamin and Betsey (Vorce)_____ 36-337
6. NATHAN, son of Isaac and Huldah (Preston)_____ 42-365
7. NATHANIEL, son of Samuel and Hannah (Ray)_____ 21-210
8. NELLIE, dau of George and Caroline (Brown)_____ 47-375
9. NELSON, son of Ebenezer and Jane (Faunce)_____ 10-114
10. NOAH, son of Joseph and Mary (Pickard)_____ 18-180

NOTES

PHINNEY:

1.	ONESIPHORUS, son of Peletiah and Mercy (Washburn)	19-185
2.	ORA, dau of George and Caroline (Brown)	48-380
3.	OTIS, son of Frank and Ida (Ferris)	47—382

PHINNEY,

1.	PATHIENCE, dau of Joseph and his 2nd wife, Esther (West) wife of ROBERT COOK. Their children.	19-67
2.	PATIENCE, dau of John and Sarah (Lumbert)	16-58
3,	PATIENCE, dau of John and Martha (Coleman)	15-150
4.	PATIENCE, dau of Thomas and Reliance (Goodspeed)	15-160
5.	PELATIAH, son of Joseph and Esther (West)	19-66
6.	PELATIAH, son of Joseph and Mary (Rickard)	18-177
7.	PETER, son of Samuel and Hannah (Ray)	21-211
8.	PHEBE dau of Joseph and Phebe (Cole)	25-234
9.	PHEBE (COLE) wife of Joseph	25-104

NOTES

PHINNEY:

1. REBECCA, dau of Ebenezer and Susanna (Linnell) _____ 21-79
2. REBECCA, dau of John and Rebecca(Bryant) _____ 18-172
3. REBECCA, dau of Joseph and Mary (Rickard) _____ 18-181
4. REBECCA, dau of Ebenezer and Rebecca (Barnes) _____ 22-219
5. REBECCA, dau of Elisha and Rebecca (Peck) _____ 37-243
6. REBECCA, dau of Daniel and Elizabeth (Coomer) _____ 35-328
7. REBECCA (BARNES) wife of Ebenezer _____ 22-81
8. REBECCA (BRYANT) wife of John _____ 18-62
9. REBECCA (PECK) wife of Elisha _____ 27-113
10. REBEKAH (GRIFFITH) wife of Gershom _____ 19-70
11. REBECCA, dau of Gershom and Rebekah (Griffith) _____ 19-198
12. RELIANCE, dau of John and Mary (Rogers) _____ 9-21
13. RENA, dau of George and Caroline (Brown) _____ 45-376
14. RHODA, dau of Samuel and Bethya (Smith) _____ 7=86
15. RHODA, dau of Gershom and Rebekah (Griffith) _____ 19-203

———————

NOTES.

PHINNEY:

1. SAMUEL C. Rev. b. 1812 d. April 16,1899, Sunday night. He was
    ome of the first settlers of Appleton, Wisconsin, coming there   in
    1853 and lived there until 1894 when he moved to Green Bay mak-
    ing his home with his dughter, Mrs. W. D. Mason.   Not too long
    after his move to Green Bay he suffered a very violent attack of
    the grip, a desease of the brain, from which he neverfully recover-
    ed.

    Mr. Phinney was in his 87th year at the time of his death. Dur-
    ing the early years of Appleton he was one of the men who   was
    most prominent at its commercial, church, and educational life.   He
    was born in Vernon, N.Y. Nov. 12, 1812 and educated at Cazenovia
    Seminary.   Upon completeing his education he entered the Methodist
    ministry and preached for seven years, until his health began to fail.
    He left the ministry and went west, and engaged in business in Ap-
    pleton.   Mr. Phinney was always the frien;d of every good thing. His
    integrity was of the best; and his disposition was of the tenderest.
    His sympathies were always enlisted for what was best and most el-
    evated in citizenship.   During the last years of his residentvy in Ap-
    pleton his age was so advanced he could take little part in the act-
    ive life of the city. He was one of the group of older men of whom
    so few now remain, who were contemperance with almost the entire
    history of Appleton.   He came here when the river ran unfettered
    from the lake to the bay, participating in the pioneer experience of
    the place, working early and late to provide for his family, and finally
    after the strain was over settling down for a few years of rest and
    quiet before obeying the summons that must come to all, calling him
    up higher.

    Mrs Phinney died in 1880 and the surviving members of the family
    are the daughters, Mrs. Stansbury and Mrs. Mason. Mr. Phinney is
    also survived by his brother, James M. Phinney of Appleton.

    ———————

1. SAMUEL son of John and Marey (Rogers)_____ 7-18
2. SAMUEL, son of Ebenezer and Susanna (Linnell) _____ 21-78
3. SAMUEL son of Joshua and Lucy (Ensworth) _____ 26-236
4. SARAH, dau of John and Sarah (:umbert)_____ 16-57
5. SARAH dau of Thomas and Reliance (Goodspeed)_____ 15-158
6. SARAH, dau of John and Martha (Coleman)._____ 15=152
7. SARAH, dau of Gershom and Rebekah (Griffith)_____ 19-195
8. SARAH, dau of Ebenezer and Rebecca (Barnes)_____ 22-214
9. SARAH, dau of Isaac and Elizabeth (Kiney) _____ 34-319
10. SARAH, dau of David and Mary (Pope)_____ 22-224
11. SARAH (SALLY) dau of Isaac and Huldah (Preston)_____ 42-361
12. SARAH (LUMBERT) wife of John_____ 5-13
13. SALMON (SOLOMON) son of Isaac and Huldah (Preston)_____ 42-366
14. SETH, son of Ebenezer and Susanna (Linnell)_____ 7-83
15. SETH, son of Benjamin and Mary (Crocker)_____ 25-101
16. SETH, son of Gershom and Rebekah (Griffith)_____ 19-202
17. SETH, son of Ebenezer and Rebecca (Barnes) _____ 22-218
18. SETH, son of Isaac and Huldah (Preston)_____ 44-362
19. SILAS, son of Benjamin and Martha (Crocker) _____ 9-99
20. STEPHEN, son of Johnand Martha (Coleman)_____ 15-148
21. SUBMIT, dau of Isaac and Huldah (Preston) _____ 42-363
22. SUSANNA, dau of Thomas and Mariah (Lumbert)_____ 20-206
23. SUSANNAH, dau of Samuel and Hannah (Ray) _____ 21-209

NOTES

PHINNEY;

NOTES

PHINNEY:

1. WARREN, kson of Benjamin and Betsey (Vorce) _____ 36-342
2. WILLIAM, son of Samuel and Hannah (Ray) _____ 21-212

Y.

Z.

PHINNEY:

1. ZACCHEUS, son of Beniamin and Martha (Crocker) _____ 24-100
2. ZACCHEUS, son of Zaccheus and Susan (Davis) _____ 24-229
3. ZERVIA, son of Pelatiah and Mercy (Washburn) _____ 19-187
4. ZERVIA, son of Peletiah and Mercy (Washburn) _____ 19-184
5. ZILPAH b. 1749 son of Seth and Bethia (Bump) _____ 25-230
6. ZENAS, son of Isaac and Elizabeth (Kiney) _____ 34-323

NOTES

INDEX
A,

INDEX
B.

BOLTON:

    44.   Grace Della (Mater) wife of Joseph David ——————— 65-630-2

BERDEN"

    45.   Beulah Blanche 2nd wife of Charles Wesley Finney ————— 71-707

BLACK:

    46.   Abigail, 2nd wife of William Finney ———————— 30-122

BLANCHARD:

    47.   Warren m. Harriet Maria Phinney ———————— 46-373

BOLLES:

    48.   Mary Dring 2nd wife of George Gibbs Clark —————— 40-265-2

BONNEY:

    49.   William ———————————————— 24-98

BOSWORTH:

    50.   Alvin, 2nd husband of Nancy Phinney —————— 35-331.
    51.   Nancy, wife of John Mason ———————— 35-331

BOURNE:

    52.   Elizabeth, wife of John Pope ———————— 22-82

BOWEN:

    53.   Avis, wife of John Finney ———————— 40-266
    54.   Ronda Ray wife of David Wesley Finney —————— 73-714
    55.   Ruth (Arnold) wife of James ————————— 40-266

BOWMAN:

    56.   Laura A. 3rd wife of William G. Finney —————— 71-688

BRADEN:

    57.   Elizabeth, wife of James Finney ———————— 57-551
    58.   Robert, m. Margaret Finney ———————— 57-577

BRADFORD:

    59.   Elizabeth (Phinney) wife of David ——————— 3-29
    60.   Sarah, wife of Jonathan Barnes ——————— 22-81

BRANT:

    61.   Marilyn, wife of Owen Engler Finney —————— 23-715

BRICE:

    62.   Mary, wife of Daniel Shepherd ——————— 23-89

BRIGGS:

    63.   Abigail, wife of Peter Carpenter ——————— 41-268

BRIGHTMAN:

    64.   Rebecca, wife of David Barton ——————— 27-242

BRISTOW:

    65.   Elizabeth, wife of Jeremiah Finney ——————— 12-44

BROADBENT:

66. Julia Pearl (Finney) dau of Dwight M. and Wave W. (Wooster) Finney. Julia was b. June 11,1908 and m. March 28, 1929 to Carl Herchel Broadbent b. Sept. 4, 1906. Their children: _____ 4DF1-3

    1. Carlton b. April 25,1930
    2. Neida Vinne b. Oct. 17, 1931.
    3. Beverly Jo b. Apriol 17, 1933.

BROOKS:

67. Nancy, wife of John Wesley Finney _____69-678

BROWN:

68. Caroline, wife of George Phinney _____45-369
69. Charlotte, wife of William Craig _____44-367
70. Elizabeth, wife of JOnathan Milliken _____66-636

BRUCE:

71. Dea__ 2nd husband of Hannah Phinney _____27-244

BRYANT:
72. Abigail, _____ 8.19
73. Jonathan, m. Mary Phinney _____ 8-19
74. Mary, _____ 8-19
75. Mercy, wife of Joseph Phinney _____ 6-15
76. Rebecca, 1st wife of John Phinney _____ 18-62

BULLOCK:

77. Hopestill, wife of Joshua Lumbert, mother of Jonathan who m. Martha Phinney _____ 17-59

BUMP or BUMPAS:

78. Bethia, wife of Seth Phinney, dau of Samuel and Joanna (Warren) Bump. Their children: _____ 25-110

BURCH:

79. Becky, wife of David Wesley Finney _____ 73-714

BUTLER:

80. Mary, wife of Abraham Taylor, m other of Jane _____ 17 60
81. Jane, wife of Jabez Phinney. Their children_____ 17-60
82. Hannah, wife of David Thompson Finney_____ 58-563
83. Rebecca, wife of John French Finney_____ 58-562
84. Sarah wife of Thomas Phinney,_____ 6-16

BUTTS:

85. Mary Belle (Farlow) wife of William_____ 70-681

INDEX
C.

1886 dau of James Scott and Alice (Flannagan) Finnwy. William d. July 1913. They were m. June 30, 1910. Their children:

1.   William was in W.W. II as a pilot. He m. an English girl.

2.   Hazel Alice.

Both children are married and have children but the names are unknown at this time.

_____

COGGESHALL

INDEX
C.

COUNTE:

154. Martha, wife of Hawkins Cook Finney _____ 60-628

COY:

155. Mary, 2nd wife of Jeremiah Finney _____ 29-118

CRAIG:

156. Charlotte (Brown) wife of William b. in Ireland _____ 44-367
157. Matilda, wife of Inglis Phinney _____ 44-367
158. Sarah, wife of Thomas Patterson _____ 2AF1-3

CRANSTON:

159. Sarah, wife of Stephen, parents of Elizabeth (Eliza) _____ 35-239
160. Elizabeth, wife of Daniel Phinney _____ 35-239

CREICHTON:

161 Dr. James Lowell, m. Wave Finney. Their children _____ 1WF5

CROCKER:

162. Alice, wife of William parents of Eleazer _____ 8-20
163. Joseph, father of Martha, wife of Benjamin Phinney _____ 9-22
164. Mercy (Phinney) wife of Eleazer _____ 8-20
165. Temperance (Bursley)wife of Joseph; mother of Martha _____ 9-22
166. William m. Alice parents of Eleazer _____ 8-20

CROWEL:

167. Lydia, wife of Ebenezer Goodspeed _____ 15-55
168. Reliance,wife of Thomas Phinney _____ 15-55

CROUCH:

169. Alphretta (Finney) wife of John _____ 2AF8

ISSUE: *CROUCH.*

1. WILLIAM WILLIS b. May 13, 1877
2. JAMES BOYD b. Feb. 15,1881

_____

170. James Boyd, son of Alphretta amd John Crouch m. June

26, 1906 Mary Estella Stantz b. Feb. 20,1882. _____ 2AF8

ISSUE:

1. William Herbert Crouch
2. Dorothy Caroline Crouch.

_____

171. William Willis Crouch m. Sept. 26,1900 Gertrude Maxwell

b. July 12,1876 dau of Sarah Boyd Anderson,said to be a

cousin to Robert E. Lee. _____ 63F

ISSUE:

1. Eleanor Elizabeth m a Mr. Rigg.
2. Charles m. Mildred _____

_____

172. William Herbert, son of James Boyd_____ IN 170-1

CRUMBAKER:

173. Corrine, dau of George and Claire (Finney) b. April 23, 1935_____ 2WF4-4
174. Claire (Finney) b. March 8, 1908 dau of William Herbert and
Susanna (Bell)Finney m. George Duncan Crumbaker. Their chil   IN 173

175. George Duncan b. Jan. 19, 1900 m. Claire Finney June 10, 1933
They have a daughter **Corrine** b. April 23, 1935._____ 21-28F

CRUNKLETON:

176. Martha, wife of James Finney _____ 57-551

CULBERTSON:

177. Elizabeth, b. 1800 d. Oct. 2, 1839 wife of Elijah Finney. Family 1EF8-5
178. Nancy sister of Elizabeth wife of Thomas Finney._____ 1TF4

CUMMINGS:

179. James, b. 1858 m. Polly Hannah Finney, dau of Wesley. She m.
James Cummings Dec. 25, 1885. She d. Dec. 12, 1886. Could she
have died in child-bed? _____ 65-677

CURTIS:

180. Hattie E. b. May 7, 1871 d. 1946 m. William Burton Simpson, son
of Mary Jane (Finney and Denney Burns Simpson. They had seven
children. No names of chidren were shown _____ 62F

NOTES

DAVID:

181. Thomas, m. Betsey Barnes, dau of Corban and Mary(Finney) Barnes 30-120-3
182. **Betsey (Barnes)** _____ **30-120=3**

DAVIS:

183. Stephen m. Rebecca Phinney. Their children _____ 21-79
184. Josiah and Ann (Taylor) parents of Stephen _____ 21-79
185. **Nathan**, m. Elizabeth Phinney. Their children _____ 14-52
186. Jabez m. Experience (Linnell) parents of Nathan _____ 14-52
187. Job, m. Mary Phinney son of Dolar and Hannah(Linnell) _____ 21-76
188. Captain Jesse m. Rebecca Finney. Their children _____ 39-264
189. Susan, wife of Zaccheus Phinney. Their children _____ 24-100
190. Jabez and Anne (Dimrock) parents of Susan _____ 24-100
191. Margaret, wife of James Madison Finney Their children _____ 2JF-7

DAVIES:

192. Rebecca, wife of Richard King Finney. Their children _____ 61-573

DENSMORE:

193. William m. Harriet Maria Phinney _____ 46-373

DERBY:

194. Elizabeth, wife of Thomas Lumbert _____ 5-13

d e WOLF:

195. Mark Anthoney and Abigail (Porter) parents of William _____ 38-251
196. William m. Charlotte Finney. Their children _____ 38-251

DEXTER:

197. Alice wife of Edward Taylor, parents of Alice _____ 40-265-1

DIAMANT:

198. Hannah (Finney) wife of Thomas. Their children _____ 11-36
199. Thomas and Hannah (James) parents of Thomas _____ 11-36

DINMOCK (DINROCK)

200. Anne, wife of Jabez Davis, mother of Susan _____ 24-100
201. Lusanna (Phinney wife of _____ D _____ 9-102

DODGE:

202. Nathan, m. Hannah (Phinney) Their family _____ 43-333
203. Nancy (Taggert) wife of Solomon parents of Nathan _____ 43-333
204. Calista (Phinney) wife of Nathan _____ 43-333

DUNHAM:

205. Elizabeth, wife of Oliver Finney. Their child _____ 31-127

DUNLEVY:

206. Mary Evanna (Patterson) dau of James and Mary (Swangie)
Patterson b. Oct. 25,1847 m. JOHN DUNLEVY b. Oct 5,1833
His first wife was Mary McKee, whome he m. NOv. 20,1856.
He d. Sept. 14, 1904 and Mary d. April 2,1927. _____ 146 F

ISSUE:

1. ETTA DUNLEVY b. July 9, 1871
2. JESSIE DUNLEVY b. May 22, 1887

DURLAND,
207.   Elizabeth, wife of Lot Phinney. Their children   42-315.

NOTES

————

NOTES

F.

FALES:

224.　John, son of Nathaniel and Sarah (Little)m. Martha Finney ___ 37-250

FALLOWELL:

225.　Gabriel, m. Catherine Finney dau. of "Mother"Finney _____ 1-1

FARLOW:

226.　Elmer, m. Clara Ellen Finney. Their children _____ 70-681
227.　Martha (Cloud) mother of Mary Ann _____ 70-680
228.　Mary Ann, wife of Daniel Webster Finney. Their children ___ 70-680
229.　Nathan, father of Mary Ann _____ 70-680

FARRELL:

230.　Margaret, wife of Samuel Alexander Gilliland. They have two

children; *1. Georgiana 2. Alexander.* Np dates. _____ IN 258

FAUNCE:

231.　Jane, wife of Ebenezer Phinney. Their child_____ 10-32

FERGUS:

232.　Mary, m. Robert Colemore Finney. Their family_____ 3RF1

FERRIS:

233.　Ida, wife of Frank Phinney. Their children _____ 47-379

FISHER:

234.　Sarah, M. 2nd wife of Joseph Davies Finney. Their children 66-636

FITCH:

235.　Oliver, b. 1775 d. Dec. 17,1839 m. Susanna Finney _____ 28-255

FLANNAGAN:

236.　Alice, wife of James Scott Patterson. She was b. June 5,1859
d. Feb. 28, 1923. James Scott Patterson was b. June 18,1852
and d. Nov. 10. 1889. They were m. in 1885. He was the son
of Joseph and Rebecca (Scott) Patterson. Their children:

ISSUE: *PATTERSON:*

237.　1.　*EDITH HAZEL b. April 19, 1886m. William Bolton Chattaway.* IN 106-2
238.　2.　*CLIFFORD SCOTT b. May 3, 1887 m 1915 Rachel Jones* IN-334
239　3,　*JOSEPH b. April 20, 1889 drowned accidently Sept 16, 1898.—*

FORSYTH:

240.　Colin L. b. March 31, 1904 m. June 9, 1925 Iva Elberta Finney b. Feb. 13,1901. She was the dau of David and his second
wife, Hariet Way. Their children_____ 1-1F-3

FOUST:

241　Paula Lee, wife of Thomas Ryan Finney _____ 74-733

FOX:

242.　Francis Aaron, b. Aug. 15,1902 m. March 20,1927 Rebecca Ruth
Finney b. Sept. 13, 1908. Their children _____ 1RF-12

NOTES

GAMBILL: 60F
249.   Grace Anna wife of William Homer Ayers. She was b. July 11, 1882. William was b. Jan 8, 1874. Theyhad two children names unknown at this time. _____ 1MF-3

GAMBLE: 132F
250.   Nancy, m. Feb. 16,1922 Howard Patterson Finney, son of David and Sarah (Patterson) Finney. _____ 1DF7-1

GARRETT: 28aF
251.   Abigail Ann (Finney) b. 1833 d. 1907 dau of Elijah and his 1st wife, Elizabeth (Culbertson)_____ 1EF8-3

GATES:
252.   Ruth, wife of Levi Phinney, dau of John and Elizabeth (Fales) Gates.   Their children _____ 44-559

GATEWOOD:
253.   Neva, wife of James Boyd Finney.   Their children _____ 1JF-11

GEIER:
254.   Barbara Jean, wife of Frank Lewis Finney_____ 75-735.

GIBBS:
255.   Martha, 2nd wife of Joseph Finney.   Their children_____ 28-115

GIFFORD:
256.   Huldah, wife of Abraham Finney.   Their children _____41-314

GILBERT:
257.   Sarah, wife of Thomas Carter_____ 33-141

GILLILAND: 138F
258.   Ada E. (Patterson) wife of William Fleming. She was born 1961, dau of James Patterson.   She m. William Fleming Gilliland March 13, 1889.   Their children _____.IN-459
ISSUE:
1.   ANN GILLILAND b. 1892
2.   MARGARET GILLILAND b. 1893 m. 1920 Walter Morris an attorney.
      A.   *ANNE LOUISE MORRIS b. Aug. 27 1920*
      B.   *MARGARET JANE (PEGGY) b. July 5, 1926.*
3.   SAMUEL ALEXANDER b. 1898 m. MARGARET FARRELL They have two chidren; Georgiana and Samuel Alexander.
4.   JAMES PATTERSON b. 1898 m. ALICE DONALDSON.

GITTINGS:
259.   Martha, wife of James Gibbs. Mother of Martha _____ 28-115

GOLDMAN:
260.   William David, m. Malinda Catherine Finney_____ 63-662

GOODSPEED:

GOODWIN:

GORDON: 60F

265. Arthur Leslie, m. Esther May Grumbling. He was born
Dec. 3, 1892 and m. Esther May Grumbling Dec. 25,1915.
Esther~ was b. March 20, 1893.

ISSUE: *GORDON.*

1. *ARTHUR WILLIAM b. Dec. 16, 1918 m. NORMA LORRAINE BELL b.
April 5, 1942. Their children:*

   A. *SHARON LORRAINE GORDON b. Oct. 9, 1943.*
   B. *Rosemary Gordon b. Jan1945.*

2. *VIOLA RUTH b. May 9, 1921 m. ORIE DAVIDSON Feb.4, 1940*
3. *FOSTER RALPH GORDON b. May 13, 1927. Served in WW II.*
4. *CLYDE DEAN b. June 27, 1931.*

GRAHAM: 137F

GRAVES:

GRAVEDONI:

GREEN[E] 143F

269. Homer, m. Katherine Brown Patterson. She was the dau of
John Watt Patterson. They had two children: *HOMER* and
MAC L.

GREENOUGH:

GRIFFITH:

GRIFFIN:

GREGGORY:

GRISWOLD:

274.   Loris, wife of Tommie Milton Finney. Their children   72-709

GROSE:

275.   Jessie, wife of Charles Edward Finney. Their children   71-695

276.   Madison m. Mary (Rader) Parents of Jessie   71-695

GRUMBLING: 60½F

277.   Esther May, b. March 20, 1893 m. Dec. 25,1915 Arthur Leslie Gordon. Their children   IN 263

278.   Eunice Evelyn b. Feb. 18, 1902 m. Roy Gilbert. They had one son: ROY b. March 21,1922. His father evidently died before his birth. She m. (2) Louis Case Lawrence Jan 6, 1933

279.   John Hiram b. March 13,1892 m. June 13, 1916 Marian Johnson b. March 4, 1898.

ISSUE:

1. Meribah Grumbling b. April 2, 1918. She was in the service WAB
2. Paul Richard Grumbling b. June 27, 1920. He was in the Navy.
3. Paul Johnson b. May 15. 1926. He was in the Navy.
4. Anna b. Nov. 10, 1929.

-----

280   William Ralph b. May 6, 1907 m. Aug. 28,1930 Mildred Ellen Summers b. May 24,1912.

ISSUE:

1. HENRY GRUMBLING b. July 23, 1932.
2. ARRET DORIS b. Sept 4, 1934.
3, ROWLAND WARREN b. Sept 15,1938.
4. RALPH WILLIAM b. Oct. 30, 1939.

These dates may not be exact. The above were all descendants of William H. Grumbling.

-----

281.   William Henry b. Aug. 23,1868 d. Oct. 23,1915. He m. Eunice Clyde Ayers, dau of Margaret (Finney) and Hiram Ayers.   1MF3-2

Their grandchildren   IN 280

GUTTEREDGE:

282.   GORDON G. b. May 24,1915 a British Army Officer m Mary Marjorie Stevenson b. May 11, 1909. They were married May 1, 1943 in Egypt.   IN 655.

GOTHRIE:

283.   Margaret, wife of Robert Finney. Their children   62-578

INDEX.
H.

HACKETT:

284,   Alice, wife of Joseph Phinney. Their children _____ 18-65

HAILE:

285.   Richard, m. Hannah Phinney. Their children _____ 26-110

HALL:

286.   S.R. m. Ada Jane Patterson, dau of William Alonzo Patterson. Ada Jane was b. Dec. 30, 1880. They had one dau. who m. John R. Erdman. The Erdmans had two children, *JOAN* and *MARGARET* Joan was b. Feb. 1928 and Margaret was b. January 1930. _____ IN 460

HALLADAY:

287.   Helen A. wife of Elmer Blanchard, son of Warren. Their children _____ 46-373

HAMLIN:

288.   Ebenezer, m. Alice Phinney, dau of JOseph and Mercy (Bryant) Phinney. _____ 6-61

289.   Eleazer, m. Mary Phinney dau of Joseph _____ 6-63

HAMILTON:

290.   C.M. m. Maxine Mason dau of R.L. and Mary (Patterson) Mason. _____ 140F

HARLOW:

291.   James, 2nd husband of Mehitable (Church) Norton _____ 24-98

HARPER:

292.   Ed, m. Martha Curry McClure, grand=daughter of Robert and Margaret (Patterson) Finney _____ 2RF2

293.   Ed, m. Martha Curry McClure dau of Alexander and Sara Jane (Finney) McClure _____ 1SF8-2

HARRIS:

294.   Samuel m. Rebecca Finney, dau of Jeremiah _____ 4-39

HARROUFF:

295.   Ray Edward b. Nov. 18, 1898 m. Minetter Elizabeth Finney b. July 29, 1903. She was the dau of William Herbert Finney and his wife, Susanna Bell. Their children _____ 4MF22

      1. MARY ELAINE HARROUFF.   *2. JAMES RAY HARROUFF.*

HART:

296.   Samuel C. m. Lydia Campbell, dau of Huldah (Phinney) and Elson Monroe Campbell. _____ 45-368-1

297.   Edna Ruth, wife of Forest Fielding Finney _____ 74-716

HAYFORD:
298. John m. Thankful Phinney. Their children. _____ 25-103

HENDERSON:
299. Andrew, m. Elizabeth Finney dau of William Finney_____51-525

HENNICKS:
300. George, M. m. Myrtle Allen dau of William M. and
Mary C. (Finney) Allen._____69-675

HICKMAN:
301. Hannah, wife of Robert Finney. Their children _____ 56-547

HIGGINS:
302. Samuel, m. Mehitable Phinney dau of Ebenezer and
Susanna (Linnell)Phinney. Their children_____ 20-75

HILBERT:
303. Stella (Finney) wife of a Mr. Hilbert._____ 69-698

HILL:
304. Charlene (Searles)m. a Mr. Hill. Their children_____48-380-3

HINKLEY:
305.
Sylvanus m. Sarah Phinney dau of Thomas_____15-158

HINSHAW:
306. Mary Matilda, wife of Wesley Finney. Their children _____65-632

HITCHCOCK:
307. Mary, first wife of Robert P. Finney_____ 62-640

HODGE:
308. He m. Lydia Phinney dau of Thomas and Reliance
(Goodspeed) Finney _____ 15-557

HODGE
309. He m. Julia Ann Chamblin _____ 37-243-3

HOLMES.
310. Ansel, m. Patty Barnes dau of Corban and Mary (Finney) ── 30-120-6
311. Eleazer, m. Mary Barnes, dau of Corban and Mary (Finney) Barnes._____ 30-120-1

HOUSEHOLDER:
312. Edna m. Porter Milroy Finney. Their children _____1PF-10

HOWARD:
313. He m. Louisa Carpenter dau of Elisha and Hannah
(Finney) Carpenter_____ 41-268-2

HOWE:

314. Jane, wife of Andrew Finney son of James and Martha
(Mayes) _____ 53-557

HOWELL: 143F

315. Maude Etta b. June 24,1884 dau of James ,wife of John
Watt Patterson b. March 8, 1883. They were m. May 5,1903.

ISSUE: *PATTERSON.*
1. Katherine Brown b. Sept. 15, 1905 m. Jan 1, 1923
   Homer Greene. Their children _____ *IN 269*

2. Arnetta May, b. Dec. 17, 1912.
3. Florence Lenore b. Juine 25. 1917.

HOWLAND:

316. Elizabeth, wife of Isaac Hamblin, mother of Eleazer _____ 6-63

HUDSON:

317. Marie, wife of Charles Copeland son of Abner and
Samanteha Jane (Finney) Copeland. Their children _____ 68-673-7

HUFFMAN:

318. Gilla, dau of Lawson, wife of Daniel William Finney _____ 63-655

HUMESTON:

319. Albert Barnes m. Nina Thornber _____ 46-372-2

HUNT:

320. Matilda, wife of Robert Finney. Their shildrem _____ 63-624
321. Parke Delaney, 2nd wife of John Long Finney _____ 60-626

HUNTER:

322. David, m. Jean Finney dau of William and Jane (Stevenson) Finney. _____ 51-534

_____

I.

INGRAHAM:

323. Lydia, wife of Bernard Miller, mother of Robert _____ 35-328
324. Rebecca, (Finney) wife of Robert _____ 35-328

K.

INDEX

L.

LONG:
368. Mary Polly, wife of Joseph Finney. _____ 60-571

LOOKER:
369. David Eugene, m. Brenda Alice Finney _____ 74-736

LOVELL:
370. Betty, 2nd wife of John Phinney. Their children _____ 18-62

LOWDON:
371. Aaron, m. Hattie Thornber _____ 46-372-3

LOWRY:
372. Emeline, wife of William, parents of Priscilla _____ 68-663
373. Mary, wife of Samuel, parents of James Patterson Finney   1SF-6
374. Priscilla, 2nd wife of John V. Finney _____ 68-663

LUMBARD/LUMBERT:
375. Abigail, 2nd wife of Thomas Phinney _____ 20-71
376. Elizabeth (Derby) and Thomas, Parents of Sarah _____ 5-13
377. John, parent of Martha _____ 17-59
378. Jonathan, m. Martha Finney. Their children _____ 17-59
379. Joshua, and Hopestill (Bullock) parents of Jonathan _____ 17-59
380. Mariah, wife of Thomas Phinney _____ 20-71
381. Sarah, wife of John Phinney. Their children _____ 5-13
382. Sarah, mother of Margaret _____ 17-59
383. Samuel and Mary (Comer) parents of Abigail _____ 20-71

LUTHER:
384. Nathan, m. Elizabeth Finney _____ 5-51

NOTES

McCLAY:

403. Mary, wife of Samuel Stewart, whom he married in Ireland. It is said they were a striking looking couple and they had a family of ten children; four which were born in Ireland. it is said that there was only one girl in the family and this might explain the countless Stewarts in America (See Stewart.) _____ 119F

McCLURE:

404. Alexander, m. Sara Jane Finney, dau of Robert and Margaret (Patterson) Finney. They have three children. _____ 1SF-8

405. Vivia Jane wife of Carl Chester Finney _____ 72-700

McCONELL:

406. Robert m. Jane Finney, dau of Robert and Polly (Pedan) Finney _____ 33F1

407. Sara; dau of Mrs. Caroline (Cobeen) McConnell, m. Joseph McKee, eldest son of her step-father. She was b. 1846 died 1920, _____ IN F-9

408. Helen, wife of David Wesley Finney _____ 67-656

McCRACKEN:

409. Mayme, d. 1920 m. 1910 Clayton Harvey Patterson. son of John Van Kirk and Mary Jane Patterson.

ISSUE:

1, Thelma M. b. Dec. 31, 1910.
2. Mildred Belle b. May 1915.
3. John Clayton b. July 1917.

McCUTCHEON:

410. Margaret (Finney) wife of James. _____ 53-554

McKEAN:

411. William b. 1707 m. Letitia Finney. Their children _____ 51-509
412. Mary (Borden) wife of Thomas _____ 51-509
413. Sarah (Armitage) 2nd wife of Thomas _____ 51-509

McKEE:

414. John m. Nancy Finney. Nancy was his first wife. He m. (2) Mrs. Caroaline (Cobeen) McConnell. _____ IN F-5

ISSUE:

1. Joseph McKee b. 1846 d. 1920. He m. Sarah McConnell.
2. William McKee.
3. John d. at the age of 13 yeares

NOTES

McKINLEY:
    415. Grace, wife of Clayton Patterson _____ IN 487

McKNIGHT:
    416. Sarah, m. Jan 14,1890 John Frank Patterson. Sarah was b. Oct. 30, 1868. John was b. Jan 15,1864 and d. March 24,1926 IN 498

        ISSUE:

        1. Mabel Patterson b. May 21,1891 d. Sept 11,1942.
        2. James McKnight Patterson b. Jan.2, 1894 m. Jewel Mischler. He d. Nov. 22, 1938 at the age of 44. He served in World War I as an instructor.
        3. Marjorie b. April 19, 1897.

McMILLIN:
    417. Elizabeth (Phinney) m.a Mr. McMillin _____ 57-580

McMULLEN:
    418. Sarah (Finney) m. French _____ 52-543

MEAD:
    419. David, m. Jeannett Finney _____ 54-559

MILLER:
    420. James, m. Elizabeth Finney _____ 52-539
    421. William, m. Ann Dorothea Finney _____ 52-540
    422. Robert. m. Rebecca Phinney. Their children _____ 35-328
    423. George Robert _____ 35-328-1

MILLIKEN:
    424. Amanda L. wife of Joseph Davies Finney. Their children ___ 66-636
    425. John and Elizabeth (Brown) parents of Amanda _____ 66-636
    426. Mildred Catherine dau of Otis and mary Ellen (Rheah) (Leavett) Milliken. She m. Rufus Finney. Children _____ 4RF-5

MISCHLER:
    427. Jewel, wife of James McKnight Patterson _____ IN-495

MORGAN:
    428. Lorena, wife of Joseph Finney _____ 60-625
    429. Kenshen and Sarah _____ 60-625

MORRIS:
    430. Anne Louise b. Aug. 21,1920 dau of Margaret (Gilliland) and Walter Morris _____ IN 258-A
    431. Margaret Jane (Peggy)b. July 5,1926 _____ IN-258B

MORSE:
    432. Theodore m. Susan Davis. widow of Zacchues Finney _____ 24-100

MORTON:
    433. Anne wife of William Finney _____ 53-553
    434. Benjamin, m. Hannah Morton _____ 4-8-1
    435. Josiah m. Melatiah Phinney _____ 24-97
    436. John, m. Reliance Phinney _____ 24-97

MURDOCK:
    437. Jean florence m. William David Finney. Children _____ 2WF3

INDEX
N.

O.

ISSUE:

1. Minnie O'Neil b. July 311878 m. Robert Lowry Steele.
   Their children (See Steele)
2. Della O'Neil b. Nov. 29, 1881 d. 1912.

ISSUE:
1. James Steele Orr.

PARKER:

455. Abigail, wife of Thomas _____ 43-332
456. Dydia Peck (Phinney) wife of Josiah. Their children _____ 43-332
457. Hannah, wife of Ezekiel Clark _____ 40-265
458. Maria (Phiney) wife of Captain Jonathan, son of James. Their children _____ IMPH-3

PATTERSON:

459. Ada E. wife of William Fleming Gilliland; dau of James ____ IN 258
460. Ada Jane wife of S.R. Hall. They had one daughter _____ IN 286
who m. John R. Erdman. Erdman's children:
ISSUE:

1. JOAN ERDMAN b. Feb. 1926
2. MARGARET ERDMAN b. Jan 1930

---

461. Agnes (Finney) wife of James _____ 2AF1
462. Alexander b. Aug. 1850 2nd child of Jamesa and his 2nd wife. He m. Barbara Engles b. Aug. 30, 1859 _____ IN 221
463. Almira (Scott) b. Nov. 11,1883 m. William A. Covert. _____ IN 553-3
464. Alice (Flannagan) wife of James Scott Patterson. Their children _____ IN 236
465. Anna Margaret b. 1859 wife of Samuel Graham. _____ IN 266
466. Arnetta May b. May 21,1910. She m. June 8,1929 Paul Shook. _____ IN 622
467. Barbara (Engles) wife of Alexander. _____ IN 221
468. Belle (Bebout) wife of William Alonzo _____ IN 41
469. Bernice (Peairs) dau of Boyd Peairs, wife of Frank Roy ____ IN 486
470. Bertha b. April 27,1885 dau of William Alonzo and Belle (Bebout) _____ IN 553-4
471. Caroline (Ayers) b. Feb. 21,1829 wife of Finney C. _____ IN 482
472. Clayton Harvey b. Oct. 10,1885 son of John VanKirk He m. 1910 Mayme McCracken who d. March 1920. Their children _____ IN 409
473. Clifford Scott b. May 3, 1887 son of James Scott m. 1915 Rachel (Jones). He was in the state legislature of Pennsylvania. They had one daughter, Mary Louise who m. June 8, 1937 Manor Johner Siljander. His parents were born in Finland. _____ IN 334
474. Cora Bell, dau of David McKibben _____ 144F
475. David McKibben b. Nov. 15, 1889 son of John VanKirk. He m. Aug. 19, 1914 Mabel Philips. Their children
ISSUE:

1. Ruth Virginia b. Aug 20, 1915
2. Mary Blanche b. June 10, 1917
3. Cora Bell b. Aug. 4, 1921.
4. June Lorraine b. May 7, 1925.
5. Mabel Jane b. June 9, 1926.
David also married Lucile Rhodes _____ IN 509

PATTERSON:

476. Dorothy Jane b. Dec. 17,1912 dau of John Watt _____ IN 499
477. Edith Hazel b. Feb. 9,1930 dau of James Scott. She m.
     June 30, 1916 William Bolton Chattaway. _____ IN 106
478. Edythe Luella dau of Thomas Clyde Patterson _____ IN 502-2
479. Elijah b. 1788 d. 1875 son of James and Agnes (Finney)_____ 2AF-1-7
480. Elijah, b. 1849 son of John Watt. He m. (1) 1870 Lillie
     Fritz who d. 1874. He m. (2) 1878 Jane McClure b. 1849
     and d. 1924 Elijah d. 1917. _____ IN 246

ISSUE by first wife.

1. Clayton Patterson b. 1872.
٤' By second wife.
2. Ruth Patterson b. 1851 m. 1873 John O'Neil_____ IN 453

481. Emma Luella b. 1863 d. Oct. 1911 dau of Thomas _____ IN 516-3
482. Finney C. b. July 27,1833 m. Feb. 2, 1859 Caroline Ayers
     b. Feb. 21, 1829. _____ IN 582-9

ISSUE:

1. Frank Munda Patterson.
2. Jane.

_____

483. Finney Henry b. c1796 son of Agnes (Finney) and James_____ 2 AF1-10

484. Florence Lenore b. June 25,1917 dau of John Watt. _____ IN 499
485. Frank Munda, son of Finney C. became a distinguished
     judge in the Ohio courts. _____ IN 482-1
486. Frank Roy b. Oct. 17, 1887 son of John VanKirk m. Nov.
     10, 1914 Bernice Peairs, dau of Boyd Peairs. No children ____ IN 469

487. Grace McKinley, wife of Clayton _____ IN 415
488. Hazel Loucile, dau of Thomas Clyde _____ IN 549-1
489. Ida Laura b. 1859 dau of John VanKirk_____ IN-516-2
490. James b. Feb. 11, 1825 son of Mary (Watt) and James. He
     m. 1848 Sarah Ann VanKirk b. 1824. He d. Dec. 25,1895.
     She d. June 16,1892 _____ IN 582-6

ISSUE:

1. Sarah Amanda Patterson d. 1848 in infancy.
2. Oliver Patterson b. 1850 d. 1868
3. Elizabeth Caroline b. 1852 d. 1910.
4. Mary Jane b. 1854 d. 1928. Never married.
5. James Patterson b. 1856 d. in infancy.
6. Anna Margaret b. 1859 m. July 24, 1901 Samuel Graham IN 465
7. Ada E. Patterson b. 1861 m. March 13,1889 William
   Fleming Gilliland _____ IN 258
8. John Frank Patterson b. Jan 15,1864 m. Jan 14, 1890
   Sarah McKnight. Their children _____ IN 416

_____

491. James Harvey and Belle (McCune) parents of Mary Jane. ____ IN 502

PATTERSON:

492.   James m. Mary Watt. Their children;

     ISSUE:

    1.   Agnes Nancy b. Nov. 26. 1813.
    2.   Jane b. April 5, 1816. m. William Stewart Finney
    3.   Margaret b. Aug. 15, 1818.
    4.   Susanna b. Feb. 1, 1821.
    5.   John Watt b. March 9, 1823.   IN 499
    6.   James S. b. Feb. 11, 1825.   IN 490
    7.   Joseph, b. May 28, 1827.   IN 503
    8.   Thomas b _Aug 19, 1831_   IN 516
    9.   Finney C. b. July 5, 1833.   IN 482
  10.   Mary b. July 5, 1833
  11.   Sarah, b. 1835.

    Children by his second wife, Mary Swangie   IN 671
  12.   Mary Evana b. April 25, 1847
  13.   Alexander b. July 11, 1850.

493.   James m. Agnes Finney. Their children   2AF-1
494.   James Scott b. June 18, 1852 m. Alice Flannigan   IN 503-1
495.   James McKnight m. Jewel Mischler. He was the son of   IN416-2
    John Frank and Sarah (McKnight) Patterson. They were
    m. in Denver, Colorado. He d. Nov. 22, 1938 aged 44.
    He served in World War II as an instructer   IN 416-2
496.   Jane, b. April 4, 1816 wife of William Stewart Finney   3JF-7
    Their children   5WF-1
497.   Jewel (Mischeler) wife of James McKnight   IN 416-2
498.   John Frank b. Jan 15,1860 m. Sarah McKnight. Their
    children   IN416
499.   John Watt b. March 9, 1823 He was named for his
    paternal grand=father, John Watt. He was the son of
    James and Mary (Watt)Patterson. He m. 1845 Susan Scott
    b. 1823 d. 1899. He d. 1909. He was prominent in McKees-
    port and a man of means. Warner's History relates much
    about him.   IN 607

    ISSUE:

    1.   Elijah Patterson b. 1849'   IN 480
    2.   Ruth Patterson b. 1851 m. John O'Neil.   IN 453

500.   John d. 1813 son of James and Agnes (Finney) Patterson;
    at his death he left his wife and four children which were
    cared for by his brother, Elijah, who never married but
    made a home for his brother's widow and her children   2AF-1
501.   John Clayton, b. July 1917 son of Clayton Harvey.   IN472

NOTES

211.

PATTERSON:

502. John VanKirk b. Jan 23, 1853 d. Jan. 20, 1918. He was the son of Thomas and Martha Jane (VanKirk)Patterson.   He m. Mary Jane Patterson b. 1855 d. Dec. 26, 1907. She was the dau. of James Harvey and Belle (McCune) Patterson _____IN 516

ISSUE:

1. Wilmer Herbert Patterson b. April 17, 1830._____ IN 554
2. Thomas Clyde b. Jan. 12,1882. _____ IN 549
3. John Watt b. March 8, 1883 m. Maude Etta Howell _____ IN 315
4. Clayton Harvey b. Oct. 10, 1885 m. Mayme McCracken ___ IN 409
5. Frank Roy b. Oct. 17,1887 m. Bernice Peairs_____ IN 486
6. David McKibben b. Nov. 15,1889 m. Mabel Philips._____ IN 475
7. Myrtle Belle b. June 15, 1892_____ IN 528
8. Luella Jane b. Feb. 17, 1896 lived with her brother Wilmer.

---

503. Joseph b. May 25, 1827 son of James and Mary (Watt) Patterson. He m. Aug. 26,1831 Rebecca Scott b. March 23,1822. She d. May 10, 1872. Her parents are unknown at this time. IN 492-7

ISSUE:

1. James Scott Patterson.
2. William Alonzo b. Aug. 22,1853 m. April 14,1880 Belle Bebout _____ IN 394
3. Mary Alice b. July 24,1855 m. Oct. 29, 1879 Adoniran Judson Yohe. He was b. Jan 22, 1848 d. Aug. 13, 1933. She d. Jan 23,1924.   (For children see YOHE)

---

504. Vivia, b. May 3, 1858 m. June 20, 1883 James Thomas Stewart. He d. March 19, 1885. She d. Nov. 13,1938. No children are listed._____ IN 551

NOTES

212.

PATTERSON;

505. Vernie Price b. Dec. 1,1865 m. April 29, 1891 Frank
   Bebput b. Dec. 28, 1865 d. Aug. 22,1940 _____IN 578

   ISSUE: *BEBOUT*

   1. RUTH b. Jan 17,1897 m. April 11,1936 James Wilbur
   Nelson as his second wife.

506. Joseph b. 1792 d. 1855 never married. Son of Agnes Finney and James Patterson _____2AF1-8
507. June Lorraine b. Nov. 7,1925 dau of David McKibben_____IN 475-4
508. Katherine Brown m. Homer Greene_____IN 269
509. Lillie (Fritz) 1st wufe if Elijah Patterson d. 1874 _____IN 480
510. Luella A. (Rhodes) wife of David McKibben_____IN 475
511. Mabel b. May 21,1891 d. Sept 11, 1942 dau of John Frank_____IN 416-1
512. Mabel Jane b. June 9, 1926 dau of David McKibben_____IN 475-5
513. Margaret, dau of Agnes (Finney) and James Patterson _____2AF1-6
514. Margaret m. Robert Finney as' his 2nd wife. Children _____2RF-2
515. Marjorie b. April 19, 1897 dau of John Frank _____IN 416-3
516. Martha Jane (VanKirk) b. March 8,1833 m. Thomas, son
   of James. Thomas was b. Sept 19,1830 and d. Nov. 18,1894.   IN 492-8

   ISSUE:

   1. John VanKirk b. Jan 23,1853 d. Jan 20, 1918 He m.
   Jan. 23,1820 Jane Patterson dau of James Harvey Patterson. She d. Dec. 26,1907 (See Mary Jane (Patterson)   IN 522
   2. Ida Laura b. 1859 d. April 2. 1915. Unmarried.
   3. Emma Luella b. 1863 d. Oct. 1911 _____IN 481

517. Mary b. March 31,1882 m. H.L. Mason. She was the dau
   of William Alonzo Patterson. (See Mason)_____IN 394
518. Mary Alice b. July 23,1895 dau of James Scott. She m.
   Oct. 29, 1879. Adoneran Judson Yohe. Their children_____IN 753
519. Mary Blanche b. June 10, 1917 dau of David McKibben _____IN 675-2
520. Mary Evanna b. Oct. 25, 1847 dau of James Patterson. She
   m June 1, 1870 John Dunlevy   Their children _____IN 206
521. Mary Jane b. 1854 d. 1928 dau of James. She lived with
   her sister in the Gilliland family_____IN 490-1
522. Mary Jane dau of James Harvey and Belle McCune. She
   was the wife to John VanKirk. Their children _____IN 502-3
523. Mary Louise dau of Clifford Scott. She m. June 8,1937
   Manor Jahnar Siljander. No children_____IN 503-3

PATTERSON:

PATTERSON.

553. William Alonzo b. Aug. 22, 1853 m. Belle Bebout _____ IN 41
ISSUE:

1. Ada Jane b. Dec. 30, 1880 m. S. R..Hall _____ IN 460
2. Mary b. March 31, 1882. m. R. L. Mason _____ IN 394
3. Almira Scott b. Nov. 11,1883 m. William Covert _____ IN 463
4. Bertha b. April 27, 1883 d. Jan 27, 1889.
5. William Alonzo b. Aug. 2, 1891 d. Jan 20 1892.

554. Wilmer Herbert b. April 17, 1830 never married. He lived
with his sister, Luella Jane _____ IN 502-8

PATTON:

555. William R. b. 1850 m. Lydia Ann Finney dau of Richard King Finney _____ 61-637
556. Isabelle, wife of David Plantz Stevenson. She was the
mother of Andrew Milton Stevenson, a soldier in the Civil
War. He m. Pearl Finney. Their children _____ _____ ⊢PF-4

PEARSE:

557. Elizabeth, (Atwood) wife of Samuel parents of Experience
Pearse wife of Loring Finney. Their children _____ 39-261

PEAIRS:

558. Bernice wife of Frank Ray Patterson _____ IN 486

PECK:

559. Henry m. Rachel Whittaker, parents of Rebecca
wife of Elisha Phinney _____ 27-113
560 Lydia wife of Ephraim Preston, parents of Huldah,
wife of Isaac Phinney. Their children _____ 42-321
561. Rebecca, wife of Elisha Phinney. _____ 35-139

PEDEN:

562. Mary(Polly) wife of Robert Finney _____ 2RF1

PHELPS:

563. Phebe, wife of Jonathan Finney. Their children , _____ 33-145

PHILLIPS :

564. Amaziah m. Lydia Finney _____ 31-281
565. Mabel, wife of David McKibben Patterson _____ IN 475

PIERCE:

566. Susannah, wife of Caleb Mathews, parents of Henrietta, wife of George Finney. Their children _____ 41-294

PLUM:

567. Charles Leroy, m. Mary Jay Finney. Their children _____ 73-710

POOL:

568. Lydia (Phinney)wife of a Mr. Poole. Her children: _____ 45-378
ISSUE:

1. Harry Pool
2. Jessie Pool
3. Clifford Pool.
4. Roy Pool.

INDEX

P.

POOLER:

569. Jane Ann b. Aug. 26, 1925 dau of Arthur Charles and Olive Virginial m. John Charles Finney b. Nov. 7 1920 Son of Dwight McDill and Charlotte Mae (Gates) _____ 4DF1-6

   ISSUE:

   1. Michael Charles Pooler Finney.

POPE:

570. Thomas m. Ann Fallowell, dau of Gabriel and Catherine (Finney) Fallowell. _____ 1-1
571. Mary, wife of David Phinney. Their children _____ 22-82
572. John and Elizabeth (Bourne) parents of Mary _____ 22-82

POLLOCK:

573. Mary (Finney) b. 1830 d. 1877 dau of Thomas l and Nancy (Culbertson) Finney _____ IN 178

PORTER:

574. Cathereine Alice wife of Joseph Harrison Finney _____ 68-661

POTTER:

575. Abigail, wife of Mark Anthony deWolf, mother of William _____ 38-251

PRESTON:

576. Huldah, wife of Isaac Phinney, dau of Ephraim and Lydia (Peck) Preston. Their children _____ 42-321

PRICE:

577. Edna, dau of Albert Phinney _____ 48-381
578. Vernie, wife of Frank Bebout _____ IN 505

NOTES

216.

RALSTON:

579   Agnes (Finney) dau of Thomas and Nancy (Culbertson) Finney _____ 78aF

RANSOPHER:

580.   Mary, wife of John V. Finney. His first wife _____ 68-663

RAY:

581.   Hannah, b. Oct. 16,1712 dau of Peter and Tabitha (Newcomb) Ray. She m. Samuel Finney. Their family _____ 21-78

READ:

582.   Josephine b. Jan 23,1909 wife of James Paul Stevenson an attorney. Their children _____ 1PF4-3

583.   Mercy, b. 1706 d. 1767 wife of Jonathan Phinney _____ 10-27

REYNOLDS:

584.   Belle McClure wife of Melvin _____ 1SF8-1

585.   Lizzie, b. 1856 wife of William Finney. Their family _____ 5WF-2

RHEAH:

586.   Mary Ellen, wife of Otis Milliken _____ 4RF-5

587.   Rebecca, 3rd wife of James Finney. Their family _____ 57-551

RHODES:

588.   Deborah (Finney) wife of Lucius _____ 29-263

589.   Lucile, 2nd wife of David McKibben Patterson _____ IN 475

590.   Sylvia, wife of Clyde Finney _____ 2CF-15

RICHMOND:

591.   Alice (Hackett-Campbell) 2nd wife of Joseph Phinney _____ 18-65

RICHARDSON:

592.   Sarah, dau of John wife of John Finney _____ 50-506

RICKARD :

593.   Joseph, father of Mary, 1st wife of Joseph Phinney. _____18-65

RING:

594.   Ruth Sylvester Cooke 3rd wife of John Phinney. She was the dau of Israel and Ruth (Turner)Sylvester._____ 18-62

RIPLEY:

595.   Phebe, wife of Robert Finney son of *Mother* Finney _____ 1-2

ROARK:

596.   Nancy (Breeding) See Family Group No. 1 _____ 5JF-4

ROGERS:

597.   John, son of Thomas, of the *Mayflower* _____ 3-4

598.   Mary, dau of Lt. John of the *Mayflower*. Wife of _____ 3-4

John Finney. Their family _____ 3-4

599   Thomas, father of Lt. John, Grandfather to Mary _____ 3-4

600.   Maria deWolf m. a Mr. Rogers. _____ 38-251-4

601.   Susanna, wife of Nathan Phinney _____ 34 -322

ROTH:

602.   Albert F. m. Zelah Finney, dau of David and Sarah
(Patterson) Finney. Zelah was b. Aug. 21,1893 dau. of
of David and Sarah (Patterspm)Finney. She m. Al=
bert R. Roth April 30, 1918. Albert was b. June 29,
1890._____LZF-4

ISSUE:

1. Albert Finney Roth b. Nov. 20,_____
2. Dorothy Leona Roth b. April 22, 1927.

NOTES

SHORT:

623. Elizabeth, dau of James and Margery (Riatt) m. James Patterson. Their family. _____ FJF 13

SHULTZ:

624. Carl Donald b. June 10, 1906 m. Sept. 12, 1933 Ruth Minnehaha Stevenson b. Aug. 26,1906. She was the granddaughter of James Patterson Finney _____ 24 &29F

ISSUE:
1. Mary Louise Shultz b. Aug. 5, 1935 d. Jan. 12, 1936.
2. Donald Carl Shultz b. June 3, 1937 d. June 25, 1942.
3. James Milton Shultz b. Feb. 20, 1939.
4. Marjorie Jean Shultz b. July 3, 1941.

SIGNS:

625. Jake, m. Nellie Phinney whom she divorce. Their family __ 47-375
626. Wesley m. Ora Phinney. Their family _____ 48-380-1
627. Bertha, dau of Wesley; m. Orin Stevens _____ 48-380-2
628. Nettie, m. William Kenney. _____ 49-380-2

SILJANDER:

629. Manor Jahner m. Mary Louise Patterson _____ IN 323.

SIMPSON:

630. Amos Glover b. Dec. 2, 1875 d. while in the Spanish American War of fever in camp. _____ 62F
631. Denny Blaine, b. Jan 13,1884 d. March 3, 1944 _____ 62F
632. Mabel, b. June 22,1879 m. Jack Carrillo. She d. Oct. 8, 1924. _____ 62F
633. Minnehaha, b. April 1, 1877 m. June 26,1909 Albert ___ 62F Bennett.
634. Ida May b. June 24,1873 m Marcg 3m 1917 Fred Wheeler. He was b. Aug. 9, 1861 d. March 3, 1926. _____ 62F
635. Mabel m. Thomas Clyde Patterson. Their family _____ IN 549
636. Mary Jane (Finney)m. Denny Burns _____ 5WF-1-4

SLOAN[E]

637. Helen Lois (Phinney) dau of James and Helen (Rich) Phinney. She was b. Nov. 19, 1848. She m. Henry Clay Sloan. She spells her name S L O A N E   She is a *Mayflower* descendant (*Leslie P. Mason records*)
    (*See appendix for further information*)

NOTES.

ISSUE:

1. William Steele Thompson d. at six years of age.
2. Ruth Ann b. April 1940
3. John b. 1942.

----

650. Minnie (O'Neil) b. July 31, 1878 m. Robert Lowry Steele She was the dau of Ruth (Patterson) and John O'Neil. Robert was b. Nov. 2, 1875.

ISSUE:

1. Ruth b. July 4, 1907 m. William S. Thompson. Her Family _____ IN 649

It is possible there were more children blut there is none known at this time.

STEWART: See Appendix

NOTES.

TRIPP:

TRIM:

TYSON:

NOTES

INDEX

U.

USHER:

V.

VALADIN:

VANKIRK.

VEZAR:

VINNICUM

VORCE:

NOTES

WELLFARE:

728. Richard Jesse, son of Jesse D. and Roberta. He m. Pauline Smith McSparran. She was b. July 7, 1924. Richard was b. Nov. 9, 1929, Lansing, Michign. Their children are; _____ IN 727

1. Pamela Ann b. May 24,1957.
2. Susan Kay b. Oct. 26, 1958
3. Michelle Jane b. Nov. 29, 1959.
4. Kimberly Jane b. Sept 4, 1961.

729. Robert Wayne, son of Jesse D and Roberta. He m. Barbara Ann Starkey b. Oct. 6, 1934. Robert was b. July 15, 1933. _____ IN 727

ISSUE:

1. Michael Robert b. March 27, 1962.
2. Jonathan Edward b. Sept. 21.1963.

   (Wellfare Familly taken from the records of Roberta Wellfare)

WEST:

730. Esther, second wife of Joseph Phinney. Their children_____ 6-15
731. Margaret, wife of Jonathan Bryant, parents of Rebecca Bryant, wife of JohnP Phinney. _____ 18-62

WESTCOTT:

732. Anne Eliza 1st wife of George Gibbs Clark, son of Mary (Finney) and Capt. Parker Clark _____ 40-265-2

WHALEY:

733. Mary LaRue, wife of David Owen Finney _____ 74-731

WHITE:

734. Anne Margaret b. Feb. 7, 1920 wife of Robert Earl_____ 3AF-19
735. Mary, (Carpenter)dau of Hannah (Finney) and Elisha She m. a Mr White. _____ 41-268-1

WHITMAN:

736. Emma G. wife of Thomas C. Finney,parents of John Edgar Finney. Their children _____ 67-653

WHITTAKER:

737. Rachel, wife of Henry Peck, parents of Rebecca, wife of Elisha Phinney. Their children _____ 27-113

WIGHTMAN:

738. Florence Virginia b. Aug. 16,1885 m. June 29,1906 Carl Judson Yohe b. April 21.1884. Carl was the son of Mary Alice (Patterson) and Adoniran Judson Yohe _____ IN 503-3 (See Yohe for children.)

WILLIAMS:

739.   Elizabeth wife of John Macomber, parents of John who m. Elizabeth Phinney. Their children _____ 26-109

740.   Harold b. March 17,1923 son of Ira and Mae (Shaler) Williams. He trained as a pilot and commissioned an officer; assigned to a P40 fighter plane but died suddenly of acute pertonitis _____ 432F

WILLIAMSON:

741.   Anna wife of Asa Finney,son of Joseph Davies Finney ___ 66-683

WILLIS:

742.   George, m. Rena Phinney, dau of George and Caroline (Brown) Phinney: _____ 45-376

WILSON:

743.   Flossie (Phinney) wife of Lewis Wilson, dau of Frank and Ida (Ferris) Finney. Their family _____ 47-384

744.   Rebecca wife of Robert Patterson _____ IN 534

745.   Sarah Agnes (Finney) b. 1856 d. 1881 m. a Mr. Wilson ___ 1SF6-4

WOOD:

746.   Elizabeth, widow of Thomas Tibbits, wife of Samuel Finney. Their children _____ 14-49

747.   Tilghman, m. Anna Finney. Their children _____ 69-676

748.   Hannah, wife of Nathaniel Finney. Their children _____ 32-130

WOODWARD:

749.   Rachel, wife of John Finney Their children _____ 31-126

WOOSTER:

750.   Charles Coffman m. Nannie Cullum, parents of Wave W. Wooster wife of Dwight MacDill Finney. Children ___ 4DF1

NOTES

YOCUM:

YOHE:

753. Adoniram Judson m. OCt. 29, Mary Alice Patterson. Mary was b. July 24,1855. Adoniram was b. Jan 22, 1848. He d. Aug. 13, 1935. and Mary Alice died Jan 23,1924. _____ IN 503-3

ISSUE:

!. Vivia Casandra Yohe never married. b. Jan 28,1882.

2. Carl Judson b. April 21,1884 m. June 29, 1906 Florence Virginia Wightman b. Aug. 16,1885.
    A. Carl, bJan 17, 1913. He was in W.W. II for 38 months in the Pacific Area. He is married and has children.
    B. William Henry b. April 20, 1920. He was in WWIIMedical Corps
    C. Florence Virginia b. Dec. 1, 1914. She m
    D. Mary Alice b. March 5, 1918.
    E. Isabelle Ruth (Twin of William Henry) b. April 20, 1920.

YOUNG:

NOTES

229.

SPECIAL SECTION

Information listed here was found in the files and some of it is in error because the person who wrote it, mentions the 2nd Robert and the 3rd John, and these people cannot be located if one uses this book to decide which person that has been mentioned. In one place it mentions the first Robert as having a son. The first Robert in this book had no children, leaving his estate to his nephews, children of John, the Pilgrim. However, this will be written as found, and it is hoped that it will be of assistance to those trying to complete their family tree.

PHINNEY, FINNEY, or FINNYE, ISAAC, Medfield 1657. JOHN, Plymouth, by w. Christian wh. d. 9 Sept.1649, had John, b. 24 Dec.1638, bapt. at Barnstable 31 July 1653, and perhaps others, rem. to Barnstable, m. 10 June 1650, Abigail, wid. of Henry Coggin, who d. 6 May 1653, and for third w. 26 June 1654, Eliz. Bayley, had Jonathan, 14 Aug. 1655; Robert, 13 Aug. 1656; Hannah, 2 Sept.1657; Eliz. 15 Mar. 1659; Josiah, 11 Jan. 1661; Jeremiah 15 Aug. 1662; and Joshua, Dec. 1665. Hannah m. the sec. Ephraim Morton. John, Barnstable, s. of the Preced. m. 10 Aug. 1664, Mary Rogers, had John, b. 5 May 1665; Melatiah, Oct. 1666 d. next yr; Joseph, 28 Jan 1668; Thomas, Jan. 1672; Ebenezer 8 Feb.1674; Samuel, 4 Nov. 1676; Mary 3 Sept.1678; Mercy, 10 July 1679; Reliance 27 Aug. 1681; Benjamin, 18 June 1682 bapt. 16 Sept. 1783; Jonathan 30 th July 1684, bapt. 26 July 1685; Hannah, 28 Mar. 1687 bapt. 7 Apr. 1689, d. young; and Eliz. bapt. 10 May 1691. Josiah, Barnstable, br of the preced. m. 19 Jan. 1688, Eliz d. of the first Joseph Warren. Robert, of Plymouth, prob. br. of John the first, and perhaps elder, came with his mo. I suppose, for the rec. says "mo Feney d. 22 Apr. 1650, aged upwards of 80," m. 1 Sept.1641 Phebe Ripley, was deac. 1667 and d. 7 Jan. 1688 near 80, and his wid.d. 9 Dec. 1710 "suppos. 92 yrs old." Robert, Barnstable, s. of John the first d. 1690, in the wild crusade of Phips against Quebec.

FINNEY, ALBERT, son of 2nd William m. 1833 Lucinda Thomas, and had Albert Thomas, 1834 m. Carrie C. Paty; Charles Harlow, 1835, m. Rebecca Diman; Costello, 1837 m. Nellie Nelus; Thomas Weston, 1838, m. Isabella Griffith; Rufus 1841 m. Maria Nelus; Emeline 1843; Frederick, 1846; Lucinda, 1848; Clara V. 1852. Benjamin Cooper, son of Daniel, m. 1833 Elizabeth D. Wood and had Elizabeth D., m. Joshua Savage and George H. Green. Caleb, son of 2nd Ephraim m. 1799, Lydia Covington, and had Ephraim 1810, m. Deborah and Susan Churchill; Benjamin D m. Mary Ann Churchill and Adeline Clark; Caleb; and Mary m. Reuben Leach. He m. 2d, 1817, Phebe Leonard. Clark son of 3rd Robert m. 1797, Polly Wethered, and had Mary, m. William Swift; Experience, m. Nathan Whiting; Everett m. Susan (Leach) Howland, wid of Henry; Susan, m. James Finney; John m. Marcia W. Doten and Deborah Swift; Clark, and George. Clark, son of 1st Elkanah m. 1837 Jeanette R. Burt and had Henriette Lucy, Clark, and Elkanah. Daniel, son of 4th Josiah m. 1795 Sarah Cooper, and had Benjamin, Cooper; Sally C. m Henry Erland; Polly, and Lydia, both m. Daniel Goddard; Harriet C. 1808; Alice m. Benjamin Dunham; Olive m. Peleg Faunce. Ebenezer, from Bristol m. 1726, Jane Faunce. Ebenezer from Barnstable, m 1730, Rebecca Barnes. Elkanah, son of 3rd Robert m. 1798 Lucy Morton, and had Josiah; Elkanah; Lucy m. Lemuel Leach; Henry; William; Clark; Betsey m. David Manter; Marcia m. Anthony S. Allen. Elkanah, son of above m. 1827 Serena Finney, and had Angeline, m. Augustus Hadaway. Elkanah C. son of

1st Seth m. 1829 Hannah Howland. He m. 2nd, Serviah Burgess, and had Elkanah and Clarinda. **Ephraim**, son of 1st Ezra m. 1804, Phebe Wright, and had Phebe, 1804 m. Johnson Davie; Harriet, m. Granville Gardner; Ephraim m. Salome B. Newell; Susan, 1819 m. James R. **Shaw. Ephraim,** son of 3rd John m. 1776 Mary Bartlett, and had Caleb, Solomon, and Sylvanus. **Ezra,** son of 3rd John, m. Hannah d. of Seth Luce, 1769, and had Hannah 1762; Ezra, 1776; Seth, Lydia, Ephraim, and Elizabeth. **Ezra,** son of above, m. Lydia, d of Andrew Bartlett, 1797 and had Lydia Bartlett,1799, m 2nd Betsey, wid. of John Bishop and dau of Eliphalet Holbrook, 1808, and had Betsey Bishop, 1809, m. William Sampson Bartlett; Mary Coville, 1811;Caroline 1822. **George,** son of 3rd Robert m. Abigail Finney, 1797, and had Sorena, m. Elkanah Finney; Eunice m. Nathaniel W. Leonard; Rebecca m. Nathaniel Clark; David m. Abigail Warner and Julia A. Morton; James m.a Wright and Susan Clark; Ezra m. Lydia Benson. **George,** son of 1st Clark, m. Mary Clark,1829, and had George, 1830 m. Abbey Warren Morton; Adaline, 1832m. Ebenezer Cobb; Alvin,m. Hannah Vaughn and Marcia W. Doten; Nancy, 1836m. Augustus Hadaway. **Gershom,** of Sandwich m. Martha Swift, 1821. **Henry,** son of 1st Elkanah m Betsey Langford 1828; Adaline Howland, 1837; Lucy Manter; Eliza Benson and Abby (Clark)Thomas; having by his 4th wife, Henry Allerton. **John,** an early settler in Plymouth, who came from England with his brother and mother, by wife Christian, had John 1638. He m. Abigail Coggin, wid of Henry1650 and 3rd Elizabeth Bayley, 1654 and had Jonathan, 1655; Robert 1656; Hannah 1657 m Ephrain Morton; Elizabeth 1650; Josiah, 1661; Jeremiah, 1662; Joshua, 1665. **John,** son of above, m. Mary Rogers, 1664 and had John,1665; Meltiah1666; Joseph, 1668; Thomas, 1672; Ebenezer, 1674; Samuel 1676; Mary 1678, m. John Erland; Mercy 1679; Rebecca 1681; Benjamin, 1682;Jonathan 1684; Hannah 1687; Elizabeth 1691 m. David Bradford. **John,**son of the first Josiah m. Sarah Bartlett,1721, and had Sarah, 1722'm. Ephraim Holmes; Phebe, 1725 m. Edward Doty; Josiah, 1727; Ruth, 1728 m. James Doten; John,1730. He m/ 2nd Susanna (Doten) Pratt, wid. of Elkanah and had Josiah. 1740; Robert, 1741; Ezra, 1743; Sylvanus, 1746 m. Mary Morton; Ephraim 1748 and William 1750. **John,** son of above, m. Rebecca Holmes 1757 and had Ruth, 1757; Sarah 1758; Elizabeth, 1761' m. Levi Paty; James 1764; John 1766. **Joseph,** son of 2nd John m. Mercy Bryant, 1693 and had Alice 1694; John 1696 m. Rebecca Bryant of Kingston; and Mary m. Samuel Clark. **Joseph** m.' Esther West1706. **Josiah,** son of 1st Robert m. Elizabeth Warren, 1688 and had Josiah,1688. Elizabeth, 1690 m. William Bradford; Robert,1693 m. Ann Morton; Priscilla 1694 m. Samuel Marshall; Josiah, 1698 m Abigail Bryant; John,1701; Phebe, 1705 m. Jonathan Barnes; and Joshua m. Elizabeth Pope. **Josiah,** son of 3rd John, m. Alice Barnes and had Alice B. 1764 m. Nathaniel Sylvester; Susanna, m. Ebenezer Sampson; Mary m. Joseph Holmes, and Daniel. **Josiah,** son of 3rd Robert, m. Rebecca Warren, 1791, and had Nancy, 1792; Nancy, 1793; Sally, 1795; Betsey,1797; George 1801. He m. 2nd Sally Sylvester, 1806 and had Josiah Morton; Joseph Sylvester;Josiah Thomas, 1810; Nathaniel Sylvester, 1813. **Josiah,** son of 1st Elkanah,m. Nancy Doten, 1821and had Nancy, m. Gustavus Dates' and Josiah. He m. 2d Betsey B. Doten 1832. **Josiah,** m. Mary Thomas 1726. **Josiah,** m. Mary Thomas, 1726, **Joshua,** m. Hannah Curtis1727. **Leavitt,** son of 2nd William m. Mary Weston1834 and had Levitt Weston 1837; Lydia W. 1840; and Mary E. 1850. **Lewis,** son of 1st William m. Betsey Weston 1804 and had Eliza Sherman, m. David Harlow; Lewis m. Rhoda Ann Wood; Pelham m. Mary Ann Burgess; Angeline m. Nathaniel Wood; and Harrison.

Robert, probably brother of 1st John came to America with his mother and m. Phebe Ripley1641 and had Josiah. Robert, son of 1st Josiah m. Ann.Morton 1746and had Lydia1818; Rebecca, m. David Morton. Josiah, Elizabeth m. William Wood; and Jerusha; m. Isaac Harlow. **Robert,** son of the 3d John m Isabella Clark 1765 and had LYdia m. Henry Cassady; Robert 1768, Clark George, Josiah, Elkanah; and Experience m. Truman Bartlett.

Families listed here were taken from the preceding pages, 23 and 232 to give a clearer picture of the information on those paes. The informationis sometimes not too clear as to who is relation to a family. Statements are made that a son or daughter is the son or daughter to the 3rd John, or the 2nd Jeremiah, and that person has no one **listed** in his family by that name. This is not too explicit but this compiler will endeavor in this section to try to unravel some of the information in a more understanding form. **It** is stated **that** the Finney is used exclusively, **but** that Phinney is also used as part of the family, but is not spelled that way. So it will be up to the reader as to the proper spelling of the name.

FINNEY: Albert, son of William 1833 m. Lucinda Thomas

    ISSUE:

1. Albert Thomas Finney b. 1834 m. Carrie C. Paty.
2. Charles Harlow! b. 1835 m. Rebecca Diman.
3. Costello b. 1837 m. Nellie Nelus.
4. Thomas Weston b. 1838 m. Isabelle Griffith.
5. Rufus, b. 1841 m. Maria Nelus
6. Emaline b. 1843
7. Frederick b. 1846
8. Lucinda b. 1848.
9. Clara L. b. 1852.

_____

FINNEY, Benjamin Cooper, son of Daniel m. 1833 Elizabeth D. Wood.

    ISSUE:

1. Elizabeth D. m. Joshua Savage and (2)George H. Green.

FINNEY: Caleb, son of Ephraim m. 1790 Lydia Covington.

    ISSUE:

1. Ephraim b. 1810 m. Deborah; and Susan Churchill. (Sisters ?)
2. Benjamin D. m. Mary Ann Churchill and Adeline Clark.
3/ Caleb.
4. Mary m. Ruebin Leach.

FINNEY: Clark, son of 3rd Robert. m. 1798 Lucy Morton.

    ISSUE.

1. Mary m. William Swift.
2. Experience m. Nathan Whiting.
3. Everett m. Susan (Leach)Howland, widow of Henry.
4. Susan m. James Finney.
5. John m. Marcia W. Doten and Deborah Swift.
6. Clark.
7. George.

_____

FINNEY, Clark, son of Elkanah m. 1847 (?)Jeanette R. Bert.

    ISSUE:

1. Jeanette   2. Lucy. 3. Clark. 4. Elkanah.

FINNEY; Daniel, son of 4th Josiah m. 1795 Sarah Cooper.

ISSUE:

1. Benjamin Cooper Finney.
2. Sally C. m. Henry Erland (Probably Eastland)
3. Polly ⎤ Both married David Goddard.
4. Lydia ⎦
5. Harriet C. b. 1805
6. Alice m. Benjamin Dunham.
7. Olive m. Peleg Faunce.

FINNEY: Elkanah, son of 3rd Robert m. 1798 Lucy Morton.

ISSUE:

1. Josiah.
2. Elkanah
3. Lucy m. Lemuel Leach.
4. Henry
5. William
6. Clark
7. Betsey m. David Manter.
8. Maracia m. Amthony S. Allen.

FINNEY, Alkanah, son of Elkanah and Lucy Morton m. 1827 Sorena Kenmey.

ISSUE;

1. Angeline m. Augustus Hadaway.

FINNEY: Elkanah C. son of 1st Seth m. 1828 Hannah Howland and Servian Burgess.

ISSUE:

1. Elkanah.
2. Clarinda.

FILNNEY: Ephraim, son of 1st Ezra m. 1904 Phebe Wright.

ISSUE:

1. Phebe b. 1904 m. Johnson David.
2. Harriet m. Granville Gardner.
3. Ephraim m. Salome B. Newell.
4. Susan b. 19191 m. James R. Shaw.

FINNEY: Ephraim son of 3rd John m. 1876 Mary Bartlett.

ISSUE:

1. Caleb.
2. Solomon.
3 Sylvanus.

FINNEY: Ezra, son of 3rd John m. 1769 Hannah, Luce dau of Seth Luce.

ISSUE:

1. Hannah b. 1769
2. Ezra, b. 1776 m. Lydia, dau of Andrew Bartlett.
3. Seth.
4. Lydia.
5. Ephraim
6. Elizabeth.

FINNEY: Ezra, son of Ezra above m. Lydia, dau of Andrew Bartlett. 1797 m. (2) Betsey (Holbrook) Bishop, widow of John, dau of Eliphalet Holbrook.

ISSUE:

1. Lydia Bartlett b. 1799 m. Lemuel Clark.
2. Ezra b. 1801.
3. Eliza b. 1804 m. John Bartlett.

By second wife.

4. Betsey Bishop b. 1809 m. William Simpson Bartlerr.
5. Mary Coville b. 1811, must have died young.
6. Caroline b. 1814 must have died young.
7. Ezra b. 1817.
8. Mary Coville b. 1819 m. Henry Mills.
9. Caroline b. 1822.

FINNEY, George, son of 3rd Robert m. Abigail Finney b. 1797.

ISSUE:

1. Sorena m. Elkanah Finney.
2. Eunice m. Nathaiel kW. Leonard.
3. Rebecca m. Nathan Clark.
4. David, m. Abigail Warner and Julia A. Morton.
5. James m. a Wright and Susan Clark.
6. Ezra m. Lydia Benson.

FINNEY: George son of 1st Clark m. Mary Clark b. 1829

ISSUE:

1. George b. 1830 m. Abby Warren Morton.
2. Adaline b. 1832 m. Ebenezer Cobb.
3. Alvin m. Hannah Vaughn and Marcia W. Doten.
4. Nancy b. 1830 m. Augustus Hadaway.

FINNEY, Gershom, of Sandwich, m. Martha Swift b. 1821.

FINNEY: Henry, son of 1st Elkanah m. Bettsey Langford 1828 and Adaline Howland 1837.

FINNEY: John, son of 1st Josiah m. Sarah Bartlett £771 and kSusanna (Doten)
Pratt.   (2-10}

ISSUE:

1. Sarah Bartlett b. £722 m. Ephraim Holmes.
2. Phebe 1723 m. Edward Doty.
3. Josiah b. 1727.
4. Ruth b. 1728 m. James Doten.
5, John, b. 1730 m. Rebecca Holmes (2) Susanna (Doty)Pratt.
By second wife:
6. Josiah.
7. Robert. b. 1741
8. Ezra b. 1743.
9. Sylvanus b. 1746 m. Mary Morton.
10. Ephraim b. 1748.
11. William b. 1750

FINNEY: John, son of John and Sarah Bartlett Finney m. Rebecca Holmes
1757.

ISSUE:

1. Ruth b. 1737
2. Sarah b. 1758
3. Elizabeth b. 1761 m. Levy   Paty
4. James, b. 1761
5. John, b. 1766.

FINNWY: Josiah, son of 1st Robert (1-2) m. Elizabeth Warner 1688.

ISSUE:

1. Josiah b. 1688
2. Elizabeth b. 1690 m. William Bradford.
3. Robert, b. 1693 m. Ann Morton.
4. Priscilla b. 1694 m. Samuel Marshall.
5. Josiah b. 1698 m. Abigail Bryant.
6. John, b. 1701
7. Phebe b. 1705 m. Jonathan Barnes.
8. Joshua m. Elizabeth Pope.

FINNEY: Josiah, son of 3rd John m. Alice Barnes 1763.

ISSUE:

1. Alicel B. b. 1764 m. Nathaniel Sylvester.
2. Susanna m, Ebenezer Sampson.
3. Mary m. Joseph Holmes.
4. Daniel.

FINNEY: Seth, son of Seth and Sally (Churchill) Finney. He m. Betsey Whiting and Ruth Dickerson Howland widow of Isaac.

ISSUE:

1. Seth m. Sarsah Finney.
2. Sarah C. b. 1844.

FINNEY: Seth of Boston m. Lydia Eaines   1742,
FINNEY; Solomon, son of 2nd Ephraim m. Patience Churchill 1797

ISSUE:

1. Solomon 1798
2. Sylvanus 1800.
3. Harvey. 1807
4. Alvin.   1811.
5.

FINNEY: Josiah of 3rd Robert m. Rebecca Warren 1791 (?) and Sally Sylvester. 1806.

ISSUE:

1. Nancy b. 1793
2. Sally b. 1795
3. Betsey b. 1797
4. George b. 1800

By 2nd wife:

5. Josiah Morton
6. Joseph Sylvester .
7. Josiah Thomas b. 1810
8. Nathaniel Sylvester b. 1813.

FINNEY: Josiah, son of 1st Hannah m. Nancy Doten 1821 Betsey Doten 1832 (Possibly No. 129-291)

ISSUE:

1, Nancy n, Gustavus D. Bates.
2/ Josiah m. Mary Thomas 1726
3. Joshua m. Hannah Curtis 1727. He was the child of the   2nd wife.

FINNEY: Leavitt, son of 2nd William m. Mary Weston 1834.
ISSUE:

1. Leavitt Weston
2. Lydia W. b. 1840.
3. Mary b. 1850.

FINNEY: Lewis, son of 1st William m. Betsey Weston 1801.

ISSUE:

1. Eliza Sherman Finney m. David Harlow.
2. Lewis m. Rhoda Ann Wood.
3. Pelham m. Mary Ann Burgess.
4. Angelie m. Nathaniel Wood.
5. Harrison.

FINNEY: Robert, son of 1st Josiah m. Ann Morton 1716

ISSUE:

1. Lydia; b. 1718.
2. Rebecca m. David Morton.
3. Josiah.
4. Elizabeth m. William Wood.
5. Jerusha m. Isaac Harlow.

FINNEY: Robert, son of 3rd John m. Lydia Clark 1765   (4-13)

ISSUE:

1. Lydia m. Henry Cassidy.
2. Robert b. 1768.
3. Clark.
4. George.
5. Josiah.
6. Elkanah
7. Experience m. Truman Bartlett.

FINNEY;   Robert, son of Roberts and Grndson of Robert and Ann(Morton) Finney. He m. Sarah Leach 1793.

ISSUE:

1. Sarah b. 1794 m. Thomas Smith.
2/ Lydia b. 1797.
3. Christiana b. 1799.
4. Susan L. b. 1802 m. Benjamin Whiting.
5. Robert b. 1804 m. Susan Holmes.

FINNEY,   Robert, son of Robert and Susan Holmesl 1877 .

ISSUE:

1. Robert m. Isabella Holmes.
2. Susan Holmes b. 1844 m. George Pierce.
3. Lydia m. John T. Morton.

FINNEY;   Seth, son of 1st Ezra m. Sally Churchill 1798

ISSUE:

1. Seth, m. Betsey Whiting and Ruth Dickerson Howland
2. Elkanah.
3. Hannah m. Ephraim Howard.
4. Mary Otis Augustus Burgess.

FINNEY: William son of 3rd John m. Elezabeth Sherman 1773.

ISSUE.

1. Elizabeth m. Abraham Howland.
2. Nathan Whiting.
3. Sally m. Ephraim Churchill and Barsilla Holmes.
4. Lewis.
5. William m. Patty Harlow.

FINNEY: William son of Thomas m. Patty Harlow 1806

ISSUE:

1. William m. Betsey Hackett.
2. Albert.
3. Leavitt.
4. Cordana m. Nathaniel Smith of New Hampshire.
5. Laura, m. Justus Harlow and Benjamin Ransom.

FINNEY: William L, son of Elkanah m. Ruth H. Churchill 1804.

ISSUE:

1. William.
2. Ruth H. m. Marsina F. Holmes.

In the records examined the H after Ruth's name looks like II and the compiler
assumed it was H.

The above special section was taken from the pages just preceding the above
information, and is to show how difficult it is to secure information as it is often
written. The compiler has left out the information this item contained that was
previously entered in the book.

Appendex

GENEALOGY OF THE FINNEY FAMILY

IN AMERICA

The original Finney Family came from Bristol, England consisted of a mother, a daughter, Catherine, and two sons, Robert and John. Robert died without children and it is from John, known as John, *THE PILGRIM*, that the family as descended. The records show John was granted land in 1631 at Plymouth, Mass. This is the first known date in this country.

John Finney, known as John, *the Pilgrim* b. 16-__ d. c1703 was b. in Bristol, England. He was one of the firs pilgrims granted land at Plymouth, Mass. in 1631 He later lived at Barnstable, Mass where he was admitted as a freeman in 1644, having received other grants of land in 1640/41. He was exciseman in 1646-1648; served on several juries; moved to Scituate and later joined a company that went to Bristol, Rhode Island in 1680. He was married three times. He had two children by his first wife, none by his second wife, and seven by his third wife. (See No. 3)

His first son, John Jr. b. in 1638 founded the Barnstable Line who spell their name *PHINNEY*. We are descended from Elizabeth Bailey, the third wife. His first wife was CHRISTINA _____. His second wife was ABIGAIL COGGIN, and his third wife, ELIZABETH BAILEY.

It was from Josiah, b. 1661 that Charles Grandison Finney, the great evangelist, was descended. The family moved to Ohio where Charles was an early president of Oberlin College where Finney Chapel bears his name.

There is a Revolutionary War record for John, son of Joshua and Martha (Carter) Finney. (No. 126)

Jonathan Sackett Finney, son of Joel and Ann (Sackett) Finney was born 1786 (No 355B) He m. Mary Richards and had some children.
1. DAMON d. Jan 13,1892   2. IRA   3. HEMAN b. Oct. 8,1809
4. GEORGE.   5. ELIZABETH.   6. RUTH. 7
7. MIRANDA   8. JONATHAN.

Jonathan, with his brothers, Joel, Anson, and Heman went to Elizabethtown, Essex County, N.Y. when the country was a wildserness. in 1812 With some of his family he went to Pennsylvania and a year later went to Ohio. They floated down the river on a raft to Butler County Ohio where he died later.

Damon, son of Jonathan Sackett and Mary (Richards) Finney died Jan 13, 1892 and was buried in Essex County, N.Y. The date of his birth is uncertain He m. Betty Kelly. His children were: 1. Augustus 2. James. 3. Benjamin 4. Jonathan 5. Webster and 6. Margaret.

In 1842 the three brothers migrated to Clark County, Illinois. Heman and Damon settled a section of land eight miles south of Casey, and Jonathan settled near Hazel Dell, Illinois. Damon was a member of the Christian Church. Heman was Universalist and Jonathan, the Baptist. Politically they were Republicans, having descended from the Old White Line.

Jonathan married Rachel White, who was a sister to Susan White, Heman's wife.

William Webster Finney b. Dec. 16, 1828 d. Feb. 19, 1902 married Louisa Shearley b. 1837 d. May 23, 1892. They had the following children: 1. James b. Feb. 17 1859. 2. Ulysses 3. Elzina. 4. Elra (Twin) 5. Elworth (Twin) 6. Olive 7. Stella (Twin) 8. Stella's twin died. 9. Frank (Twin) died. 10. Perry (Twin) died.

JAMES MADISON FINNEY, b. Feb. 17, 1859 in Jasper County. He died Aug. 23. 1936 m. Margaret Davis. Their family is listed on page 2JF-7.

JAMES OVAL FINNEY b. November 11, 1918 Clark county, Illinois. He was to leave for the army Nov. 11, 1918, his 21st bortjday, but received word that morning that the Armistice for World War I had been signed, so he didn't have to go. On October 1918 he went to work in the oil fields near Bellair, Ill. He also begam work for the Marathon Oil Company on November 24, 1924. He m. Helen Alexander b. June 12, 1904. They were married Dec. 10, 1924.

In May 1948 James was transferred to the Robinson district and he retired January 1961 after 37 years of service. They had one daughter, Marion Frances. who married Lowell Livingston in 1948. She lives near her parents in Bellaire, Ill (*See 2JF-8) From the records of Mrs. Marion (Finney) Livingston, Route 1 Box 267 Oblong, Ill, 62449)*

CHARLES KEY FINNEY

****

Charles Key Finney, and old resident of New Orleans died of old age at his residence 2709 Dryades Street, this city, Saturday afternoon at 4:30 o'clock.

Mr Finney was born in Westmoreland County, Virginia, eighty-two years ago, and at the outbreak of the Civil War was living in Texas. He enlisted in the Eighth Texas Calvary, Col. Terry's famous regiment, and served with distinction during the entire period of the war. At the close of the war he came to New Orleans and engaged in the distillery business in which he remained several years. Later he became associated with the New Orleans Ice Company. as manager and bookkeeper. For the past twenty years Mr. Finney had led a retired life, and had not been engaged in active business.

Mr. Finney was related to some of the best known families of Virginia and Maryland. He was a cousin to Francis Scott Key as well as being closely related with the Patterson family of Baltimore, Maryland.

A wife and six children, three sons and three daughters survive him all of whom are married except one son.

The funeral took place at 5 o'clock Sunday afternoon from the family residence, internment being at Greenwood Cemetery. Rev. Dr. William H Chase of the St. Charles Avenue M.E. Church officiated

Death Notice. Times Picayune Newspaper, New Orleans Feb. 27,1905
New Orleans, La.

Charles Key Finney married Frances Mary Cook about 1861 in Texas probably close to Matagorda, Texas. He took her as a bride to Vera Cruz, Mexico, where she had her first daughter, Nina Finney. When the Civil War broke but he went back to Texas joining the Texas Eighth Calvary, probably leaving his bride in Vera Cruz. Following the war he went back after her and left Vera Cruz, soon after the death of Emperor Maxmillan 1867. A letter written by his wife states that he was wounded severely during the war. He died at home in New Orleans, La. 1905.

The children: NINA b. 1861 Vera Cruz, Mexico.
REBECCA b. 1869 New Orleans, La.
CHARLES WILLIAM b. 1872 New Orleans, La.
VIRGINIA b. 1873 New Orleans, La.
DAVID PURCELL b. 1876 New Orleans, La.
ANTHONY KENNER b. 1879 New Orleans, La.

Charles K. Finney's father was b. in Pennsylvania and his mother was born in Maryland.

Records of Frances Finney Mills of 11556 Archery Drive, Baton Rouge La 70815.

AN OPTIMIST AT 90
****

Mrs. Frances Cooke Finney, the oldest member of the Napoleon Avenue Methodist church of New Orleans, at the age of 90 years, and the widow of Charles Key Finney says she is optimistic about the future and that is one reason she has lived so long.

"I've seen New Orleans go through war, occupation by enemy troops, reconstruction, and starvation and yellow fever plagues when there were too many dead for them to be buried properly. Why should the city worry over this thing they call 'depression'?" she queried. " This old city will get over the depression as she's gotten over everything else. Only God knows why it was sent and only God knows how it will go, but go it will."

Mrs. Finney's face was lined with wrinkles and her eyes no longer see but she says that she has lived as long as she has because of an incurable optimism.

"I've learned in 90 years that things are never as bad as they say they are."

The members of her Bible glass of the Napoleon Avenue Methodist church were giving her a party at her daughter's home, where she lives. Someone put on her favorite song "Old Grey Bonnet, With The Blue Ribbons On it" Her wrinkled face was wreathed in smiles ands jerked her head in time to the music. Patting her foot in time she said,"Ain't that lovely?"

She liked to talk about the time she had seen the Empress Charlotta and the Emperor Maxmillian of Mexico when she was a bride living in Mexico

"I first saw Carlotta with Maxmillian driving through the streets. She was fair and rosy cheeked. Shortly after this she went to France to get help for her poor husband. In the meantime he was shot and she went crazy."

Shortly after this Mrs. Finney left Vera Cruz for New Orleans on a ship with her husband and child. The boat was cast on the rocks near the coast of Mexico and a special rescue was made by a French man of war. Her husband came to New Orleans to to be superintendent of the New Orleans Ice Works., and she has lived there ever since.

———————

(Grand-children of <u>William Stewart</u> Finney and)
(   )
(his wife Jane (Patterson) Finney as follows:-)

Children of their eldest son, James Patterson Finney given

elsewhere so will not be repeated here.

****

Children of <u>Margaret (Finney) Ayers</u> and her husband <u>Hiram</u>

<u>Ayers</u> as follows:--

<u>Ida Dora</u>, born Oct. 17, 1866 at Mansfield, Ohio where she

died Apr. 28, 1867 and is buried in Mansfield Cemetery.

<u>Eunice Clyde</u>, born Feb. 25, 1868 at Mansfield, Ohio. Married

Feb. 3, 1891 <u>William Henry Grumbling</u>, born Aug. 23, 1868, died

Oct. 23, 1915 at Newton, Kansas and is buried there. Eunice

now lives in Visalia, Calif. with her son William Grumbling.

<u>James Craig Ayers</u>, born June 17, 1871 at Mansfield, Ohio.

Unmarried.

<u>William Homer Ayers</u>, born Jan. 8, 1874 at Mansfield Ohio.

Married Nov. 26, 1902 <u>Grace Anna Gambill</u>, born July 11, 1882.

They have two children. Live in Topeka, Kansas.

<u>Ralph Erskine Ayers</u>, born in Walton, Harvey Co. Ks. Feb. 11, 1880.

His mother died when he was only 3 years of age. He later

studied for the ministry and went out to India as a missionary,

where he married (1) Apr. 2, 1913 <u>Violet May Scott,</u> who died June

19, 1914. Married (2) <u>Mary Elizabeth Lawrence</u>, Apr. 12, 1916.

They have three children - Mary Eunice, Sarah Margaret and

John Lawrence - All are now married. John Lawrence is like his

father, a minister of the Gospel. Ralph and Elizabeth live at

Ezel, Ky. (1946)

NOTE: <u>Hiram Ayers</u> was a soldier in the Civil War.

BIBLE RECORD

Written by father (Rev. James Patterson Finney) in the large

Family Bible, now owned by his son Dwight MacDill Finney,

422 West Court Street, Beloit, Kansas.

The Following is copied from the Bible record.

James P. Finney and Elizabeth Short were married the 22nd

of March 1865 at Haysville, Ohio, by Rev. J. A. Ashenhurst,

pastor of United Presbyterian Church at Haysville and Savannah, O.

"BIRTHS"

James P. Finney, Feb. 29, 1837 at Mt. Pleasant, Ohio.

Elizabeth S. Finney, May 8, 1841 at Ashland, Ohio.

"THEIR CHILDREN"

Minnehaha Olive Finney, Jan. 24 (Thurs.) 1867 at Pittsburg,

Indiana, baptized by Rev. George Mitchell.

William Herbert Finney, born March 21 (Sabbath) 1869 at

Manhattan, Kansas, baptized by Rev. D. H. Pollack.

Roscoe Raitt Finney, born Aug. 13 (Sabbath) 1871 at Mansfield,

Ohio, baptized by Rev. David MacDill, D.D. Roscoe died Feb. 4,

1885 at Beloit, Mitchell Co. Kansas.

Sarah Jane Pearl Finney, born July 15 (Tuesday) 1873 at

Wheat, Adams Co., Ohio, baptized by Rev. D. MacDill, D.D.

Dwight MacDill Finney, born May 27 (Saturday) 1876 at

Wheat, Adams Co., Ohio, baptized by Rev. David MacDill, D.D.

Copied by Minnehaha Finney
Oct. 1946
121 N. 7th Sterling, Kansas

****

Death Record is added:--

Mrs. Elizabeth (Short) Finney died Dec. 8, 1916 at their home,

307 N. Campbell Ave., Beloit, Kansas. Funeral service at their

home and burial in Elmwood Cemetery, Beloit, Kansas.

Rev. James Patterson Finney died at the home of his son
Herbert, near Beloit, Kansas, Turkey Creek Twp., Aug. 16, 1918.
Funeral service was held in his son Herbert's house and burial
in Elmwood. The obituaries, as printed in Beloit local press
have been copied to go with these records.

NOTES

Anniversaries MAY 30, 1982

Forrest & Ruth Finney

Mr. and Mrs. Forrest Finney, 2304 N. Hollywood Ave., will celebrate their 50th wedding anniversary during a 2-4 p.m. reception June 6 in Muncie Church of the Brethren, 1714 Royale Drive.

Family and friends are invited to attend. The couple request that gifts be omitted.

They were married June 4, 1932, in Yorktown. Rev. S.H. Caylor officiated. Mrs. Finney is the former Ruth Hart.

They are the parents of David Finney, Plano, Texas; Wallace Finney, Key West, Fla., and Mrs. Shirley Liby, Muncie. They have nine grandchildren.

Mrs. Finney works at The Handcrafter. She is a member of Muncie Quilters Guild and Muncie Weavers Study Group.

Finney retired in 1974 from The Muncie Star and Muncie Evening Press, where he had been a printer for 32 years.

Both are active members of Muncie Church of the Brethren.

MR., MRS. FORREST FINNEY, 1932

MR., MRS. FORREST FINNEY, 1982

THE DEPARTMENT OF THE TREASURY

Bureau of Alcohol, Tobacco and Firearms

DAVID O. FINNEY
Special Agent in Charge
Dallas District

Suite 330
1200 Main Tower Building
Dallas, Texas 75202

Ofc. Com. 214-767-2250
Ofc. FTS 729-2250
24 Hr. 214-767-0527

FINNEYS OF SCOTLAND OR ENGLAND
****

Robert Finney b. either in Scotland or England c1630, known to be a large landowner in both Scotland and Londonderry, Ireland as early as 1650 married Isabell (   ) about 1650. Their children are as follows:

1.   Henry, born Nov. 30,1657 in Ireland.
2.   James born July 4, 1659 in Ireland.
3.   William b. May 6, 1664 in Ireland.
4.   Marye, b. Aug. 29 1668 in Ireland.
5.   Robert b. 1668 Londonderry, Ireland.

****

The folliwing is the history of the 5th child of Robert and Dorothea Finney.

Robert II   Robert was one of the defenders of Londonderry, and in the Boyne 1690, he was wounded and left on the field as dead. Regaining consciousness in the night, he mounted a horse grazing near by' and rode away. It is said that at the burial of some one year after his sepulcher his skull was discovered with a hole in it, showing where he had been wounded.   Another oft repeated tradition is to the effect that before leaving Ireland he dreamed that he had emigrated and purchased land in America and when he actually came he recognized in *THUNDER-HILL* The home of his dreams.

****

Robert Finney II married Dorothea (   ) in Ireland. She was born in 1670 in Ireland. Robert and his wife Dorothea died and were buried at *THUNDER-HILL* He d on March 1755 and Dorothea in May 1752. New London Township Chester County, Pennsylvania. Their children were as follows:

1.   Dr. John Finney. 2. Dr. Robert Finney 3. Lazarus 4. Letitia and 5. William.

****

NOTES.

The Conococheague area locality of some early Reformed Presbyterian or Covenanter ministers Journal of Rev. John Cuthbertson, the pioneer Covenanter minister. There is noted an entry: 1760 Mar. 16. Sabath-preached Psalm 147: 1-6. Lectured Nahum 3: 1-8, Preached Ephesians 1:7 and baptized Rachel daughter of Robt. Love; Hanna daughter of Bartho. Ha...: William son of John Wallace; Hugh son of Hugh Stewart; John son of James Finey; Martha daughter of James Colhoun; and Henry , son to James McKnaught.

****

It will be observed that the following list of Capt. Thomas Morton's Company of Rangers on the Frontiers from Westmoreland County as shown on 330-331 of vol. 23 of the Pennsylvania Archives includes.

Thomas Morton, Capt.	Isaac Greer	William Allen
Philip Howell	Thomas Samson, Jr.	Henry McGlaughlin
George Shields	Thomas Samson, Sen.	Nehimiah Hayton
John Neal	James Willson	Alex. Stewart
William Smith	James Hamilton	John Bigart
Adam McConnell, Sen.	Robt. Jameson	Amos Weddle
Adam McConnell, Jr.	Henry Westley	James Steel
John McConnell	William Ritchey	Thomas Owens
William Finney	Oliver McDuff	Nathaniel Boyd
William Morton	Samuel Laramore	John Maxwell
		John McIlduff

****

The Forefathers and Families of Certain Settlers in Western Pennsylvania. By Wm. Boyd Duff 1200 Center Street Pittsburgh, Pa. 15221

*****

ELIJAH STEWART
****

HE WAS A SOLDIER IN THE AMERICAN REVOLUTION

RECORDED IN PENNSYLVANIA ARCHIVES
FIFTH SERIES
VOLUME SEVEN   PAGES 337 338.
****

The wife of Elijah Stewart was Mary Patterson. Once I stood beside her grave in Union Cemetery in Ohio:19 miles N. of Cincinnati, Ohio, and I thought that it would have been a privilege to talk to her about those early days we know so little about. The tombstone record is as follows; *MARY (PATTERSON) STEWART WHO DEPARTED THIS LIFE Feb. 7, 1826 aged 79 years.* Note: Her name was given simply Mary Stewart. I inserted "Patterson"to show her maiden name. We do not know where she fits into any of the Patterson genealogical lines. From the dates on her tombstone we know she was born in 1747.
(copied from THE HISTORY OF THE FINNEY FAMILY by Minnehaha Finney)

Elijah Stewart was born in Lancaster County, Pennsylvania. The exact date of his birth is unknown but it would be aount the year 1736. HE died in 1807 in Paxtang Township, Dauphin County, Pennsylvania and lies buried in an old country cemetery several miles out from Harrisburg.:

Elijah's ancestry can be traced back to John Stewart of the seventeenth century who fled from Scotland to County Down, Ireland 1720, to escape penalties incurred for non-compliance with Royal edicts respecting religious worship and attendance at the Parish Church.

The north of Ireland had become a refuse for Protestants and condemned covenanters, and John Stewart sought refuse there, preferring to abandon his native hills in dear old Scotland than return to the Solemn League entered into by the Scottish people in 1643. John Stewart died in 1720. He had one son, Robert, b. near Glasgow, Scotland in 1665 (the oldest date in these records) and died 1730 in Ireland.   The lives of these two men, father and son, embraces that period in the history of England, commencing with the reighn of Charles I through the commonwealth under Cromwell, Charles II, James II, William and Mary, Queen Anne, George I, and into the reign of George II.1625-1730.

Mary Patterson, wife of Elijah Stewart is buried in Union Cemetery, in Ohio, near **Cincinnati** After the death of Elijah Mary went with her daughter, Sarah (Stewart) Finneyto Southwestern Ohio and there lived the remainder of her days. She died Feb. 7, 1826 age 79 years as recorded on her tombstone. She is buried only a few feet from the grave of Jeremiah Morrow, the sixth governor of Ohio. According to the dates on the tombstone she would have been born in 1747, but her parents are unknown at this time. Among the early baptisms of

251

the Rev. John Cuthbertson, when he first arrived in America and had many children to baptize., her name does not appear among them. She would have been about four years old in 1751.

Elijah Stewart was the fourth son of Samuel and Mary (McClay) Stewart. A record of their marriage is found in the diary of Rev. John Cuthbertson who was the first missionary to come to America of the Reformed Presbyterian Missions. This diary is interesting reading and is very full of valuable information. Under the date of March 29, 1768 there is this record; *TRAMPED ONE MILE, MARRIED ELIJAH SJEWART AND MARY PATTERSON.*

There is a public record of Elijah Stewart's war record in the State Library in Harrisburg, Pa. See later.

The children of Elijah and Mary (Patterson) Stewart is given as follows:

1. SARAH baptized June 17, 1770.
2. JOHN, baptized Jan 31, 1771.
3. SAMUEL, baptized Nov. 9, 1772.
4. SUSANNA, Baptized June 29, 1783.
5. JAMES, Baptised June 29, 1783.
6. MARGARET   The baptism of these four children is not given in
7. MARY   the John Cuthbertson diary for Rev. Matthew Lind for .ir
8. NANCY   (or Linn) was pastor at Paxtang 1774-
9. JANE   1783

Sarah married James Finney.

John m. a lady whose last name was Wilson. They had a daughter Nannie, Margaret m. William Finney.

Mary married William Stewart her cousin.

Nancy married a Mr. Clark.

The definite service of Elijah Stewart in the Revolutionary War is given in the copy of the record furnished by the Custodian of the Public Records in the State Library of Pennsylvania at Harrisburg, which states as follows;

To Whom It May Concern;

 I hereby certify tht one, Elijah Stewart, was a Private to Captain James Gordon's Company, Fourth Battalion, Lancaster County Militia, commanded by Colonel James Burd, Esqr. March 23, 1776.

Signed--H. H. Shenk

Custodian of the PUblic Records

March 6, 1923.

(See pages 337,338 Volume seven Pennsylvania Archives Fifth Series.

Seal of the Dept.
Affixed here
_____

The William H. Grumbling Family
****

Their Children;

1. Esther May Grumbling, born March 20, 1893 married Dec. 25,1915
    Arthur Leslie Gordon, born in Anderson Co., Kans December 3,1892.
    Esther was born in Newton, Kansas. Their children;

    1. Arthur William Gordon, b in Troy, Ohio, Dec. 16, 1918.
        He m. Norma Loraine Bell, b. in Santa Monica, Califor-
        nia, April 5,1942. Their childrn as of this writing are:
        A. Sharon Lorraine Gordon, b. Santa Monica. Oct.9,
            1943.
        B. Rosemary Gordon, b. Jan 1945 in Santa Monica.
    2. Viola Ruth Gordon, b. May 9, 1921 Troy, Ohio. She m.
        Orie Davidson, Feb. 4, 1940. He was b. in Pratt, Kan.
    3. Foster Ralph Gordon, b. May 13,1927, Newton, Kansas.
        He served in the Navy during World War II April 30,1945
        to Aug. 17, 1946.
    4. Clyde Dean Gordon b. June 29, 1931 at Newton, Kansas.
    NOTE: Arthus William served in the' Navy Air Corps for over two
    years.

2. John Hiram Grumbling, b. March 23,1892 Newton, Kansas, or Troy,
    Ohio. He was raised in Newton, Kansas and m. June 13, 1916 to
    Marian Johnson, b. March 4, 1898. Both; in 1911, graduated from
    Newton High School. Their children are;

    1. Meribah, b. April 3, 1918 in Los Angeles. She was in
        the Service , W.A.B.
    2. John Richard, b. June 27, 1920 in Los Angeles. He was
        in the Navy.
    3   Paul Johnson, b. in Van Nuys, Cal. May 15,£926.   .He
        was in the Navy, and went to Japan andother places in
        photography work.
    4. Anne, b. NOv. 10, 1929 in Van Nuys, Cal.

3, Eunice Evelyn Grumbling born Feb. 18,1902 in Newton, Kans. She
    m. (1) Roy Gilbert and had one son named Roy b. March 21,1922
    in Oklahoma City, Oklahoma but his father suddenly died before
    his birth so has always gone by the surname of Grumbling,. his
    mother's maiden name. Eunice m. (2) Louis Case Lawrence Jan. 6,
    1933 and at presnet live in Mendocine, California. Roy Myers Gil-
    bert was in the Navy under the name of Grumbling, being sponsored
    by his jother's brother, William Ralph Grumbling.

4. William Ralph Grumbling, b. May 16, 1907 Newton, Kansas, married
    Aug. 28,1930 Mildred Ellen Summers, b. May 24,1912 or 1908. in
    California. Their children are;

    1. Henry Grumbling b.July 23,1932.
    2. Arret Doris Grumbling b. Sept. 4, 1934
    3. Rowland Warren Grumbling b. Sept. 15,1938.
    4. Ralph William Grumbling, b. Oct. 30, 1939.
    The above dates may not be exact.

Thomas Finney b. July 9, 1795, son of William and Margaret (Stewart) Finney. He was born in Pennsylvania and marraied Jan. 4, 1827 Nancy Culbertson b. Jan 29, 1806. Thomas d. May 26,1854 and Nancy died Feb. 11, 1877   1-TF4

ISSUE:

1. William Shannon b. 1843 d. 1884.
2. Mary.
3. Agnes m. a Mr. Ralston.
4. James born 1833.

James Finney, amd severa; pf jos spms were om tje

James Finney and several of his sons were in the Revolutionary War. It is interesting to note that James Finney's wife, Martha Mayes on July 1,1784 patented *BLOOMING GROVE* the same day tracts were patented by John Finney, Sr, John Jr., Walter, Robert and William Finney. *Blooming Grove* is where Robert and Margaret (Patterson) Finney lived and is in Allegan Co. Pennsylvania.

Margaret Stewart married her cousin William Finney. Their children are listed at 6WFl.

NOTES

Chart No. _____

Name _____

James Finney
b. 1726
d. 8-3-1802
Martha May---
b.
d.

b/o James Finney 2nd
Robert Finney
b. 1765
m. 1785/6
d. 7-16-1850
(Polly)
Co., PA. Mary Peden
b.
d.

1st cousin of Robert Finney
William Finney
b. 10-30-1801
w: Eliz. Tp. Allegheny Co., PA.
m: 3-20-1828
w.
d. 1-3-1886
w. Eliz. Tp. Allegheny Co., PA.

2nd cousin of Thomas G. Finney
Samuel Finney
b. 7-17-1832
w. Elizabeth Twp Allegheny Co., PA.
m. 11-25-1862
w.
d. 8-8-1914
w. Greensburg, PA.

Lucinda Nicholls *
b. 2-13-1811
w.
d. 11-2-1830
w. Elizabeth Twp.
Allegheny, Co. PA.

b.
m.
d.

b.
d.

b.
m.
d.

b.
d.

b.
m.
d.

b.
w.
m.
w.
d.
w.

Susannah Shrader *
b. 1-29-1841
w. Elizabeth Tp. Allegheny Co., PA.
d. 9-3-1924
w. Greensburg, PA.

3rd cousin of William G. Finney
Ella Wood Finney
Born
Where
Married
where
Died
Where

Ella Wood Finney s/o William Shrader Finney
William f/o William Rutlege Finney, he 4th cousin of Joseph F. Finney.
William Rutledge's children are Thomas R. Finney's 5th cousins.
256

FAMILY ___Finney - Crunkleton - A___

Husband's Name ___Robert Crunkleton___

Address ___Antrim Twp. Cumberland County, PA.___

Date of Birth _____ Where _____

Date of Marriage _____ Where _____

Other Wives _____

Date of Death _____ Where _____

Cemetery _____

Father's Name _____

Mother's Maiden Name _____

GENERATION

Wife's Maiden Name ___Margaret (   )___

Address ___Same___

Date of Birth _____ Where _____

Date of Death _____ Where _____

Cemetery _____

Other Marriages _____

Father's Name _____

Mother's Maiden Name _____

M or F	CHILDREN Arrange in order of birth	When Born			Where	Married To	When Married			Where	When Died			Where	Chart
		Mo.	Day	Year			Mo.	Day	Year		Mo.	Day	Year		
M	Joseph														
M	Robert Jr.														
M	Samuel														
F	Rebeccah					( ) Miller									
F	Mary					Robert Crooks									
F	Martha					James Finney 2nd	4	20	1774	Cumberland Co., PA.				Cumberland Co., PA.	
F	Susan														
F	Elizabeth					( ) Prater									
F	Sarah					Robert McCutchen									

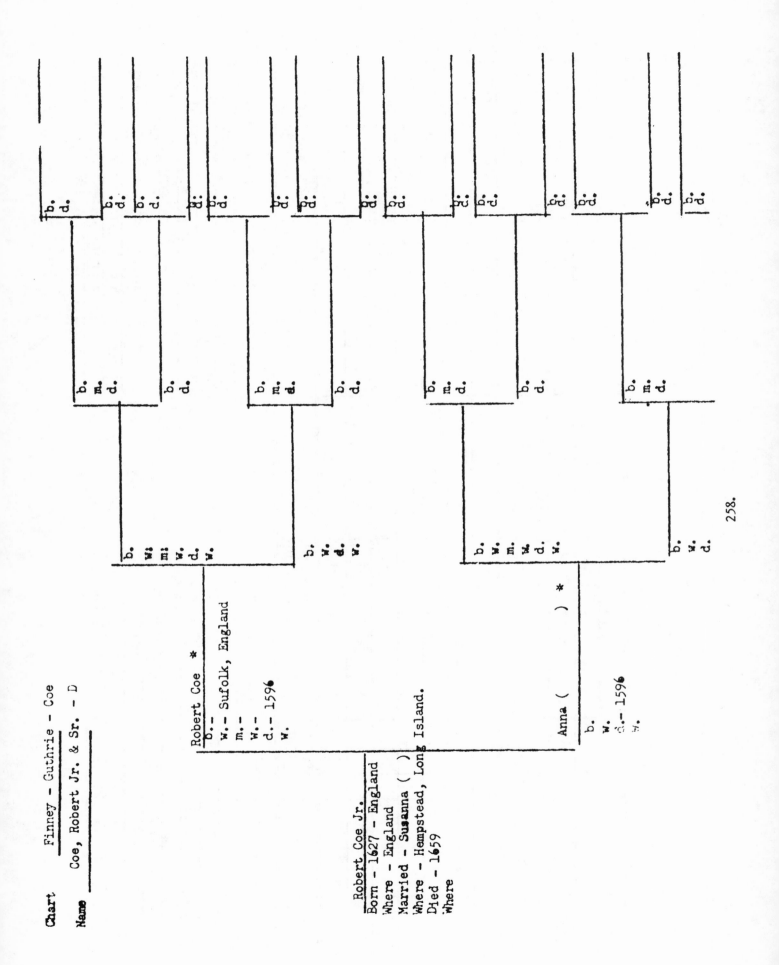

Chart.   Finney – Guthrie – Coe

Name   Coe, Robert Jr. & Sr. – D

Robert Coe *
b.–
w.– Sufolk, England
m.–
w.–
d.– 1596
w.

Anna (   ) *
b.
w.
d.– 1596
w.

Robert Coe Jr.
Born – 1627 – England
Where – England
Married – Susanna (   )
Where – Hempstead, Long Island.
Died – 1659
Where

258.

Chart No. __Finney - Guthrie - Coe__

Name __Guthrie - Caldwell - Davis - Coe - C__

(The Martyr)
James Guthrie - *

John Guthrie

b.
m.
d.

Captain John Coe
b.- 5-10-1658
m. - 12-20-1682
d. - 4-19-1741

Mary Hawley
b.
d.- 10-9-1731

d:Robert Coe Jr. - I
b.- 1627- England
d.- 1659

Susanna ( )   *

Joseph Hawley *

John Guthrie 2nd

b.
w:
m:
w.
d.
w.

2nd Susanna ( )
Abigail Coe

b.
w.
d.
w.

John Guthrie 3rd

b.
w.
m.
w.
d.
w.

(Son of Sarah (Davis)Guthrie)
Robert Guthrie
Born - 1752
Where
Married - 5-4th-1778 ——— Elizabeth Caldwell, d/o William Caldwell.
Where
Died - 5-6th-1815
Where

2nd wife Sarah Davis *
1st wife Patience Knapp

b.
w.
d.
w.

259

Name   Joseph Fielding Finney to James Finney 2nd. - A

James Finney - B
b.   1750
d. Lancaster Co., Ohio
Martha Crunkleton   #1

Robert Finney
b. About 1780
m.   "   1806
d.

Robert Guthrie - C
b.
d. d/o William
Elizabeth J. Caldwell
Caldwell *

Thomas G. Finney
b.   6-3-1826
w: Harrison Co., Ohio
m: 5-4-1848
w. Harrison Co., Ohio
d.   2-12-1919
w. Petersburg, IN.

Margret Guthrie
b. 12-11-1784
d.

Margret J. Nash *
b.   5-28-1829
w.
d.   5-2-1906

William G. Finney
b.   12-7-1855
w. Dubois Co., IN.
m. #2- 9-23-1875
w. Alba, Missouri
d.   2-7-1941
w. Petersburg, IN.

Robert Guthrie, above is the son of John & Sarah (Davis) Guthrie,
Rev. War Soldier, (Mahoning Co.,Ohio) D.A.R. No. 77,619 - Information
Mahoning Chapter. -"Ohio D.A.R. Revolutionary Soldiers Roster" Volumes
I & II 1929-1938 - Trumbull Co. (Location Page 167 Vol. I - John
Guthrie (Mahoning Co.) D.A.R. Records, PA. Archives Series 2 Vol.13
P-89. Series 3- Vol. 23 - P-14 & Series 4 -
P-43. This John Guthrie is John Guthrie 3rd
Joseph Lester *

b.   4-23-1818
1841

Mary Blocksom *
b. 1-10-1820

#2- Susan Rosine Lester
b.   12-21-1854
w. Washington Co., IN.
d.   9-9-1933
w. Melrose, Kansas

Joseph Fielding Finney
Born   11-25-1876
Where Alba, Missouri
Married   7-11-1908
Where Logansport, IN.
Died   7-27-1949
Where Fayetteville, Ark.

Married-Stella S. Engler

Finney lineage from

Char

Name   James Finney 2nd to Robert Finney from Ireland. - B

Robert Finney
b.- About 1620.
d- 8- -1672.
Isabell ( ) *

Robert Finney
b.- 1668
m. - About 1690
d.= 3- -1755
Dorothea ( ) *

William Finney
b.- 1700--1710
w.- North Ireland
m.- About 1725
w.- Chester Co., PA.
d.- 1751
w.- Chester Co., PA.

(In the forks of Youghiogheny)
(Yough.)
One of the first families in the (Youghiogheny.)
In this Finney line,--1st American born Finney.
James Finney

b.- 1720
w.- Chester Co., PA.
m.- 1747
w.- Chester Co., PA.
d.- 8-3-1802
w.- Allegheny Co., PA.

Jean Stephanson *
b.
w.
d.
w.- Chester Co., PA.

James Finney 2nd
Born- 1750
Where -Lancaster Co.,PA   1st wife Martha Crunkleton.
Married- 4-20-1774 --
Where- Conococheague -- (Conny-ga-gee,) Lancaster Co.,PA.
Died- 9-1-1829
Where- Harrison Co.,OH.

Thomas Mayes *
b.
w.
m.
w.
d.
w.

Martha Mayes
b.
w.
d.- 7-8-1804
w.-Allegheny Co., PA.

Margaret ( ) *
b.
w.
d.

261.

Chart No. _____

Name _____

This James Finney b/o James that maried Martha Crunkleton

This Wm. 1st cousin/o James that m. Martha Crunkleton

This Wm. S. 2nd cousin/o Robert that m. Margaret (Guthrie)

Rev. James P. Finney below was a
2nd cousin/o Thomas G. Finney

Rev. James Patterson Finney
  Born 2-29-1837
  Where Mt. Pleasant, Ohio
  Married 3-22-1865
  Where Haysville, Ohio
  Died 5-16-1918
  Where Beloit, Kansas

James Finney 1st.

Martha Mayes
  b.
  d.

  b.
  d.

d: Samuel Stewart
  d.

Mary McClay
  b.
  d.

  b.
  d.

  b.
  d.

d: Thomas Finney
  b.
  c.

Susanna Stewart
  b.
  d.

  b.
  d.

d. Wm. Orr
  b.
  d.

Thomas Finney
  b.
  m.
  d.

Susana Stewart
  b.
  d.

Elijah Stewart
  b.
  d.

Mary Patterson
  b.
  m.
  d.

James Patterson Sr.
  b.
  m.
  d.

Agnes Finney
  b.
  d.

John Watt
  b.
  m.
  d.

Jane Orr
  b.

Wm. Finney
  b.
  Wi
  d.
  W.

Margaret Stewart
  b.
  W.
  d.
  W.

James Patterson
  b.
  W.
  m.
  M.
  d.
  W.

Mary Watt
  b.

Brother & Sister

Wm. Finney
  b.
  W.
  m.
  W.
  d.
  W.

1st cousins

1st cousins once removed

James Patterson

Jane Patterson

James Patterson Finney m. Elizabeth Short their
children, Minnehaha Olive, William Herbert, Roscoe
Watt, Sarah Jane Pearl and Dwight MacDill Finney are
4th cousins/o William G. Finney. And that makes
Minnehaha Olive Finney my 4th cousin 2 times removed.
****

Minnehaha Compiled the " Finney Family History."
Minnehaha the d/o James Patterson Finney above, b. 1-21-d-867-
at Pittsburg, Indiana. Carrol Co. N.W. of Delphi, In.

262.

ZENAS PHINNEY
1752 1848
Bible Record

I

Zenas Phinney died March 4, 1848 aged 95 years, 5 months,10 days. On the flyleaf is written: *I have given this Bible at my decease to Captain Daniel Ruggles, my grandson Septr 14 day 1846.* This seems to be in the handwriting of Zenas Phinney as are most of the other entries.

On the two inside covers of the Bible Zenas Phinney has left a record of jos ;ofe written inhis 93rd year. Some placesthe record is extremely difficult to read or decipher. The following is what was able to be deciphered.:

I was born September the 2d day 1752—was a poor boy without money or friends to get me forward in the fareing line. When

I was born September the 2d day 1752==was a poor boy without money or friends to get me forward in the fareing line. When I first went to sea I was in my twentieth year. Went a whaling to the Westtin Islands in the year 1772 and was in the same business when Bunker Hill battle was 1775. We heard of it at sea, returned home then listed and joined the Army at Roxbury, January the first 1776 when the English Left Boston marched to New York where we soon met the English had several small engagements. We retreated into New Jersey crost the Delaware. They divided their army in 3 divisions viz; Morristown, Prince town and Trenton on the 25 of December at night we crost the Delaware back and went against Trinton in a thick snow storm at 8 in the morning gave them battle took 918 prisoners, about 1000 small arms, sum brass cannon Left the dead on the field of Battle. . . . . to camp on the second day of January 1777. I was discharged set out for home was sick on the road was 1 month gong home. No Mortal case have an idea what I underwent—Glory to be God for returning me in safety.

My misfortunes at sea from the beginning of 1777 to the end of 1788.

I was 3 times taken by the English in the War.

! was 2 times shipwreck at sea, taken of our vessel--soon sank.

I was 1 rime Drive ashore by the English--lost our vessel near Cape Henry.

I was one time put ashore in Spain sick among the Spaniards.

I was 1 time sent to New York Prison Ship treated as a Rebbel.

I travel 3 times from the Southern States with my deck for Cape Cod.

One time I sail^d from North Carolina for Boston in December 1788 only two men before the mast first night out lost one man overboard. Our vessel sprang a leak, had to keep one to the pump, one to the relm and when we.. could find a chance for one to sleep--- Lay down on deck an hour or two and in about 10 days we got into the Vinyard.---.where I got help and went to Boston. All these misfortunes happened when I was mate and prise master on voyage except the Last then; by the Blessings of God my luck turned Blessed be God for preserving me through all the Dangers I have Past through.

I wrote this when I was 93 years old.

APPENDIX

On the back of the last sheet between the Old and New Testament is written; *This Bible was left by me to the care of my lamented Father Gardner Ruggles in 1851 and at his decease was placed in the care of my Mrs. Mercy Allen who has taken care of it for me and in whose han;ds I now leave it for presentation to my son Mortimer Bainbridge in case it shall plesse providence he shall attain to man's estate and if not to the eldest surviving son.*
Westminster, Mass

June 9, 1857.
Daniel Ruggles
bvt Lt Col U.S. Army.

In the Confederate Cemetery in Fredericksburg, Va is the handsome granite tombstone bearing the following inscription:

DANIEL RUGGLES
January 31, 1810-June 2, 1897
Lt. Col. U. S. A.-Major General C. S. A.
Richardetta Mason Hooe Ruggles
November 19, 1821-4 January 1904
Edward S. Ruggles
July 10, 1843-March 1, 1919
Major, C. S. A.

Phinney Bible Records of Zenas Phinney (1782-1848) of Massachusetts Transcribed from the original record in the Bible printed at broorfield by E. Merriam & Co in the year 1815.

BIRTHS

Zenas Phinney born Sept. 13, day in the year 1752.
And Sarah his wife was born October the 7th day in the year 1756 born att
    Harwick on Cape Codd now called Brewster.
Thankful Phinney born Tuesday June the 19 day in the year 1781.
Lydia Phinney born on Wednesday February the 12 day in the year 1783.
Patty Phinney born on Friday November the 12 day in the year 1784.
Sally Phinney born on Sunday May the 6; day in the year 1787
Lucy Phinney born on Tuesday August the 12 day in the year 1788.
Zenas Phinney born on Saturday Janaway the 28 day in the year 1792.
Sally Phinney born Janaway the 20 day in the year 1793.
Zenas Phinney born Janaway the 10 day in the year 1794.

A record of Zenas Phinney Junr children age;
Sarah Berry Phinney born June 3 day in the year 1822 att Harwick, Cape Codd
William Henry Phinney born OCtober 24 day in the year 1823 at Hardwick.
Charles Freeman Phinney Born Sept 21 day1825 att Hardwick
Squire Zenas Phinney born February 20 day1831 at Pawtucket.
Thomas Russell Phin;ney born November 23 day 1832 at Pawtuckit.
Julaan (? Susan) Phinney born July day 1835.

APPENDIX

Deaths

Sally Phinney Departed thisLife on Wednesday June the 13 day in the year
1787 age 38 days.

Zenas Phinney departed this life on the 17 day of February in the year 1792.
aged 20 days.

Sally Phinney departed this life on the 7 day of February in the year 1793 aged
19 days.

My wife Sarah Departed this life December the 20 day 1832 aged 76 years
2 months and 13 days.

My daughter Lydia, Gardner Ruggles wife departed this life September 23 dau
1833 aged 50 years 7 months and 17 days,

Gardner Ruggles departed this life Aug. the 5th 1853 aged 71 years (Thrown
from his carriage and killed)

Zenas Phinney Bartlett departed this life August the 11 day 1838 aged in his
16 year.

Luke Bartlett departed this life August 25 day 1838 aged 44 years.

Elbridge Bartlett departed this life September the 6 day 1838 aged 11 years.

David Aikin and Gardner Ruggles little daughters, I have forgot wjem.

(On the margin, apparently after writing the above Zenas Phinney writes): *viz*
I find by my records Anne Aiken departed this life April the 2 day 1813
aged 2 years.

Martha Haskell departed this life May the 5d 1837 aged 16 years.

Sarah Berry Haskell Departed this life September 2d 1836 aged 23 years.

Mary Haskell departed this life October 3d day 1838 aged 28 years.

Febuary 1 day 1840 Forister Aikins little daughter departed this life aged
1 year.

My daughter Thankful, Ephraim Haskels wife, Departed this life November the
15 day 1841 aged 60 years 4 months and 26 days.

Zenas Phinney died March 4th 1848 aged 95 years 5 months and 10 days.

On the fly leaf " I have given this Bible at my Decease to Captain
Daniel Ruggles, my grandson--Sept 14 day 1846." (This seems to be in the
handing of Zenas Phinney 1752-1848 as are most of the above mentioned
entries)

On the two inside covers of this Bible Zenas Phinney (1752-1848) has left
a record of his life, written in his 93rd year. For one dreason or another in
places this record is extremely difficult to decipher. (See previous page)

NOTES

Jabez Phinney, b in Barnstable, Mass: Feb. 27,1777 son of John and Abigail (Blish)Phinney. They had nine children. Names unknown at this time.

Mary Finney, b in Norton, Mass Nov. 12, 1727 dau of John and Mary (Campbel) Finney. She m. m. Ebenezer Jones son of Joseph born in Raynham, Mass.Oct 1, 1726. He was a sergeant in the local militia in 1754. Mary probably died in Easton Mass. in 1819 age 90. Their children: ; Recorded in Easton:

1. Isaac Jones b. in Raynham March 6, 1750
2. **Ebenezer** Jones b. in Norton March 27, 1752.
3. Joseph Jones b. February 21, 1757.
4. Mary Jones b. in Easton Nov. 14,k 1758.

Phinney Onon Co History: At South Bay, April 15, by Rev. N. D. Williamson of Cicero, Hiram Phinney of Cazenovia to Miss. Maria, dau of Simon Driesback of South Bay (Married) *Syracuse Standard April 19, 1850)*

May 7, 1872 married in St. Peters Church, Cazenovia, by Rev. A. P. Smith D.D. the Rector, David N. Phinney of Syracuse to Frances E. dau of Sylvester Coin of former place.

JOURNAL 5,5, 9,72

David Phinney d. at Eagle Village on Wed. 29th Ult ae. 76. (near Manlius, next town to Cazinovia but in(Onon Co)Manlius Repository, Sept 4 1832.

B. Anna Phinney, Jan 23, 1840 to Ansil N and Abigail Phinney, Van Buren, Onon Co.

Rep. Meeting in Manlius--including Lorenzo Phinney--Sept 31828. (Onon Register.)

Wampsville Co. Clerks Office, Madison Coiunty, N.Y.

Grantee 1854-1873.
No Nathan Phinney. No Cathereine.

Grantee; 1806-1853.
1853 Nathan A1 P 408
1848 Nathan Av P. 345

Grantee; 1873-1880
No Nathan No. Catherine.

Grantor 1806-1852
1838 Nathan and wife AS P 73
1839 Nathan and wife - Salomon Phinney AS p 374 &375
1838 Salmon and wife et al AS p 73

Grantor 1852-1873
1866 Nathan & Wife 107 o, 204
No Hiram.
Same Book 1852-1873
1856 Salman and wife- Hiram Phinney CF p 485
1866 Salman and wife 108 P 95

APPENDIX
DEED BOOK

AL 406-Nov. 30, 1830 bet. Parmelee and Phebe, his wife of Cazenovia, Mad. Co (1) and Solomon Phinney and Nathan Phinney of same place (2) $700.00 Lot 24 purchased of the Onedia Indians bounded --beg at center of road on N. side of said lot E to land owned by Isaac Phinney:S 50 rods W parallel with N. line to center of said road N on road to ::beg. 34 acres.; Reserving the wheat now growing with priviledge pf cutting. stoking the same off when ripe. Rec. Sept. 25,1835.

AS P.73. Sept. 15,1838 bet. Salman Finney and Nathan Finney of CAzenovia and Catherine Finney and Betsey Finney wives of said Salmon and Nathan of the first part and Samuel Peck (Same place)(2) $850.00 Fourth allotment. New Petersburg tract in said town lot 26 beg. at stake and stones standing 38 links S of house formerly owned by John Jinks on S. Side of the E and W. road S 3 degrees W to the low water mark of the Lake Westerly to head of the lake waters thence along the line of the road 16 chains 74 links to place of begining 35 acres. Signed Salman Phinney, Nathan Rhinney, Betsey Phinney and Catherine Phinney. Witness Justin Dwinell. who says he knows them all. Rec. Sept 24,1838.

AS p373 Sept. 15,1838 bet. Nathan Phinney and Catherine Phinney his wife of Cazenovia Da. Co (1) and Salman Phinney of same place (2) $425.00, All that equal undivided ½ of all that certain piece of land known as Lot 24 purchased of the Oneidia Indians bounded as follows, beg.in the center of road on the N. line of said lot E on N line of said lot to land owned by Isaac Phinney to a stake and stones S 50 rods to stake and stones with N. line to center of the said -----N on center of said road to beg. 34 acres situated in town of aforesaid. Nathan Phinney, Catherine Phinney, witness Justin Dwinell. Mad. Co. Sept. 15,1838 Rec. Feb. 4, 1839.

AS p 374 Sept. 15, 1838 bet. Isaac Phinney of Cazenovia, Mad. Co (1) Salman Phinney of same place (2) $3000.00 All that piece of land in town aforesaid and being the farm on which said Isaac Phinney now resides and being part of lots 23 and 24 bounded N. by said Salman Phinney land and (Scanton) and Youngs land on the E by Charles Parmeles land S by Hestes and Richards land on W. by Albert Prestons land 100 acres, reserving the right to the said Isaac the -------and the use and profit of the said farm and premises for and during the natural life of the said Isaac and Huldah his wife and the life of the survivor of them. Justine Dwinell witness. REc. Feb. 4, 1839.

AS p 345 Sept 24, 1838 bet. Samuel Morey and wife of Cazenovia, Mad Co (1) Nathan. Phinney of same place (2) $2,509.60 all of that tract in town of Cazenovia part of lot 22 and 23 in the 4th allotment of "New Petersburgh tract" bounded----beginning at S.W. corner of Lot 23 N. along W. line 12 chains 50 links. E. parallel with S line thereof 40 chains to E. line therefore thence N. along the line of said Lot 22 and 23 8 chains 36 links E parallel with S. Line of Lot 22 4 chains thence S 15 degrees E 16 chains 52 links thence W parallel with S. line of said lot 22 8 chains 90 links thence S parallelwith W. line of lot 22 5 chains 33 links to the S line thereof thence W along S line of lot 22 2 chains 21 links to W. corner thence W along S line lot 23 40 chains 8 links to place of beg. 62 acres 74/100 Witness Enos Cushing Sept. 26,1838 Rec. July 8, 1840

CF p 485 Nov. 25,1845 bet. Salman Phinney of town of Cazenovia and
Betsey, his wife (1) and Hiram Phinney of the same place(2) $200.00
land situated in town and county of aforsaid beig part of farm on which
the said Salman now resides and being25 acres on the W¡and of said farm
to be taken off of the W and beg. by running a line parallel with W line
of said farm so far E. therefrom through said farm W to S shall include
just 25 acres bet. N by M.Scantons land, S. by A.Rickards land E by the
residue of the said farm.   Witness; Justin Dwinel. Sup court Commissioner.
Nov. 25,1845 Rec. Sept. 15,1856.

107 p.204 March 1, £866 bet. Nathan Phinney and Catherine his wife of
Cazenovia, and Washington F. Brown of Cuyler, Cortland Co (2) $3,760.00
land in town of Cazenovia part of lot 22 and 23 in 4th allotment of New
Petersburgh Tract bounded beg. S.W.korner of lot 23 N. along W. line 12
chains   50 links E Parallel with S. line of said lot 22 and 23 8 chains 36
links E parallel with S. line of lot 2 , 4 Chains 93 links S. 15 degrees E
16 chains 52 links W parallel with S line Lot 22 8 Chains 90 links S. parallel with W line lot 22; 5 chains 33 links S. line W. along south line Lot
22 2 chains 21 links to SW corner W along S lineof lot 23 40 chains 8
links to plance of beg. 62 acres 74/1oo acre Rec. March 12,1866

108 p 95. April 2, 1866 bet. Solomon Phinney and Betsey, his wife of
town of Cazenovia, Madison Co (1) and Francis Everson of town of Manlius, Onon. Co(2) for $5,155.15 land in Cazenovia being part of lots 23
 and 24 purchased of Oneida Indians beg. center of Lake Road leading
to Cazenovia N line of lot 24 S 83½ degrees E along said N line 38 chains
95 links to N.E. corner S. 5½ degrees 25 chains 7 links to a stake N. 83½
degrees W 37 chains 85 links to a stake N 4½ degrees W) 6 chains 61 links
along a board fence to a stake S 83½ degrees E 4 chains 5 links to the
center of said road E along thecenter therof to beg. 93 acres 73/100
acre Rec. May 19, 1866

1855 Madison Co, Cazenovia 1st Election District.
111-123 James Phinney 78 b Conn 18 years in T. farmer.
             Mary Phinney 70 wife b. Mass.
             Sarah Phinney 9 child b. Mad. Co.

Village of Woodstock   in 1st Dist. of Cazenovia.
2nd Dist of Cazenovia.
109-119 Lorenzo N. Phinney 52 servant b. Mass 20 years in town
farmer in home of Henry Thompson.

370-401 Gaylord Phinney 58 b. Mass 25 years in town farmer
      Ann Phinney 47 wife b. R.I. 40 years in town
      Rhoda A. Phinney 23 chd b. Mad. Co, 21 years in town
      Benjamin F. Phinney 2 0 chd b. Mad. Co 19 years in town
      David N. Phinney 17 chd b. Mad. Co 15 years in town clerk.
      Jackson Phinney 14 chd b. Mad Co
      R. Dewitt Phinney 12 xhs v. Mad. Co

APPENDIX

SPECIAL SCHEDULE 3   Business.
       Loomis and (S) Phinney   Tanning   Real estate 600   2 men emp.
Wm. H.D. Dwinelle is a Dentist.
Village of Cazenovia within the limits of this district and district 3.

CENSUS 1855

70-75 Salmon Phinney 58 b. Mad. Co 54 years in Town Farmer
      Betsey Phinney 54 wife b. Herkimer 50 years in Town
      Isaac Phinney 90 father b. Mass 51 years in Town farmer.
      Lucretia MIlls 18 servant b. Mad Co 6 years in Town.

71-76 Hiram Phinney 35 b. Mad. Co 35 years in Town farmer.
      Maria Phinney 27 wife b. Herkimer 5 years in Town.
      Minerva Phinney 10 daughter b. Mad Co. 10 years in Town.
      P.S. Phinney 6 son b. Mad Co. 3 years in Town.
      Florence Phinney 3   dau b. Mad. Co.

3rd Election Dis Caz. Mad.
109-118   Nathan Phinney   50 b. Mad. Co 48 years in Twon farmer.
      Katherine Phinney   49 b. Montgomery 29 years in Town

DEED BOOK

F10. May 31,1811 bet. Noah Joslin Caz and D.(Ammus) his wife (1)
Zenas Phinney of same place $60.00 Lot 38 in 4th Allotment
of new Petersburg beg. at SW corner of a------of land deeded
to Noah Joslin by Zenas Phinney in 1810 W 3 degrees --------
N. 98 Rods to a stake and stone fence N. 3 deg. E 6 rods 13
links to a stake and stones E 3 deg S 98 rods to a stake and
stones---the west line of Allen Dryer jun'r.land thence 3 deg
W 6 rods 13 linka to beg   4 acres and No more or less.
Rec. Dec. 10, 1811.

K29 April 26, 1810 bet. John Lincklaen and Helen,his wife of T
of Caz (1) and Zenas Phinney of same place $900.00.   New
Petersburgh tract in T Caz part of lot 38 and part of Lot 40
of 4th Allotment beg. S.W. corner lot 38 at a Maple Sapling
marked 38 N 3 deg E. 13 ch 30 links S. 87 deg E 46 chains
45 (44) links S 3 deg W. 38 chaines 90 links to a stake stamd-
ing on S. boundary of lot 40 thence N. 87 deg W 36 chains
45 links to a stake it being the SW corner lot 40 thence N. 3
deg E 25 chains to a maple tree marked 38,839 N. 87 deg W.
10 chains to beg. agreeable to a survey made thereof by Elisha Johnson in Nov. 1805 155 agrees 8/10 acre. Be the same
more or less == reserving nevetheless out of thesaid Lot farther use of the preident directors and company of the third
Great Western Turnpike. Road Company   The turnpike Road
leading through the same. Rec. Feb. 20, 1815.

PHINNEY.

The surname, Finn, and its variants, Phin, Phinn, and Phinney, have two possible origins, according to Bardsley, surname authority. One is that they have a baptismal significance and indicate "the son of Phin." Another is that they were applied originally as nicknames, meaning "the fine," refined, delicate, exquisite.

(Bardsley: "Dictionary of English and Welsh-Surnames.")

According to a tradition among descendants of James Phinney, who lived in Oneida County, New York, in the early nineteenth century, the founder of this Phinney family settled early at Cape Cod. He was the owner of several vessels but lost them and, with them, his entire fortune in a terrific storm at sea. He had a large family, but, following his disaster, his children became scattered. Bearers of the name lived early in Rhode Island, Connecticut, Massachusetts, and Vermont.

The name Phinney (in its variant spelling of Finney) is found in Oneida County, New York, records, as early as 1794, in a purchase of land in what is now Oneida County, but was at that time included in Herkimer County. By a deed dated September 13, 1794, Marinus Willett of the city of New York conveyed to Ebenezer Finney of Herkimer County, yeoman, for £125, land in Herkimer County, "in what is called the Twentieth Town, one of the Towns lately laid out on the Unadilla River and sold by the State of New York, two hundred fifty acres. Witnesses, J. Pearsee and John J. Morgan."

Levi Gardner Pinny (perhaps a misspelling of Phinney), of Deerfield, Oneida County, New York, died intestate, and administration on his estate was granted January 5, 1799 (record says 1798, an obvious error as shown by context), to Moses Barnard. Witness, Arthur Breese. Signed by Arthur Breese, Surrogate.

Sylvester Finney (who so signed) deeded to Joshua Smith, both of the town of Paris (then in Herkimer but now in Oneida County), February 28, 1798, for $88.50 (paid to said Finney) and $25.06, with interest (to be paid to the State of New York), land in said town, "a part of the Land lately set off from Brothertown," lot No. 68, containing fourteen acres, one hundred thirty-nine rods. On September 7, 1799, Sylvester Finney and wife Rebekah, of the town of Paris, Oneida County, deeded to Salmon Wedge of Warren, Litchfield County, Connecticut, for $250, land in the town of Paris, Oneida County, a part of the land set off from Brotherton, in Lot Number 68, sixty acres.

Oneida County, whence the Phinneys emigrated to Wisconsin, was formed from Herkimer County, March 15, 1798. The town (township) of Vernon, where these Phinneys lived, lies on the western border of Oneida County, south of the center. The territory of this town was included in the original Oneida Indian Reservation. Through the eastern part of the town flows Skanandoa Creek, upon which is located Vernon village. This creek was named from the celebrated Oneida chief, the name signifying hemlock, or stream of hemlocks. This chief once made a striking remark: "I am an aged hemlock. An hundred winters have whistled through my branches. I am dead at the top!" Vernon Center, where James Milton Phinney was born, is in Vernon Township, and in 1860 contained two churches and thirty dwellings.

("Oneida County, New York, Deeds," Book V, p. 224; Book XVII, p. 309. "Oneida County, New York, Letters of Administration," Book I, p. 13. J. H. French: "Gazeteer of the State of New York," pp. 458, 469. Family data.)

I.

JAMES PHINNEY, earliest definitely known ancestor of this line, was born, probably, before 1785, and died at Vernon Center, Oneida County, New York, between May 16, 1850, and January 23, 1854. He resided in the town of Vernon, Oneida County, New York, in 1809, 1814, 1823, 1827, 1835, 1839, and 1850, and doubtless was a continuous resident there during that whole period.

James Phinney and his wife, Lois, of the town of Vernon, Oneida County, New York, deeded June 28, 1809, to David Picksley of the town of Paris, same county, for a consideration of $400, eight acres and sixty-seven rods of land in said town of Vernon, known as lot two hundred thirty-four on the late Oneida reservation, bounded by land then occupied by Samuel Cady (Cody) and Joseph Freeman. One boundary led "to the center of a well of water." The deed was witnessed by Samuel Cady (Cody) and Levi Skinner.

February 24, 1814, James Phinney of Vernon became possessed of four acres and seven rods of land in that same lot, number two hundred thirty-four, by a deed from Levi Skinner of the same town, consideration, $200. The land was near the house then occupied by Samuel Cady, and was subject to a mortgage given to the people of the State of New York.

July 8, 1823, James Phinney and wife Lois of the town of Vernon, for $200, deeded to Jared Moss of the town of Augusta, same county, land in the latter town, "part of Lot Number fifteen in the first allotment of New Petersburgh—beginning five feet south of the head of the floom which conducts the water to the Grist Mill on said lot," the line running "along the east bank of a mill dyke." Its area was one rood and twenty perches, and it was "subject to the incumbrance of said mill dyke and the right of the owners thereof to repair the same." The witnesses were Samuel Cady and Pitt Cady.

April 17, 1827, James Phinney, of Vernon, acquired by deed from David Tuttle and wife Polly of the same place, for $150, land in the town of Vernon, "commencing at the point where the road leading from the Oneida Glass factory to Vernon centre meeting house intersects with the road leading from Stephen Brigham's Inn to said Vernon centre meeting house"; adjoining the land of Daniel Pettebone, "being in the form of a triangle," one and one-half acres. Witness, Asahel Gridley.

The State census of 1835 shows James Phinney as then residing in the town of Vernon, Oneida County, New York, the family consisting of four males (three besides himself) and three females; two of the males being entitled to vote; two of the females being between sixteen and twenty-five years of age and married. One death had occurred

PHINNEY

in the family during the year preceding.   (No other Phinney is recorded as living in the said town in 1835.)

April 1, 1839, James Phinney of Vernon, Oneida County, New York, became the owner, by deed, from Hannah Sturges of Marshall, Oneida County, for $912, of land in Vernon, part of Lot No. Eight in Baschard's location (so-called), beginning at the center of Schenandoa Creek on the line of the late Samuel Wetmore's land and adjoining land formerly owned by Huet Hills, deceased, twenty-seven and one-half acres.   Witness, William W. Buckley.

James Phinney and wife Lois, of Vernon, Oneida County, New York, on May 16, 1850, deeded to Samuel C. Phinney of the same place, for $1,000, the same twenty-seven and one-half acres described above, "subject to a mortgage given by James Phinney to Hannah Sturges for $657, dated April 1, 1839, of which $500 is now due."   Witness, Levi T. Marshall, Justice of the Peace.   April 20, 1852, Lois Phinney (then either the wife or possibly the widow of James Phinney) and Clarissa Phinney (whose name precedes that of Lois in the deed), both of Vernon, were deeded by Thomas Wilson and wife, Mary, of Vernon, for $700, twenty acres and three rods of land in Vernon on the west side of the "highway from Seneca Plank Road to the residence of James Phinney," and on the north side of lands owned by Samuel C. Phinney, and bordering the Mill pond.

James Phinney's widow, Lois, having died in 1853, her heirs made a quit-claim deed to the above-mentioned twenty acres, of which she was joint owner with Clarissa A. Phinney.   A verbatim copy of the deed follows:

This Indenture Made this Twenty third day of January Eighteen hundred and fifty four Between Samuel C. Phinney & Lorian S. his wife & Jared Alling & Julia ann his wife & James M. Phinney & Helen L. his wife & Hiram A. Phinney of the first part and Clarissa A. Phinney of Vernon Centre Oneida County & State of New York of the Second part Witnesseth that the said party of the first part in consideration of the sum of one hundred and fifty Dollars to them in hand paid the receipt of which is hereby acknowledged have Sold and Quit claimed unto the Said party of the Second part and to her heirs and assigns the following described land.   Commencing at the Centre of the highway running (by lands of James Bartholomew) from Vernon Centre to Vernon village and bounded on the East by Said highway, on the North and South by lands owned by James Bartholomew and on the west by the Shenandoah Creek, Said land being the land owned by Clarissa A. Phinney and the heirs of Lois Phinney deceased and containing twenty acres.   To have and To hold with the appurtenances thereof forever.   And the said Party of the first part covenants to Warrant and Defend the Said granted premises to the Said party of the Second part against all claims under the Said party of the first part.

In Witness Whereof the said party of the first part has hereunto Set their hands and Seals the day and year before written.

| Signed Sealed and delivered in presence of | | | SAMᴸ C. PHINNEY (L. S.) |
| | | | H. A. PHINNEY (L. S.) |

ANSON BALLARD	LORIAN S. PHINNEY (L. S.)	JARED ALLING (L. S.)
G. H. MALSTON	JA's M. PHINNEY (L. S.)	JULIA A. ALLING (L. S.)
J. W. HOYT	HELEN L. PHINNEY (L. S.)	
E. D. MASTERS		

State of Wisconsin
Outagamie County ss.

On the twenty third day of January A. D. 1854 Samuel C. Phinney & Lorian S. his wife & Ja's M. Phinney & Helen L his wife & Hiram A. Phinney to me known as the persons named as Grantors in the foregoing Instrument, freely acknowledged the execution thereof.

ANSON BALLARD, Notary Public, Wisconsin.

State of Wisconsin
Outagamie County ss.

I Henry S. Eggleston Clerk of the Circuit Court of Said County do hereby certify that the annexed instrument is executed and acknowledged in due form according to the laws of this State, Also that Anson Ballard, Esqr before whom the same was acknowledged, was at the time of taking the same Notary Public in and for Said State, duly qualified and authorized to take said acknowledgment, and also that I am acquainted with the handwriting of the said Ballard, and believe his Signature to the annexed instrument to be genuine.

In Witness whereof I hereunto Set my hand, and affix the Seal of our Said
L. S.   Court at Appleton this 25 day of January A. D. 1854.

HENRY S. EGGLESTON Clerk

State of Wisconsin
Jefferson County ss.

On the twenty seventh day of February A. D. 1854, Jared Alling and Julia A. Alling his wife to me known as the persons named as Granters in the foregoing instrument, freely acknowledged the execution thereof.   E. D. MASTERS,
Justice of the Peace.

State of Wisconsin
County of Jefferson ss.

I Walter H. Besly, Clerk of the Circuit Court for the county and State aforesaid do hereby certify that E. D. Masters to me known as the person named as Granter in the foregoing instrument, freely acknowledged the execution thereof.   WALTER H. BESLY   Clerk
L. S.

Recorded March 13, 1854 a 1 h 45 m P. M.   RICHARD HULBERT   Clerk

James Phinney married, about 1805-12, Lois Cody.   (Cody V.)
Children (as deduced from quit-claim deed dated January 23, 1854):

1. (perhaps) Susanna C., died August 31, 1826, buried in Skinner Cemetery, Vernon, New York.

2. Rev. Samuel C., born 1812; he was of Vernon, New York, on April 7, 1835, when, for $300, Alpheus I. Grover and his wife, Elizabeth B., of Westmoreland, Oneida County, New York, deeded to "Samuel C. Phiney" of Vernon, land in Westmoreland and in the village of Hampton, adjoining Samuel Clark and the center of Deans Creek. July 10, 1839, Samuel C. Phinney, of Vernon (no wife signing) deeded to James M. Buell, of Westmoreland, for $400, the same land which he had bought in 1835, as shown above. By deed dated February 4, 1848, Samuel C. Phinney of Vernon, bought for $600, from Robert L. Wells and "wife Caroline C." (signed C. M. Wells) land in Vernon adjoining Matthew Pennock, and another parcel, part of Lot No. 8, adjoining Elisha Pettibone, six and one-half acres. March 20, 1851, Samuel C. Phinney and wife Lorian S., of Vernon, deeded to Esau Youngs of the same place, for $700, land in Vernon, beginning in

the center of the highway leading from James Phinney's to the Seneca Plank Road and adjoining Matthew Pennock; also other land in Lot No. 8, adjoining that of Hiram D. Tuttle, six and one-half acres. Samuel Phinney moved to Appleton in 1853 and engaged in business with his brothers. He was a Methodist minister until his voice failed. On October 26, 1853, "Saml C. Phinney and wife Lorian S.," of Vernon, deeded to James Bartholomew, of Kirkland, for $1,200, land in the town of Vernon, part of Lot No. 8 on Baschard's Location (so-called), beginning in the center of Schenandoah Creek, on the west line of lands formerly owned by Samuel Westmore deceased, and adjoining land formerly owned by "heirs of Hills deceased," twenty-seven and one-quarter acres. Samuel C. Phinney married, in 1840, Lorian Sheldon, who died in 1880. They had two daughters:

     i. Mary Ann, born October 5, 1842, in Vernon Center, New York, died January 7, 1928. She came with her parents to Appleton, Wisconsin, in 1853 and entered Lawrence Academy, having previously been taught by her father and mother. In 1859, at sixteen, she received the degree of A. B. from Lawrence University and later that of A. M. She taught for short periods at Lawrence and was elected to Phi Beta Kappa. Mrs. Stansbury was active in charitable and civic work, besides her literary work. She was the author of many short stories and one volume of collected poems, "The Path of Years," published in 1907 Her work appeared in "The New England Magazine," "The Critic," "The Outlook," "Scribner's," "Youth's Companion," and other periodicals. She wrote the poem "How He Saved St. Michael's." She married (first), August 12, 1862, Edward P. Humphrey, of Athol, Massachusetts, who died in 1865. She married (second), June 13, 1872, Dr. Emory Stansbury, of Baltimore, Maryland, who died April 3, 1899; child of first marriage:

        (a) Edward P., Jr., born in 1865, living in Los Angeles, California.

Children of second marriage:

        (b) Clara, graduate of Lawrence College, and attended State University of Wisconsin one year for graduate work; married Frank P. Young, county superintendent of Outagamie County, Wisconsin, schools; they had one son:

           (1) Frank Stansbury.

        (c) Karl, graduate of Lawrence College and vice-president of the Thilmany Pulp and Paper Company, of Kaukauna, Wisconsin; married and is the father of:

           (1) Mary Ann.

           (2) Helen.

        (d) George J., graduate of Lawrence College, and secretary and treasurer of the Thilmany Pulp and Paper Company.

    ii. Lora E., born at Appleton, Wisconsin, August 10, 1858; now resides in Los Angeles, California; married W. D. Mason; children:

        (a) Harry, now deceased; gassed during the World War.

        (b) Rex.

        (c) Beatrice.

   3. Clarissa A., who, with Lois Phinney, of Vernon, was a grantee, April 20, 1852, from Thomas Wilson and wife Mary of the same place, for $700, of land in Vernon on the west side of the highway from Seneca Plank Road to the residence of James Phinney, on the north side of lands owned by Samuel C. Phinney, and bordering the Mill Pond, twenty acres and three rods. January 23, 1854, Clarissa A. Phinney, of Vernon Centre, received a quit-claim deed from the heirs of Lois Phinney, as has already been shown. And on March 24, 1854, Clarissa A. Phinney, of Ver-

non, deeded to James Bartholomew of the same place, for $700, land in Vernon on the west side of the highway leading from the residence of Matthew Pennock, twenty acres and three rods.

4. *James Milton*, of whom further.

5. Hiram A. He and his brother, Samuel C. Phinney, of Vernon, were grantees, April 1, 1848, from Pitt Cody and wife Phebe E., of the same place, for $1,300, of thirty-eight and sixty-eight one-hundredths acres in Vernon, parts of Lots No. 8 and 12, Baschard's location, adjoining the road from James Phinney's to the Seneca Turnpike, also adjoining the land of Matthew Pennock and of the heirs of David Tuttle. Hiram A. Phinney was also a pioneer settler of Appleton, coming there in 1853 with his brothers. For many years he was a merchant, and for several years postmaster. He was twice married.

6. Julia A., married Jared Alling; they resided, in 1854, in Jefferson County, Wisconsin.

(E. B. Swanscott: "Bible, Cemetery and Church Records," typed copy at Oneida Historical Society, Utica, New York, p. 158. "State Census, Town of Vernon, Oneida County, New York," 1835, in Library of Oneida Historical Society, Utica, New York. "Oneida County, New York, Deeds," Book XIX, p. 409; Book XXVII, p. 401; Book XXXVII, p. 222; Book XLIV, p. 331; Book LXIX, p. 361; Book XCV, p. 237; Book CV, p. 123; Book CXXXV, pp. 434, 455; Book CLIII, p. 417; Book CLXVII. p. 89; Book CLXXVIII, pp. 132, 178, 181, 479, 480; Book CLXXIX, p. 50; Book CLXXXVII, p. 329.)

II.

JAMES MILTON PHINNEY, son of James and Lois (Cody) Phinney, was born in Vernon Center, Oneida County, New York, July 4, 1821. He received his education in the common schools of New York and was graduated from Wesleyan College, Middletown, Connecticut. He was an exceptionally well educated man. He was a member of Psi Upsilon Fraternity. He borrowed from his father $300.00, which he used for his education, paying it back by getting up at three and four o'clock in the morning and working on the shoe bench. James Milton Phinney taught for a time at Bowling Green, Kentucky, though he was much younger than most of his pupils. In 1848 he and his wife went to Wisconsin, where he was associated with his brother-in-law, who operated a mill at Green Lake. Prior to that he had been county superintendent of schools in Monroe County, New York, for two years. In November, 1849, he moved to Appleton, Wisconsin, and he became one of the first professors at Lawrence University, which was opened at Appleton November 12, 1849. He served as a trustee for twenty-one years and for fifteen years was in business with his brothers. He was a man of rare and exceptional talent.

James Milton Phinney was residing in Outagamie County, Wisconsin, January 23, 1854, when, wtih his wife, Helen L., and other heirs of Lois Phinney, he signed a quitclaim deed to Clarissa A. Phinney, of land in Vernon, Oneida County, New York.

James Milton Phinney married, in Penfield, Monroe County, New York, November 24, 1847, Helen Linklane Rich. (Rich V.) (Mayflower Descent VIII.)

Children:

1 *Helen Lois*, of whom further.

2. Clarissa A., born August 16, 1852, died January 2, 1880; was graduated from Lawrence University with the degree of Master of Science, and taught school for a time; she married, in 1876, G. V. Nash; child:

> i. Clarence, who was killed by a fall at the age of seven years.

("Oneida County, New York, Deeds," Book CLXXVIII, pp. 479, 480. "Outagamie County, Pioneers," p. 297. Alumni Records of Wesleyan University, Middletown, Connecticut, and Lawrence College, Appleton, Wisconsin. Family data.)

III.

HELEN LOIS PHINNEY, daughter of James Milton and Helen Linklane (Rich) Phinney, was born November 19, 1848, in Dartford, Green Lake County, Wisconsin. She is a wonderful woman and much interested in aiding young people to secure an academic education. She married Henry Clay Sloan. (She spells her name Sloane.) (Sloan IV.)

("Outagamie County Pioneers," p. 296. Family records.)

RICH.

Rich Arms -- Gules, a chevron between three crosses botonnée or.

(Burke: "General Armory.")

Authorities seem to disagree on the origin and meaning of the name Rich. One states it designates a person of wealth, power, or might; a second that it is more probably an abbreviation of the baptismal name Richard than an epithet implying wealth, while a third says that it is a nickname for Richard.

Family tradition claims that Captain John Rich (generation III of the following line), was a grand-nephew of the Earl of Warwick, and came to America in charge of the ships of his great-uncle, who had received a grant for some of the land between the Connecticut River and Cape Cod, originally owned by Lord Sayre and Brooke, but genealogical research proves that if this family was connected with the Earl of Warwick, the connection was apparently through Richard Rich, founder of this family in America, rather than through his grandson.

(Harrison: "Surnames of the United Kingdom." Lower: "Patronymica Britannica." Bardsley: "Dictionary of English and Welsh Surnames." Family record.)

APPENDIX

1855 Madison County Czaenovia 1st Election District

111-123 James Phinney 78 b. Conn 18 years in T. Farmer.
Mary Phinney 70 wife b. Mass.
Sarah Phinney 9 child b. Mad. Co.

Village of Woodstock is in 1st Dist of Caz.

2nd District of Caz.
109-119 Lorenso N. Phinney 62 servant b. Mass 20 years in Town. Farmer in home of Henry Thompson.
370-401. Gaylord Phinney 58 b Mass 25 years in Town farmer.
Ann Phinney 47 wife B.R.I. 40 years in Town
Rhoda A Phinney 23 chd b. Mad. Co 18 years in Town
Benjamin F. Phinney 20 chd b. Mad Co 18 years in Town
David N. Phinney 17 chd b. Mad. Co 15 years in Town clerk
Jackson Phinney 14 chd b. Mad. Co
R. Dewitt Phinney 12 chd b. Mad Co.

Special Schedule 3. Business
Loomis and (S) Phinney tanning Realestate 600 2 men emp.

MARRIAGE RECORDS BEFORE 1699 by Olemens.

FINNEY, John & Mary Bryant 14 June 1693 Plymouth, Mass.
Jonathan & Joana Kinnecut 18 Oct. 1682 Britsol, R.I.
Josua & Mercy Watts 31, May 1688 Bristol, R.I.
Jeremiah & Esther Lewis 7 Jan 1684 Bristol R.I.

NOTES

APPENDIX

Copied from the Fall 1964 issue of the Detroit Society for genealogy Research
Magazine   v.266 No 1

CITATION TO HEIRS AND THE WILL OF NATHAN PHINNEY
OF MANLIUS, ONONDAGA COUNTY, NEW YORK
Contributed by Mrs. Herbert W. Beck of Manitou Beach, Michigan

A Citation to Heirs, dated 16 September 1887, from the Surrogate's Court at Syracuse, Onondaga County, New York is among family papers. It names the executor of the will of Nathan Phinney and 105 then living next of kin, legatees, and creditors.

The contributor wishes to determine the parentage of Harriet Maria Phinney whose son, Chauncey L. Blanchard, was named in this paper. He was the son of Warren Blanchard and Harriet Maria Phinney married at Eagle in Clinton County, Michigan on 1 January 1850. Also named in this paper was Merrit Densmore believed to have been another son of Harriet Maria Phinney, widow of Warren Blanchard; she had married 2nd in 1867, William Darius Dinsmore of Portland in Ionia County, Michigan.

The will of Nathan Phinney shows that he had a brother Seth Phinney and sisters, Sally Davis, Mercy Gridley, and Submit Culver, all having children. Does someone know who were the children of Seth Phinney and who were the parents of Nathan and Seth Phinney? Was Harriet Maria Phinney a daughter of Seth?

The persons listed in the Citation to Heirs, with their places of residences, have been arranged alphabetically:

ALDRICH	Clarissa	Clayton, Mich	CHAPPELL	Cynthia	Jordon, NY
ANDERSON	Jennie	Portland, Mich	COLBY	Lottie	Hepworth, Canada
APPLEBY	Artemus	Holmwood. Kans	CRISSEY	Jessie	West Bay City, Mich
	Bert	Geneva, Iowa		Louisa	Chicago, Ill
	Charles	Chicago, Ill	CROSS	Hattie	Weedsport, NY
	Eli	Geneva, Iowa	CULVER	Artemus B.	Chicago, Ill
	Emerson	Brimfield, Ill		Artemus	Pittsburgh, Pa
	George	Chicago, Ill		Charles W.	Cazenovia, NY
	John	Ebony, Missouri		Charles	Milwaukee. Wis
	Lucien H.	Holmwood, Kans		George	address unknown
	Myron	Geneva, Iowa			by Surrogate
	Warren	Clifton, Iowa		Nellie	New York City
	Warner	address unknown		Orlando	Waukesha, Wis
		by Surrogate		Submit	deceased-no location
					given. Job Reynolds
BALDWIN	Isadore	Omaha, Nebr			executor of her will
BLAKE	Alice	Auburn, NY			
	Bloomfield	address unknown	CURTIS	Libius	Lansing, NY
		by Surrogate	DAVIS	Robert	Allegan, Mich
	Hattie	Auburn, NY		Maria	deceased-no location
	Isaac O.	Lysander, NY	DENSMORE	Merrit	Portland, Mich.
	Jabez C.	Meridian, NY			
BLANCHARD	Chauncey L.	Groton, Mich(sic)	GRIDLEY	Charles W.	Omaha, Nebr
	Elmer E.	Sebawa(sic)		Findley P.	" "
		Sebewaing, Mich		Frank R.	Rapid City, Dak
BRADLEY	Emily M.	Kalida, Ohio		James U.	" " "
BLATHERWICK	Emeline	Des Moines, Iowa		Leonard	Garrettsville, Ohio
BUCK	Isaac N.	Elgin, Ill		Mary B.	Rapid City, Dak
	Jonas L.	New York City			
	Julia	Worthington, Ohio	HALL	Flora C.	Rapid City, Dak
	Kittie E.	Joliet, Ill	HEATH	Douglas	Cadillac, Ill
	Lorenzo D.	Abilene, Kans	HESSLER	Sally Ann	St. Paul, Minn
	Nathan P.	St. Paul, Minn	HOLMES	Victoria	Allegan, Mich
	Ralph P.	Wilber, Nebr	HUMISTON	Nina	Gaylord, Mich
	Rena	Worthington, Ohio	HUNTINGTON	Seth P.	Barrington, Ill
	Sally	Elgin, Ill	HURT	Hulda E.	Valparaiso, Ind
CAMPBELL	Emma Jane	Marine City, Mich	LOSEE	Minnie	Woodstock, Ill
	Huldah	Wacousta, Mich			

APPENDIX

McCAUSEY	Allen N.	West Sebawa(sic) W. Sebewaing, Mich	REYNOLDS	Job	Executor of will of Submit Culver
	Charles	Scot Station, Mich	RICHARDSON	George	Baskin Creek, Mich
	Frank	West Sebawa(sic) W. Sebewaing, Mich	ROBINSON	John	South West Oswego, NY
	George	" "	ROGERS	Edmund S.	Allegan, Mich
	Gilbert	" "		Josephine	" "
	Henry	" "			
	James	" "	SEWARD	Elizabeth H.	Syracuse, NY
NICHOLS	Harriet	Fenner, NY	SMITH	Hattie	Big Rapids. Mich
			SPICER	Emily	Geneva. Kans
OLIVER	Florence	New York City	STANLEY	Cornelia H.	Chittenango Falls, NY
	Nellie	Oswego, NY		James A.	Cazenovia, NY
PAINE	Finley K.	Cleveland, Ohio			Executor of will of Nathan Phinney
	James	" "		Marietta	Cazenovia, NY
	Robert F.	" "	TAYLOR	Jennie	Port Byron, NY
PERKINS	Emily L.	Lake Preston, Dak		Lavenia(Lovina?)	address unknown by Surrogate
PHINNEY	Catharine	Manlius, NY	THORNBUR	Wesley	Big Rapids. Mich
	George	Wacousta, Mich	THROOP	Lillian	Allegan, Mich
	Hiram	St. Cloud, Wis	TURPENEY	Clarissa M.	Winters, Ill
	Nathan	Manlius, NY the testator	VANDERHEYDEN	Nancy	Mount Carroll, Ill
POST	Collins	New London, Ohio		Clarissa	Winters, Ill
	Maud M.	Chicago, Ill	WARNER	Mary A.	Pitcherville, Ill
	Orlando	New London, Ohio	WELFARE	Lydia A.	Danby, Mich
	Susan R.	Chicago, Ill	WOOD	Jane	Cleveland, Ohio

**Chauncey L. Blanchard lived at that time at Langford, Dakota Territory, 20 miles from Groton, Dakota. He had previously lived in Clinton County, Michigan.

*Named as administrators of the estate of Maria Davis were: Josephine Rogers, Victoria Holmes, Lillian Throop, Robert Davis, and Edmund S. Rogers all of Allegan, Michigan.

The will of Nathan Phinney states his relationship to some of the persons shown in the Citation to Heirs: "I NATHAN PHINNEY of the town of Manlius, Onondaga County New York. Mindful of the uncertainties of human life do make publish declare and acknowledge this my last will and testament in manner following: First After the payment of my just debts and funeral expenses and the erection of a suitable Tombstone to my memory I give, devise and bequeath to my wife CATHARINE PHINNEY the use, occupation and uninterrupted enjoyment of my house and premises where I now reside on Seneca Street in Manlius Village in the town of Manlius aforesaid and the interest on the sum of six hundred dollars to be paid to her semiannually during the term of her natural life in lieu of Dower. Second I give and bequeath to my nephew GEORGE PHINNEY all my Clothing and wearing apparel and the sum of fifty dollars. Third I give and bequeath to NATHAN PHINNEY, son of my said nephew George Phinney, the sum of fifty dollars. Fourth I give and bequeath to my nephews and nieces as follows, to wit: To HARRIET NICHOLS, wife of ALEXANDER NICHOLAS - CORNELIA STANLEY wife of JAMES STANLEY - and ARTEMAS CULVER, daughters and son of my sister SUBMIT CULVER. HULDAH PHINNEY and LOVINA PHINNEY, daughters of my deceased brother SETH PHINNEY. JAMES GRIDLEY and EMELINE BLATHERWICK, wife of MARTIN BLATHERWICK, son and daughter of my sister MERCY GRIDLEY. MARIA DAVIS, daughter of my deceased sister SALLY DAVIS, and EMERSON APPLEBY the Sum of fifty dollars each. Fifth After the payment of the bequests mentioned in items 2, 3 & 4, and after the decease of my wife Catharine Phinney, I give, devise and bequeath all the rest residue and remainder of my estate real and personal to my nephews and nieces named in items 2 and 4 to be divided equally between them share and share alike. Lastly I nominate constitute and appoint my friend James Stanley, husband of my niece Cornelia Stanley of Cazenovia, N.Y. Sole Executor of this my last will and testament giving and granting to him full power to Sell and convey any real estate I may own at my decease execute acknowledge and deliver deed or deeds of conveyance therefor(sic) and to do any other act or thing necessary and requisite to carry into effect all the provisions of this my last will and testament hereby revoking all former wills by me made. Witness whereof I have hereunto set my hand and seal this 17th day of June A.D. 1884. Witnesses: Franklin H. Dewey of Manlius, Onondaga Co., N.Y. SS Nathan Phinney" Charles E. Cole of Manlius, Onondaga Co., N.Y. [Probated 13 April 1885] [From County of Onondaga, Surrogate's Court, Syracuse, New York. Will Book Z, pages 539-41]

(See settlement of the Will at page 291)

Mrs. L. E. Hendrix
14 Mill St.
Cazenovia, N.Y.

Dear Mrs. Hendrix:

I have made a complete search of our records and I find no record of marriage of Isaac Phinney, Jr. and Huldah. You state probably about 1785-1790. I think it would have been before since the first child's birth date is given as August 22, 1785.

The births of children of Isaac and Huldah Phinney are given as follows in Book 1, page 10:

Clarasa, daughter was born August 22, 1785
Sarah, daughter was born August 30, 1788
Seth, son was born May 27, 1791
Submit, daughter was born August 17, 1793
Mercy, daughter was born July 20, 1796

There is no record of a marriage of Seth Phinney and Lydia.

There is no record of death of Isaac Phinney, Sr. and his wife.

Before Williamsburg was incorporated in 1771 it was a part of the town of Hatfield. You might possibly find some earlier records there. If you know the married names of any of the daughters listed above there might be information in later records of marriages, deaths, etc.

Very truly yours,

[signature]

Asst. Town Clerk

APPENDIX

FINNEY/PHINNEY
FAMILIES IN AMERICA
Decendants of John Finney of Plymouth
and Barnstable, Mass, and Bristol, R.I.
of Samuel Finney of Philadelphia, Pa.
and of Robert Finney of New London, Pa
From the Notebooks of
Howard Finney Sr.
Printed in the U.S.A.
The William Byrd Press, Inc.,
Richmond, Va.

Page 26 of the book

228. Isaac [5]Phinney b. May 10, 1733, in Harwich, Mass; m. Jan. 3, 1754
Elizabeth Kiney of Chatham, Mass. She d. 1710. He was a soldier in the
in the Revolutionary WAr.

ISSUE:

1. Heman, b. Aug. 2, 1754 He served in the Revolutionary War.
2. David, b. March 28,1756 'm/ Kidotj Masj. ,adospm Co, N. Y.
3. Mary b. Nov. 18, 1758 m. Nathan Atwood.
4. Sarah b. Aug. 8, 1760 m. Elisha Graves (?)
5. Temperance b. March 31, 1762 d. June 13, 1824 in Madison Co.
   Cazenovia, N.Y. m July 30. 17---Roswell Cleveland.
6. Isaac, b. May, 1, 1764   m) Huldah Preston, Madison Co. N.Y.
7. Nathan b. Aug. 14, 1766.
8. Zrnas b. 1770 d. Oct 28,1846 m. Rhoda Cleveland, who was born
   1774 and d. July 13, 1830 in Manlius, N. Y.

From Mrs. L.E. Hendrix 14 Mill St, Cazenovia, N.Y. Genealogical Research.

" I have spent a little time searching for cemetery records and other
data in an effort to find the maiden name of Huldah, wife of Isaac, but
have been unable to do so. The records of an abanded cemetery in the vicinity
of the Phinney home have yielded the followng death dates for Isaac and
Huldah.

Peck Hill Cemetery, Peck Hill Rd. CAzenovia, N.Y.

Phinney, Huldah, wife of Isaac Phinney, died July 10, 1853.
       ae 79 y 11 mo 19 d

Isaac Phinney d. Aug. 5,1860.   Stone down. (This stone was replaced by
Mr. and Mrs Jesse Wellfare , descendants, who visited the cemetery. After
replacing the fallen stone, cementing it together, Mrs. Roberta Wellfare
outlined the lettering on the stone in black enamel.)

APPENDIX

DEED TO THE FARM OF WILLIAM S. FINNEY
WHO DIED NIGHT OF DEC. 6, 1877, NEAR
MANSFIELD, OHIO

The transfer was made by the heirs of William S. Finney

to Robert Newton Stewart. April 1, 1878, Mansfield, Ohio.

Names of heirs as follows:---

SARAH T. FINNEY, WIDOW OF THE DECEASED,
JAMES P. FINNEY, ONLY SON OF THE DECEASED.
ELIZABETH S. FINNEY, WIFE OF JAMES P. FINNEY.
MARGARET R. AYERS, ELDEST DAUGHTER OF THE DECEASED.
HIRAM S. AYERS, HUSBAND OF MARGARET AYERS,
MARY J. SIMPSON, SECOND DAUGHTER OF THE DECEASED.
D. B. SIMPSON, HUSBAND OF MARY J. SIMPSON.
ALPHA CROUCH, YOUNGEST DAUGHTER OF THE DECEASED.
JOHN R. CROUCH, HUSBAND OF ALPHA CROUCH.

The farm was bought by Robert Newton Stewart, a son of

Sarah T. Finney, by her first husband, Samuel Stewart.

He bought the farm for 12,800 dollars and a good many years

later sold it for 40,000 dollars when the city of Mansfield

had grown to the extent that farms in near by sections

were in demand for city lots. This farm was well improved,

a fine new house having been built on it by R. N. Stewart

and now makes a most presentable city residence, well

situated as it is. The farm was well-wooded especially

with extensive sugar maple groves. Now beautiful residences

are scattered about among these beautiful clumps of ancient

trees of different kinds.

Hovey Bradford Campbell's obituary to his Mother, Huldah (Phinney) Campbell.

OBITUARY.

On last Wednesday morning at 3:15 a. m. there passed from this life to the great beyond, our beloved mother, Huldah Campbell. The subject of this sketch was born in Casnovia Madison Co, N.Y. May 2, 1811, and died at Delta December 10, 1891, aged 80 years 7months and 17 days.

Her maiden name was Huldah Phinney. At the age of 17 she married Elson Campbell of her native state. Together with her husband and parents moved to Michigan in 1836, and located near Wacousta, at that an almost unbroken wilderness, where they built them a log cabin with blankets hung up at the doors and windows. Here she spent many a night all alone with the bears growling and wolves howling at the very door. She was a helpmate in every sense of the word, in sharing the hardships of pioneer life; many times bearing more than her share of the burden, yet we never heard her complain under the most adverse circumstances, bearing everything with a christian fortitude. with a kindly welcome and word of cheer and comfort to those in trouble, and a ministering angel for the sick.

Truly she was a mother in Israel, and no one knew her but to love.

For the last 50 years she has been a sufferer from a complication of diseases. and we had thought many times near death's door; and in every instance she had been resigned and submissive to the Lord's will--ready to bear all her sufferings for His sake, and when the time came we found her willing to depart with the assurance that "all is well". her lasd words.

We have consolation in believing that our mother has gone to receive a christian's reward; that she will hear that welcome voice "come up higher".

She and her companion had traveled life's journey together for over sixty-three years and the fruit of this union was two daughters amd four sons; one daughter and three sons with the aged husband survive her.

The funeral was held at the M.E. church of which denomination she was a member. and was buried, in the village cemetery the services having been conducted by the Rev. C. L. Miller, of Grand Ledge, from Revelations 11 chapter and 13 verse.

                                    H. B. Campbell.

APPENDIX

Last Will of JOHN WATT of Elizabeth Twp. Allegheny Co., Pa.

Made June 24, 1839, proved April 18, 1844

Recorded at Pittsburgh, WB Vol. 5, page 475

In the name of God, Amen, the 24th day of June 1839, I, John Watt, of Elizabeth Township, Allegheny County and State of Pennsylvania, being in usual health, etc. . . . . .

I give and bequeath to my beloved wife Jean the income of both the farms during her life if she needs it and choice of a house or which of them may best sute her and in case William Watt and Nancy should take the care of her they may have the possession of the Jamison Farm at my death and the incomes of the one I live on during her life. This, however, is not to infringe on the privileges of any renter that may be in possession until their Leace is out. And I hereby appoint William Watt to see to the putting it to her use also. I alow her the choice of one horse creture, saddle and bridle, one cow her choice, the cupboard and furniture, so much of the kitchen furniture as she may choose to keep, two beds and beding, One wheel and reel, Large Bible & Psalm Book, Eskins Sermons, the Confession of & one testimony of the reformed decenting Presbetry, with the use of what other Books she may wish to keep that are not otherwise disposed of her lifetime and at her death to be equally divided among my grandchildren. She I alow to her six chairs, two chests, the use of the desk during her lifetime and at her death I alow it to my grandson John Miller. I also alow her one table and

---

Note: William Watt was a nephew of John Watt and his wife Nancy was John Watt's grand-daughter, daughter of Polly Watt and James Patterson.

stand with one third of all the cash that may be found by cash
notes, sale of property or otherwise, also the disposing of such
provision as is laid in for the present use of the family,
namely all kinds of food.

Item, I give and bequeath to Nancy Watt, my granddaughter,
one share in the Jamison farm at her grandmother's death, and
if William chuses to take the whole of it, that is, the
remaining shers at thirty dollars per acre, he may pay the
other shers in the following manner. Namely, one year after
he gets the full possession $100 to <u>John Patterson,</u> the remaining
money to be equally divided among my daughter Polley's children,
and to be paid in annual payments, beginning at the oldest,
these payments to be clear of interest till they become due
by this Testament. If William Watt should not chuse this way,
I alow the place to be sold and after John gets his hundred,
the rest of the price to be equally divided to the rest of the
family, viz., of Polly's children.

I also alow to Nancy "Dunham on the Joug." Item, I alow
to my daughter Peggy her lifetime the farm I presently live
in and at her death to be appraised and sold and the price of
it equally divided among her children, her oldest son to have
the offer of it at the appraisement, if he should not accept
of the offer, any of her sons may, still giving preference to
the oldest. I also alow to her all papers of a privet nature,
such as privet letters, memorandums, etc. Also Owen on

Note by M. F. :- John Patterson was a son of Polly Watt and her
husband James Patterson – his name was John Watt Patterson and
<u>somewhat a favorite of his maternal grandfather, John Watt.</u>

Communion and on the 130 Psalm, beside her divide of all books not otherwise disposed of; the possession of the land and part of the Books to be limited by Item first. Also I do alow her one third of the money that may be found. Item Furst.

Item, It is my will that my grandsons Jos. Miller have one horse, his choice after his grandmother has got hers, saddle, bridle, saddlebags, boots and spurs, Henry's Commentary on the Scripture. Item I give and bequeath to my grandson John Miller my shere of the crop that may be found in the ground at my decease with what carpenter tools may be found, Goss Arithmetic, Hanys Mensuration Scale, and dividers, Sliding rule and book of directions to work it, English Dictionary, my pocket bible and watch.

Item, I give to Mary Miller one Cow, Prichats Commentary and Gospel Sonnets.

I give and bequeath to Margaret Patterson one cow and three sheep, Gospel truth.

Item, I give and bequeath to James Patterson one entire suit of clothes the best.

Item, I give and bequeath to Joseph Patterson the little colt, one pocket bible to be bought.

Item, the remainder of my wearing apparel to be disposed of as my wife may see proper. Item, the remainder third of money to be equally divided as equally as possible between Polly's children and Peggy, the last to descend to her children after her death.

Note: James Patterson, son-in-law of John Watt, husband of Polly Watt.

Item, It is my will that the bureau and bedding mentioned

in the memorandum between John Pangburn and me with all other

things that have been called Ratchel Pangburns be faithfully

given to her with such things as she may purchase with the

old woman's concert and if she chooses stay the time named in

the memorandum, Sat ur her (three preceding words seem illegible

and do not make sense} the New Woman's Sader, with two little

books, persents to Early Piety by I. Pike, and a guide to

young disciples, same author, all and sundry the remainder of

my property to be put to public sale and the money disposed of

as directed above.

Lastly, I do nominate and appoint Thomas Miller my son-

in-law and William Watt my brother's son Executors of this

my last Will and Testament, hereby revoking all other wills,

legacies and bequests by me heretofore made. In witness whereof

I have hereunto set my hand and seal the day and year above

written.

JOHN WATT (seal)

Witnesses:
  ISAAC WILSON
  MOSES D. WILSON
  DAVID WILSON

Allegheny County, 18 April 1844, came Isaac and Moses Wilson

and proved the will.

Letters Testamentary were granted to Thomas Millar and William

Watt, Executors.

> This will copied from the originally recorded
> instrument in the Register of Wills Office,
> Pittsburgh, Penna. October 1944, by
> Kenyon Stevenson, 82 Aurora St. Hudson, Ohio
> for Miss Minnehaha Finney.

WILL OF ELIJAH PATTERSON, WILL BOOK NO. 6, PAGE 70.

GREENSBURG, PA., WESTMORELAND CO.

No. 48 of 1875   :   In the name of God Amen, I Elijah
:
will of   : Patterson of the Borough of West Newton
:
Elijah Patterson late: Westmoreland County and state of
:
of West Newton Borough:Pennsylvania being advanced in life but
:
dec'd 33"   : of a sound mind, memory and judgment
:
blessed be God for the same, considering

the uncertainty of this life do make and publish this my last

will and testament (Hereby revoking and setting aside all former

wills by me made.)   In the manner and form as follows to wit:

1st.   I will my immortal spirit to God that gave it, and

my body to the dust from whence it came. 2nd. Concerning

my worldly effecta. It is my will and I do order and direct that

all my just debts as shall be by me owing at my death together

with my funeral expenses and all charges touching the proving

or otherwise concerning this my will shall in the first place

out of my personal estate and effects be fully paid and satisfied.

I will and bequeath unto the heirs of my Brother John Patterson

dec'd three hundred dollars to them their heirs and assigns for

ever, to them share and share alike. I will and bequeath unto

the heirs of my sister Susannah Patterson Dec'd four hundred

dollars to them their heirs and assigns forever to them share

and share alike. I will and bequeath unto the heirs of my

Brother Thomas Patterson of the State of West Virginia, Deceased,

four hundred dollars to them their heirs and assigns for ever
to them share and share alike.

I will and bequeath unto the heirs of my Brother James Patterson
late of Elizabeth Twp. Allegheny County Pa. dec'd three hundred
dollars to the heirs of his first wife to them their heirs and
assigns forever to them share and share alike. And also I will
and bequeath unto the two minor heirs of the said James Patterson
dec'd to wit Mary E. and Alexander Patterson one hundred dollars
each to them their heirs and assigns forever.

I will and bequeath unto the heirs of my Brother William
Patterson of Crawford County Pa. dec'd four hundred dollars to them
their heirs and assigns forever to them share and share alike.

I will and bequeath unto the heirs of my Brother Samuel
Patterson late of South Huntingdon Township Westmoreland County
Pa. deceased four hundred dollars to them their heirs and
assigns forever to them share and share alike. I will and
bequeath unto the heirs of my Brother Robert Patterson late of
the state of Indiana, Deceased, three hundred dollars to them
their heirs and assigns for ever to them share and share alike.

It is my will that my executor hereafter named make sale
of all my real and personal estate not otherwise disposed of as
soon after my deceased as conveniently be done. And farther
it is my will that all the above bequeaths be paid to the
legitees in one year after my decease or as soon as can
conceniently be done by my executor.

And provided that there should remain in the hands of my

executor any money after paying all the above named bequests together with all debts or charges concerning the settling of my estate together with collateral inheritance tax then it is my will that my executor pay ove one half of said balance to the trustees of the United Presbyterian Congregation of West Newton to be used to the best interests of the congregation, and the other half of said balance to be paid over to the Home, Foreign, and Freedmens Missions Fund, share and share alike.

And lastly I nominate constitute and appoint James Patterson Jr. son of my Brother James Patterson of Elizabeth Township Allegheny County Pa. executor of this my last will and testament, reposing full confidence in his integrity to perform the trust committed to his charge. In witness whereof I Elijah Patterson the testator have here unto set my hand and seal this eighteenth day of February A.D. one thousand eight hundred and sixty seven.

Elijah Patterson   Seal

Signed, sealed and declared by the above named Elijah Patterson as and for his last will and testament in presence of us and in the presence of each other who at his request have signed our names as witness to the same.

David Shreder

H. P. Hofer

Oct. 8, 1875. Legally proved and approved; same day recorded and letters testamentary granted to within named Executor who was sworn to the same this day before me.

J. W. Laird, Register

Testator died 4, Oct. A.D. 1875, about 4 o'clock P.M.

COPY OF CITATION OF SETTLEMENT
OF
THE WILL OF NATHAN PHINNEY

Surrogate's Court held in and for the County of Onondaga, at the Surrogate's Office in the City of Syracuse, on the 16th day of September, AD 1887.

PRESENT, GEORGE R. COOK, SURROGATE.

In the matter of the Final Settlement of the Accounts of James H. Stanley of
the last will and testament
of
NATHAN PHINNEY deceased.

It appearing to the satisfication of the Surrogate of the County of Onondaga, New York, by the affidavit of JAMES H. STANLEY, the petitioner, the executor
of the estate of NATHAN PHINNEY
late of Manlius, in said County deceased, now on file in the Surrogate's office of said County, that the following named persons are heirs at law, next of kin, legatees, devisees, creditors, or are persons otherwise interested in the estate of said deceased, and are necessary parties to the final judicial settlement of the estate of said deceased, now pending before the Surrogate of said County, and are severally non-residents of the State of New York, and that they respectively reside at the several places hereinafter set opposite their names to-wit:

Artimus B. Culver	Chicago,	Illinois
Louise Crissey	Chicago,	Illinois
Susan R. Post	Chicago,	Illinois
Maud M. Post	Chicago,	Illinois
Louise R. Post	Chicago,	Illinois
Charles Appleby	Chicago,	Illinois
George Appleby	Chicago,	Illinois
Orlando Culver	Waukeaha,	Wisconsin
Artimus Culver	Pittsburg,	Pennsylvania.
Charles Culver	Milwaukee,	Wisconsin.
Emma Jane Campbell	Marine City,	Michigan.
Orlando Post	New London,	Ohio.
Collins Post	New London,	Ohio.
Emiline Blatherwick	Demoines,	Iowa
Leonard Gria(?)could be Gridley	Garrettsville,	Ohio
Isadore Baldwin	Omaha,	Nebraska
Findley P. Gridley	Omaha,	Nebraska
Charles W. Gridley	Omaha,	Nebraska
Frank B. Gridley	Rapid City	Dakota
James W. Gridley	Rapid City,	Dakota
Flora C. Hall	Rapid City,	Dakota
Mary B. Gridley	Rapid City,	Dakota
Robert F. Paine	Cleveland,	Ohio
Findley R. Paine	Cleveland,	Ohio
James Paine	Cleveland,	Ohio
Jane Wood	Cleveland,	Ohio
Hiram Phinney	St. Cloud,	Wisconsin
Sally Ann Hessler	St. Paul,	Minnesota.

Nathan P Buck	St. Paul,	Minnesota
Huldah E. Hunt	Valparaiso,	Indiana.
George Phinney	Wacousta,	Michigan.
Huldah Campbell	Wacousta,	Michigan.
Emily Spicer	Geneva,	Kansas
Lydia A. Welfare	Danby,	Michigan
Henry McCausey	West Sebewa	Michigan
George McCausey	West Sebewa	Michigan
James McCausey	West Sebewa.	Michigan.
Allen N. McCausey	West Sebewa,	Michigan.
Frank McCausey	West Sebewa,	Michigan.
Gilbert McCausey	West Sebewa,	Michigan.
Charles McCausey	Scot Station;	Michigan.
Elmer E. Blanchard	Sebewa,	Michigan.
Chauncey L. Blanchard	Groton,	Michigan.
Merritt Dinsmore.	Portland,	Michigan.
Jennie Anderson	Portland,	Michigan.
Nina Humiston	Gaylord,	Michigan.
Wesley Thornbur	Big Rapids,	Michigan.
Hattie Smith	Big Rapids,	Michigan.
Ralph P. Buck,	Wilbur,	Nebrasla.
Lorenzo D. Buck,	Abilene,	Kansas.
Isaac N. Buck	Elgin,	Illinois.
Sally Buck	Elgin,	Illinois.
Josephine Rogers	Allegan;	Michigan..
Victoria Holmes	Allegan,	Michigan.
Lillian Throop	Allegan,	Michigan.
Robert Davis	Allegan,	Michigan.
Edmund S. Rogers	Allegan,	Michigan
Emily L. Perkins	Lake Preston;	Dakota
Seth P. Huntington	Barrington Station,	Illinois.
Minnie Losel	Woodstock,	Illinois.
Douglas Heath	Cadillac,	Illinois.
Jessie Crissey	West Bay City,	Michigan.
Kittie E. Buck	Joliet,	Illinois.
Rena Buck	Worthington,	Ohio.
Julia Buck	Worthington,	Ohio.
Emerson Appleby	Worthington,	Ohio.
Warren Appleby	Clifton,	Iowa.
John Appleby	Ebony,	Missouri,
Nancy Jane Vanderheyden	Mount Carroll,	Illinois.
Clarissa M.Turpeny	Winters;	Illinois.
Clarissa Vanderheyden	Winters,	Illinois.
Eli Appleby,	Geneva	Iowa
Myron Appleby,	Geneva,	Iowa.
Bert Appleby,	Geneva,	Iowa.
Mary A. Warner	Pitcherville,	Illinois.
Lottie Colby,	Hepworth,	Canada.
Lucien H. Appleby	Holmwood,	Kansas.
Artimus Appleby	Holmwood,	Kansas.
Emily M. Bradley	Kalida,	Ohio.
Clarissa Aldrich	Clayton,	Michigan
George Richardson	Baskin Creek,	Michigan.

That the several places of residence of George Culver, Lovina
Taylor, Warner Appleby and Bloomfield Blake are unknown

GEORGE R. COOK
Surrogate.

A sister off NATHAN PHINNEY was SUBMIT PHINNEY b. August
1793, Williamsburg, Mass. who married RICHARD CULVER. This is
a copy of information received from the Surrogate's office of
the County of Onondaga, N.Y.

THE PEOPLE OF THE STATE OF NEW YORK by the GRACE OF GOD Free
and independent.
Catherine Phinney of Manlius, N.Y. Job Reynolds as Executrix of
last will and testament of SUBMIT CULVER, deceased,

Cornelia H. Stanley of Chittenango Falls, N.Y.
Artimus B. Culver
Louisa Crissby
Susan R. Post.
Maud H. Post.
Louisa R. Post.
Charles Appleby.
George Appleby Severally of Chicago, Illinois.
Charles W. Culver
Marietta Stanley severally of Cazenovia, N.Y.
Elizabeth H. Seward of Syracuse, N.Y.
Harriet Nichols of Fenner, N.Y.
Orlando Culver of Waukesha, Wisconsin.
Artimus Culver of Pittsburg, Pa.
Charles Culver of Milwaukee, Wisconsin.
Emma Jane Campbell of Marine City, Michigan.
Orlando Post
Collins Post severally of New London, Ohio.
Florence Oliver.
Nellie Culver
Jonas L. Buck severally of New York City
Emeline Blatherwick of Desmoines, Iowa
Leonard Gridley of Garrettsville, Ohio
Isadore Baldwin
Findley P. Gridley
Charles W. Gridley severally of Omaha, Nebraska.
Frank P. Gridley
James U. Gridley
Flora C. Hall
Mary B. Gridley severally of Rapids City, Dakota.
Robert F. Paine.
Findley K. Paine.
James Paine, Jane Wood severally of Cleveland, Ohio.
Hiram Phinney of St. Cloud, Wisconsin.
Sally Ann Hessler
Nathan P. Buck severally of St. Paul, Minnesota.
Huldah E. Hunt of Valparaiso, Indiana.
George Phinney
Huldah Campbell, severally of Wacousta, Michigan.
Emily Spicer of Geneva, Kansas.
Lydia A. Welfare of Danby, Michigan.
Henry McCausey
George McCausey
James McCausey
Allen N. McCausey.
Frank McCausey
Gilbert McCausey severally of West Sebewe, Michigan.
Charles McCausey of Scott Station, Michigan
Elmer E. Blanchard of Sebewa, Michigan.
Chauncey L. Blanchard of Groton, Michigan.

Merritt Densmore
Jennie Anderson severally of Portland, Michigan.
Nina Humeston of Gaylord, Michigan.
Wesley Thornburl
Hattie Smith severally of Big Rapids, Michigan.
Ralph P. Buck of Wilbur, Nebraska.
Lorenzo D. Buck of Abilene, Kansas
Isaac N. Buck
Sally Buck sverally of Elgin, Illinois.
Josephene Rogers
Victoria Holmes
Lillian Throop
Robert Davis and
Edmund S. Rogers as administrator of the ESTATE OF MARIE DAVIS
deceased, severally of Allegan, Michigan.
Emily L. Perkins of Lake Preston, Dakota.
Seth P. Huntington of Barrington Station, Illinois
Minnie Losee (Losel) of Woodstock, Illinois.
Douglas Heath of Cadillac, Illinois.
Jessie Crissey of West Bay, Michigan.
Kittid E. Buck of Joliet, Illinois.
Rena Buck
Julia Buck severally of Worthington, Ohio.
Emmerson Appleby of Brimfield, Illinois
Warren Appleby
Bert Appleby severally of Geneva, Iowa
Mary A. Warner of Pitcherville, Illinois.
Isaac O. Blake of Lysander, N. Y.
Jabez G. Blake of Meridian, N. Y.
Mattoe B;ale
Alice Blake severally of Auborn, N.Y.
Nellie Oliver of Oswego, N.Y.
John Robinson of South West Oswego, N.Y.
Hattie Cross of Weedsport, N.Y.
Jennie Taylor of Port Bryan, N.Y.
Cynthia Chappell of Jordon, N.Y.
Libius C rtis of Lansing, N.Y.
Lottie Colby of Hepworth, Canada
Lucian M. Appleby
Artimus Appleby severally of Holenwood (Holmwood) Kansas.
Emily M. Bradley of Kaliden, Ohio.
Clarissa Aldrich of Clayton; Michigan
George Richardson of Baskin Creek, Michigan

Merritt Densmore
Jennie Anderson severally of Portland, Michigan.
Nina Humeston of Gaylord, Michigan.
Wesley Thornburl
Hattie Smith severally of Big Rapids, Michigan.
Ralph P. Buck of Wilbur, Nebraska.
Lorenzo D. Buck; of Abilene, Kansas
Isaac N. Buck
Sally Buck sverally of Elgin, Illinois.
Josephene Rogers
Victoria Holmes
Lillian Throop
Robert Davis and
Edmund S. Rogers as administrator of the ESTATE OF MARIE DAVIS
deceased, severally of Allegan, Michigan.
Emily L. Perkins of Lake Preston, Dakota.
Seth P. Huntington of Barrington Station, Illinois
Minnie Losee (Losel) of Woodstock, Illinois.
Douglas Heath of Cadillac, Illinois.
Jessie Crissey of West Bay, Michigan.
Kittid E. Buck of Joliet, Illinois.
Rena Buck :
Julia Buck severally of Worthington, Ohio.
Emmerson Appleby of Brimfield, Illinois
Warren Appleby
Bert Appleby severally of Geneva, Iowa
Mary A. Warner of Pitcherville, Illinois.
Isaac O. Blake of Lysander, N. Y.
Jabez G. Blake of Meridian, N. Y.
Mattoe B;ale
Alice Blake severally of Auborn, N.Y.
Nellie Oliver of Oswego, N.Y.
John Robinson of South West Oswego, N.Y.
Hattie Cross of Weedsport, N.Y.
Jennie Taylor of Port Bryan, N.Y.
Cynthia Chappell of Jordon, N.Y.
Libius C rtis of Lansing, N.Y.
Lottie Colby of Hepworth, Canada
Lucian M. Appleby
Artimus Appleby severally of Holenwood (Holmwood) Kansas.
Emily M. Bradley of Kaliden, Ohio.
Clarissa Aldrich of Clayton; Michigan
George Richardson of Baskin Creek, Michigan

———————

A VISIT TO SOME FOREFATHERS
*****

By Mrs. Jesse Wellfare   (Roberta Rosalie)

On September 1, 1966 Jesse D. Wellfare and his wife Roberta
started on a trip to Cazenovia, N.Y. to locate the graves of
ISAAC JR. and HULDAH PHINNEY, our great,great,great grandpar-
ents. Through a New York genealogist, Mrs. Lester Hendryx, they
knew where to go. They found the private cemetery, on a hill,
that had run wild with myrtle and wild roses. Isaac's and
Hulda's stones were broken and face down in the dirt, as were
all be three of the other stones. This is not surprising with
the severe winters and clear sweep of the wind.

EPHRIAM PRESTON'S was the most imposing of the upright stones.
Since our records showed he did much land trading with the
Phinneys, we wondered if he was Hulda's father. This would
explain why they were buried here rather than in the Cazenovia
or Manlius cemeteries as were other members of their families.
Jesse reclaimed their stones and cemented them in an upright
position while Roberta traced the worn lettering with black
enamel.

The information about ISAAC PHINNEY, JR and wife HULDAH 'has
come from various sources: The will of Nathan Phinney, family
records, but most from the town of Williamsburg, Mass., office
of the Town Clerk, Haydensville, Mass. ahd the land records of
Madison and Onondaga Counties in New York.

ISAAC PHINNEY, Jr and his wife, HULDAH, must have come to
New York about 1801 or 1804. NATHON was born about 1805, as he
is not mentioned in the birth records of the children of Isaac
Jr and Huldah Phinney, born between Williamsburg and Madison Co,
N.Y. He received the paternal farm so we are justified in be-
lieving him to be a son.

APPEMDIX

The records of this abandoned cemetery in the vicinity of the Phinney home have the following dates for the death of IsaacJr and Huldah Phinney:

> PECK HILL CEMETERY, PECK HILL ROAD
>
> CAZENOVIA, NEW YORK
>
> PHINNEY, HULDAH, WIFE OF
>
>   ISAAC PHINNEY, died July 10,1853
>
>   ae 73 (or 79)y. 11 mo. 19 d. .
>
>   ISAAC PHINNEY d. Aug. 5(or15)1860

The land records of Madison Co, N.Y. and Onondaga Co inform us that Zenas Phinney and wife, Rhoda, bought land in April 1810 (Zenas was a brother of Isaac Jr). On February 1815, Seth Phinney of Cazenovia, bought part of Lot 21 on Mile Strip of Oneida Indians (Seth was a son of Isaac Jr and Huldah) Recorded 1824, Seth Phinney and Lydia of Ira, Cayuga Co, N.Y. sold Lot on Mile Strip to IsaacPhinney of Cazenovia, Madison County and Salmon Phinney of the same place "--all that pice of land in town aforesaid and being the farm on which Isaac Phinney now resides, 100 acres reserving to the said Isaac the possession and the use and profit of the said farm and premises for and during the natural life of the survivor of them". Recorded Feb. 4, 1839.

Material copied from The Finney Family History by Minnehaha Finney.

GRANDFATHER

WILLIAM STEWART FINNEY OF MANSFIELD OHIO

died a tragic death Dec. 6, 1877. Even to the present day
the event of his death is remembered and every once in a while
is brought to notice by alert Newspaper reporters.

Shortly after my return to the United States in the
summer of 1937 and when I was being entertained in the home
of some cousins in Ashland, Ohio, The Ashland Times Gazette
sent in one of their staff, William A. Duff, to interview me.
The following is the result of the interview which was printed
in the above mentioned newspaper at the date given.

The event of my grandfather's tragic death was always
a terrible memory to me and I have always tried to avoid
telling the story as he was such a dear old man and much loved
by his grand-children. So since Mr. Duff got the story out
of me and wrote it up so well and toned it down by relating
other of my more pleasant experiences, I thought it would be
an easy way to show respect to my grandfather by just quoting
Mr. W. A. Duff's well written article in our Genealogical
Records. As a matter of fact, a story of this sort is a real
Genealogical Landmark. This is my only reason for using the
story.

Sincerely, and Respectfully

Minnehaha Finney

P. S. The tragic event happened when I was a child 10 years of
age.

APPENDIX.

ASHLAND TIMES GAZETTE
Friday evening, October 29, 1937

William A. Duff--OBSERVES TODAY

Miss Minnehaha Finney, whom I interviewed at the residence
of her cousins, Mrs. Frank N. Patterson and Miss Ada Patterson
on Center street, was for 43 years in active highly successful
missionary work in Lower Egypt and in the heart of the delta
of the Nile. She traveled in various other regions rich in
history, visited India, journeyed to Ur of the Chaldees, early
home, in Mesopotamia, of the patriarch Abraham; also to Mount
Sinai: and to that ancient city of Bagdad, now the capital of
Iraq. In her girlhood, out in Kansas, where her father was
engaged in missionary work, there were many Indians. But the
most perilous experience of all her life, I think, was the one
on that December night, nearly 60 years ago, in the Finney
farmhouse southwest of Mansfield when her grandfather, William
S. Finney, was murdered, her grandmother so terribly beaten that
for severval days her life was despaired of, and her mother
rendered unconscious when the midnight marauder struck her down.

Miss Finney preferred to speak of phases of her missionary
experience in Egypt--evangelistic work, teaching in schools for
girls; installation, when she was superintendent of the high
school on the United Presbyterian mission in Alexandria, of a
trained worker to conduct the first kindergarten classes in
Egypt; instruction to mothers in the care of children, in health
and hygiene and in the training of evangelistic workers.

Though Miss Finney, after 43 years of foreign missionary
work in Egypt, is now retired and lives at the home of her

sister, Mrs. Pearl Stevenson at Sterling, Kansas, she has been responding to calls for speaking engagements on missionary work.

Miss Finney, who is a cousin of the late Appellate Judge Frank N. Patterson, had the pleasure, while visiting in Ashland of seeing in Milton township, near the Nelson schoolhouse and not far from Sprott's Hill, Clearcreek township, the stone residence which her grandfather, James Short, soldier of the war of 1812 and an early settler on Milton township, erected some time before his death in 1861, and in which her Grandmother Short lived the rest of her life. James Short was married twice. After the death of his first wife he married in 1825, Miss Margery Raitt, whose parents came from Dundee, Scotland. One time, on a visit to Scotland Miss Finney visited Dundee from which her great-grandparents came to this country. She found there some interesting records of the family.

Miss Finney's mother, Elizabeth Short, was the youngest daughter of James and Margery Short. In 1865 she married James Patterson Finney, son of Mr. and Mrs. William S. Finney who lived near the Lexington road, about two miles southwest of Mansfield. James Patterson Finney entered the United Presbyterian ministry and it was at Pittsburg, Carroll county, Ind., that Miss Finney was born. To do home missionary work out in Kansas, the Rev. and Mrs. Finney journeyed to what was then Westport, Mo., but now the metropolis, Kansas City. There everybody got off except the Finneys and some Indians. The mission station at which they took up their work was at Manhattan, Kans. The site of the house in which they lived is now just across the road from the campus of the Kansas State College. The country was full of Indians, Miss Finney recalls.

Miss Finney's father was the only son of Mr. and Mrs. William S. Finney and as the parents were becoming advanced in years they urged their son to take up pastoral work in Ohio. So the Rev. James Finney finally took a pastorate in Adams county, was there for a while and then owing to his father becoming more feeble he and his family were at the Finney farm. Miss Finney attended the Pollock district school near her grandfather's home and frequently saw passing along the road a big Negro who worked for a neighboring farmer named Cook. In the Finney family he was usually referred to as "Cook's darkey".

And now we come to the tragedy at the Finney farmhouse on the night of December 6, 1877 when Miss Finney's grandfather was so terribly beaten with a gun in the hands of a midnight marauder that he died before medical aid could arrive, the grandmother so badly injured that she was unconscious for three days during which it was thought she could not survive, and Miss Finney's mother stunned by a blow over the head. In the files of Mansfield and Ashland papers, also in the columns of various other papers in north-central Ohio can be found long articles about the Finney murder. Miss Finney's parents were reluctant for a long time to mention the tragedy and after all these years she doesn't like to talk about it, but she told me all the circumstances which I shall touch upon as briefly as possible.

In one of the downstairs bedrooms on the night of the murder, Grandfather and Grandmother Finney were sleeping. In another downstairs room were Rev. and Mrs. Finney and three children and upstairs were the hired man named Lindsay and

thinking that Grandmother Finney was ill started for the
bedroom. She had reached the door when she was struck
over the head. The assailant next attacked Rev. Finney, dealt
him a blow with the butt end of the gun. The victim warded off
a second blow, wrenched the gun from the murderer's hands,
then summoned the hired man. The assailant, with a lamp in
his hand stood over the bed where 10-year-old Minnehaha lay.
He evidently thought her asleep but she wasn't. By the light
of the lamp she recognized him as "Cook's darkey." The slayer,
hearing Lindsay say; "Here's my revolver," jumped out of the
window, taking the lamp with him. The slayer's tracks in the
light snow led toward the Cook darkey's home. Uncle Ayers, at a
neighboring farm, was informed of the midnight attack, went to town
and secured a physician but Grandfather Finney was dead before
the doctor arrived.

"Cook's darkey", Edward Webb, was arrested, some stolen
articles were found in his home, a newspaper account said.
The gun used in the murder was one that had been stolen the
previous fall from H. S. Ayers. The 10-year-old Minnehaha
positively identified Webb as the murderer, he was convicted
and on the 31st of May, 1878, was hanged at Mansfield, the only
execution in the history of that city. Webb had known that the
aged Finney had sold his hogs and probably had the money,
about $100, in the house, hence the robbery attempt that re-
sulted in murder.

In the spring of 1878, Rev. James Finney and his family
returned to Kansas and he took up a land claim. The family

remained at Lawrence until the following year when they joined
him. Miss Finney graduated from the Beloit, Kans. high school
in 1886 with first honors, taught school a year or two,
graduated in 1891 from Tarkio, Mo., College, taught school at
Red Oak, Ia., was engaged in the Freedmen's Mission at Knoxville,
Tenn., and in 1894 went to Egypt as a United Presbyterian
missionary, being supported in the work by the Allegheny
Presbyterial. She was first located at Mansoura in Lower Egypt,
along the Nile, taught in a school for girls and did evangelistic
work. She studied the Arabic language and in her later work
was superintendent of the high school in the United Presbyterian
mission at Alexandria where, as I have said, she introduced
kindergarten work, securing for this a trained worker. There
was an interruption of her work at the time of the breaking
out of the World war, but at the end of 1914 she took up work
at Tanta in the heart of the Nile delta. In connection with
other work later she developed district work, established training
schools and did evangelistic work. After the World War with
the new world movement there was a great advance in mission
activities. A new building was secured for a training school
for women workers. Miss Finney told me some features of the
district work, the construction of a house car that was operated
on a railroad in the Nile delta. Some 50 or 60 villages were
regularly visited, evangelistic work done and, by charts, health
and hygiene taught, cleanliness in the home, the care of
children, how to avoid diseases that were especially prevalent.

Last July, Miss Finney returned to the United States and
has retired from work in the foreign field. When Miss Finney

came here she was desirous of seeing the old home of her
Grandfather Short. T. V. Simanton gave the desired information
and Mrs. and Miss Patterson took her to see it. A nephew of
Mrs. John Herschler is tenant on the farm and lives in the
stone mansion which is excellently preserved.

Two cousins, Mr. and Mrs. W. W. Crouch of Mansfield were
guests with Miss Finney at dinner Wednesday evening at the
Patterson home.

An Appreciation of
JUDGE FRANK N. PATTERSON
published at the time of his death in the
Ashland Times-Gazette, Ashland, Ohio.

Born in Hayesville, Ohio, December 28, 1863.

Attended rural and district schools and Wooster College.

Principal of Loudonville high school while reading law.

Admitted to bar and started practicing law in Loudonville
in 1890.

Married to Mary Schauweker in 1892 (Apr. 13)

Served as presecuting attorney for one term starting in 1894.

Served as city solicitor of Ashland for two terms.

Served as state senator in 77th and 78th general
assemblies, 1906-10.

Elected judge fifth appellate district in 1918 and re-
elected in 1924 by majority of 24,000.

Author of Patterson's Criminal Code.

Died April 12, at age of 63 years. (1926)

8**********************

Judge Patterson was an able attorney, a fair and impartial
judge, well known author, prudent law maker and a loyal American
citizen. His judgment and counsel were sought by such men as
Senator Frank B. Willis, Senator Simeon D. Fess and the late
Warren G. Harding.

When he was in the state senate representing the joint
27-29th Ohio District, he was one of the leaders among the
Republicans. He was active in the fight for prohibition.

He was the son of Finney C. and Caroline (Ayers) Patterson.
His father preceded him in death November 17, 1865, when he was
less than two years of age.

During his early life, he worked on the farm and attended the rural school. Later he taught district school and provided for himself and mother. At the age of 20, he entered Wooster College, where he attended school for two years.

After leaving school he secured the position of principal of Loudonville high school. During his terms of teaching, Judge Patterson read law and was admitted to the bar atarting active practice of law in 1890 in Loudonville.

For many years, Patterson was associated with the late Harry Mykrantz in the law firm of Patterson and Mykrantz. This partnership was broken when Patterson was elected appellate Judge.

Patterson's Criminal Code was regarded as an authority not only by attorneys throughout this state, but by others who had occasion to refer to Ohio laws.

The eleventh edition of the work includes all the laws relating to crimes and criminal procedure as enacted to and including Volume 110 of the Ohio laws.

Judge Patterson was president of the local Chamber of Commerce for two years. He was a charter member of the Rotary Club and was president of the organization for a year. He was active in patriotic activities and was one of the local leaders in Liberty Loan drives during the World War I.

He was a member of Ashland lodge number 151 Free and Accepted Masons, the local Chapter of Masons, the Knight Templar lodge at Mansfield and the local Colonial Club.

He was an active member of the Presbyterian Church.

APPENDIX

FAMILY BIBLE RECORD

The following is a list of the children of James Patterson and his wife Mary Watt:--

NOTE added: All were born in Elizabeth Twp. Alleg. Co., Penn.

       I   Agnes Nancy, born Nov. 26, 1813

      II   Jane, born April 5, 1816

     III   Margaret, born Aug. 15, 1818

      IV   Suaanna, born Feb. 1, 1881

       V   John Watt, born March 9, 1823

      VI   James S., born Feb. 11, 1825

     VII   Joseph, born May 28, 1827

    VIII   Thomas, born Sept. 19, 1830

      IX   Finney C., born July 5, 1833

       X   Mary, born July 5, 1833

      XI   Sarah, born   1835.

NOTE:-- The above exactly as found is the Family Bible which is now owned by Miss Marjorie Patterson, grand-daughter of James (see above). Her address is Elizabeth, Pa. Alleg. Co., Penn. Rock Run Road.

****

NOTE:-- Their first child was named William but his name was not recorded in the Bible. He died in infancy. Also there is no record in the above mentioned Bible of the children of the 2nd. wife, Mary Swanger. She had two children as follows:--

       Mary Evana, born Apr. 25, 1847

       Alexander, born July 11, 1850

****

FAMILY GROUP No. _____	Husband's Full Name			David Purcell Finney		*my father*

Printer

This Information Obtained From:	Husband's Data	Day Month Year	City, Town or Place	County or Province, etc.	State or Country	Add. Info. on Husband
Book of Marriages #22	Birth	21 Oct 1876	New Orleans	Orleans	La.	
Folio 851 New Orleans	Chr'nd	Meth				
La. Deputy Rec. Birth	Mar.	11 March 1901	"	"	"	
and death marriage	Death	9 Oct 1949	Hattiesburg	Forrest	Mississippi	
Orleans Parish	Burial	10 Oct 1949	"	"	Highland Cemetary	
Information obtained	Places of Residence		Hattiesburg	Forrest	Miss.	
from living family	Occupation Printer		Church Affiliation Meth		Military Rec Spanish A. War	
	Other wives, if any. No. (1) (2) etc. Make separate sheet for each mar.					
	His Father Charles Key Finney			Mother's Maiden Name Frances Cooke		

	Wife's Full Maiden Name			Emma Liddle Munro		
	Wife's Data	Day Month Year	City, Town or Place	County or Province, etc.	State or Country	Add. Info. on Wife
	Birth	10 Aug. 1877	New Orleans	Orleans	La.	
	Chr'nd	Meth				
	Death	6 Aug 1940	Hattiesburg	Forrest	Miss.	
	Burial	7 Aug 1940	"	Highland Cemetary	"	
Compiler	Places of Residence		New Orleans, La. Hattiesburg, Miss.			
Address	Occupation if other than Housewife			Church Affiliation Methodist		
City, State	Other husbands, if any. No. (1)(2) etc. Make separate sheet for each mar.					
Date	Her Father John Munro, Jr.			Mother's Maiden Name Emma Louisa Schreede		

Sex	Children's Names in Full (Arrange in order of birth)	Children's Data	Day Month Year	City, Town or Place	County or Province, etc.	State or Country	Add. Info. on Children
1	David Purcell Jr.	Birth	1903	New Orleans	Orleans	La	
	Full Name of Spouse	Death	1903	Died at seven months			
		Burial					
2	Miriam Finney	Birth	5 May 1904	New Orleans	Orleans	La.	
		Mar.	21 Aug. 1928	Hattiesburg	Forrest	Miss.	
	Full Name of Spouse	Death	21 Jan 1957	"	"	"	
	Louis E. Wicht	Burial	22 Jan 1957	Highland Cemetary	"	"	
3	Emma Liddle Finney	Birth	25 Nov 1906	Mobile		Alabama	
		Mar.		Hattiesburg	Forrest	Miss.	
	Full Name of Spouse	Death					
	Harris C. Jones	Burial					
4	Frances Key Finney	Birth	27 Nov 1909	Jackson	Hinds	Miss.	
		Mar.	18 Nov 1933	Richton (by Judge Mills)	"		
	Full Name of Spouse	Death					
	William Ward Mills	Burial					
5	Ruth Grace Finney	Birth	29 Nov 1910	Jackson	Hinds	Miss.	
		Mar.	15 July 1933	Hattiesburg	Forrest		
	Full Name of Spouse	Death	14 Nov 1970	Highland Cemetary (Bay St. Louis Hospital			
	Robert W. Wyatt	Burial	15 Nov 1970	Hattiesburg	Forrest		
6	James Finney	Birth	born about 1913 and died six months afterwards				
		Mar.	of whooping cough (twin)				
	Full Name of Spouse	Death	1913	Ashville		North Carolina	Born
		Burial	1913	New Orleans	Orleans	La.	
7	John Finney	Birth	Twin 1913	died in 1913 of whooping cough in			
		Mar.		New Orleans, La at six months of age			
	Full Name of Spouse	Death	1913	Ashville		North, Carolina	
		Burial		New Orleans Orleans		La.	
8	one son	Birth		Name unknown, possibly stillborn			
		Mar.		between Miriam and Emma			
	Full Name of Spouse	Death					
		Burial					
9		Birth					
		Mar.					
	Full Name of Spouse	Death					
		Burial					
10		Birth					
		Mar.					
	Full Name of Spouse	Death					
		Burial					

*If married more than once No. each mar. (1) (2) etc. and list in "Add. info. on children" column. Use reverse side for additional children, other notes, references or information.

William Ward Mills and
Name of Compiler Frances Finney Mills Person No. 1 on this chart is the same
Address 11556 Archery Drive   person as No. 1 on chart No. 1.
City, State Baton Rouge, La.
Date _____

b. Date of Birth
p.b. Place of Birth
m. Date of Marriage
d. Date of Death
p.d. Place of Death

Form A2, Copyright 1963 by The Everton Publishers, Inc., P.O. Box 506, Logan, Utah, publishers of THE GENEALOGICAL HELPER. Send for a free catalogue with lists and full descriptions of many genealogical aids.

Chart No. 1

16 James A. Mills
b. 6 Jan. 1805 (Father of No. 8) Cont. on chart No. 3
m.
d. 11 Nov. 1890

17 Harriet Bunch (Mother of No. 8) Cont. on chart No. 6
b. 12 Oct. 1811
d. September 1868

18 William Issac Henderson
b. 1802 (Father of No. 9) Cont. on chart No. 4
m.
d. 11 June 1858

19 Elizabeth Strickland (Mother of No. 9) Cont. on chart No. 5
b. 26 Jan. 1806
d. 9 Oct. 1894

20 Phillip James (M)
b. 5 May 1811 (Father of No. 10) Cont. on chart No. 4
m. 4 Aug. 1862

21 Mary Ann Smith (Mother of No. 10) Cont. on chart No. 4
b. 8 Dec. 1811
d. 29 Aug. 1889

22 Edward Washington Davis
b. 26 Aug. 1810 (Father of No. 11) Cont. on chart No. 2
m. 31 Oct. 1891 1832
d.

23 Mary Caroline Dunn (Mother of No. 11) Cont. on chart No. 2
b. 29 Aug. 1817
d. 5 June, 1893

24
b. (Father of No. 12, Cont. on chart No. ___)
m.
d.

25 (Mother of No. 12 Cont. on chart No. ___)
b.
d.

26 Hamilton Leon Cooke (Lenno
b. 16 Feb. 1901 (Father of No. 13, Cont. on chart No. ___)
m. 17 Nov. 1837
d. c 1857-1859

27 Temperance Ann Haley (Mother of No. 13, Cont. on chart No. ___)
b.
d.

28 John Munro, Sr. (Scotland)
b. 1805 (Father of No. 14, Cont. on chart No. ___)
m.
d. 15 Aug., 1845

29 Emma Liddle (Scotland) (Mother of No. 14, Cont. on chart No. ___)
b. 1806
d. 11 July, 1876

30 Henry Schroeder (Germany)
b. 1814 (Father of No. 15, Cont. on chart No. ___)
m.
d. 10 Feb. 1892

31 Martha Charlotte W. Indies (Mother of No. 15, Cont. on chart No. ___)
b. 1827
d. 30 Sept 1888

---

8 William J. Mills (Father of No. 4)
b. 1831
p.b. Greene County, Miss.
m.
d. 18 June, 1862
p.d Columbus, Mississippi

9 Dorcas Henderson (Mother of No. 4)
b. 1836
p.b. Greene County, Miss.
d. 9 January 1879
p.d Greene County, Miss.

10 Patrick James (Father of No. 5)
b. 29 June, 1837
p.b. Greene County, Miss.
m.
d. 5 February, 1909
p.d G. C. Miss. Clark Cem.

11 Louarchy Davis (Mother of No. 5)
b. 14 Jan. 1941
p.b. Greene County, Miss.
d. 30 Jan. 1918
p.d. G. C. Miss. Clark Cem.

12 Charles Key Finney (Father of No. 6)
b. 1823
p.b. Westmoreland Co. Virginia
m. c 1861
d. 26 Feb. 1905
p.d New Orleans, La.

13 Frances Cooke (Mother of No. 6)
b. 29 Jan. 1842
p.b. Metagorda, Texas
d. 20 September, 1933
p.d. New Orleans, La.
Greenwood Cem.

14 John Munro, Jr. (Father of No. 7)
b. 5 February, 1846
p.b. New Orleans, La.
m. 3 July, 1872
d. 18 November, 1920
p.d New Orleans, La.

15 Emma Louise Schroeder (Mother of No. 7)
b. 4 September 1850
p.b. New Orleans, La.
d. 11 December, 1937
p.d. New Orleans, La.

---

4 William David Mills (Father of No. 2)
b. 24 Aug. 1861
p.b. Greene County, Miss.
m. 20 January 1887
d. 6 Aug. 1942
p.d Meridan, Miss.

5 Mary M. James (Mother of No. 2)
b. 18 Nov. 1868
p.b. Greene County, Miss.
d. 22 October, 1940
p.d. Hattiesburg, Miss.

6 David Purcell Finney (Father of No. 3)
b. 21 October 1876
New Orleans, La.
p.b.
m. 9 March 1901
d. 9 October 1949
p.d Hattiesburg, Miss.

7 Emma Liddle Munro (Mother of No. 3)
b. 10 August 1877
p.b. New Orleans, La
d. 6 August, 1940
p.d. Hattiesburg, Miss.

---

2 William Ward Mills, Sr. (Father of No. 1)
b. 31 January, 1908
p.b. Richton, Miss.
m. 18 November, 1933
d.
p.d

3 Frances Key Finney (Mother of No. 1)
b. 27 Nov. 1909
p.b. Jackson, Miss.
d.
p.d.

---

1 William Ward Mills, Jr.
b. 17 June, 1935
p.b. Hattiesburg, Miss.
m. 4 March, 1961
d.
p.d.

Sylvia Richard (Spouse of No. 1)
b. 11 Dec. 1941 d.
p.b. Beaufort, S. Carolina p.d.

APPENDIX

REV. J. P. FINNEY PASSES AWAY
From Saturday's Daily Call
Beloit, Kansas

It is with sorrow that we are this evening called upon to chronicle the passing of another of Kansas' pioneer settlers and an early day settler of Beloit, in the death of the Rev. James Patterson Finney, who passed away at 11:30 o'clock last night at the home of his eldest son, W. H. Finney, from the effects of paralysis. He had been in declining health for some months, but the end came suddenly, he having been stricken three weeks ago.

James Patterson Finney was born Feb. 27, 1837, at Mt. Pleasant, Jefferson County, Ohio, and passes away at Beloit, Kansas, August 16, 1918, at the age of 81 years, 5 months and 19 days.

Mr. Finney was educated at Westminster college, New Wilmington, Pa., graduating in 1861, also graduating from the theological seminary in 1865, his first charge being at Wabash, Ind.

He was united in marriage to Elizabeth Short, March 22, 1865. A long married life was spent happily, they having celebrated their golden wedding anniversary, March 2, 1915, at their Beloit home on N. Campbell avenue.

He came to Kansas in 1868, locating at Manhattan, where he lived, engaging in home missionary work until 1871, when he returned to Ohio to care for his aged parents. Served as Pastor at Unity, Adams Co. Ohio, U.P. Church 5 years.

Being attracted by the west, he returned to Kansas, after his father's death, living at Lawrence; then coming to Beloit in 1879, where he had been since that date, excepting a few years spent in Tarkio, Mo., educating his children. The early days were spent on the homestead, 7 miles southwest of Beloit, where his younger son, D. M. Finney, now resides. At that time he was pastor of Hopewell church. His life as a minister was full of experience of pioneer life and his jovial, happy, disposition made the work exceedingly pleasant. He held prominent offices in the church, giving up his office of clerk of Presbytery only two years ago.

Mr. and Mrs. Finney spent their retired life in Beloit where they made hosts of friends and where their children and grandchildren were always royally welcomed. Mrs. Finney passed away 21 months ago. Since that time Mr. Finney has lived with his daughter, Pearl, of Pretty Prairie, Kansas, having come to spend the summer with his sons, D. M. and W. H. Finney, at which latter home he died Aug. 16, 1918.

APPENDIX

BELOIT GAZETTE
Beloit, Kansas, December 13, 1916

Finney,-- At 7 o'clock on the evening of Friday, December 8, 1916, occurred the death of Mrs. Elizabeth Short Finney, wife of Rev. J. P. Finney of this city. About six or seven weeks ago Mrs. Finney caught a slight cold while visiting in the southern part of the state, which resulted in her finally getting the grip. She kept gradually getting worse all the time, and at no time from the time she took sick until she passed away did her condition improve although everything that loving relatives and friends and skilled physicians could possibly do was done for her. Towards the last she was also bothered with her heart, and heart failure was given as the direct cause of her death.

Miss Elizabeth Short was born May 8, 1841, in Ashland county, Ohio, and at the time of her death was aged 75 years and 7 months. She was the youngest of ten children of James and Marjorie Short, and was the last of the children to pass away. She received her education at the academy at Haysville, Ohio, and at the university in Canonsburg, Penn. She was married March 22, 1865, in Ashland county, Ohio, to Rev. James Patterson Finney. They lived for two years in Indiana, in which state, Rev. Finney did missionary work. In 1867 Rev. and Mrs. Finney and their six-months old daughter, Minnehaha, came to Kansas and located at Manhattan, the Finneys were the only people on the train excepting some Indians. Rev. and Mrs. Finney worked considerably among the pioneer settlers during their five years residence at Manhattan, in and around which place they established missions and did missionary work.

They then returned to the East and lived for five years at Unity, Ohio, where Rev. Finney had charge of a congregation of more than two hundred members. His parents at Mansfield, Richland County, Ohio, were in such poor health that Rev. Finney had to give up the charge to take care of them. In 1878 the Finneys came to Kansas the second time, and lived for one year at Lawrence, after which they came to Mitchell county. Rev. Finney homesteaded the farm in the south edge of Turkey Creek township on which his son, D. M. Finney, now lives. When Rev. and Mrs. Finney moved to the Hopewell neighborhood there was already a church there, it having been erected about two years previously. Rev. Finney had charge of the church for about twelve years, and, during that time, Mrs. Finney did a great amount of work in the cause of the missions.

Mrs. Finney was ever a great help and inspiration to her husband, family, friends and all who knew her. She was a devout Christian and a strong member of the United Presbyterian church. Her large number of friends always knew her to be a lady greatly devoted to her family, jovial at all times and a very pleasing entertainer until her feebleness commenced to get the better of her in her declining years. At the time of her death Mrs. Finney was treasurer of the Concordia branch of the United Presbyterial missionary association, and had been for many years previously. She was an intelligent lady, and a tireless worker in the cause of her Master.

Mr. and Mrs. Finney became the parents of five children. Roscoe, the third child, passed away in 1884. Miss Minnehaha Finney, who is at the present time working as a foreign missionary and stationed at Tanta, Egypt, is the oldest child. She was cabled the sad news of her mother's death, but of course was unable to come home. William Herbert Finney of south of Beloit is the second child; Mrs. Pearl Finney Stevenson of Pretty Prairie, Kansas, the third; and Dwight MacDill Finney, county commissioner-elect from the second district, is the youngest. There are also seventeen grandchildren, in whom their grandmother always took a great deal of pride and interest, left to mourn her death.

The funeral services were held Sunday afternoon at 2 o'clock at the residence, 307 North Campbell Ave., Beloit, Kansas, where Rev. and Mrs. Finney have resided for many years. They were conducted by Rev. W. B. Watson, pastor of the Hopewell church. It was a large funeral, and the many friends for miles around came to pay their last mark of respect to the memory of the late Mrs. Finney. Interment was made in Elmwood cemetery.

APPENDIX

REVOLUTIONARY WAR ANCESTORS IN THE FINNEY LINE.

ELIJAH STEWART, his service as follows:-- Elijah Stewart was
a Private in Captain James Cowden's Company, Fourth Battalion
Lancaster County, Penn. Militia, commanded by Colonel James
Burd Esq. March 13th, 1776. Military Record is found in Penn.
Archives, Vol. VII, Pages 337 and 338. Also see National D.A.R.
Numbers as follows in the Lineage Books-37001,37004,103969,260406.

****

JOHN WATT, his service as follows:-- John Watt served in Captain
Brisben's Company 1st Battalion L.C.M. His name appears on a
Muster Roll in 1782, Penn. Archives, Series fifth, Vol. VII,
page 51. "A true and exact list of the names of each and' every
male white person inhabiting or residing within my district in
the eighth company of the first Battalion of Lancaster County
Militia, between the ages of eighteen and fifty-three years".
Taken for the year 1782. (Penn. Archives, Series fifth, Vol.
VII, page 70.)

****

WILLIAM ORR, his service as follows:-- William Orr served as
a Ranger on the frontiers of Westmoreland County in Captain
Andrew Swearingen's Company. (Pennsylvania Archives, Series 3,
Volume 23, page 312.)

His name appears on a Depreciation Pay list on file in the
Division of Public Records, State Library, in Harrisburg, Pa.
(Pennsylvania Archives, Second Series, Vol. XIII, page 177).
He also served as a Private in Captain Reed's Company, in West-
moreland County, Pa. and was a member of the Sandusky Expedition.
(Penn. Archives, Series Six, Vol. II, page 398).

APPENDIX

See D. A. R. Lineage Records, National Number 317257 for both John Watt and William Orr. There may be others.

****

There may be others whom I do not know about so will be interested in obtaining further information. I feel rather sure that the first James Patterson given in the record (wife Agnes Finney) would have a Revolutionary record, living as he did during the war in Westmoreland County, Penn. This information has not been found, however, for the simple reason that the name "James Patterson" was the name of so many different individuals at that time, it seemed impossible to sort them out, unless there was a definite clue given.

****

COLONIAL WARS

THOMAS FINNEY SR was in the French and Indian War and his record is as follows:--

"Thomas Finney (Corporal)

age 24 years

Enlisted March 6th, 1756

Before whom attested

Richard Walker Esq.

"Officers and soldiers, Province of Pennsylvania, 1744-1765 Muster Roll of Major James Burd's Company in the 1st. Regiment of Foot of the Province of Pennsylvania."

Reference-- Penn. Archives, Series 5, Vol. I, page 60.

****

APPENDIX

BIBLE RECORDS OF
Rev. James Patterson Finney.

****

Rev. James Patterson Finney was born February 27,1837 near Mt. Pleasant, Jefferson Co., Ohio. His parents were William Stewart Finney and Jand (Patterson) Finney, members of the Reformed Dissenting Presbytery and whose pastor at that time was Rev. John Anderson by whom their son James was baptized.

The dying request of a godly mother had its weight with thi son, (she died before he was 16)pointing him to the Gospel Ministry.

After attending the Academies of Monroe under Dr. Richard Gailey, and Vermillion Institute at Haysville, Ohio, he graduated with honors at Westminster College, New Wilmington, Penn, June 1860.

(Note.--The family several years previous to this time had moved from Jefferson County, Ohio to Richland County, Ohio., buying a farm two or three miles south of Mansfield in 1846. Now 100 years later in 1946 at the time when these records alre being reviewed, the old Finney farm is within the city limits of Mansfield, Ohio with fine residences built here and there on it. After the death of the father of James Finney, the old home place was sold to his step-brother who later built a beautiful residence on it which is at present occupied by Mr. Dickson, the man who bought the farm from Newton Stewart and laid it out to city lots.)

The subject of this sketch connected with the church, The Associated Reformed Church at Mansfield, Ohio, about 1858. This church later became an United Presbyterian Church aet the time of the union of the two branches, Associate and The Associate Reformed Churches and called the United Presbyterian Church.

After teaching school for a session and then after a long spell of sickness (diptheria, which paralized the limbs and the organs of speech) he began the private study of Theology under Rev. David Paul. During this time nothing but feeble health urged by his friends as a reason, kept him from joining his comsrades on the battle field for God and his country.

315

After spending the usual time in the study of Theology he graduated at the Allegheny Theological Seminary, March 1866 and was licensed as a probationer, April 1865. (Note: The Allegheny Seminary, located in Allegheny City is now, in 1946larger Pittsburgh, is the Divinity School of the United Presbyterian Church.)

He was married to Elizabeth Short of Ashland, Ohio, March 22, 1865, a graduate of Vermillion Institute, located at Haysville, Ohio. She was a successful school-teacher for a short time.

After leaving the Allegheny Theological Seminary, he with his wife , went to Pittsburg, Indiana to fill the appointment of stated supply made by the General Assembly of the United Presbyterian Church, for a year. Here he was ordained to the Gospel Ministry, Nov. 15, 1866. After this they with their six months old daughter, Minnehaha, went to fill an appointment from the same source at Carnahan Creek, Karrsas Presbytery   (Near Manhattan, Kansas) which appointment was continued three years and three months when in a few months he received a call

to become pastor of a flourishing congregation, called Unity, in Chillecothe Presbytery, Adams Co, Ohio. (Post Office was Wheat Ridge, now called Wheat.) He was installed there Oct. 19, 1871 and after a very successful pastorate was released Aug. 23,1876. This congregation was the last pastorate of good old Father Arbuthnot. (This aged minister and the young minister were close friends as revealed in the last sentence.)

He remained with his aged parents at Mansfield, Ohio, for a period of one year, when God in thunder tones called him forth to go back to the ministry. (It is only fair to say that the reason for his giving up his fine work in the fine congregation of Unity, Adams Co., Ohio. was to fill a place of urgent need in the home of his aged parents who needed the help of the only son to settle up their affairs, so that they could lived a life of greater ease to their old age. Then the catastrophe which even to this day,, 1947, seventy years ao is known as the "Finney Tragedy" took place. Old grand=father, William S. Finney was brutally murdered in the middle of the night by a negro. The murderer was quickly found, tried and hanged. Grandt=mother Finney went to lieve with her son by her first husband, who bought the Dinnwy farm which was know in later years as the Newton Stewart farm.)

316.

Now we find him with his devoted wife and five little children returning to the plains of Kansas as a Home Missionary. He was called to take charge of Hopewell congregation, ten miles S.W. of Beloit, Mitchell Co., Kansas and a rural church of the Concordia Presbytery of the United Presbyterian Church, where he was installed June 19, 1879.

He says, "Wherever I go I find souls to be saved". (Note:-- He traveled as a "Horse and Buggy" Home Missionary over nearly all the counties in the north-western part of Kansas and ministered to little groups of pioneer settlers, living yet in their primitive "sod" houses, and held meetings for them, baptizing their children, and holding Communion Services as well. His wife and children stayed behind to keep things going on the "Home-stead", the 160 acre plot of ground on which he had filed his "Home-stead-Rights" and which is still held by his youngest son, Dwight MacDill Finney.) M.F.

To go back to his narrative-- "Many have been received into the church communion and many children have been baptized at different times. "Would to God I could reach the "ten-thousand" lost souls around me and take them captive for Christ. Oh, God help me, make me a better and more devoted preacher and pastor and God helping, the captive chains forged by Satan shall and must be broken. I hear the cry 'Come over and help us'".

NOTE:-- Here the record closes and I, his daughter, wish to add a line or two in tribute to his faithful ministry during his long life of 81 years. He wielded a fine influence among all classes of men in the community where he lived. He was most upright, genial, and always willing to help any who were in need or in trouble of any sort. He was very strong in prayer and was lmpwm as a "man of prayer." Medical doctors were scarce in those early days, but everybody knew that Rev. Finney kept a "medicine chest" even to remedies for "rattle-snake bites ,". sp it was a frequent sight to see a hurried horse-back rider galloping on the drive-way asking for the needed medicine and he always got it.

No wonder just when the above brief autobiography was written it was found in his well-thumbed Bible after his death in 1918, at Beloit, Kansas.

Copied and commended on by his eldest daughter,

Minnehaha Finney
Sept. 1946
Sterling, Kansas.

Father wrote the following Obituary on the death of his eldest grand-daughter, Elizabeth Isabel Stevenson, daughter of Rev. Andrew Milton and Mrs. A. M. Pearl (Finney) Stevenson, who died at the age pf 8 years amd 9 months. Elizabeth was a lovely girl. Her whole life was one sweet song. Her day school teacher testified that she always excelled in everything she undertook. In her compasionable way she was a cheer to her parents, helpful and kind to others, and especially toher little sisters and brother. The grandfather of this little girl closed a rather lengthy tribute to her with the following poem of his own composition:

> Darling Elizabeth, how we miss thee,
> > The voice we loved is stilled
> The chair is vacant and they place
> > Can never more be filled.

> Thy cheerful voice is hushed,
> > No more we hear thy tread;
> Dear Elizabeth, how we miss thee,
> > But we cannot call thee dead.

> Grandparents.

APPENDIX

FATHER AND MOTHER

REV. AND MRS. JAMES PATTERSON FINNEY

(Printed in "THE UNITED PRESBYTERIAN")

Written by

Minnehaha Finney (Egypt)

Only this evening (August 20, 1918) a cablegram came bringing to me here in Tanta, Egypt, the sad news of the death of my dear father over there at Beloit, Kansas, U. S. A. It took sixteen hours for the cablegram to reach me, and that is remarkably quick time for these war-time days, (World War I).

Mother passed away twenty months ago. I wish to write this little tribute to their precious memory, for I suppose that there is no one else who knows better than I, their oldest

daughter, the value and self-sacrifice of their rather quiet and humdrum lives hidden away in uneventful but nevertheless valuable work for the advancement of Christ's Kingdom on the sunny plains of Kansas.

More than fifty years ago they together went to the home mission field in the then unknown Middle West. I have heard them relate how, when they reached Kansas City and took the train for their destination, Manhattan, Kansas, they found on passing Lawrence that they themselves and several rather savage looking Indians were the only occupants of the car.

But nothing daunted they went on and soon found themselves located and ready for pioneer work in and about Manhattan. The house they occupied was located near what is now the beautiful campus of the Agriculture College of the State of Kansas.

I have heard them tell how, when father would go away
on a trip among the lonely settlers scattered here and there
along the valley, mother bravely stayed alone quite often,
as it would not always be convenient for her to accompany him.
But she was of the plucky sort and quite willing to do her
part. She often laughingly told one experience, using it as an
illustration of the fact that we never need to be afraid if we
trust God to care for us. She heard a queer noise in the middle
of the night - a queer rubbing noise on the window. Saying to
herself, "I'll have no peace of mind till I find out what it is"
She went outside to the guilty window and found the old horse,
"Baldie", calmly rubbing his nose up and down the window pane.

Another story I have often heard them tell was "Fording
the Blue River". There were few bridges in those early days and
the only way to get across the river was to ford it. This time
the water was higher than it gave evidence of when they drove
down into it and before they knew it the wagon was floating and
the horses swimming for all they were worth. But they got
across and went on their way rejoicing to hold the church service
as arranged for at a certain district school house up the valley

The days when my memory serves me best are those when we
moved west to Beloit, Kansas. An interval of five years had
been spent back in Ohio when father was pastor of the Unity
Congregation in Adams County. Father and mother made some rare
and happy friendships in this Unity Congregation which lasted
all along through the years of their lives.

At Beloit, Kansas, father became pastor of Hopewell Congregation, ten miles southwest of Beloit. It is considered one
of the model rural churches in the Middle West; and I personally,

as I observe methods of home and foreign mission work at home and abroad and have lived long enough to observe results of methods, am not slow to give my father much credit in his ways and methods of work. To spend and be spent was his chief method, and never to let an opportunity pass to help someone in some way. And mother was a true helpmete in this.

When we first went to this new field, such a thing as a parsonage for the preacher was unheard of. The only thing for the country preacher to do was to "take up a claim" as all the members of his congregation were doing. And in doing that he identified himself with all the interests of the community and the county in a way which otherwise would not have happened.

Our country home was the free rendezvous of all travelers, and especially the stopping place of all sorts of young men "going west" to see the country, or to cast in lots to "grow up with it". Generous, Sympathetic, simple and sincere hospitality was what the "homeseeker" found at the "preacher's house", and I always look back upon those days with a sort of wonder, of delight and pride -- thankful for such a father and mother who unheralded and unknown in any very wide sense of the word, did faithfully and quietly, without any evident reward, this sort of foundation work in a new country, the sort of work that today is being chanted and lauded in fiction and story and verse.

Well do I remember the trips my father made over those northwestern counties of Kansas when he was Presbyterial missionary and in his genial, kindly way, bringing cheer and spiritual help into many a home planted lonely and isolated out on a far reaching prairie. It wasn't an easy work and often

the trips had to be made across country with his team of horses,
"Pet and Nell", and the old "express wagon", as the vehicle was
called. Once, I remember, I went along, and when we were cros-
sing the Solomon River "Nell" lay down in mid-stream. Fortunately
the river was low, and the day was hot and the flies were bad,
so who can blame "Nell"?

Father was clerk of Concordia Presbytery for many years,
I am sure I do not know how many. He was a loyal supporter of
the principles of the United Presbyterian Church, but he was
liberal and hearty in his appreciation of the work of all the
Evangelical denominational bodies, and in the community where
he spent between thirty and forty years, I can safely say that
he had the highest respect and love of all classes of people.
They had been closely identified with the temperance movement
in Kansas during all these years.

Father and mother are the sort whom their children even to
the second generation or third will rise up and call them blessed.
"Their godly lives, their strong faith and devotion to Jesus Christ,
their sacrifices on our behalf and their wide interests in the
advancement of the Kingdom of God at home and in the foreign
lands are memories which will always be sweet and refreshing
and uplifting and we thank God for our dear parents,

American Mission, Tanta, Egypt, Aug. 20, 1918.

WILLS
Court House, Lancaster Co. Pa.
James Finney - 26th July 1770

"I James Finney of Hanover Township, Lancaster Co., and
Province of Pennsylvania etc. etc. and as touching my worldly
estate which it pleases God to endow me with, I do bequeath in
manner following:---

I give and bequeath to my wife Jane Finney the 1/3 part
of all my movable estate etc. etc. also I give and bequeath to
my son Thomas Finney 2/3's of my Real Estate and at his mother's
death the other 1/3 of my said Real Estate, also I give and
bequeath to my said son Thomas the 2/3's of all my moveable
estate, out of which he is to pay the following bequeathments--
I give to my daughter Jane Ritchledge ten pounds, also I give
to my daughter Mary McGuire twenty pounds, also I give and
bequeath to my daughter Rebecca Caldwell eight pounds, also
I give to Jane Sturgeon twenty shillings and also I give to
Mary Robinsin twenty shillings, and also I give to Rebecca Green
twenty shillings -- The above to be paid in two years after my
decease and I do appoint my wife Jane Finney and my son Thomas
Finney my executors, etc. etc. etc. -- Witness my hand and seal
the 26th of July 1770

James Finney   (Seal)

Signed, sealed and Delivered in Presence of Witnesses

Benj. Wallace
Mich. Wallace

State of Pennsylvania   )
County of Lancaster   ) SS

etc. etc. etc. -- duly sworn May 4th 1774, and among files of
records in Registers Office of Lancaster Co."

1774, May 4 — The will of JAMES FINNEY, of Hanover Twp., Lancaster Co., was proved in Court and his son THOMAS FINNEY, named executor in the will, was granted Letters Testamentary. The widow Jane (or Jean) renounced her right of executorship. This will had been made by James on July 26, 1770, and left to his son THOMAS all his real estate (one-third after the widos's death). Money bequests were left to James' daughters Jane Ritchledge, Mary McGuire and Rebecca Caldwell, and to children of his deceased daughter Effie, who had married (1) Thomas Robinson in 1750 and

* (2) Col Timothy Green in 1760. Effie had been born in 1735 and died Dec. 28, 1765, buried at Old Hanover Church. Her children were Jane Robinson, b. 1751, mar. Robert Sturgeon; Mary Robinson, b. 1753; Elizabeth Robinson, b. 1756; Joseph Green, b. 1761; Rebecca Green, b. 1763; and Timothy Green Jr., b. 1765.

THOMAS FINEY exhibited his father's will at the Registrar's Office at Lancaster on May 4, 1774, at the same time the will was proved. The inventory showed "one plantation of about 100 acres of watered land, "valued at 400 pounds.

1779 — Taxpayers of Hanover Twp. (Pa. Arch. III, 17, 621) shows:

THOMAS FINNY   — 110 acres
Samuel Finny   — 90 acres

NOTE that Susanna Finney, widow of the other Thomas, does not appear in this 1779 tax list, because she had married William Brandon in 1778. Tax is paid by Samuel, eldest son of Thos. deed.

1782 — Taxpayers in Hanover Twp. (Pa. Arch. III, 17, 690) shows:

THOMAS FINNEY   — 135a — 4h — 4c — 7.5.0 tax.
  Rent to Fleming 175a —   5.0.0 tax
Samuel Finney   — 90a — 1h — 1c   5.0.0 tax

1784, Sept. 15 — THOMAS FINNEY, of Hanover Twp., Lancaster Co., made will, leaving his property as follows:

To ISABELLA FINNEY, wife, one-third of real estate for life.
To JOHN FINNEY, son, his lower Plantation.

* Timothy Green (wife Effie Finney) and Thomas Finney (wife Susanna Stewart) were together in the same company in the French and Indian War, under Col. James Burd. See Penn. Archives.

WILLS.

1784, Sept. 15   — THOMAS FINNEY, of Hanover twp., Lancaster Co.,
made will, leaving his property as follows: (cont.)

> To HERVEY FINNEY, son, Plantation "that I
> now live on."
> Two sons, John and Hervey, to pay 125 pounds
> each to his daughters as follows:
>> MARTHA, to be paid first
>> MARY, to be paid second
>> JANE, to be paid third
>> ISABELLA, to be paid fourth
>> MARGARET, to be paid fifth
>> EFFEY, to be paid sixth
>
> Six children to be "schooled and maintained
> off the whole head until they arrive at
> maturity," are named in this order: JOHN,
> JANE, ISABELLA, MARGARET, HERVEY, EFFEY.
> From this provision, we may assume that the
> two daughters, Martha and Mary were already
> grown in 1784 when the will was made.

1786, Mar. 22   — THOMAS FINNEY'S will was proved in Dauphin
County Court by testimony of two of the three
witnesses: John Cooper and Samuel Sturgeon,
Jos. Green not appearing.

> NOTE - The writer's copy of the will does not
> show that the widow ISABELLA was granted the
> Executorship, but we may assume that she became
> executor, as was so named in the will.

1786, Sept. 19   — "Upon the application of William Brandon administrator of all and singular the goods and
chattels rights and credits which were of THOMAS
FINEY late of Hanover township deceased, the
Court appoints John Barnett of the said township
Guardian over the person and estate of JOHN FINEY
a minor sonunder the age of fourteen years of
the said deceased during his minority." This
is as reported to the writer years ago, from
Dauphin Book A-61.

> NOTE - The above reference can be confusing,
> inasmuch as Wm. Brandon had married Susanna
> Finney, widow of the other Thomas Finney, back
> in 1778, and the natural assumption would be
> that this John, under 14, was a son of Thomas
> and Susanna. They did not have a son JOHN,
> however, whereas Thomas and Isabella did.

790   – First Federal Census shows in Dauphin County, Penna.:

ISABEL FINNEY, head of a family comprising 1 male over 16, 1 male under 16, and 7 females. Those figures check out as being Isabella herself, her 2 sons and 6 daughters.

1799, Jan. 16   – PEGGY FINNEY over 14 years of age, daughter of THOMAS FINNEY dec'd, comes into court and chooses Benjamin Wallace guardian.

HARVEY FINNEY and EFFY FINNEY over 14 years choose Timothy Green as their guardian. (These two references are from Dauphin County Orphans Court Docket, Book B, pages 78 and 79). Colonel Timothy Green was Uncle of these children.

1810, Apr. 20   – HERVEY FINNEY deeded to Agnes Stewart 135 acres in Dauphin County, bounded by the lands of John Line, James Martin, and others. This was the property left Hervey by the will of his father, Thomas Finney, described as the plantation "that I now live on." THOMAS FINNEY had bought this 135 acres by deed dated Nov. 15, 1775, from Eliab and Barbara Negley. Its prior history had been this: It was warranted to George Gillaspy on Aug. 1, 1759, then described as bounded by lands of John Line, Jacob Martin, William Cooper, James Murphy and Robert Curry. On Oct. 13, 1762, Gillaspy deed this land to JAMES FINNEY. Then on May 18, 1767, JAMES FINNEY and wife JANE deeded the 135 acres to David Caldwell (probably their son-in-law, husband of their daughter Rebecca.) David Caldwell deeded the land to Benjamine Wallace, who in turn deeded it to Eliab Negley.

1813   – HARVEY FINNEY deeded to George Bower Sr. for 750 pounds a tract measuring 68½ acres and 38 perches neat measure, bounded by lands of Benjamin Wallace's estate, Peter Krum, Stophel Noacre, Robert Stewart and Widow Stewart. This also is said to be a part of the land inherited by Harvey Finney from his father, Thomas Finney, by the 1784 will.

HARVEY FINNEY has not been traced further and the names of his wife and children, if any, have not been ascertained.

Neither have any of the 6 daughters of Thomas and Isabella Finney been traced, as to marriages and descendants.

1813

JOHN FINNEY, son of Thomas and Isabella, was born about 1782 or later (he was under 14 when John Barnett was made his guardian in Sept. 1786.

JOHN FINNEY is shown as a member of the Hanover Congregation from 1796 to 1811 in Robinson's History of Old Hanover Church. In Egle's reprint of Notes & Queries, 1st Series, Vol. 1, page 95, it is stated that among the members of Paxtang Church who subscribed in 1808 was JOHN FINNEY, who removed to Ohio in 1811.

In Xenia, Greene County, Ohio, Miss Minnehaha Finney has found a JOHN FINNEY, born about 1781, died 1862, who came there from Allegheny Co., Pa. This writer believes that this JOHN of Xenia is identical with John, son of Thomas.

JOHN, of Xenia, according to Mrs. Austin M. Patterson, of Xenia, served in the War of 1812 and afterwards belonged to a militia company. He was a farmer, tall, dark, a Scotchman and a Covenanter. He married Isabel McDowell (1783-1838), dau. of Archibald, son of John, of Mifflin Twp., Allegheny Co. Penna. There were 8 children: Thomas, Jane, Sarah Ann, Susan Armstrong, Isabella, Louisa Ann, John and Julia Anna. John Finney married (2) Eleanor W. Harper, but they had no children. The Greene County land records show that John Finney purchased land in 1814, 1816, 1822 and 1829.

THIS ENDS THE ACCOUNT OF THE FAMILY OF THOMAS

& ISABELLA.

APPENDIX

Harrisburg, Pa.
Dauphin Co., Office of the Register of Wills
Book A - 45

15th Sept. 1784 - Thos. Finney and wife Isabella

This 15th day of Sept. 1784 -- I Thomas Finney of the Township of Hanover, Lancaster Co., Pa. etc. etc. etc. I will and bequeath to my wife Isabella Finney 1/3 of the whole of my Real Estate - etc. etc.

I will and bequeath to my son John Finney my lower plantation.

I will and bequeath to my son Hervey Finney the plantation that I now live on.

I will and bequeath to my wife Isabella Finney the one full 1/3 of the whole of my Personal Estate etc. etc.

I give and bequeath to my daughters Martha, Mary, Jane, Isabelle, Margaret and Effy etc. etc.

It is my will and I allow that John, Jane, Isabella, Margaret, Hervey and Effy be schooled and maintained off the whole Head until they arrive to maturity etc. etc. etc.

Signed Thos. Finney   (Seal)

Witnesses: John Cuper
            Samuel Sturgeion
            Jos. Green

NOTE: (reference) Thomas Finney and wife Isabella.

Children:

1. Martha   m. Harbison
2. John
3. Jane
4. Isabella
5. Margaret
6. Effy

APPENDIX

WILLS.

22 Mar. 1786

This 22nd day of March 1786 came John Cuper and Samuel Sturgeon two of the subscribing witnesses to foregoing will—and being duly sworn according to law doth depose and say they were present and heard and saw Thos. Finney sign, seal will etc. etc.

Signed <u>Jos. Montgomery</u>
Register.

APPENDIX

WILLS.

FINNEY

Wills on file in Dauphin Co., Pa. File 1 - 6
Office of Register of Wills, Harrisburg

THOMAS dated Sept. 15, 1784. See page 110.

ELIJAH dated Aug. 18, 1788. Heirs mentioned are his sisters
Sarah and Jennet and his brother James. The executor was James
Finney. Witnesses to this will were Andrew Stewart, Sarah
Stewart and Elijah Stewart. See Note in "Additions" - end of Vol.

ISABELLA dated July 30, 1803. Leaves to John, Harvey and
Martha (Harbison) brothers and sister, each 7s-6d and the remainder of the estate among her four sisters Jean, Margaret, Mary
and Effey. The executrix is Jean, her sister.

EFFEY dated Aug. 30, 1803. Leaves her property to be equally
divided between her sisters Jean, Margaret, Martha Harbison,
Mary and her brothers John and Hervey.

THOMAS dated April 17, 1847. Heirs mentioned, his wife Margaret;
daughters Mary Ann (Richards), Susanna (wife of Washington
Sturgeon), Sarah Elizabeth (Ann). His farm is divided between
his sons John Crawford Finney and Thomas Washington Finney,

SUSANNA dated Hanover Aug. 25, 1853. Heirs are her sister
Elizabeth, and Anne and Washington Finney's boys Wm.S., Isaac S.
James B., Thos. J., and J. F. Hassiager.

ANNA OR ANNE dated 1864. Left everything to Susan Engle.

APPENDIX

MINNEHAHA FINNEY (AUTOBIOGRAPHY)

A SHORT SKETCH OF HER WORK IN EGYPT WHERE SHE

WAS SENT BY THE UNITED PRESBYTERIAN CHURCH IN

NOVEMBER 1894

Since I was honorably retired in 1937 at the age of retirement prescribed by the Women's Board, which is 70, my date of birth being Jan. 24, 1867, I have been making my home in Sterling Kansas with my younger sister. I left Egypt June 30th, 1937 with a very sad heart because it was hard to give up all my dear Egyptian friends with whom I had worked for forty-three years and with whom I had formed many close friendships.

In 1926 the editor of the United Presbyterian asked me to make a contribution to their pages called "Who's Who in the United Presbyterian Church", which meant that I was to write my own life's history up to that date. I am making a copy of that page but with a few additions to bring the story up to date.

"Minnehaha Finney was born in Pittsburg, Carol County, Indiana. Her father was James Patterson Finney and her mother Elizabeth Short Finney. The families of both her parents are of the good old Scotch-Irish and pure Scotch stock of Colonial times, and all along the line have figured largely in the pioneer life, in turn of western Pennsylvania, Ohio, and Kansas. Her father went to Kansas in 1867 with his wife and one child sent as a Home Missionary to Manhattan, Kansas where he organized the work of the United Presbyterian Church in those parts and that was at the time when the Indians and great herds of buffalo roamed the nearby prairies. Except for a period of five years

state of Mrs. Finney where he was called to become pastor of
Unity Congregation, Adams County, Ohio, Miss Finney with her
three brothers and one sister, spent the days of their youth
on the Kansas plains and went to church at Hopewell, ten miles
southwest of Beloit, Mitchell Co., where their father was pastor.

She graduated in the High School at Beloit, Kansas in 1886,
receiving first honor. After teaching two years she entered
Tarkio College, Tarkio Mo., and graduated with honors in 1891.
She taught in Red Oak, Iowa, for one year, and then took up
work in the English Department of Knoxville College, Knoxville,
Tenn., which position she acceptably filled for two years.
Then the call came to go to Egypt and she was appointed to
that great work by the Women's Board of the United Presbyterian
Church, under Mrs. W. J. Reid who was Foreign Secretary of the
Board at that time.

In addition to the careful and godly training received
from her consecrated parents, three books were largely influential
in arousing and intensifying her interest in Foreign Missions.
These books were "Our India Mission", "The Three Mrs. Judsons",
and Dr. Scudder's "Tales for Little Readers". The latter book
she read over and over when a very small child, and it left
a lasting impression upon her mind. This little book had been
presented to her father by his mother, who died before he was
sixteen years old.

Miss Finney landed in Egypt, November 9, 1894, and the
next day was introduced to a definite piece of work, the Mission
School for Girls, in Mansoura, which she superintended during
her first term of seven years and in addition to her study of
the Arabic language which is always the most important task

of the new missionary. On her return from her first furlough,
she was located in Alexandria, where she spent many happy years.
During that time, in connection with the development of the
Central School for girls into a High School, located in the
new Mission building in Alexandria, she was instrumental in
putting into existence the Kindergarten Department, which has,
as a result of her vision, been developed into a Kindergarten
Training School for Kindergarten teachers. Not having training
along the line of Kindergarten work herself, she was most for-
tunate in getting the assistance of a trained Kindergartner
from the Pittsburgh Kindergarten Training School, in the person
of Miss Katherine Graham, later Mrs. Stauffer.

Miss Finney with others also gave much real study and hard
work towards the initiating of a uniform course of study for the
Mission Schools for Girls in Egypt and in the campaign for higher
education among girls and women she helped develop the present
uniform system of Mission Graded Schools and High Schools for
girls all over Egypt.

In 1915, the Editor of the Women's Missionary Magazine,
the late Mrs. George Moore of Xenia, Ohio, asked Miss Finney to
become the Egyptian Editor of the Magazine which meant gathering
monthly material for the Correspondence Department of the
Magazine, now days called "Good News from Far Countries".
Also it meant doing the necessary special work (the getting of
photographs, etc.) for the Egyptian Number of the Magazine.
This position she held for twenty-five years or up to the time
of her retirement in 1937.

Although school work on the Mission Field held many at-
tractions for Miss Finney, yet, as she saw the great undeveloped

field of evangelistic work for women all about her, she longed
to do something which would help carry the gospel to these who
had not heard it. As a result of a trip to India, where she
was sent as a delegate to the Lucknow conference for workers
in Moslem lands, she was led to offer herself for special appointment to evangelistic work among women in the neglected
Delta of Egypt, where two-thirds of Egypt's 16,000,000 live,
choosing Tanta as a strategic center. The Missionary Association
gave her the appointment she so ardently desired, and in 1915
she entered upon this work. The original idea in her own mind
was that she would work in connection with Tanta Hospital, doing
the follow up work among women patients who had left the hospital
and gone back to their homes in the surrounding villages and
towns. This she began to do but the using of the hospital
for her evangelistic head-quarters was frustrated for a time
during the period of the First World War, when the hospital had
to be closed for much needed repairs already begun, but could
not be finished because of the impossibility of obtaining the
necessary materials.

Miss Finney, through her activities carried on by means
of an occasional use of the Delta Car, and other means of getting
out among the villages (riding a donkey, for instance) and into
the homes of the people, saw the great need of well-trained
Egyptian women workers to help in the important and ever urgent
task of evangelizing and teaching the women of Egypt. The
Missionary Association's committee on women's work was appealed
to, as every woman of this committee doing evangelistic work
among women in other parts of Egypt had likewise experienced

the need for trained helpers from among the Egyptian women,
they were quite sympathetic with the appeal. So plans were
made and presented to the Women's Board, which after a period
of much waiting and prayer resulted in the establishing of a
training school for Bible Women Teachers to be conducted along
very simple lines in the residence occupied by Miss Finney,
and later housed in one of the New World Movement buildings
of the Women's Board erected in Tanta in 1923. The success of
the effort speaks for itself in the many Egyptian girls who are
products of this Training School and doing splendid work both
in the Delta villages and in many different places all up and
down the Valley of the Nile. God has richly blessed this effort
and we praise Him for it. I may say at this point that I have
made a few additions to the page called "Who's Who in the
United Presbyterian Church", printed in 1926 in "The United
Presbyterian" to bring the story up to date. So now, in 1946,
I am giving some items not in that printed story.

Miss Finney always desired to get out among the women in
the large and populous districts of the Egyptian Delta, so in
1928 she turned over the Bible Women Teacher's Training School
to other well-trained American Superintendents, and began to
develop the District work.

The Delta Car (a railway car fitted up as a little house
and with good stout wheels to run on the railway lines) was at
my disposal and so I started out always with one or more trained
workers with me, taking along a lot of Christian literature,
perchance meeting some who could read, generally men, stopping
at village after village, some of them very populous-- ten-

thousand inhabitants more or less, shunting our little house
off on a rail-road siding, then starting out to visit home after
home and holding many evangelistic meetings in homes and quite
often right out in the street with crowds of women and men
ready to listen.

We visited regularly in fifty and sixty villages with the
Gospel message, and talks on Temperance, care of children,
duties of mothers, value of learning to read God's Word for
themselves, etc.. As a result of these visits several per-
manent centers were opened with a little school and Kindergarten
department. How the villagers heartily welcomed us and loved to
listen and loved our little schools !

****

A SOLDIERS CLUB IN EGYPT

During World War I Egypt was full of British, Australian
and New Zealand soldiers making many demands upon both English
and American residents to open Tea Rooms and Recreation rooms
for the troops. The American Mission communities in Egypt did
their part well, both in the large cities and in the cities of
the outlying Provinces. At that time I was in Tanta which is
called the Heart of the Egyptian Delta and a large railway center.
It is a city of 100,000 inhabitants and during most of the
war years between 1915 and 1918 a contingent of the British
Rifle Brigade was located in Tanta to guard the bridges of the
net-work of the canal system of that part of the Delta in order
to protect the transportation of soldiers and war materials
between Alexandria, Cairo and Port Said.

APPENDIX

Our Mission Center in Tanta, opened what was then called a Tea Room as English soldiers are real tea drinkers and love their evening "cup of tea" with cakes and sandwiches, so our Tea Room was well patronized by the Rifle Brigade during the evening after their day's work.

Miss Minnehaha Finney was the main stay of this Tea Room every evening for several years since mission work out in the district was impossible and unsafe during the war years. But when the war ended and the Rifle Brigade left town, before their departure their Colonel in a very charmingly written note presented it as a sort of "Honorable Mention" to Miss Finney for the part she had played in making the soldiers Tea Room such a success. Also the Y. M. C. A. Secretary who often visited the camps in connection with his work among the troops all over Egypt wrote Miss Finney a letter of high appreciation for her faithful piece of work there in Tanta, and especially as it turned out to be rather a strenuous piece of work on account of the riots and uprisings in Egypt at that time.

Once 3000 soldiers were sent to Tanta to protect the town and surrounding country-side. Communications were cut off by the rioters so that their supplies did not even reach them at once so Miss Finney was appealed to for a rather big supply of bread for 3000 hungry men. Fortunately she was well acquainted with the efficient Greek baker in Tanta who had been baking the nice tea cakes and cookies for the Rifle Brigade Club several years and when she requested him to supply bread for 3000 soldiers, the bread was forth coming in no time at all,

APPENDIX

So the Tea Room was really put on the map in no time and the demand was great for sandwiches, and all kinds of cookies and sweet-cakes which vanished like snow on a summer day. It was a real job to make the stacks and stacks of sandwiches day by day. Egg sandwiches were most popular and it kept several loyal Egyptian helpers busy scouring the surrounding country for fresh eggs, getting them by the crate. Milk was also an important item, but again the faithful Egyptian helpers had it brought in from, one wonders where. Egyptian cream is very heavy and it substituted splendidly for butter for the sandwiches and went over big with the soldiers. Of course there were books and papers and an old Phonograph which played its part valiantly. The religious services were well attended and enjoyed if the way those soldiers sang is any evidence.

FINNEY/PHINNEY FAMILIES
NOTES.

FINNEY/PHINNEY FAMILIES
NOTES.

FINNEY/PHINNEY FAMILIES
NOTES.

FINNEY/PHINNEY FAMILIES
NOTES.